Musings

Musings

Musings

Daily Encouragement for the Lord's People

William F. Powers

BLUE CAT PUBLISHING
SOUTHWESTERN OHIO, USA

Edited by Jerian R. Powers

All Images © 2016 Patti Smith Photography, except the cover and February photos © William F. Powers

Cover Poem: "When Morning Gilds the Skies;" Author Unknown, translated by Edward Caswall

Cover Design © 2018 by William F. Powers

Published by Blue Cat Publishing
ISBN-13: 9781792062742

Bible quotations are from The King James Translation (KJV), Oxford University Press.

Dedication

This book is dedicated to the Lord Jesus Christ, who loved me before I loved Him and who paid for my sins and redeemed me to Himself. (1 John 4:19, Galatians 2:20) Thank you, dear Savior.

This work is also dedicated to God's precious gift to me, my wife Jerian. As a bonus, she also edits my writings and makes me look like I know what I am doing. <smile> I love you.

This book is also dedicated to all who read it. Each of us, regardless of fame, wealth, station in life, or lack of those things, rejoice in the pleasures and delights of life, but also struggle with its pains, sorrows, and losses. It is my earnest prayer that the Heavenly Father will override the imperfections in these writings and that through them He will challenge you with the Savior's holy splendor; awe you with His majestic grace; and encourage you with His loving kindness.

Musings

Table of Contents

Musings

FORWARD

I lost the quote long ago, but I believe it was the late Francis Schaeffer who referred to "The true and living God who created the heavens and the Earth." As I recall, Mr. Schaeffer's reason for using that phrase was that there are so many ideas today of who God is or what He is like that he didn't want anyone to be unsure about the One of whom he was speaking.

The very thought of the majestic Creator—who the whole universe cannot contain and before whom every knee shall one day bow—should humble our hearts in awe, even as it did Isaiah (chapter 6), John (Revelation 1), and many others before and since. As I reflect on the magnificence of His being, it is a matter of utter amazement to me that He would use feeble people to carry out His work; however, that is what He has purposed to do.

I thank Him for His grace and help in this project; it is with a sense of reliance upon Him for His wisdom and guidance that I offer these daily thoughts. My prayer is that God would be glorified and that the reader would be encouraged to consider the wonder and majesty of the Savior who loved us and laid down His life to pay for our sins.

Finally, an editorial note: There are special days that are not always on the same calendar date, such as the American day of Thanksgiving, and days that always fall on a particular date but are celebrated on a Monday to allow for a three-day weekend. I have placed a few thoughts in the general vicinity of those holidays, coupling the reality of shifting dates with the desire to acknowledge those societal events.

I pray the Lord's richest blessings for you as you consider Him, who to know is life eternal. (John 17:3)

William F. Powers
December, 2018

Galatians 2:20

Musings

JANUARY

1

One of Our Greatest "Kneeds"

Psalm 95:1-6 "O come, let us sing unto the LORD: let us make a joyful noise to the rock of our salvation. Let us come before his presence with thanksgiving, and make a joyful noise unto him with psalms. For the LORD is a great God, and a great King above all gods. In his hand are the deep places of the earth: the strength of the hills is his also. The sea is his, and he made it: and his hands formed the dry land. O come, let us worship and bow down: let us kneel before the LORD our maker."

Since my mid-teens, I have had knee trouble. In my thirties and forties, I underwent two separate surgeries on my right knee, and it needs surgery again. My left one will soon be ready for some work also. My current weight does not help the situation, but in my own defense, when my trouble started I was a young man barely over one hundred pounds soaking wet. As helpful as shedding some of these extra pounds might be, they were not the beginning of my troubles.

With my background, I suppose it is normal that I recently noticed an advertisement for an e-book titled, "The Knee Book - A Guide to Healthy Knees." However, as I contemplated that ad, I realized there is *another* "knee" trouble that we struggle with, and that is our *need* to bend our *knees*. Today's Scripture lists the remedy: "O come, let us worship and bow down: let us kneel before the LORD our maker."

Age or physical conditions may make bowing and kneeling difficult or even impossible; however, we *all* should at least humble our hearts and minds before "the LORD our maker" and worship Him, for He indeed is worthy.

"The four and twenty elders fall down before him that sat on the throne, and worship him that liveth for ever and ever, and cast their crowns before the throne, saying, 'Thou art worthy, O Lord, to receive glory and honour and power: for thou hast created all things, and for thy pleasure they are and were created.'" (Revelation 4:10-11)

"O come, let us worship and bow down: let us kneel before the LORD our maker." (Psalm 95:6)

1

2

The Persistent Panda

Luke 18:1-6 "And he spake a parable unto them to this end, that men ought always to pray, and not to faint; Saying, There was in a city a judge, which feared not God, neither regarded man: And there was a widow in that city; and she came unto him, saying, Avenge me of mine adversary. And he would not for a while: but afterward he said within himself, Though I fear not God, nor regard man; Yet because this widow troubleth me, I will avenge her, lest by her continual coming she weary me. And the Lord said, Hear what the unjust judge saith."

I saw an online video where a photographer was trying to take some pictures in a zoo setting. Unfortunately, he was in an area with a baby panda. No matter what the poor fellow did, the panda followed and tried to wrap its forepaws around the man's ankle. He gently worked his way out of the panda's grasp and walked away, but the little animal waddled after him and attempted another "bear hug."

Watching the persistent panda reminded me of the widow in today's verses. Her adversary oppressed her, and yet the only one who could help didn't care at all about her plight. Still she came, and in the midst of her continuous complaints, the judge gave in, lest she continue to petition him.

After telling the story, the Lord Jesus said that God was *not* unjust like that judge. Instead, God *would* avenge His people, and He *would* answer our prayers. Jesus also implied that He wouldn't do it grudgingly, but willingly. He also illustrated that God's timing might be different than we expect.

I find it interesting that Jesus then continued in the chapter with a parable contrasting two men who went to the temple to pray: the Pharisee who "prayed", letting God and others know what a good and worthy person he himself was; then, the publican who acknowledged his own sinfulness and need for mercy. (Luke 18: 9-14)

Perhaps the lesson we can draw from these two parables is that we should petition God; have faith in His goodness and faithfulness; and that we should always do so with humble and contrite hearts because "The LORD is nigh unto them that are of a broken heart; and saveth such as be of a contrite spirit." (Psalm 34:18)

3

One More Thing

Psalm 5:4-6 "For thou art not a God that hath pleasure in wickedness: neither shall evil dwell with thee. The foolish shall not stand in thy sight: thou hatest all workers of iniquity. Thou shalt destroy them that speak leasing: the LORD will abhor the bloody and deceitful man."

Have you ever thought about God's gifts of mercy compared to what He "owes us?" His mercy is only offered to the ungodly, not to those who think they are "not that bad." (Luke 5:31-32) In light of today's verses, I want us to consider something else along that same line of reasoning.

God does not like wickedness, evil, foolishness, iniquity, leasing (lying and falsehoods), and bloody, deceitful men. However, David was all of those things! He committed adultery with Bathsheba, which was wicked, evil, and foolish iniquity. Then he murdered her husband, a bloody act to be sure. Finally, David covered up his crimes, which was deceitful falsehood.

Was David thinking about his enemies when he wrote this psalm, or was he thinking about himself? In either case, instead of shrinking in fear of his own sinful failings, David recognized the truth he wrote in Psalm 19:9a: "The fear of the LORD is clean, enduring for ever." Perhaps that was his thought when he also wrote in Psalm 5: "But as for me, I will come into thy house in the multitude of thy mercy: and in thy fear will I worship toward thy holy temple." (v 7) He then went on to ask God to keep him from straying: "Lead me, O LORD, in thy righteousness because of mine enemies; make thy way straight before my face." (v 8)

King David recognized that the only difference between him and his enemies was that he had a reverent fear of God and therefore had placed his trust in the Lord and His mercy. (v11) He came to the same "Logical Conclusion" that Paul did; David knew he was—in and of himself—an ungodly man who needed God's mercy rather than what he was due.

Let me ask you this question, my friend. Have you recognized your own need for forgiveness, or are you still satisfied with your own righteousness and believe that God owes you something? Think carefully; your entire forever will be reflected in your answer.

4

Hard Places and Pleasant Places

Psalm 16:5-7: "The LORD is the portion of mine inheritance and of my cup: thou maintainest my lot. The lines are fallen unto me in pleasant places; yea, I have a goodly heritage. I will bless the LORD, who hath given me counsel: my reins also instruct me in the night seasons."

How is your life? Is everything perfect? Is everything as you wish it was? My guess is you and I would probably say no. Even the psalmist seems to acknowledge there are hard places in his life when he writes the words that Peter later applies to Jesus in Acts 2:27: "For thou wilt not leave my soul in hell; neither wilt thou suffer thine Holy One to see corruption." (Psalm 16:10)

However, David also sees something underlying his struggles when he writes, "The lines are fallen unto me in pleasant places; yea, I have a goodly heritage." He seems to say, "Even in my struggles, I have an inheritance that has me on a good path." In fact, he even anticipates a good END to that path, for he concludes, "Thou wilt show me the path of life: in thy presence is fullness of joy; at thy right hand there are pleasures forevermore." (Psalm 16:11)

David describes parts of his life as "hell", a place that would end in corruption if he were not rescued from it. (Psalm 16:10) However, his fears are assuaged in knowing he is on a straight path from a goodly heritage to the presence of God where there is fullness of joy and pleasures forevermore.

Knowing by grace that we are on that kind of path is a great comfort.

5

Unstoppable

Isaiah 14:26-27 "This is the purpose that is purposed upon the whole earth: and this is the hand that is stretched out upon all the nations. For the LORD of hosts hath purposed, and who shall disannul it? and his hand is stretched out, and who shall turn it back?"

Who can resist the hand of God?

Ever since the fall of Eden, the pride of the human heart has been our main enemy. It causes us to deny reality and assume more intelligence, power, and authority than we actually possess.

One of the most powerful passages in Scripture is a letter. It is not one of the New Testament epistles; it is a letter written by a king to all the people of the Earth. That includes us today.

"Nebuchadnezzar the king, unto all people, nations, and languages, that dwell in all the earth; Peace be multiplied unto you. I thought it good to shew the signs and wonders that the high God hath wrought toward me." (Daniel 4:1-2) The king goes on to describe his own pride and conceit. He then tells how the most High God broke him of his own foolishness by removing his sanity for a period of time, causing him to live in a field and eat grass like a wild beast.

"And at the end of the days I Nebuchadnezzar lifted up mine eyes unto heaven, and mine understanding returned unto me, and I blessed the most High, and I praised and honoured him that liveth for ever, whose dominion is an everlasting dominion, and his kingdom is from generation to generation: And all the inhabitants of the earth are reputed as nothing: and he doeth according to his will in the army of heaven, and among the inhabitants of the earth: and none can stay his hand, or say unto him, What doest thou? ... Now I Nebuchadnezzar praise and extol and honour the King of heaven, all whose works are truth, and his ways judgment: and those that walk in pride he is able to abase." (Daniel 4:34-35, 37)

Is our own arrogance the cause for the insanity we see in our society today?

"He hath shewed thee, O man, what is good; and what doth the LORD require of thee, but to do justly, and to love mercy, and to walk humbly with thy God?" (Micah 6:8)

6

A Tree Planted by the River

Psalm 1:1-3 "Blessed is the man that walketh not in the counsel of the ungodly, nor standeth in the way of sinners, nor sitteth in the seat of the scornful. But his delight is in the law of the LORD; and in his law doth he meditate day and night. And he shall be like a tree planted by the rivers of water, that bringeth forth his fruit in his season; his leaf also shall not wither; and whatsoever he doeth shall prosper."

We had a real windstorm here the other day. Two rather heavy pieces of deck furniture were thrown out into our backyard as if they were made of cardboard.

During the storm, I was watching one particular tree. I call it a tree, but it was hardly more than a bush. As I watched, the wind put that little thing through a real trial. I wondered how it had any leaves left on it.

When we go through trials, we sometimes wonder what we did to deserve the struggle and if we are even going to make it through in one piece. Not that little tree, however; it just stands where it is planted with seemingly no regard for storms, rain, or wind.

According to today's verses, a believer should be that way. We are likened to a tree that is planted by rivers of water, which grows, flourishes, and prospers. Now, that does not mean we **don't** worry and fuss, but it sure means we don't have to. The believer in God has His promise that everything will turn out all right. One person said it this way, "I have read the last chapter, and the good guys win."

As Horatio Spafford put it after great personal tragedy:

> When peace, like a river, attendeth my way,
> When sorrows like sea billows roll;
> Whatever my lot, Thou hast taught me to say,
> It is well, it is well, with my soul.

7

Good and Evil

Isaiah 5:20-23 "Woe unto them that call evil good, and good evil; that put darkness for light, and light for darkness; that put bitter for sweet, and sweet for bitter! Woe unto them that are wise in their own eyes, and prudent in their own sight! Woe unto them that are mighty to drink wine, and men of strength to mingle strong drink: Which justify the wicked for reward, and take away the righteousness of the righteous from him!"

Friedrich Nietzsche (nee-chee) was a German philosopher in the late 1800s. His father was a pastor, and both of his grandfathers were in the ministry too. I do not know how strong his background was in Christian teaching, nor do I know why he abandoned that teaching. What *is* clear is that he became a vehement and outspoken critic of Christianity.

Nietzsche popularized the phrase, "God is dead." Did he actually believe in God at one time and later gave up on that, or did he just believe the concept of God was a nice idea that helped people keep their unhealthy and violent passions under control? I don't know. Either way, however, as his philosophy developed, he began to realize that a culture devoid of a God-conscience would produce a society of great catastrophes.

In the Ravi Zacharias YouTube video titled "The Incoherence of Atheism," Mr. Zacharias mentioned two conclusions Nietzsche derived as he saw the decline of a God-awareness in the late nineteenth century. His first conclusion was that the twentieth century would become the bloodiest century in history. His second prediction was that a universal madness would take hold: evil would be called good, abnormal would become normal, and truth would be labeled a lie.

Nietzsche was astonishingly correct about the bloody twentieth century, and as the twenty-first century unfolds, we see the fulfillment of his second forecast. We see it in the confusion of the sexes, the insanity of political correctness, the rejection of absolute truth, and the replacing of ageless wisdom by human reasoning. That madness is unavoidable when God is rejected and mocked. It even happened to Nietzsche; he became insane in his final decade.

How can our generation ever return to a realistic and healthy mindset? The psalmist asks, then answers that question. "Wherewithal shall a young man cleanse his way? By taking heed thereto according to thy (God's) word." (Psalm 119:9)

8

Reality and the Concept of Moral Ideas

Psalm 119: 9-13 "Wherewithal shall a young man cleanse his way? by taking heed thereto according to thy word. With my whole heart have I sought thee: O let me not wander from thy commandments. Thy word have I hid in mine heart, that I might not sin against thee. Blessed art thou, O LORD: teach me thy statutes. With my lips have I declared all the judgments of thy mouth."

The book of Psalms is the Hebrew songbook. The book is not actually divided into 'chapters'; however, each psalm (song) is separated unto itself. The longest song is Psalm 119, and its theme is God's Word. Though it has been a while since I did the research, if I recall correctly, only three of Psalm 119's 176 verses do not contain "word," "law," "precepts," "judgments," or some other reference to God's instructions to us.

Throughout this psalm, as well as throughout the entire Scripture, God is communicating to people, the pinnacle of His creation. That is exactly what He did millennia ago when He told Adam how to behave in the world into which God placed him. Adam chose his own path instead, throwing the world into chaos. All of Adam's sons and daughters have followed in his footsteps, for "All we like sheep have gone astray; we have turned every one to his own way;" (Isaiah 53:6)

Mankind has been following his own path ever since, acting as if he is accountable to no one. Aside from disobedience to God, another problem in this is that *each* of us wants *our* own way, but without an objective standard, how can I be sure my way is better than yours is? C. S. Lewis said it this way: "If no set of moral ideas were truer or better than any other, there would be no sense in preferring civilized morality to savage morality or Christian morality to Nazi morality."

Some prefer getting along with others, while some prefer murdering others. In either case, if we do not follow *God's* way, we have "gone astray" and "turned to our own way." Thankfully, that is not where Isaiah 53:6 ends, for it continues, "and the LORD hath laid on him (Jesus) the iniquity of us all."

My friend, trust God for His mercy and grace and follow His ways. He truly knows best.

9

Opinions

Matthew 25:20-23 "And so he that had received five talents came and brought other five talents, saying, Lord, thou deliveredst unto me five talents: behold, I have gained beside them five talents more. His lord said unto him, Well done, thou good and faithful servant: thou hast been faithful over a few things, I will make thee ruler over many things: enter thou into the joy of thy lord. He also that had received two talents came and said, Lord, thou deliveredst unto me two talents: behold, I have gained two other talents beside them. His lord said unto him, Well done, good and faithful servant; thou hast been faithful over a few things, I will make thee ruler over many things: enter thou into the joy of thy lord."

I read a quote the other day suggesting that those who care the most about what other people think of them are usually quite unhappy.

The opinions of others may have value. For example, if someone I trust—someone who actually has my best interest at heart—tells me that something I am doing or saying is hurting me or others around me, it may cause me to change my conduct, thereby improving myself. However, we mortals tend to crave the endorsement of other mortals, even to the point of being willing to forfeit our principles in order to gain that approval. That creates problems.

Today's passage in Matthew is part of a parable Jesus told. A man was about to leave town, perhaps on a business trip. As a test, he gave some money to three of his servants, two of whom used the marketplace to increase their holdings while their master was away. Upon the master's return, the profitable servants presented their gains, and the master's response was the same to both, "Well done, thou good and faithful servant."

As I mentioned, the opinions of others can be beneficial, even to the point of helping us in our walk with the Lord; however, we can lose focus of what is really important if we place the opinions of others ahead of God's approval. Let us be like Paul who said, "I press toward the mark for the prize of the high calling of God in Christ Jesus." (Philippians 3:14)

God's "well done" is infinitely better than the approval of mortals.

10

Seeing Correctly

1 Samuel 16:4-7 "And Samuel did that which the LORD spake, and came to Bethlehem. And the elders of the town trembled at his coming, and said, Comest thou peaceably? And he said, Peaceably: I am come to sacrifice unto the LORD: sanctify yourselves, and come with me to the sacrifice. And he sanctified Jesse and his sons, and called them to the sacrifice. And it came to pass, when they were come, that he looked on Eliab, and said, Surely the LORD'S anointed is before him. But the LORD said unto Samuel, Look not on his countenance, or on the height of his stature; because I have refused him: for the LORD seeth not as man seeth; for man looketh on the outward appearance, but the LORD looketh on the heart."

I find the eye to be incredibly intriguing. It is made up of the cornea, lens, iris, pupil, sclera, optic nerve, and various fluids—all of which are transparent—and a retina at the back onto which light paints an image. With the eye, we can look upon our world and gain some understanding of its wonders.

However, our brains, minds, and preconceptions influence how we interpret the images. For example, we all have the same geological data (rocks, layers, fossils, and frozen extinct animals, etc.). However, some will interpret that data as evolutionary, while others see it fitting into a creation model.

The same kind of thing happens when we look at people. We may view them with favor or suspicion; with openness or apprehension; pleasantly or with hostility. All this is not because we actually *see* something with our eyes but because our presumptions distort what we see. That happens with the color of a person's skin, and it happens with the grayness of their hair. It happens when we compare a person with a striking appearance with someone who looks plain.

This is what happened to Samuel in today's verses. Eliab must have had a striking appearance (tall, handsome, rugged, etc.), and Samuel assumes him to be God's choice. However, God tells the prophet to bypass Eliab, and later tells him that Eliab's younger brother David is the right man.

This is a good reminder: "Man looketh on the outward appearance, but the LORD looketh on the heart." As we seek to be more godly, it would be wise to see as He sees.

11

Getting a Vision

Isaiah 6:1-4 "In the year that king Uzziah died I saw also the Lord sitting upon a throne, high and lifted up, and his train filled the temple. Above it stood the seraphims: each one had six wings; with twain he covered his face, and with twain he covered his feet, and with twain he did fly. And one cried unto another, and said, Holy, holy, holy, is the LORD of hosts: the whole earth is full of his glory. And the posts of the door moved at the voice of him that cried, and the house was filled with smoke."

This passage records the time when God gave a vision to Isaiah. The prophet glimpsed Heaven where he saw seraphim proclaiming God's holiness. He also saw quaking doorposts in a room full of smoke. The most startling and majestic sight was the Lord sitting on His throne, "high and lifted up."

Please understand me as I share this because I am not trying to pretend to be what I am not. I am just like most of you; I too struggle with keeping my focus on God. However, I believe the single, most intense need for the Lord's people today is to see God for the magnificent person that He is. He is unlike anything and anyone we can see. He is high; He is lifted up; He is God!

I recently saw one of the most moving videos I have ever seen. One at a time, it featured six or eight people who were colorblind. Each reacted in amazement as they put on a recent invention, a pair of glasses that filters the light so they could see colors like non-colorblind people do. One gentleman looked around with his mouth agape; then slowly, in a stunned voice, he asked his friends, "Is this what you see all the time?"

Oh, that we comprehended God in all His glory "all the time"; our worship would flow more freely, and our service would be more passionate and joyful.

> Majestic sweetness sits enthroned
> Upon the Savior's brow;
> His head with radiant glories crowned,
> His lips with grace overflow,
>
> No mortal can with Him compare,
> Among the sons of men;
> Fairer is He than all the fair
> Who fill the heavenly train.
> ~ Samuel Stennett

12

Misdirected Fear Causes Misguided Action

Galatians 2:11-12 "But when Peter was come to Antioch, I withstood him to the face, because he was to be blamed. For before that certain [men] came from James, he did eat with the Gentiles: but when they were come, he withdrew and separated himself, fearing them which were of the circumcision."

I don't know if Paul was an especially feisty man, but you didn't want to play loose with the gospel around him. The people of Galatia had started to mix grace with their own works as part of their salvation. As a result, the most intense of Paul's letters in the Scriptures is this one that he wrote to the Galatians.

Paul marveled that the Galatians had turned away from the true gospel to a mixed imitation. (Galatians 1:6) In today's verses, Paul tells us he had to get up in Peter's face for the same kind of thing.

Peter had been in Antioch, eating and mixing socially with the Gentile Christians there. All was fine until James sent some representatives to the region; Peter suddenly changed his ways and only ate with the people James sent. That might not seem that egregious at first, but what made Paul so upset was the implication that the gospel of Christ could not save the Antioch believers as effectively as it saved the Jews who had the law and its customs.

Peter's fear of what men might think caused him to act differently than he did when he was living in the freedom he had in Christ. He was afraid of men and was willing to compromise the message of the gospel because of that fear.

Now, works are good. The Bible teaches that changed lives and good works are the evidence—the fruit—of a redeemed soul; however, we must **never** think that works are what **make** us right with God, for the free flow of good works is only a *sign* of a redeemed life, not the cause of it.

Grace and works for salvation did not mix in Paul's day, (Romans 11:6) and they do not mix today. The gospel of God's grace *always* stands on its own merit, free from any human efforts. Let us bow before the Almighty in humble reverence, worshiping the true and living God for His goodness, mercy, and His grace.

13

Sad Consequences

Galatians 2:11-13 "But when Peter was come to Antioch, I withstood him to the face, because he was to be blamed. For before that certain came from James, he did eat with the Gentiles: but when they were come, he withdrew and separated himself, fearing them which were of the circumcision. And the other Jews dissembled likewise with him; insomuch that Barnabas also was carried away with their dissimulation."

Last time we saw that Peter muddied the waters about the gospel. Peter ate and fellowshipped with the Gentile believers at Antioch, but when James sent certain Jewish men, presumably to find out how things were going there, Peter acted as if the gospel worked a little bit better for the Jews than it did for believers at Antioch. It is interesting—and perhaps ironic, considering Peter's foolishness—that the first place where followers of Jesus were called Christians was at Antioch. (Acts 11:26)

However, there is another sad fact revealed in the same passage: *other* Christian Jews followed Peter's lead and separated from the Antioch believers, and even compassionate Barnabas was drawn into Peter's folly. (verse 13)

We as Christians don't live alone. By birth and by adoption, God has brought us into His family, and He tells us to love one another. We do not have any Biblical right or authority to separate ourselves from other believers who are seeking—even imperfectly—to live godly lives.

However, we must be ***especially*** mindful that when we treat other Christian believers as second-class citizens, someone will see OUR sin and may follow us into that tragic rebellion against Christ's law of love.

Now, as always, we must understand the larger picture too. God ***does*** call us to be separated from the world; (Romans 12:2, 21) from worldly believers; (1 Corinthians 5) and from false teachers. (2 Peter 2) It is good if we can encourage someone like that to align themselves with Christ and follow Him in righteousness; however, we should be on guard to prevent them from enticing us away from the Lord.

So then, since we are Christ-followers, let us be diligent to separate ourselves from those He says to separate from but be just as diligent to love and cherish those who are His children, even if they are a little different from us. After all, we ***all*** are a little different in some way, aren't we? <smile>

14

Not "All about John" Anymore

2 Corinthians 5:14 -15 "For the love of Christ constraineth us; because we thus judge, that if one died for all, then were all dead: And that he died for all, that they which live should not henceforth live unto themselves, but unto him which died for them, and rose again."

My wife used to teach third and fourth grade. One year she had a student who I will call Jack (not his real name). When she would give out an assignment, Jack would ask, "But what about me?" as if the general assignment did not apply to him. When awards were passed out, he would ask the same question as if he was being intentionally left out of a tribute he was due, even though he had not earned any specific recognition.

I do not know what became of Jack, but I do know that the mindset he had is far more common than we might think. We mortals crave recognition and long for the endorsement of our peers; however, there is also a temptation to think that the rules for others don't apply to us. That is something from which ***all*** of us must guard ourselves, but it seems to be more pronounced among those who attain some level of notoriety. Politicians and performers seem to have a bigger struggle with this problem, along with those who have gained some level of social standing by wealth or other achievements.

Although I have not been able to confirm it with any other source, I saw a quote attributed to actor and singer, John Schneider: "Becoming a Christian changed my life completely. My life wasn't 'all about John'

13

anymore." Another John who was the predecessor of Christ expressed the same sentiment in John 3:30: "He (Christ) must increase, but I (John the Baptist) must decrease."

I do not know a lot about Mr. Schneider; I do know that, like all of us, he has struggled with pain and suffering in his life. However, the thoughts expressed in the quote are significant. I don't need to ask, "What about me?" because life is not all about me. The questions I should ask are these: "How can I bring more glory to God? How can I direct people's attention to Him?"

I wish I asked those questions more and answered them better. Lord, help me. Lord, help all of us.

15

Evolution and Intelligent Design

Psalm 139:1-4, 14 "O Lord, thou hast searched me, and known me. Thou knowest my downsitting and mine uprising, thou understandest my thought afar off. Thou compassest my path and my lying down, and art acquainted with all my ways. For there is not a word in my tongue, but, lo, O Lord, thou knowest it altogether... I will praise thee; for I am fearfully and wonderfully made: marvelous are thy works; and that my soul knoweth right well."

The human body is amazing. The eye is amazing, and the ear is amazing. The hand is amazing, and the brain is amazing. The five senses are amazing, and the coordination between all these things is amazing. In fact, when you stop to think about it, there isn't anything about the human body that *isn't* amazing!

We take all this for granted without even thinking about it. Almost automatically, my brain is conceiving this musing while my fingers are typing my brain's thoughts into my computer.

I am reasonably certain that people who accept evolution also find this all amazing. The intricacies of our bodies shout out the intelligence of our design. The difference between the believer in evolution and the believer in creation is that the evolutionist ascribes all that amazing creativity to the creature, whereas the believer in creation ascribes that creativity to the Creator.

The late Professor Fred Jiles of South Carolina was speaking with an evolutionist. When the man found out Fred was a creationist he said, "You have a problem," to which Fred replied, "Yes, but I wouldn't trade my wheelbarrow full for your truckload."

I have said previously I don't want to be insulting or unkind to evolutionists, but we must be clear on reality. Either the blob of cells that first developed an eye already had the intelligence to know there was light to see; that all in the light's path must be transparent; and knew what transparent was; *or* that intelligence resided in a Maker who was distinctly separate from His designs.

Let us not be caustic or malicious in stating our beliefs; however, let us never be ashamed of the reasonableness of creation. The existence of a Creator makes all else comprehensible. The only alternative is that the intelligence to develop every new organ or capability resided in the blob of cells from which all evolved.

16

Perspective on Life

Psalm 33:1-5 "Rejoice in the LORD, O ye righteous: for praise is comely for the upright. Praise the LORD with harp: sing unto him with the psaltery and an instrument of ten strings. Sing unto him a new song; play skillfully with a loud noise. For the word of the LORD is right; and all his works are done in truth. He loveth righteousness and judgment: the earth is full of the goodness of the LORD."

I recently saw a cartoon of the character Charlie Brown and his dog Snoopy. They were sitting on a dock, looking out over a pond. Charlie says, "Some day, we will all die, Snoopy!" The beagle answers back, "True, but on all the other days, we will not."

Some of us have a naturally pessimistic outlook on life, while some find it easy to be positive. Some are anxious about the last day of our lives, while others realize that every day we awake is an opportunity to live abundantly and thankfully before God.

David, the second king of Israel and a man after God's own heart (Acts 13:22) was discouraged about many things. His psalms record his frustrations and apprehensions; however, he also acknowledged the Lord's gracious providence, just like the psalmist in today's passage.

As much as some of us might struggle with pessimistic feelings— and I do too at times—let us all rejoice regularly, holding to the promise that "the earth is full of the goodness of the LORD". (Psalm 33:5b)

It is easier to sleep, to awake, and to live when we embrace that.

17

Take Good Heed Therefore

Joshua 23:9-11 "For the LORD hath driven out from before you great nations and strong: but as for you, no man hath been able to stand before you unto this day. One man of you shall chase a thousand: for the LORD your God, he it is that fighteth for you, as he hath promised you. Take good heed therefore unto yourselves, that ye love the LORD your God."

Joshua had gotten old and was in his final days. Here he tells the people of Israel to take God seriously. He reminds them that God has used even small numbers of them to rout large enemy encampments, and he instructs them to remain faithful to God.

This is a command to the people of Israel, but the Old Testament was also written for our learning. (Romans 15:4) We should be aware of the greatness of the True and Living God who Created the heavens and the Earth, and we should love Him with all our hearts, minds, and souls.

I struggle with something that crosses my mind from time to time; perhaps you have thought the same thing. Yes, we ARE to love God with all that we are. However, when I sin, I am not loving God; I am not trusting God; and I am not fearing God. It hurts me to say it, but at that very moment, I am placing my will above His will, my thoughts above His truth, and my passions above His purposes.

We fallen, broken humans tend to trust ourselves above any advice, even good advice. "Follow your heart," we are told, but God warns us about that advice in Jeremiah 17:9-10. "The heart is deceitful above all things, and desperately wicked: who can know it? I the LORD search the heart, I try the reins [an old word for the seat of the emotions], even to give every man according to his ways, and according to the fruit of his doings."

We are tempted to follow our own insight, whether about money, relationships, or other matters. I pray we all pull back from that precipice and turn to the Lord and His Word, thereby preventing our being pierced through with many sorrows. (1 Timothy 6:10)

18
What a Waste

Mark 8:34-37 "And when he had called the people unto him with his disciples also, he said unto them, Whosoever will come after me, let him deny himself, and take up his cross, and follow me. For whosoever will save his life shall lose it; but whosoever shall lose his life for my sake and the gospel's, the same shall save it. For what shall it profit a man, if he shall gain the whole world, and lose his own soul? Or what shall a man give in exchange for his soul?"

On January 8, 1956, missionary pilot Nate Saint flew four other missionaries to a landing strip on the beach of a river in eastern Ecuador. The goal was to present the gospel of Christ to the indigenous people, sometimes referred to as the Aucas. On that day, the Aucas killed Saint and his four friends.

I recently came across a quote by Mr. Saint that was almost prophetic: "People who do not know the Lord ask why in the world we waste our lives as missionaries. They forget that they too are expending their lives ... and when the bubble has burst, they will have nothing of eternal significance to show for the years they have wasted."

Did those five missionaries waste their lives? Hardly. They laid the groundwork for Elisabeth Elliot, the wife of one of those missionaries, and Nate's sister Rachel who returned later and made that gospel presentation. As a result, a number of the Auca people came to know the living God.

As much good as has been accomplished by Western civilization, we often miss the mark when it comes to distinguishing the temporal from the eternal. Today in the Western world, there is a large-scale abandonment of the gospel and the Bible; however, even in Saint's day, some had begun to drift in that direction. Sadly, there is more interest in the temporal 'here and now' and less in the eternal 'there and then.'

One of the ways we bring glory to God is by being a witness to His saving power through the gospel. Far from being a waste, it is part of what the Christian life is all about. Nate Saint had it right. Jesus said, "Go ye into all the world, and preach the gospel to every creature." (Mark 16:15) Nate Saint and his friends took Christ seriously.

19

The Way, the Truth, and the Life

John 14:5-6 "Thomas saith unto him, Lord, we know not whither thou goest; and how can we know the way? Jesus saith unto him, I am the way, the truth, and the life: no man cometh unto the Father, but by me."

Several years ago, a famous man passed away. He had been raised in the Christian community but later abandoned it for a completely different belief system.

People often quote (and misquote) Matthew 7:1—"Judge not, that ye be not judged"—in a negative or defensive way, implying "You don't have the right to judge me." There is significantly more to that command than such a simplistic interpretation (see John 7:24), but there is also a positive aspect to that verse—I do not have the right *or responsibility* to determine anyone's eternal guilt, innocence, or fate.

I say all that to say this: after he died, I saw a number of posts expressing assurance that he had gone to Heaven. I will tell you with all my heart that I hope he did, but in accordance with Matthew 7:1, I cannot say one way or the other. It is very natural for us to wish Heaven on those we love, respect, or admire, or with whom we identify in some way. It is equally natural to want some sort of condemnation for those we do *not* like for some reason. My point is that we do not have the power or the responsibility to determine either outcome. That is God's job, and He will fulfill it righteously.

According to Jesus, we cannot base our eternal destination on what others say or think, but rather on the completed work of Christ on the cross. *No one* comes to the Father any other way. To embrace that gift is to be saved; to reject it is to be lost. All of us, "good" or "bad", rich or poor, famous or unknown, need a Savior.

No one knows what happens in the heart of someone in their last hours. A person *can* trust Christ on their deathbed; however, since we don't know when—or how suddenly—we will die, waiting until the end is wasteful at best, not to mention extremely dangerous.

Jesus said He is the *only* way; that is a sobering claim. Choose wisely, dear reader. *everything* depends on it!

20
Piercings and Other Pains

Mark 15:25-27, 33-34 "And it was the third hour, and they crucified him. And the superscription of his accusation was written over, THE KING OF THE JEWS. And with him they crucify two thieves; the one on his right hand, and the other on his left ... And when the sixth hour was come, there was darkness over the whole land until the ninth hour. And at the ninth hour Jesus cried with a loud voice, saying, Eloi, Eloi, lama sabachthani? which is, being interpreted, My God, my God, why hast thou forsaken me?"

The thought of personally enduring a crucifixion is an unimaginably horrible one. I think it would be very excruciating just to watch, but to go through it would be unbearable.

However, there is another element in the crucifixion of the Lord Jesus, for He didn't just endure the physical pain; He endured the punishment that was rightly due me for my sins. He endured the punishment due to all those who believe in Him. He endured the punishment required to redeem His universe from the curse of sin.

I fear we sometimes minimize the work of Christ on the cross, not intentionally, but it is difficult not to. The magnitude of the effort, coupled with the fact that He was separated from the Father, is more than we can fully comprehend; nevertheless, let us be diligent to study and appreciate, as much as possible, the work Christ did on our behalf.

It took an incomprehensible price to redeem us from the curse of Adam's fall and from our own folly. Yet, just because it is incomprehensible doesn't mean we cannot ponder, delight in, and be awed by His gracious gift.

21
The Conflict Within

Romans 8:38-39 "For I am persuaded, that neither death, nor life, nor angels, nor principalities, nor powers, nor things present, nor things to come, Nor height, nor depth, nor any other creature, shall be able to separate us from the love of God, which is in Christ Jesus our Lord."

Self-esteem is a major quest for many. Several years ago, one advertisement for a hair treatment product featured a pretty, young lady who supposedly looked like she did because she used that product. As I recall, toward the end of the commercial, she said, "I deserve it because I'm worth it."

Our society seems to be in a death struggle between self-loathing and narcissism. On the one hand, people have contempt for themselves, a loathing, almost a hatred. On the other hand, they boast about their abilities, appearance, wealth, or social status in some desperate attempt to convince others of their intrinsic worth. Then again, perhaps it is to convince themselves.

I understand the craving for self-esteem. We pick at ourselves or even beat on ourselves. Then enemies, society, or even friends kick us while we are down. Interestingly enough though, there is one cure for both of those conditions—self-loathing *and* narcissism—and that is to trust in God and draw close to Him.

Professional golfer Webb Simpson said it very well, "If we knew what we really deserved from God because of our sin, we wouldn't live with any sense of entitlement." Now perhaps that excludes us from boasting, but it does nothing to help us feel better about ourselves.

Consider this: we know "what we really deserved from God" and we know we are not entitled to *anything*. Now take a moment to realize that in His love, He has given us everything worth having, in spite of ourselves. Furthermore, He has done so at a staggering personal cost.

We don't *need* to be rich or famous, or powerful, or beautiful to enjoy God's love. What we *really* need is to trust in God's goodness and forgiveness, yielding to His wisdom and truth. As the song says, "Trust and obey, for there's no other way to be happy in Jesus but to trust and obey."

"O come, let us worship and bow down: let us kneel before the LORD our maker." (Psalm 95:6) He *is* worthy of our trust *and* our praise.

22

Regret and Repentance

Matthew 26:74-75 "Then began he to curse and to swear, saying, I know not the man. And immediately the cock crew. And Peter remembered the word of Jesus, which said unto him, Before the cock crow, thou shalt deny me thrice. And he went out, and wept bitterly."

God cautions us against judging others. I think the reason is that we can't see into the heart, so we don't know motive. That said, I acknowledge that I don't know what was in Peter's heart, but the wording in these verses and Peter's later conversation with Jesus suggest that his denial of Christ grieved him greatly, and he repented.

Again, not knowing what was in the heart, Judas *seemed* to have a different response to his betrayal, for he grew angry and then took his own life.

I don't want to draw absolute conclusions from each man's reaction to his earlier bad decision, but it does *seem* to indicate a distinction between the two. Peter, as much as he may have struggled with it, repented and came back to Christ. In contrast, Judas did not and took a more destructive path.

For several reasons, I have always assumed Judas never was actually a genuine believer in Christ; I am glad I don't have to make that call. However, it *is* safe to say that repenting and coming to God for forgiveness and cleansing is *much* better than despairing and being desolate. It is also infinitely better than ending the precious life that God Himself gave you.

23

Allegiance, the Church, and God

Lamentations 5:16-21 "The crown is fallen from our head: woe unto us, that we have sinned! For this our heart is faint; for these things our eyes are dim. Because of the mountain of Zion, which is desolate, the foxes walk upon it. Thou, O LORD, remainest for ever; thy throne from generation to generation. Wherefore dost thou forget us for ever, and forsake us so long time? Turn thou us unto thee, O LORD, and we shall be turned; renew our days as of old."

My mother was born in Cameroun, West Africa. Since then, the 'u' in the name has been replaced with a second 'o'. Mom's parents were missionaries to their dear friends in Cameroon and expressed their love for God by loving His people there.

Like many missionaries, then and now, my grandparents were sent out under the sponsorship of one of the main denominations. At that time, denominations had different understandings of what we might call the "non-essential" beliefs, but for the most part, the main church groups had a general agreement on what are sometimes called "essentials." An example of non-essentials is whether or not to use pianos and other musical instruments in public worship; the structure of church government; the format of the service, etc. Essential doctrines include the deity of Christ, His death, burial and physical resurrection, the trinity, and other principles of the Bible.

Over the years, adherence to the essentials has weakened, even to the point of abandonment by many groups. Various main denominations, and to a lesser extent individual independent churches, have started drifting away from positions they held just a generation ago. Clear biblical admonitions and even essentials are being set aside and forsaken in the interest of fitting into the present culture.

One of the things for which I will always be grateful is that my parents never taught me to give my allegiance to a specific church or denomination. Instead, they taught me to follow God and honor His Word, and align myself with churches that do the same. It is discouraging to see so many formerly faithful groups fall away from God's truth, but it is good to know that we, as individuals and as churches, can remain on solid ground by always standing with His revealed will, even if others forsake God and walk away from Him.

24
Deep Love

Song of Solomon 8:5-7 "Who is this that cometh up from the wilderness, leaning upon her beloved? I raised thee up under the apple tree: there thy mother brought thee forth: there she brought thee forth that bare thee. Set me as a seal upon thine heart, as a seal upon thine arm: for love is strong as death; jealousy is cruel as the grave: the coals thereof are coals of fire, which hath a most vehement flame. Many waters cannot quench love, neither can the floods drown it: if a man would give all the substance of his house for love, it would utterly be contemned."

Recently, I heard about an upcoming play. The announcer finished before I realized what he was talking about, but as much as I recall, the play was about a young woman who had been disfigured. She felt discouraged and unlovable. As the outline of the story was presented, the announcer said the young lady searches for a preacher who can heal her. However, in her search, she meets a soldier and a romance blossoms between them in spite of her appearance.

When I heard the brief outline of the play, I was also reminded of the sad reality that many who find themselves spiritually broken and lost chase after a preacher, or a healer, or even a church, only to be further disillusioned or even further broken.

Can a preacher or other church member help guide us toward Christ? Yes, they can, and in many cases, that is what happens, but let us all, seeker and believer alike, realize that we may get good guidance and advice from another mortal, but the goal is not to stop there. Instead, we all need to seek the Savior and find our love, our security, and our salvation in Him. Seekers should be seeking—and believers should be pointing to—the Lord Jesus Christ. Only through Him can the unforgivable be forgiven, and it is He who will love us in spite of our being unlovely.

That reminded me of another story—a true story. It is a story of disfigurement and distortion. It is a story of disgrace and humiliation. It is the story of a whole world that has been destroyed by sin. It is also a story of a Savior who loved His bride—the Church—and laid down His life for her.

25
Mr. Humility

Philippians 2:8 "And being found in fashion as a man, he humbled himself, and became obedient unto death, even the death of the cross."

I saw a tee shirt a while back that said, "I can't hear you over the sound of how epic I am." Things like that cause me to chuckle. I am sure the young man wearing that shirt didn't take that quip seriously, but even in its humor, it addresses a sad inclination of the human heart.

The apostle Paul wrote today's verse about the Lord Jesus Christ: "And being found in fashion as a man, he humbled himself, and became obedient unto death, even the death of the cross." Let that sink in for a moment. That was not some criminal on that cross; that was not just a good man or even a prophet who hung there in shame, bearing our sins; that was God *Himself* who suffered and died so He could deliver us from all unrighteousness and make us fit to stand before the throne of His Father in Heaven.

Now, what was the outcome of that humble submission? Yes, our salvation was one result, but there was so much more. Paul's letter goes on: "Wherefore"—because of His willing submission—"God also hath highly exalted him, and given him a name which is above every name: That at the name of Jesus every knee should bow, of things in heaven, and things in earth, and things under the earth; And that every tongue should confess that Jesus Christ is Lord, to the glory of God the Father." (verses 9-11) His submission and obedience resulted in exaltation and honor.

How does that apply to us, you may ask? Well, let's go back several verses: "***Let this mind be in you***, which was also in Christ Jesus: Who, being in the form of God, thought it not robbery to be equal with God: But made himself of no reputation, and took upon him the form of a servant, and was made in the likeness of men." (verses 5-7, emphasis mine)

God in the flesh humbled Himself to serve. He calls you and me to do the same, and He will reward our obedience in His perfect time.

26

The Good, the Bad, and the Beautiful

Hebrews 7:25 "Wherefore he is able also to save them to the uttermost that come unto God by him, seeing he ever liveth to make intercession for them."

The gangster film ***Road to Perdition*** is set in 1931 Chicago and depicts the violent underworld of organized crime. One scene shows a leading character saying, "This is the life we chose … and there is only one guarantee: none of us will see Heaven."

In contrast to the men shown in that movie, John 3 tells us of a ***good*** man, Nicodemus, a Pharisee and ruler of the Jews. You know his type, a man with a fine reputation in the community, most likely a kind and gentle person who always does what is right. What catches us off guard is Jesus' initial comment before Nicodemus even asks a question: "Verily, verily, I say unto thee, Except a man be born again, he cannot see the kingdom of God." (v5) Jesus later reemphasizes that thought: "Marvel not that I said unto thee, Ye must be born again." (v7) Surely Jesus was not saying there was something missing in this "good" man's life. Or was He?

I find it interesting that in the very next chapter after Nicodemus, John 4 tells of a promiscuous woman. You know her type too. Oh, she is different from the murderous gangsters in the movie, but late at night, in the depth of her solitude, she probably thought the same thing as the mobster in that film: "I will never see Heaven."

I believe that part of what God is telling us by putting these accounts together is that "good" people have the same need as the promiscuous and gangsters. Whether we think of ourselves as good or bad, everyone needs a Savior. Living a good life does not make it "easier" for God to save you, and falling to the depths does not make it harder, except on yourself. There is no one so good that they do not need God's salvation or so bad that God cannot save them.

Lord willing, we can look at this a little more tomorrow. Until then, I leave you with this thought: "This is a faithful saying, and worthy of all acceptation, that Christ Jesus came into the world to save sinners; of whom I am chief." (1 Timothy 1:15)

That is a beautiful thing.

27
The Good, the Bad, and the Beautiful, Part 2

Matthew 19:16-17, 20-22 "And, behold, one came and said unto him, Good Master, what good thing shall I do, that I may have eternal life? And he said unto him, Why callest thou me good? there is none good but one, that is, God: but if thou wilt enter into life, keep the commandments … The young man saith unto him, All these things have I kept from my youth up: what lack I yet? Jesus said unto him, If thou wilt be perfect, go and sell that thou hast, and give to the poor, and thou shalt have treasure in heaven: and come and follow me. But when the young man heard that saying, he went away sorrowful: for he had great possessions."

Last time, we saw that all people—from the best to the worst—need to be saved. It makes sense that "wicked sinners" would have the same resignation to their destiny as the murderous gangster I quoted yesterday: "This is the life we chose … and there is only one guarantee: none of us will see Heaven." Many others may think they will "get in some how," but I suspect that number shrinks considerably as they lay on their pillow at night, trying to reconcile their actions to what little they know of God's righteousness.

Today's verses show us another "good" man. He came to Jesus asking about obtaining eternal life. Jesus told him to keep the commandments. When he said he had always done that, Jesus gave him the *big* test: "Go and sell that thou hast, and give to the poor." The man left because of his great possessions, but by leaving, he failed to keep: Commandment 10 (coveting, even his own things, as Nebuchadnezzar did); Commandment 1 (placing his wealth before his allegiance to God); and Commandment 9 (lying about keeping all ten from his youth up).

No one is as good as we think we are. Are some better than others? More civil? More gracious? More kind? Yes, but by God's standard, "all have sinned, and come short of the glory of God." (Romans 3:23)

That is why we *all* need a Savior. "For the wages of sin is death; but the gift of God is eternal life through Jesus Christ our Lord." (Romans 6:23)

That *too* is a beautiful thing.

28

The Good, the Bad, and the Beautiful, Part 3

Ephesians 5:15 "See then that ye walk circumspectly, not as fools, but as wise,"

I keep these Musings brief; they can usually be read in about a minute and a half. However, being brief sometimes leaves the subject lacking. Radio bible teacher Chuck Swindoll said he wants his ministry to be remembered as being balanced. In the same way, today I hope to bring balance to my two preceding Musings.

Previously we looked at the man in John 3 who was good and the woman in John 4 who was not. What we saw was that the woman was not beyond the *power* of the cross and the man was not beyond his *need* for the cross. Despite all claims to the contrary, Jesus is the *only* way to God. However, whether you think you are good or bad, Jesus said, "him that cometh to me I will in no wise cast out." (John 6:37b) Whoever, whatever, and wherever we are, when we come to God in repentance and faith, we find acceptance and forgiveness, hope, and rest.

That brings me to the need for balance. Some seem to think that praying a few "religious words" creates a get-out-of-hell-free-pass that buys them the right to live any way they want and do anything they please without consequence. I beg my readers not to follow that deceitful way of thinking.

Remember, God tells us to walk worthy. (Ephesians 4:1; Colossians 1:10; 1Thesalonians 2:12) He even uses Paul to ask, "Shall we continue in sin, that grace may abound?" (Romans 6:1b) He then answers that question: "God forbid. How shall we, that are dead to sin, live any longer therein?" (Romans 6:2)

We know we are all sinners. That is still a fact, even after salvation; as long as we live, we will struggle with the flesh. Whether we think we "lean toward good enough" or know that we are "nowhere near good enough," the truth is we are *not* good enough. The good news is that it doesn't matter. As the old gospel song says, "Just as I am, I come."

However, let us realize as was said many years ago, "We are saved by faith alone, but the faith that saves is never alone." We should *never* trust our actions to save us, but if our sin doesn't bother us, we might be kidding ourselves.

29

Best Friend

Proverbs 18:24 "A man that hath friends must shew himself friendly: and there is a friend that sticketh closer than a brother."

Some Christians seem to be happy all the time. Not fake-happy—genuinely happy. The same for some non-Christians. They are almost always upbeat. I suppose they have moments of discouragement or self-doubt, but they are generally positive.

I think I am a relatively upbeat person, but honestly, I struggle sometimes. With deep struggles. Additionally, during my discouragements, I am most likely to speak sharply or harshly or to make bad decisions or take actions I should not take. When I am down, my mind focuses more on my troubles than on my precious Savior, and I am tempted to act or think differently than when I am more aware of His presence.

I struggled like that the other day. I was listening to some music at the time, and as I asked the Lord to help me get out of my downcast mood, what do you suppose flowed into my ears that very moment?

> What a Friend we have in Jesus,
>   All our sins and griefs to bear!
> What a privilege to carry
>   Everything to God in prayer!
> O what peace we often forfeit,
>   O what needless pain we bear,
> All because we do not carry
>   Everything to God in prayer.

Although Irish-born Joseph Scriven lost two fiancés to death—one to a drowning accident the day before his wedding and one to illness—he offered comfort to his dying mother through his poem, "What a Friend We Have in Jesus". He became a teacher and preacher, spending the rest of his life offering Jesus' compassionate love to others in Canada and beyond.

The Lord of Glory has purposed to be the friend of sinners. (Matt. 11:19) There is no better friend than the Lord Jesus. If I—or you—struggle with discouragement, especially if it makes us more likely to fall into sin, we would always do well to draw close to "the friend of sinners."

Mr. Scriven had it right: "What a friend we have in Jesus!"

> Have we trials and temptations?
> Is there trouble anywhere?
> We should never be discouraged,
> Take it to the Lord in prayer.
> Can we find a friend so faithful
> Who will all our sorrows share?
> Jesus knows our every weakness,
> Take it to the Lord in prayer.

30
Babel and the Twenty-first Century

Genesis 11:1-9 "And the whole earth was of one language, and of one speech. And it came to pass, as they journeyed from the east, that they found a plain in the land of Shinar; and they dwelt there. And they said one to another, Go to, let us make brick, and burn them throughly. And they had brick for stone, and slime had they for morter. And they said, Go to, let us build us a city and a tower, whose top may reach unto heaven; and let us make us a name, lest we be scattered abroad upon the face of the whole earth. And the LORD came down to see the city and the tower, which the children of men builded. And the LORD said, Behold, the people is one, and they have all one language; and this they begin to do: and now nothing will be restrained from them, which they have imagined to do. Go to, let us go down, and there confound their language, that they may not understand one another's speech. So the LORD scattered them abroad from thence upon the face of all the earth: and they left off to build the city. Therefore is the name of it called Babel; because the LORD did there confound the language of all the earth: and from thence did the LORD scatter them abroad upon the face of all the earth."

Today's verses give the account of the people of Shinar. At the time, the whole Earth spoke one language. In their arrogance, these people rebelled against God, so He interrupted their folly by giving them multiple languages. Later, Shinar became known as Babel, which means "confused voices."

We as Christians must not be dogmatic about subjects on which the Scriptures are unclear or silent; however, we can make observations about events around us. From that perspective, let me point out that God saw rebellion in Shinar and confused their languages; as a result, they dispersed and stopped building the city and the tower. Now, in the twenty-first century, more and more people from many different cultures are speaking the common language of English. At the same time, the world seems to be rising up again in almost wholesale rebellion against God and His revealed will, trying to build its own little "utopia."

Have we learned nothing from the experience at Shinar?

31

The Calm and the Storm

Revelation 1:17-19 "And when I saw him, I fell at his feet as dead. And he laid his right hand upon me, saying unto me, Fear not; I am the first and the last: I am he that liveth, and was dead; and, behold, I am alive for evermore, Amen; and have the keys of hell and of death. Write the things which thou hast seen, and the things which are, and the things which shall be hereafter;"

"The things which shall be hereafter." That is an interesting phrase, isn't it? Here Jesus tells John that He is going to reveal things that are going to happen "hereafter." That is, Jesus is going to tell John the future.

I just started reading the book of Revelation in my devotions. Currently I am reading in chapters two and three which are the seven letters that Jesus dictated to John to be sent to the seven churches in what is now western Turkey.

We sometimes use the phrase "the calm before the storm;" it is often used for a tense situation that is about to reach a volatile stage. However, as I did a little research on the internet, one of the pages I visited created a clever play on that phrase by referring to Revelation as "The Storm Before the Calm."

That is an appropriate subtitle for the book of Revelation because starting in chapter four, a terrible unfolding occurs, an unfolding of the events of the end-times. Those events include the seven years of tribulation, the last half of which are going to be horrible catastrophes. However, once the storm is finished and all the end-time events have played out, there will be peace and calm for us who have placed our faith, trust, and confidence in the forgiveness of God through the work of the Lord Jesus on the cross. Amen!

FEBRUARY

1

Unfathomable Riches

Romans 11:33-36 "O the depth of the riches both of the wisdom and knowledge of God! how unsearchable are his judgments, and his ways past finding out! For who hath known the mind of the Lord? or who hath been his counsellor? Or who hath first given to him, and it shall be recompensed unto him again? For of him, and through him, and to him, are all things: to whom be glory for ever. Amen."

Chapters 9 through 11 of Romans unfold some of the most profound thoughts in all of Scripture. While choosing verses for this Musing, I kept reading and rereading, wondering which to use and where to stop; I finally selected the final verses of chapter 11. They do not sum up the thoughts of the previous verses; instead, they sum up the unfathomable "wisdom and knowledge of God" that **bring about** the events of the previous verses.

In chapters 9 and 10, Paul longs for his fellow Jews to come to the saving knowledge of God's grace. He acknowledges their zeal for God but says their misguided passion is leading them to depend on their own righteousness rather than the righteousness available through the cross of Christ. As a result, they have grown distant from God.

Paul then lays out God's intricate design whereby He is using the salvation of the Gentiles to create jealousy in the Jews. They have not fallen permanently; instead, the profound plan of the all-knowing God is to woo the Jews back by also saving the Gentiles.

Everything God does is for a reason, and His actions have no unintended consequences. Every detail is purposeful; every detail also accounts for every ripple it creates. Indeed, even the ripples are part of His plan. God purposed to save Abraham's seed and put one of them—Jesus Christ—on the eternal throne of King David. He did so by sending Jesus to redeem all who trust in Him, Jew and Gentile alike, and stirring the hearts of mortals to accomplish His good purposes.

"O the depth of the riches both of the wisdom and knowledge of God! how unsearchable are his judgments, and his ways past finding out!"

2

Still Looking

2 Timothy 4:6-8 "For I am now ready to be offered, and the time of my departure is at hand. I have fought a good fight, I have finished my course, I have kept the faith: Henceforth there is laid up for me a crown of righteousness, which the Lord, the righteous judge, shall give me at that day: and not to me only, but unto all them also that love his appearing."

In 2 Timothy 4, Paul exhorts his young student and friend Timothy, telling him to remain strong and preach the truth because a time would come when people would rather hear what is pleasing to them than to hear the truth.

Paul continues in today's verses, saying that he himself has done what he is instructing Timothy to do, but he sees that his own time for earthly ministry is almost over. Even so, he is assured of a crown of righteousness that will be given to all who love the Lord's appearing.

Whether that "appearing" was a desire to behold God's power in Paul's ministry or, as I suspect, a longing for Christ's return for His church, the result was the same—a crown for a loving anticipation of His arrival.

I saw something the other day that reminded me of that anticipation. I was in the parking lot of a small store. The weather was cool but not cold, so the owner left his dog in the car while he ran in for a few items. I noticed in particular that though the dog would look around at other people as they came and went, his intent focus always returned to the door of the convenience store. His master had disappeared through that door, and the dog expected his return at any moment.

Can we say that about our anticipation of Christ? I pray our loving gaze shall always remain that centered on Christ and His appearing. If it is, I suspect we will also be more diligent and faithful in the work He has given us to do for as long as He leaves us here in this world.

3

The Smell of Smoldering Gods

Psalm 115:4-8 "Their idols are silver and gold, the work of men's hands. They have mouths, but they speak not: eyes have they, but they see not: They have ears, but they hear not: noses have they, but they smell not: They have hands, but they handle not: feet have they, but they walk not:

neither speak they through their throat. They that make them are like unto them; so is every one that trusteth in them."

In David Platt's thought-provoking book *Follow Me*, he told the story of a time he was preaching at a small church in Asia. A woman who came from a life of idol worship was gloriously saved. She told Platt and the church's pastor that her house was full of false gods, and she wanted to get rid of them. They went to her house and gathered all the idols and posters together; then they took them to the place where the church met and burned them. Platt wrote that they started their Bible study that day "amidst the smell of smoldering gods."

Whether precious metals, stone statues or wooden carvings, idols cannot speak, see or hear. Such "gods" cannot even save themselves from being destroyed. However, other "gods"—such as shiny cars, large bank accounts, or big houses—are also powerless and helpless. Those in the deepest jungles of Africa and on uncharted islands do not have a monopoly on idol worship; we—the "educated and sophisticated" of the Western world—have the same tendency toward 'thing-ism'.

Are money and the things it can buy bad in and of themselves? No. Remember, it is not money that is the root of all evil; it is the *love* of money. (1 Timothy 6:10) Nevertheless, elevating money or things—so they compete with our affections for God—is sin.

It is not wrong to own possessions; the problem comes when those possessions own us. If we place more importance on our possessions than we do on God and His will, His love may remove them so He can turn our focus back to Himself where it belongs. Nazi-death-camp survivor Corrie ten Boom said it well: "Hold everything in your hands lightly, otherwise it hurts when God pries your fingers open."

4

The Amazing Memory

Ecclesiastes 12:1, 6-7 "Remember now thy Creator in the days of thy youth, while the evil days come not, nor the years draw nigh, when thou shalt say, I have no pleasure in them; … Or ever the silver cord be loosed, or the golden bowl be broken, or the pitcher be broken at the fountain, or the wheel broken at the cistern. Then shall the dust return to the earth as it was: and the spirit shall return unto God who gave it."

Many years ago, the company where I worked had our Christmas lunch at a Mexican restaurant; there were eighteen of us in the group. The server took the food and drink order ***without writing anything down*** and only made one error, that being a dish that was ordered with beef but made with chicken. I was astounded.

I suppose I have an average memory, but as I age, I find I forget things more. My mind also wanders easily although for me that has been a lifelong problem to one degree or another.

Did you notice the command in the passage above? "**Remember** now thy Creator in the days of thy youth, while the evil days come not, nor the years draw nigh, when thou shalt say, I have no pleasure in them." (emphasis mine) The writer goes on to mention that *after* the days of our youth, "the strong men shall bow themselves (walk bent over), and the grinders cease because they are few (teeth), and those that look out of the windows be darkened (eyes).

We mortals are tempted to use our lives for ourselves, in essence saying, "I will be interested in God later; I am too busy now." Take advice from one who has lived more than seven decades; I wish now that I had focused more on my God and Savior when I was younger.

I once heard someone say, "I have never met a man who was sorry he was a Christian, but I have met some sorry Christians." I am one of those who is not sorry I am a Christian; I just wish I had understood God's glory earlier. Even at this age, I am still learning.

None of us will ever be any younger. My encouragement to all is, "Remember *now* thy Creator in the days of thy youth."

5

More Than Just Substance

Hebrews 11:1 "Now faith is the substance of things hoped for, the evidence of things not seen."

Sometime ago, my friend and mentor Wayne Schlichter published his excellent devotional on Hebrews 11, "The Faith Chapter." Of course, his focus was on faith and several important things our faith teaches us; however, my mind was also drawn to the use of the word "substance" in verse 1.

I have long enjoyed the sense of that word regarding faith. Faith is the "stuff"—the handle we can hold on to, the evidence of the things we hope for but cannot yet see.

However, there is another sense to "substance." I have looked up that word before, but either I forgot or the other aspect of the meaning never fully settled into my mind. That other flavor to the Greek word translated substance is the idea of a building's underpinning. The Greek dictionary tells us this word describes something that has actual existence and is put under something else as its foundation. In other words, faith not only gives us something to grab hold of, but it is the stable platform for all we believe.

Doesn't that add power to the idea in this verse? What God says is true whether we believe it or not, but faith is the tool God has given whereby we can embrace God's truth and whereby we find it to be solid and dependable.

"For by grace are ye saved through faith; and that not of yourselves: it is the gift of God:" (Ephesians 2:8)

Praise God for *all* His truth, including the truth of faith.

6

Silver and Gold

1 Peter 2:7-10 "Unto you therefore which believe he is precious: but unto them which be disobedient, the stone which the builders disallowed, the same is made the head of the corner, And a stone of stumbling, and a rock of offence, even to them which stumble at the word, being disobedient: whereunto also they were appointed. But ye are a chosen generation, a royal priesthood, an holy nation, a peculiar people; that ye should shew forth the praises of him who hath called you out of darkness into his marvellous light: Which in time past were not a people, but are now the people of God: which had not obtained mercy, but now have obtained mercy."

Many years ago, I was listening to a speaker who read these verses and commented how unusual it was that a rough, impetuous sailor and fisherman would use the word "precious." I am sure the speaker was thinking about the way one might refer to a picture of a child or a cute animal as "precious." Using the word in that context does seem to be a little soft for Peter, a rugged, professional fisherman.

However, just a few verses earlier, Peter uses that word to indicate a different meaning: "Forasmuch as ye know that ye were not redeemed with corruptible things, as silver and gold, from your vain conversation received by tradition from your fathers; But with the precious blood of Christ, as of a lamb without blemish and without spot." (1 Peter 1:18-19) In this context, Peter is not using the word to mean something cute or endearing; he is using the word to indicate that our salvation was purchased with something inconceivably valuable—something of great worth.

May we never lose the wonder of that thought. God has purposed to redeem us at such a costly price as the lifeblood of Jesus, God manifested in the flesh. Think of that for a moment: ***God in the flesh died for sinners like us!***

Let us embrace that truth and hold to it dearly. As Paul wrote in his first letter to Timothy, "This is a faithful saying, and worthy of all acceptation, that Christ Jesus came into the world to save sinners." (1 Timothy 1:15)

Amen!

7

Keeping up Appearances

Luke 12:15 "And he said unto them, Take heed, and beware of covetousness: for a man's life consisteth not in the abundance of the things which he possesseth."

Some years ago, my parents introduced us to the British television comedy ***Keeping up Appearances***. The central character, Hyacinth Bucket (She defensively pronounces it "Bouquet.") is engrossed in her social standing and tries to manipulate her husband, neighbors, and friends to fit in. She considers herself to be a lady of class and breeding; she expresses distain for those of a lower station in life including two sisters and a brother-in-law. However, she regularly extols those who have attained a higher status or obtained more stuff.

It is funny to watch Hyacinth's meddling manipulation and try to imagine how she is going to get out of the dilemmas she creates. In another way though, it is sad to recognize those self-centered tendencies within our own hearts, many times squeezing their way out at embarrassing moments. Sadder still is the fact that sometimes we are ***not*** embarrassed because we ***do*** have an inflated sense of importance.

Whether our craving is for status or stuff, there is a reason why God forbids covetousness in the Ten Commandments: whatever we crave more than God becomes our idol. In addition, lest we think that is an Old Testament issue, God also lists coveting in the New Testament right along side what we might consider more serious and scandalous transgressions. (See Romans 13:9; 1 Corinthians 5:10-11; 1 Corinthians 6:10; Ephesians 5:5; 1 Timothy 3:3; 2 Timothy 3:2; 2 Peter 2:14.)

Jesus gave a parable following today's verse, wherein a farmer had so much stuff he didn't know where to put it all. That evening God pronounced the solution to his predicament: "This night thy soul shall be required of thee: then whose shall those things be?" (Luke 12:20)

I have said before that money, status, and things are not the problem; instead, it is our heart attitude toward money, status, and things. Our obsession with status and stuff is not to blame. The disease is a self-centered heart. The cure is falling in love with the Lord Jesus who loved us and gave Himself for us. (Galatians 2:20)

8

Act Your Age

Isaiah 46:3-5 "Hearken unto me, O house of Jacob, and all the remnant of the house of Israel, which are borne by me from the belly, which are carried from the womb: And even to your old age I am he; and even to hoar hairs (gray-headed; same Hebrew word as in Psalm 71:18) will I carry you: I have made, and I will bear; even I will carry, and will deliver you. To whom will ye liken me, and make me equal, and compare me, that we may be like?"

While trying to create this Musing, I felt like a rabbit in a carrot patch: I knew what to do, but I didn't know where to start. Isaiah 46 is one of those rich passages that overflows with the majesty of God. I encourage you to read the entire brief chapter, but I want to settle specifically on verses 3-5 and 9.

In this chapter, God is speaking of those who make idols out of silver and gold (v 6). They transport their "god" by beasts of burden (v1), set it up in a prominent place (v7), and worship it (v6). The trouble arises when they need their god to help them; it cannot move on their behalf, answer their pleas for help, or save them from their troubles (v7).

In verse 3, God interrupts His discourse as if to say, 'Listen to Me, Israel. In contrast to those who make gods and carry *them* around, I made *you*, and I carry *you* from the time you are in your mother's womb to the time of your old age, even to the days of your gray hair.' Then He asks if there is any comparison between Himself and manmade gods. He goes on to answer His own question in verse 9: "I am God, and there is none else; I am God, and there is none like me."

What we learn from this is that whatever our age—from the womb to the gray hair—God undertakes for those who trust in Him in ways no one else can.

It honors God when we work for our money, but let us not ***trust*** in our riches, regardless how much or how little we have. Let us trust in Him who carries us for "Without faith it is impossible to please him." (Hebrews 11:6)

9

Only a Temporary Condition

Philippians 2:10-11 "That at the name of Jesus every knee should bow, of things in heaven, and things in earth, and things under the earth; And that every tongue should confess that Jesus Christ is Lord, to the glory of God the Father."

A visitor at a blacksmith's shop questioned the smithy about a pile of old hammers in the corner. "Those are the hammers I have worn out over the years," the blacksmith answered. The guest inquired further, "And how many anvils have you had over that time?" "Just one," came the reply.

The Word of God is truth, even though we live in an age when it is not popular to say that. The countless hammers of human arrogance have struck the anvil of God's truth many times, but it is always the hammer that suffers damage, never the anvil.

A meme I have seen several times said, "I would rather be made uncomfortable by the truth than soothed with a lie." I was reminded of these things recently by a sign: "Atheism is a temporary condition." Beneath that, it quoted today's scripture that declares every knee will bow and every tongue will confess that Jesus Christ is Lord.

Some say, "You can't judge me!" True, but you would not call a fire alarm a "judge." Instead, you would be thankful for the warning that saved you from injury and possible death.

Please note that the biblical warning is not addressed at "you," but rather to "us"—*every* knee and *every* tongue. I am not your judge, but as a fellow human being, I lovingly tell you the truth. Witnessing is like telling someone who is thirsty where to find water. The Scripture says, "In the last day, that great day of the feast, Jesus stood and cried, saying, If any man thirst, let him come unto me, and drink." (John 7:37)

Please don't wait my friend, "For he saith, I have heard thee in a time accepted, and in the day of salvation have I helped thee: behold, now is the accepted time; behold, now is the day of salvation." (2 Corinthians 6:2)

10

How Fallen This World Is

Ruth 1:12-14 "Turn again, my daughters, go your way; for I am too old to have an husband. If I should say, I have hope, if I should have an husband also to night, and should also bear sons; Would ye tarry for them till they were grown? would ye stay for them from having husbands? nay, my daughters; for it grieveth me much for your sakes that the hand of the LORD is gone out against me. And they lifted up their voice, and wept again: and Orpah kissed her mother in law; but Ruth clave unto her."

Gino, a friend in Ireland, regularly talks to others about the Lord. I admire his boldness in his witness to our fellow mortals. Sometimes Gino mentions someone for prayer who has been open to the gospel, but sometimes his requests for prayer are for people who are struggling with sickness. One time, he asked for prayer for two people who have cancer and one who has Parkinson's disease.

How terribly fallen this world is: cancer, Parkinson's disease, heart trouble, not to mention crime, murder, terrorism, and the almost endless list of human woes. We are indeed terribly fallen.

Naomi lived in this fallen world. She had experienced the death of her husband and two sons, and in today's verses, we see her trying to convince her daughters-in-law to go back to their Moabite people while she returns to the land of her Hebrew heritage. What grief must have burdened her dear soul!

Interestingly, verse 12 is the first time in the Bible that the word "hope" is used; however, here it is used in a negative sense, almost suggesting more hopelessness than hope.

Living without hope is drudgery at best and much worse in the extreme. And yet, where is there hope but in God? It is He who loves; it is He who redeems; it is He who gives us hope. Not a false hope, mind you, but a hope based on His promises that He is able and resolved to keep.

"Why art thou cast down, O my soul? and why art thou disquieted within me? hope thou in God: for I shall yet praise him, who is the health of my countenance, and my God." (Psalm 42:11)

11
From the Rising of the Sun

Psalm 113:1-3 "Praise ye the LORD. Praise, O ye servants of the LORD, praise the name of the LORD. Blessed be the name of the LORD from this time forth and for evermore. From the rising of the sun unto the going down of the same the LORD'S name is to be praised."

I have made many friends through these Musings. I appreciate each of you and am encouraged by your comments and posts. One friend recently quoted the third verse of this psalm. She used a translation with which I am not familiar. Her post read, "From the raising of the sun to its setting, the name of the Lord is adorable."

I had never heard it put that way before. We often think of "adorable" as being appropriate for a cute puppy or kitten, but we don't think of using that word to describe God. However, as I mused on the word, I realized that in the English language, we often put the suffix "able" at the end of a verb to use it as an adjective. Someone who is easy to love is loveable; something that we can afford is affordable; a road that is not hard to drive on is drivable. Then the words of that old carol came to mind: "O come, let us adore Him, Christ the Lord."

The dictionary defines adore as "[1] to regard with the utmost esteem, love, and respect; to honor" and "[2] to pay divine honor to; to worship: to adore God."

God is to be praised; that is clear throughout Scripture. But it is not just that He *should* be praised or that He *should* be exalted. The reality is the He is *worthy* of praise. He is WORTHY of exaltation. He is *worthy* of adoration. In that pure and very holy sense, He *is* adorable.

On any day, and at any time of the year, "O come, let us adore Him, Christ the Lord!"

12
Things That Matter

Micah 6:6-8 "Wherewith shall I come before the LORD, and bow myself before the high God? shall I come before him with burnt offerings, with calves of a year old? Will the LORD be pleased with thousands of rams, or with ten thousands of rivers of oil? shall I give my firstborn for my transgression, the fruit of my body for the sin of my soul? He hath shewed thee, O man, what is good; and what doth the LORD require of thee, but to do justly, and to love mercy, and to walk humbly with thy God?"

Of all the things that are important in this world, there is **none** as important as our standing with God. Why? Because one day our standing with God will be all we have left. Our friends will be gone, our houses will be gone, our cars will be gone, our bank accounts will be gone, and our cell phones will be gone. One day, everything will be gone, and we will stand before the throne of God.

This is true of unbelievers at the judgment that the Bible calls "The Great White Throne." (Revelation 20:11) However, there is also a different judgment for us as believers. (Romans 14:10) The believer's judgment won't be for eternal destination since that will have already been settled; however, rewards will be given for obedience. Did we grow? Did we seek to be what we were designed to be? Did we do justly, love mercy, and walk humbly with our God?

The tendency of the mortal heart is to think that activity is what is important. We thus busy ourselves, thinking it is our "doing" that pleases God. By saying that, I am not suggesting that doing is wrong in and of itself; in fact, our works **can** be a part of our worship and obedience. What I **am** saying however, is that we should always keep our priorities in order. It does not honor God if we put our religion—or our religious activity— ahead of God Himself.

"He hath shewed thee, O man, what is good; and what doth the LORD require of thee, but to do justly, and to love mercy, and to walk humbly with thy God?"

13
The Details of an Excellent Plan

Micah 6:8 "He hath shewed thee, O man, what is good; and what doth the LORD require of thee, but to do justly, and to love mercy, and to walk humbly with thy God?"

Previously, we looked at this verse and the two verses before it. We saw specifically how our hearts sometime trick us in to a flurry of activity, thinking that God is pleased with our "doing" for Him. I was clear that activity itself is not necessarily wrong; however, our efforts either can be acts of obedience, gratitude, and worship to God, or simply works of human pride. Since righteousness can **only** be ours by grace through faith, (Ephesians 2:8-9) we must **not** do things in an attempt to earn righteousness or to boast in our own works or goodness, like the Pharisee in Luke 18:11-12.

However, there is another aspect to today's verse that we shouldn't miss. Even during the time of the Ten Commandments and the Law, this verse presents a big picture view of our responsibility in two sets of three phrases.

The first set gives an overview of the other set:

- "He hath shewed thee" — God has not left us to guess; He has revealed His will.
- "What is good" — His will is good.
- "Require of thee" — These are not suggestions.

The other three are the specific actions He requires:

- "Do justly." — No preferential treatment; for good or bad, do what is right.
- "Love mercy." — Whenever you can, temper any firm justice with kindness, even if it costs you personally to do so.
- "Walk humbly with thy God." — This one is obvious enough, but it is good to understand that if we are doing this one right, doing justly and loving mercy will come far more easily.

Think about this: Jesus was always just; He was always merciful when dealing with a tender, broken, or repentant heart; and He always walked with His heavenly Father, doing so humbly while here on Earth. Now consider this: That is what Jesus is like, and Paul tells us we are to be conformed to Christ's image. (Romans 8:29) In the beginning, God made man in His image; He requires that we cooperate with Him as He *re*-makes us into the beautiful image of His dear Son.

That, my friends, is an excellent plan.

14
Love and Lovable

Ephesians 2:1-10 "And you hath he quickened, who were dead in trespasses and sins; Wherein in time past ye walked according to the course of this world, according to the prince of the power of the air, the spirit that now worketh in the children of disobedience: Among whom also we all had our conversation in times past in the lusts of our flesh, fulfilling the desires of the flesh and of the mind; and were by nature the children of wrath, even as others. But God, who is rich in mercy, for his great love wherewith he loved us, Even when we were dead in sins, hath quickened us together with Christ, (by grace ye are saved;) And hath raised us up together, and made us sit together in heavenly places in Christ Jesus: That in the ages to come he might shew the exceeding riches of his grace in his kindness toward us through Christ Jesus. For by grace are ye saved through faith; and that not of yourselves: it is the gift of God: Not of works, lest any man should boast. For we are his workmanship, created in Christ Jesus unto good works, which God hath before ordained that we should walk in them."

It is remarkable that God loves sinners after He has cleansed us and made us worthy of His love; what is inconceivable is that He loved us *before* He cleansed us and made us worthy of His love!

"For when we were yet without strength, in due time Christ died for the ungodly. For scarcely for a righteous man will one die: yet peradventure for a good man some would even dare to die. But God commendeth his love toward us, in that, while we were yet sinners, Christ died for us. Much more then, being now justified by his blood, we shall be saved from wrath through him. For if, when we were enemies, we were reconciled to God by the death of his Son, much more, being reconciled, we shall be saved by his life." (Romans 5:6-10)

"Greater love hath no man than this, that a man lay down his life for his friends." (John 15:13) Amazing love. Amazing grace.

15

Seeds, the Sower, and You

1 Corinthians 3:5 "Who then is Paul, and who is Apollos, but ministers by whom ye believed, even as the Lord gave to every man? I have planted, Apollos watered; but God gave the increase. So then neither is he that planteth any thing, neither he that watereth; but God that giveth the increase."

Jesus' parable of the sower is recorded in Matthew 13, Mark 4, and Luke 8. As the story unfolds, some of the seeds fell on good ground and produced increase; other seeds failed to bring forth any gain because they were devoured by birds or the young plants were scorched by the sun or choked out by thorny weeds. Jesus then went on to clarify the parable as a picture of someone presenting the Word of God. Some of those who heard it believed; however, other hearers were distracted by Satan, affliction, and the cares of this world, and they failed to continue in their walk with God.

As I pondered this illustration, I thought of how that applies to me. If I go out into my backyard and plant a seed, I cannot make it grow into a cornstalk or a bean bush or an apple tree. All I can do is plant the seed. If I *do* plant the seed, there is a chance it may not grow, but if I do *not* plant the seed, I am *sure* it will not grow.

You will notice that the sower never attempted to make his seeds grow; all he did was sow them. In the same way, in today's verses, Paul says that he and Apollos were merely partners in the planting and watering process; it was up to the Lord to bring success out of their efforts.

We can glean something else from this parable. We must realize that some of our sincere efforts will not produce the desired result; even if it does, sometimes it might not be in our presence or even within our lifetime. Paul planted, and Apollos watered. Then both of them, and a host of other fellow-laborers, trusted God for the results.

God does not instruct us to measure our success by our results. He calls us to be faithful in using our gifts and abilities to glorify Him. He will take it from there.

16

No Weapon Formed against thee Shall Prosper

Isaiah 54:17 "No weapon that is formed against thee shall prosper; and every tongue that shall rise against thee in judgment thou shalt condemn. This is the heritage of the servants of the LORD, and their righteousness is of me, saith the LORD."

Isaiah 54 is a rather somber chapter. In it, God acknowledges that the people of Israel are in difficult times and enduring unusual hardships. He says they are "forsaken and grieved... afflicted, tossed with tempest, and not comforted." (verses 6, 11) He also tells them that though He has pulled away from them at times, He is still their provider and their redeemer—that He is watching over them and protecting them. The chapter ends with today's verse, in which God tells them, "No weapon that is formed against thee shall prosper."

I see that passage quoted often; however, using the verse outside of any specific context implies that we Christians are invincible and that nothing can cut our skin, break our bones, or end our lives. In all fairness, that may not be the *intent* when people quote that verse, but in the interest of helping young Christians understand a little better, that is not what God is saying to the church.

God warns us that Christians would suffer for their faith, and we see that in the news regularly. Even in the apostle's time we find that some believers—including apostles—suffered mightily even to the point of death. (Hebrews 11: 36-37)

Well, if this verse doesn't teach Christian invincibility, what **does** it teach? I believe God is assuring us that He oversees the affairs of men, and we don't need to fear that things are out of control. Any harm that man—or Satan—wishes to do to us is subject to the purposes of Almighty God, and He only permits that for which He has purpose. Someone once said, "The man who fears God does not need to fear anything else." God truly IS in control. That is not just a saying, a song, or a sermon; that is a *reality*.

We will not always **understand** what He does or allows, but we can rest assured that evil men and their weapons can only operate within the framework of God's permission, for **He** is The King, and **He** is in control.

17

Sunk Down in the Pit They Made

Psalm 9:15-16 "The heathen are sunk down in the pit that they made: in the net which they hid is their own foot taken. The LORD is known by the judgment which he executeth: the wicked is snared in the work of his own hands. Higgaion. Selah."

A.W. Tozer wrote the book *The Knowledge of the Holy*. Such knowledge of God requires that we understand—at least insomuch as we are able—that God is infinitely vast in His being. That magnitude includes not just His love, grace and mercy, but His holiness, righteousness and justice. Tozer said it this way, "What comes into our minds when we think about God is the most important thing about us."

It should be a great sorrow to us that our world has become mostly unaware of the true character of God. Selfishness, greed, and indifference are marks of our time. Even many of the Lord's people don't have a clear view of the lofty One before whom we must all one day stand.

Please understand; that is not a blanket condemnation. Many Christians *do* seek God with a humble heart and long to walk rightly before Him, but on too large a scale, humanity has dismissed Him as irrelevant or even imaginary.

Look again at today's verses. Their own devices become the very trap of those who reject God; that which they design for their own pleasure or enrichment becomes their very downfall. Christian artist and songwriter Twila Paris expressed this irony in one of her songs: "You (God) knew the sturdy walls I hid behind were nothing but a prison cell." We are often trapped by "the work of our own hands." Verse 16 ends with "Higgaion. Selah"—old Hebrew words meaning to lift this thought up, perhaps in front of our eyes, and consider it very carefully.

King David continues in this psalm saying God will judge wickedness and watch over the needy, but then closes it with this request: "Put them in fear, O Lord: that the nations may know themselves to be but men. Selah." (verse 20)

We are only men and women—mere mortals. It is the beginning of wisdom to fear God and be in awe of Him. It is the depth of human folly to forget that we are "but men" (and women), and go on our way, ignoring God.

18
God Is Not Dead, But Guess Who Is

1 Corinthians 15:51-58: "Behold, I shew you a mystery; We shall not all sleep, but we shall all be changed, In a moment, in the twinkling of an eye, at the last trump: for the trumpet shall sound, and the dead shall be raised incorruptible, and we shall be changed. For this corruptible must put on incorruption, and this mortal must put on immortality. So when this corruptible shall have put on incorruption, and this mortal shall have put on immortality, then shall be brought to pass the saying that is written, Death is swallowed up in victory. O death, where is thy sting? O grave, where is thy victory? The sting of death is sin; and the strength of sin is the law. But thanks be to God, which giveth us the victory through our Lord Jesus Christ. Therefore, my beloved brethren, be ye stedfast, unmoveable, always abounding in the work of the Lord, forasmuch as ye know that your labour is not in vain in the Lord."

In these verses, Paul presents Death as a person; however, the Lord Jesus Christ, ever bold in the face of Death, interrupted a funeral procession and brought the widow's son back to life. (Luke 7:11-15) He again robbed Death when he commanded Lazarus to come from the tomb (John 11:1- 44) and brought life back to did the daughter of Jairus who had died. (Luke 8:41- 42; 49-56) If I may say it this way, Jesus was the mortal enemy of Grim Reaper and still is.

Continuing Paul's personification, Jesus' victories must have infuriated Death. On the hill of Golgotha, he eyed Christ angrily, then suddenly rose up in a rage, and murdered the Lord of glory. However, by that very act, Death was defeated. Forever! William Romaine, the eighteenth-century British preacher and author, paraphrased today's passage saying, "Death stung himself to death when he stung Christ."

Today's headlines are convincing many that the Lord's return may be very near. Whether it is or not, whether we go at His coming, or if we face the cold, clammy hand of that ignoble monster Death, we know our Lord has removed his stinger. Now he is no more than God's servant to usher us out of this life and into God's glorious presence.

Praise God for His marvelous grace!

19

Believers and Unbelievers, Here and There

1 Corinthians 15:51-52, 55-57 "Behold, I shew you a mystery; We shall not all sleep, but we shall all be changed, In a moment, in the twinkling of an eye, at the last trump: for the trumpet shall sound, and the dead shall be raised incorruptible, and we shall be changed … O death, where is thy sting? O grave, where is thy victory? The sting of death is sin; and the strength of sin is the law. But thanks be to God, which giveth us the victory through our Lord Jesus Christ."

After losing several family members over a couple years, my sister Debbie said, "I sure wish the Lord would come back and take all of us home at once. This one-at-a-time thing is getting old." Last year, Debbie went home to join those who have gone before us.

The Bible tells us that this life is brief, like a vapor "that appeareth for a little time, and then vanisheth away." (James 4:14) None of us knows when the time will come when we shall close our eyes here and wake up somewhere else. However, even as Debbie longed for, there is another way that believers may be ushered into the afterlife, and that is God's promise of Christ's return to take His people home.

While we are here on Earth, all of us have good times and bad, pleasant and unpleasant, but there is a difference between the afterlife for believers in Jesus, and the one awaiting those who do not trust Him. The other day, I saw a quote from an unidentified source: "For a Christian, this world is the only hell they will know; for the unbeliever, this world is the only heaven they will know." That reminded me of a similar thought I have had for a while: "When a believer dies, everything becomes bright; when an unbeliever dies, everything becomes dark."

There is a reason God tells us, "I have heard thee in a time accepted, and in the day of salvation have I succoured [helped] thee: behold, ***now*** is the accepted time; behold, ***now*** is the day of salvation." (2 Corinthians 6:2, emphasis mine)

What a shame that verse will go unheeded by so many. Please don't be one of them. Become serious with God today.

20

He Made the Stars Also

Genesis 1:16-19 "And God made two great lights; the greater light to rule the day, and the lesser light to rule the night: he made the stars also. And God set them in the firmament of the heaven to give light upon the earth, And to rule over the day and over the night, and to divide the light from the darkness: and God saw that it was good. And the evening and the morning were the fourth day."

We live in a rather rural neighborhood with very little in the way of city lights or even street lamps. On a clear night, you can see enough stars to dazzle the imagination.

I recently awoke at about 2:30 in the morning. As I turned over to go back to sleep, I could see the stars through the slats in the window blinds, so I interrupted my slumber to get up, go out on the front porch, and behold the handiwork of God for a few minutes. In the evening of the following day, I took the garbage to the curb. Again, it was clear, as in the early morning hours, and there were stars, stars, and more stars.

Stars often remind me of today's verses, which are part of the description of the fourth day of creation. Verse 16 includes the phrase, "He made the stars also."

Another passage I think of when I see the stars—or any number of amazing things God has made—is Psalm 8:3-5: "When I consider thy heavens, the work of thy fingers, the moon and the stars, which thou hast ordained; What is man, that thou art mindful of him? and the son of man, that thou visitest him? For thou hast made him a little lower than the angels, and hast crowned him with glory and honour."

If I can say it this way, it seems God has purposed to regard human beings as the crowning achievement of creation. Even in our fallen, distorted state, He ***still*** refers to us as having been made in His image. The

God who made us and the stars and everything that is, takes pity on us and bestows His loving kindness on His broken creation, mankind.

Lord, what is man, that Thou art mindful of him?

21

The Light Shineth in Darkness

John 1:4-5 "In him was life; and the life was the light of men. And the light shineth in darkness; and the darkness comprehended it not."

Have you ever been in total darkness? I have. A number of years ago, my wife and I went for a short excursion into a cavern. The cavern was naturally flooded with enough water that the excursion was via a group of four or five aluminum fishing boats. As we ventured into the cavern, the guide pointed out its various features. Once we were far enough from the entrance that there was no outside light coming in, the guide notified us that he was going to turn off his flashlight. When he did so, the guide continued to speak as we waited for our eyes to adjust to the dark so that we could at least see shapes or silhouettes. It was *so* dark that we were not able to see again until he turned his flashlight on again several minutes later.

Darkness is not actually something in and of itself; darkness is simply the natural condition when there is no light. It might be frightening to consider, but that is the condition of the natural human heart.

Strong's Concordance describes the Greek word translated "comprehended" in today's verses as meaning "to lay hold of with the mind; to seize upon, take possession of." Jesus *is* spiritual light, but the natural man cannot get hold of it. (1 Corinthians 2:14) We were in the same condition spiritually as we were physically when we were deep in that cavern. Our natural tendency as sinners was to sin. I recently heard a quote by the late R.C. Sproul: "Sin is not simply making bad choices or mistakes. Sin is having the desire in our hearts to do the will of the enemy."

What a stark contrast! We were in abject spiritual darkness to the point that we couldn't even grasp how badly we were ruined. (Jeremiah 17:9) That complete and total darkness was the setting into which God introduced the glorious light of the gospel. In our darkness, we could not see; but God who is *"rich in mercy"* (Ephesians 2:4) has opened our dark hearts—as He did Lydia's—to allow the light of the gospel of Christ to flow in. (See Acts 16:14.)

How spectacular is the God of Light!

22
Two Curses

Genesis 3:17 "And unto Adam he said, … cursed is the ground for thy sake; in sorrow shalt thou eat of it all the days of thy life;"

This world is under a curse. Sin has stained the Earth with a darkness that permeates even the good and the beautiful that remains. However, there is a second curse, one that allures many who wish to escape the first one. Paul warns the Galatians about that trap:

"Know ye therefore that they which are of faith, the same are the children of Abraham. And the scripture, foreseeing that God would justify the heathen through faith, preached before the gospel unto Abraham, saying, In thee shall all nations be blessed. So then they which be of faith are blessed with faithful Abraham. For as many as are of the works of the law are under the curse: for it is written, Cursed is every one that continueth not in all things which are written in the book of the law to do them." (Galatians 3:7-10)

What is the first curse? The ruin that came into this world through the sin and disobedience of Adam. What is the second curse? The useless attempt to remove the effects of the first curse through human effort.

Please hear my plea. Mortal teachers and denominations will emphasize the need for good works, as will other religious groups and secular organizations; however, today's verses, though penned by Paul, are the very words of God. We must be diligent not to allow any person or group to supersede the voice of the Almighty as He warns us that anyone who plans to obtain, maintain, or enhance their righteousness by keeping the Law places themselves under the obligation—the curse—to keep every command of the Law. Not part, not most, not even almost all, but they must obey "all things which are written in the book of the law to do them."

Now, we must acknowledge that a redeemed heart will result in a changed life. However, we must guard against the arrogant assumption that we can do what only God Himself can do "for God so loved the world, that he gave his only begotten Son, that whosoever believeth in him should not perish, but have everlasting life." (John 3:16)

That alone is sufficient for our salvation.

23
One Other Curse

Last time we considered two curses: the curse of sin (Genesis 3:17) and the curse under which we place ourselves if we attempt to solve our own sin curse by following a path of self-righteousness in keeping of the Law. (Galatians 3:7-10) However, there is a third curse I want to consider today.

In the Genesis passage (3:17), we see that Adam's disobedience placed us under the curse of sin. What could be done to remove that curse? Well, as we saw last time, some think that keeping the Law will solve the problem, but as we also learned that you would have to keep all of the Law, not just the parts you find easy or sensible.

Having said that, there are at least two other issues:

- Romans 14:23 teaches that "whatsoever is not of faith is sin." If I am "keeping all the Law," is my faith in God or in my own ability?
- Even if I *do* keep the Law perfectly, and even if I do so in a perfect attitude of faith toward God so that I never sin again, and even if that fixes my problem of future sin, what about past sins? Not breaking the Law anymore does not undo sins I have already committed.

So, we find that we are under the curse of the Law, and we cannot fix that. Now what? The answer is found in Paul's letter to the Galatians: "Christ hath redeemed us from the curse of the Law, being made a curse for us: for it is written, Cursed is every one that hangeth on a tree:" (3:13) The Lord Jesus Christ removed the curse from us, by taking the curse upon Himself. Paul said it another way in his second letter to the Corinthians: "For he hath made him [Jesus] to be sin for us, who knew no sin; that we might be made the righteousness of God in him." (5:21)

As Isaac Watts put it in his Christmas song, "Joy to the World:"

> No more let sin and sorrow grow
> Nor thorns infest the ground:
> He comes to make his blessings flow
> Far as the curse is found.

As far as the curse is found, so far flows our Savior's blessings for all who trust in Him. He has removed our curse by taking it upon Himself. Hallelujah! What a Savior!

24

Too Many Men for the Job

Judges 7:2-3 "And the LORD said unto Gideon, The people that are with thee are too many for me to give the Midianites into their hands, lest Israel vaunt themselves against me, saying, Mine own hand hath saved me. Now therefore go to, proclaim in the ears of the people, saying, Whosoever is fearful and afraid, let him return and depart early from mount Gilead. And there returned of the people twenty and two thousand; and there remained ten thousand."

Gideon had gathered 32,000 men to go to battle against the Midianites. God told him that he had too many soldiers. I am not a military strategist, but my initial reaction is that too many is usually better in battle than not enough.

In this passage, God tells Gideon to send home anyone who is afraid. Once the fearful depart, the army is reduced to 10,000 men. In the verses that follow, God says that is still too many and tells Gideon to send the remaining men to the nearby water to drink. If they cup the water from their hands to their mouths, they are to remain, but if they get down on their knees and drink directly from the water, they are to be sent home with the others.

That sounds like a strange way to select the members of a military excursion; however, the 300 remaining men won the battle and did so in spectacular style.

Why did God reduce Gideon's army to less than one percent of its original size? The Lord tells us the answer: "lest Israel vaunt themselves against me, saying, Mine own hand hath saved me."

I know it is not very flattering for us to be reminded of this fact, but the truth is that our feeble hearts tend toward pride, even to the point of taking credit for things that God has done. On the other hand, there is comfort in knowing that our weaknesses do not limit God; instead, He does great things that overcome our frailties. It is our happy responsibility to acknowledge His actions on our behalf and to praise and thank Him for His kindness.

25

Into the Looking Glass

James 1:22-24 "But be ye doers of the word, and not hearers only, deceiving your own selves. For if any be a hearer of the word, and not a doer, he is like unto a man beholding his natural face in a glass: For he beholdeth himself, and goeth his way, and straightway forgetteth what manner of man he was."

As a hobby, my late mother built miniature rooms complete with furniture, wall decorations, and illuminated light fixtures. She used a few pre-made items, but she was quite creative in making things from raw materials. As an example, she made a room that required a 'large' mirror on one of the walls. For that, she bought a sizable sheet of plastic with a mirror-like backing and cut out the three by four-inch piece that would complete the scene. My mom passed away before using any more of that reflective material, and I ended up with it.

I check our cars several times a month, reviewing the fluid and tire pressure levels. I also set up that mirror sheet and use it to conveniently make sure the front and rear lights are all working properly. However, something that is very apparent is that the plastic material warped with age, and the image it gives is distorted.

That is not a problem for my purposes; I am only looking for lights to come on and the mirror handles that task very well. On the other hand, when a person "beholds his natural face in a glass," as James puts it, two things become critical:

- The mirror must show an accurate reflection of the way things really are, and
- A wise person must accept what the mirror shows and change accordingly.

The Bible is an undistorted mirror; through it, God always shows a true picture. As James tells us in today's verses, we dare not look into it and then walk away as if what it tells us is not important.

"Thy word is a lamp unto my feet, and a light unto my path." (Psalm 119:105) If God's Word is an accurate reflection of our condition and it also enlightens the right path, then wisdom compels us to heed it and obey when it says, "This is the way, walk ye in it." (Isaiah 30:21)

26
Discipline and Purpose

Hebrews 12:5-11"And ye have forgotten the exhortation which speaketh unto you as unto children, My son, despise not thou the chastening of the Lord, nor faint when thou art rebuked of him: For whom the Lord loveth he chasteneth, and scourgeth every son whom he receiveth. If ye endure chastening, God dealeth with you as with sons; for what son is he whom the father chasteneth not? But if ye be without chastisement, whereof all are partakers, then are ye bastards [illegitimate], and not sons. Furthermore we have had fathers of our flesh which corrected us, and we gave them reverence: shall we not much rather be in subjection unto the Father of spirits, and live? For they verily for a few days chastened us after their own pleasure; but he for our profit, that we might be partakers of his holiness. Now no chastening for the present seemeth to be joyous, but grievous: nevertheless afterward it yieldeth the peaceable fruit of righteousness unto them which are exercised thereby."

Some years ago, a newspaper cartoon showed a wife talking to her widowed mother. The young woman complained her husband's snoring kept her awake. The mother acknowledged that *her* husband's snoring used to keep her up too; then with a wistful look, she said, "I sure do miss that." What one person perceives as worthless, even annoying, may be valuable to someone else, even snoring, as in the case of this reflective mother. That gives a different perspective, doesn't it?

Regarding today's verses, I have long thought about the difference between punishment and discipline. Punishment is getting back at someone for doing wrong; discipline is shaping a person's understanding and attitude so they no longer *want* to do wrong. One looks back at the past. The other looks forward to the future.

God does not punish His children; He disciplines us. He is not "getting even." He is growing us in the same way a farmer cultivates for a good crop.

Do not be discouraged when the Lord's hand rests a little heavy on you. He is working to perfect you—to mature you—to conform you to the image of His Son. Cooperate with Him and give in to His leading. In the end, you will find a surprise answer to an old saying, for in your case, the end will indeed justify God's means.

27
A Date and Time Yet Future

Matthew 24:44 "Therefore be ye also ready: for in such an hour as ye think not the Son of man cometh."

Several months ago, I saw a photograph of a man with the caption, "RIP" (Rest In Peace) followed by the man's name. We see that kind of thing from time to time, but what caught my attention was that the date of death that accompanied the picture was still several months into the future. No, I did not mistype that; the date of death accompanying the photograph would not occur until several months after I saw the announcement.

Someone may have mistyped that or posted it as a prank, but I found it rather bazaar. I looked at it again, and I am sure I understood it correctly. I suppose if a person was determined to end their own life, they could pick a specific date and time, but even then they might come to death before the set time by illness or accident, or perhaps they might even change their mind.

Most of us do not spend very much time thinking about dying. To let that become a consuming thought is not likely to create a healthy mindset; however, refusing to ponder the subject at all is not healthy either. To make death a constant thought may lead to discouragement or depression, but *never* to think about it is to risk not being prepared for it.

The balance to the subject is not to let it dominate our thoughts, but at least to be aware that a day in the future does have our name on it. By illness, accident, violence, or the Lord's return, anyone could be ushered into eternity at any moment.

When you are prepared for death, you are prepared to live life fully.

28
Death in the Wheatfield

John 12:23-26 "And Jesus answered them, saying, The hour is come, that the Son of man should be glorified. Verily, verily, I say unto you, Except a corn of wheat fall into the ground and die, it abideth alone: but if it die, it bringeth forth much fruit. He that loveth his life shall lose it; and he that hateth his life in this world shall keep it unto life eternal. If any man serve me, let him follow me; and where I am, there shall also my servant be: if any man serve me, him will my Father honour."

We in the United States typically use the word "corn" to refer to the usually yellow grain that grows on an ear and is also called maize; however, many years ago the word was used for any grain. In this setting, Jesus speaks of a kernel (corn) of wheat as an illustration.

Like many grains, a kernel of wheat serves a genuine purpose by functioning as a small piece of food. When wheat is used like that, each grain can only contribute one kernel's worth of nutrition. The Lord's remarks indicate a power we may easily overlook because the kernel contains more than just a tiny bit of nutrition. If the farmer is willing to give up the small benefit that one tiny particle can give him, he can plant it in his field. When he does that, the little seed will die, but from that sacrifice, many new kernels will spring forth.

Even though His disciples did not understand what Jesus was saying at the time, by giving this illustration, He was revealing to them that He was going to die, and in so doing, His death would bring forth new life in many others.

Is there something else here too? Yes. In verses 25 and 26, Jesus tells us that likewise, we too are to die to our own will and self-centered ambitions. He tells us that those who use their lives for themselves will eventually find their life to be worthless, but those who use their lives to serve Him will find their life will actually take on eternal value. He even says that God would honor that person.

Did He say it would be easy? No, He didn't say that. But would it be worth it? Yes, He *did* say that.

29

Real Value, Real Hope

Psalm 78:2-3, 6-7 "I will open my mouth in a parable: I will utter dark sayings of old: Which we have heard and known, and our fathers have told us ... That the generation to come might know them, even the children which should be born; who should arise and declare them to their children: That they might set their hope in God, and not forget the works of God, but keep his commandments:"

Objects on Earth have mass and weight. In outer space, they still have mass, but without the force of gravity, they have no weight. We add "less" at the end of the word—weightless—to convey the opposite of the original meaning. A manufacturer might give a warranty on their product, but if the manufacturer goes out of business, instead of the warranty being worth something, it is worthless.

Have you ever pondered the word "hopeless?" Hope must have something external that gives it value, as gravity affects an object or a thriving business secures a warranty.

The last report I saw cited suicide as the third largest cause of teen deaths in America; it also charms older generations. What causes a person to despair of life? I submit that it is being hopeless. A number of things are factors of hopelessness: bullying; fear of the future; emotional or physical pain. However, allow me to suggest an overarching factor that probably plays a bigger part than we might think.

For a significant portion of my 70-plus years, there has been a growing public assumption that life developed from some cosmic accident. We're told that we are little more than animals with no intrinsic value and no ultimate accountability. Why would someone with that view of life *not* make a disastrous choice when life becomes a struggle? In glorious contrast, what stability comes to life—yes, even a troubled life—when we embrace God's truth.

Today's verses tell us that we are to pass on to our children and grandchildren the reason for our hope in God, and encourage them to pass on to their generation—and the ones that follow—the reason for the hope that we have.

"But sanctify the Lord God in your hearts: and be ready always to give an answer to every man that asketh you a reason of the hope that is in you with meekness and fear." (1 Peter 3:15)

MARCH

1
Imagine That

Romans 8:32 "He that spared not his own Son, but delivered him up for us all, how shall he not with him also freely give us all things?"

For a moment, imagine that you are God. Imagine that you have created the universe and everything in it, and that you as the Almighty God sustain your creation in eternal righteous.

Now imagine that your creation rebels against you. Imagine that your entire creation is wrecked and ruined by this revolt so that the creatures you created in your own image begin hating, defrauding, and murdering each other. Furthermore, the animals you made begin fighting and devouring one another, and the plants you made to provide food, beauty, shade, and more begin to die.

Imagine that your righteousness demands that judgment be served upon those rebels, and the only sentence that would satisfy your righteousness is a sentence of death to those who had brought death to your creation.

Now imagine that you, in the counsel of your own wisdom, purpose a plan whereby you can forgive any rebel who repents, thereby saving them from your just judgment. However, since your righteousness requires that all crimes must be paid for—that all accounts must be settled in full—the only way you can save the rebels and redeem your creation is to call on your only begotten Son to die in the place of those who spurned you, lashed out at you, and revolted against you. Also, imagine that your plan requires that your son must die a humiliating death at the hands of the rebels. Further, imagine that while your creation humiliates your son and despitefully uses him, your plan requires you to turn your back upon your only begotten son and pour out—on your son—your anger, which rightfully belongs to the rebels!

That is what God did.

Now what do you think of Him? *Now* what do you think of what He did? *Now* what do you think of the price He paid for you?

Take time to ponder that.

2

A Poem Written over a Grave

Galatians 2:20 "I am crucified with Christ: nevertheless I live; yet not I, but Christ liveth in me: and the life which I now live in the flesh I live by the faith of the Son of God, who loved me, and gave himself for me."

I became a Christian about two months before I turned twenty-four. Early in my new life, I took today's Scripture as my life's verse. I wish I had lived it out better.

You may recall the story of the Great Chicago Fire of 1871, which is sometimes blamed on Mrs. O'Leary's cow kicking over a lantern although the exact cause was never determined. The fire killed several hundred people and destroyed more than three square miles of the Windy City.

Horatio Spafford was a lawyer and investor in Chicago at the time and lost a number of buildings, which took a heavy toll on his financial holdings. A year or two later, scarlet fever took their four-year-old son. To soften their grief, Spafford's wife and four daughters boarded a ship for vacation in England; Mr. Spafford was to join them later after tending to some business. On the voyage, their ship was struck by another vessel and sank, killing all four girls and leaving Mrs. Spafford all alone. Mr. Spafford sailed to be with his wife, and as his ship traveled through the waters in which his daughters perished, he wrote the poem, "It Is Well With My Soul." Philip Bliss later set it to music.

We sang that song at church recently. One of the verses struck me as particularly precious that morning:

> Though Satan should buffet, though trials should come,
> Let this blest assurance control,
> That Christ hath regarded my helpless estate,
> And hath shed His own blood for my soul.

Whether we know it or not, we were as helpless as those precious girls were in that watery abyss; however, knowing our plight, Christ took notice of our completely helpless condition and laid down His life that we may live. Wow! What grace!

Our sinful nature and the sins we commit have us in a helpless condition. However, Jesus paid for our sins so we can be forgiven and live.

In today's verse, God calls us to identify with Christ in His death **and** in His resurrection to new life. (Also, see Romans 6:11)

What a wonderful plan God has!

3

The Permanent and the Passing Away

1 Corinthians 15:51-54, 58 "Behold, I shew you a mystery; We shall not all sleep, but we shall all be changed, In a moment, in the twinkling of an eye, at the last trump: for the trumpet shall sound, and the dead shall be raised incorruptible, and we shall be changed. For this corruptible must put on incorruption, and this mortal must put on immortality. So when this corruptible shall have put on incorruption, and this mortal shall have put on immortality, then shall be brought to pass the saying that is written, Death is swallowed up in victory. … Therefore, my beloved brethren, be ye stedfast, unmoveable, always abounding in the work of the Lord, forasmuch as ye know that your labour is not in vain in the Lord."

Today's verses remind me of a precious and encouraging paragraph by an unknown author that is worth sharing:

"Doubting and inconsistency and unbelief are but passing away. Sorrow and pain and trial are not permanent. A few more turns of the clock and swings of the pendulum, and then farewell forever to sin and failures. Farewell to doubts and fears—a final farewell. We are to be conformed to the image of His Son. We shall be ushered into the region of light and of eternal realities. Then goodbye Faith. Farewell Hope. I am launched out into one great eternal sea of Love. Faith and Hope make very good companions on the road, but not for eternity. They go with us to the gate, but Love is inside. God is Love. We shall be plunged into the ocean of Love, lost in it, never to come out. It is shoreless, bottomless, and infinite. We shall soon be in a region where we shall know as known, and there will not be thought or a feeling that will be unlike Christ. No trouble or sorrow, all will have for ever passed away. The first thousand years in glory will roll along with Hallelujah to the Lamb! Another thousand comes, and we are still praising the Lord together. The pendulum of praise never ceases to swing. He will be the object of our adoring praise and worship for ever. Eternity! Eternity! Eternity! How long art thou? Not too long to gaze on the Lamb. Then the permanent. Nothing but Christ—the Christ of God, forever, forever, and forever."

4

When Fear Does Not Subside

Genesis 44:16-18 "And Judah said, What shall we say unto my lord? what shall we speak? or how shall we clear ourselves? God hath found out the iniquity of thy servants: behold, we are my lord's servants, both we, and he also with whom the cup is found. And he [Joseph] said, God forbid that I should do so: but the man in whose hand the cup is found, he shall be my servant; and as for you, get you up in peace unto your father. Then Judah came near unto him, and said, Oh my lord, let thy servant, I pray thee, speak a word in my lord's ears, and let not thine anger burn against thy servant: for thou art even as Pharaoh."

The story of Joseph is legendary; his brothers had sold him into slavery, and Joseph ended up in Egypt. (Genesis 37 and following) You may recall that later the Pharaoh had a dream his wise men could not interpret. When Joseph told him the dream meant seven years of good harvest followed by seven years of famine, Pharaoh put Joseph in charge of collecting the food during the years of plenty and rationing the supplies during the years of shortage.

The rationing went well until Joseph's brothers came to Egypt to buy food. Joseph recognized them, but they did not recognize him. Joseph initiated a series of manipulations, and as the story unfolded, the brothers discussed the uneasy fear that started to press in on them. Finally, Joseph sprang his trap, forcing Judah to face the disastrous evil he and his brothers had committed.

That moment was terrifying to the brothers; they knew their deceptions could kill their father. However, in the midst of his helpless panic, Judah stood up and finally did the right thing, pleading for his young brother Benjamin and even offering his own servitude for Benjamin's freedom.

Missionary and widow of a Christian martyr, the late Elisabeth Elliot said, "Sometimes fear does not subside, and one must choose to do it afraid." Just like Judah, we will face times of great fear. Whether correcting our own failures or facing injustice at the hands of others, let us be humble *and* bold—meek in ourselves, but strong in God.

"Ye are of God, little children … greater is he that is in you, than he that is in the world." (1 John 4:4)

5

Patient Anger

Psalm 7:11b "God is angry with the wicked every day."

Here is a question: If God is angry with the wicked every day, as it says in this verse, why doesn't He just express that anger now? Why doesn't God just kill the wicked and end all their wickedness? I mean, *right now!*

I don't understand how or why God does everything He does, but I *do* know that among all His wondrous attributes is one called longsuffering or patience. Exodus 34:6 and Psalm 86:15 are clear examples.

God teaches us there are at least two purposes for which He uses His longsuffering. We find one in Romans 2:4: "Or despisest thou the riches of his goodness and forbearance and longsuffering; not knowing that the goodness of God leadeth thee to repentance?" God uses His longsuffering along with His goodness as a matched set to bring many to Himself. I dare not question or "despise" His wisdom for doing that.

Now, that is for those who will, in time, come to Him. But what of those who He knows, in His infinite knowledge, will never come? Paul covers that question later. These three verses are a single sentence that asks a profound question. "What if God, willing to shew his wrath, and to make his power known, endured with much longsuffering the vessels of wrath fitted to destruction: And that he might make known the riches of his glory on the vessels of mercy, which he had afore prepared unto glory, Even us, whom he hath called, not of the Jews only, but also of the Gentiles?" (Romans 9:22-24) The verse before that asks (I paraphrase) if the Potter wants to make an ashtray and a Ming vase from the same lump of clay, am I really in a position to question His judgment? (Also see Daniel 4:35.)

One day, we will understand better than we do now that God is completely righteous and has wise purpose in everything He does. Until then, what we know is that He doesn't discharge complete wrath immediately because He wills to use longsuffering to display His power in the ashtray and His inconceivable and undeserved mercy in the vase.

I cannot speak for you, but personally, I am staggeringly grateful for His longsuffering to me.

6
491

Matthew 18:21-22 "Then came Peter to him, and said, Lord, how oft shall my brother sin against me, and I forgive him? till seven times? Jesus saith unto him, I say not unto thee, Until seven times: but, Until seventy times seven."

Have you ever done the math on the statement Jesus made to Peter? Seventy times seven equals 490. I think Jesus was giving Peter a word picture of the longsuffering God exercises when He forgives us. However, Jason Roy of the Christian musical group, Building 429, asked a poignant question, "What happens to God's forgiveness when I get to 491?"

Occasionally I see a meme that says, "Repentance is not when you cry; repentance is when you change." It is true we don't want to mistake some emotional experience for a spiritual one. We should not trifle with sin or take it lightly. God didn't take sin lightly when Christ died to pay for it. Repentance is genuinely turning away from sin and clinging to the grace and mercy of God in Christ who is our only hope.

However, the question remains: What happens when we fail? And what happens when we fail again? It would be nice if we repented of a sin once and that sin never attacked us again, or if it did, we didn't give in to it. However, it doesn't seem to work that way.

When I get to that haunting number, will God forgive me? I really couldn't put a number on it, but I am certain that in my more than four decades of Christian life, I have well surpassed the seventy-times-seven standard Jesus gave to Peter. In that case, does God just give up on me? Does He just say, "Bill, when I saved you, I had no idea how much trouble you would be. I'm sorry son, but you're on your own?"

Again, let us not minimize our sin; we must seek *His* strength whereby we may live a life that honors Him. At the same time, let's not minimize His grace either. Let us come to Him boldly "that we may obtain mercy, and find grace to help in time of need," (Hebrews 4:16) for we are helpless without His grace.

7

The Highest Place

Mark 9:33-37   "And he came to Capernaum: and being in the house he asked them, What was it that ye disputed among yourselves by the way? But they held their peace: for by the way they had disputed among themselves, who should be the greatest. And he sat down, and called the twelve, and saith unto them, If any man desire to be first, the same shall be last of all, and servant of all. And he took a child, and set him in the midst of them: and when he had taken him in his arms, he said unto them, Whosoever shall receive one of such children in my name, receiveth me: and whosoever shall receive me, receiveth not me, but him that sent me."

What is it about our mortal pride, arrogance, and narcissism that draws us like a moth to a flame? Oh, how hard we find God's command to "humble yourselves in the sight of the Lord," even though it comes with the promise that "he shall lift you up." (James 4:10)

When will we learn what Jesus was teaching His disciples in today's verses? Here, the master of the universe uses the trusting heart of a little child to expose their pettiness. After all, these grown men should have learned better as they walked day after day with God incarnate. Note also that they didn't tell Him what they were arguing about, for "they held their peace." Even so, Jesus knew. There is nothing we can hide from Him; He sees into the very depths of our hearts, and He knows.

Please do not misunderstand. I don't say this as if God is just looking for a chance to point His finger and shout, "You *sinner*!" I am also not pretending that I have it all together; just like each of us, I struggle with the pride and weaknesses of my fallen humanity.

This lesson may be difficult to grasp, but how much actual spiritual growth do we expect if we bypass this critical step? The flesh is tempted to believe that we deserve a position of prominence that feeds our pride. In reality, the greatest place that a mortal soul can occupy is prostrate before a pair of nail-scarred feet.

8

Weather or Not

James 1:17 "Every good gift and every perfect gift is from above, and cometh down from the Father of lights, with whom is no variableness, neither shadow of turning."

No, the title of this Musing is not misspelled. Let me explain.

I have a weather app on my phone. It predicts the weather for today and several days into the future; however, when I refresh the app to the latest data, yesterday's forecast sometimes still shows as part of the five-day page, and the weather information for tomorrow may be completely wrong by the time tomorrow gets here.

I am glad God is not erratic like that. The writer to the Hebrews concurs with what James says today about God's reliability: "Jesus Christ the same yesterday, and to day, and for ever." (Hebrews 13:8)

God commands us to trust Him, but He does not make that demand without giving us evidence that He is trustworthy. He requires faith, but He does not do so without giving us evidence that He is faithful. Twice in Isaiah 43, God told the Hebrew people, "Ye are my witnesses." He was telling them they could have confidence in Him because He had delivered them previously. He was not telling them to have faith in some unknown being, but in the God who *could* be trusted in the future because He had proven Himself to be dependable in the past.

He also tells them something else two times in the Isaiah 43 passage; He tells them not to be afraid: "Fear not: for I have redeemed thee," (v1) and "Fear not: for I am with thee." (v5) However, as I mentioned above, the reason He gives them for trusting Him for their tomorrows is that they have seen Him work in their yesterdays.

God is faithful, dear friend. Don't let your circumstances distract you from Him. He *will* allow you to go through trials, but He will *not* abandon you. He is faithful!

9

For Better or Worse

Psalm 19: 9 -11 "The fear of the LORD is clean, enduring for ever: the judgments of the LORD are true and righteous altogether. More to be desired are they than gold, yea, than much fine gold: sweeter also than honey and the honeycomb. Moreover by them is thy servant warned: and in keeping of them there is great reward."

In Western tradition, marriage vows often include the phrase "for better or worse." By saying this, the bride and the groom are committing to weather the storms of life together. Not just when circumstances are good, but also when difficulties arise, we will remain with each other; we will enjoy the good times together and work through the troubles together.

In 2017, reports arose that a huge iceberg the size of a small state might break away from Antarctica and become adrift, creating a problem for shipping lanes. As truly important as human commitments and huge icebergs are, there is an ultimate "better and worst" scenario, and it is this: The West as a culture has largely abandoned a long-held commitment to God Himself, or at least to His principles, and has broken away, becoming adrift from our biblical heritage and values.

Part of that is the result of modern teaching that God loves everyone and would never be upset with anyone. Those who teach such things only speak about God's love, mercy, grace, and kindness. Sadly, that paints a distorted picture of the true and living God, for though those words are indeed true of Him, they are no more true than other words, such as holy, righteous, just, and sinless.

In our drifting state, we are forgetting that God "commandeth all men every where to repent." (Acts 17:30) God would not have given such a command unless there was something from which to repent and significant consequences for not doing so.

Instead of putting all our spiritual "eggs" in our culture's basket, we would do well to reconnect to the wisdom of God as found in His Word. Let us seek Him and follow Him, lest we drift ever closer to His righteous judgment.

10

Addition and Subtraction

Ecclesiastes 3:14 "I know that, whatsoever God doeth, it shall be for ever: nothing can be put to it, nor any thing taken from it: and God doeth it, that men should fear before him."

How profound are the points in that verse:
- Whatever God does lasts forever.
- No one can add to it.
- No one can subtract from it.

- God's purposes in His actions are to produce reverential fear.

The use of the word "whatsoever" tells us that those points apply to *everything* God does, but I particularly want to draw your attention to the gospel of Christ.

In the same way as in today's verse, God also gives several points when He tells us what the gospel is. In 1 Corinthians 15:1-8, He declares that the gospel is:

- Christ died for our sins.
- He was buried.
- He arose.
- He was seen in His resurrected body by many witnesses.

I believe there is a reason why God gives that list and in that order. Christ died as a sacrifice to pay for our transgressions. The fact that He was buried for three days confirms that He was indeed dead, not just fainted as some suppose. The gospel is incomplete without the resurrection, for by it God declares His approval with the finished work of Christ. (Romans 4:25) Finally, a number of eyewitnesses saw the resurrected Christ, confirming it was not just an illusion or a dream.

We mortals tend to think we must "do" something to complete that work—to 'seal the deal' so to speak; however, may I respectfully ask you this? What is it that you are going to do that will impress God more than the blood of Christ, His Son?

The verse in Ecclesiastes is so applicable to the gospel of Christ: it will last forever; no one can add to it or take from it; and God has accomplished this great feat so that mortals should bow before Him in fear, reverence, and honor.

God has purpose for our lives, and He calls Christians to act on His behalf in order to bring glory to Himself and good to others. Nevertheless, regarding our salvation—that which makes us right with Him—ours is not to "*do*," but rather to trust in Him and His perfect work that is already "*done*."

11
What Good Are Good Works?

Romans 4:1-5 "What shall we say then that Abraham our father, as pertaining to the flesh, hath found? For if Abraham were justified by works, he hath whereof to glory; but not before God. For what saith the scripture? Abraham believed God, and it was counted unto him for righteousness. Now to him that worketh is the reward not reckoned of grace, but of debt. But to him that worketh not, but believeth on him that justifieth the ungodly, his faith is counted for righteousness."

The idea of works is one of the often-misunderstood concepts in the Bible. The Scriptures teach that followers of the Lord Jesus will have a change in their hearts that results in a change in their behavior—their works. (Ephesians 2:8-10; James 1:22-27, 2:14-26) The misunderstanding comes when we think that our works are what give us right standing before God; that is dangerously false.

Verse 4 of today's reading is relatively short, but it is drenched with both wisdom and warning: "Now to him that worketh is the reward not reckoned of grace, but of debt." The wisdom is in the distinction it makes between works and grace; the warning is consistent with what Paul says later in this same epistle: "And if by grace, then is it no more of works: otherwise grace is no more grace. But if it be of works, then is it no more grace: otherwise work is no more work." (11:6)

Works are good as an evidence of faith, as expressions of gratitude to God, and as attempts to glorify the Lord. However, if we depend on our works to appease God and as bargaining chips whereby we can win His forgiveness, then we must obey the whole Law from the time of our birth. We have locked ourselves into a salvation by works alone, for as we saw above in Romans 11:6, we cannot mix works and grace! I don't know about your works, but I know my own well enough that I dare not trust them as the basis of my forgiveness.

We cannot meet God's standard by being better than somebody down the street; instead, God's standard is for us to be perfect. Our works will never get us there. By God's marvelous grace, faith in Christ will.

12
The Logical Conclusion

Romans 4: "4 Now to him that worketh is the reward not reckoned of grace, but of debt. 5 But to him that worketh not, but believeth on him that justifieth the ungodly, his faith is counted for righteousness. 6 Even as David also describeth the blessedness of the man, unto whom God imputeth righteousness without works, 7 Saying, Blessed are they whose iniquities are forgiven, and whose sins are covered. 8 Blessed is the man to whom the Lord will not impute sin."

In today's verses, Paul is writing about whether we are justified by works or by faith. He uses an interesting Greek word five times in these verses. Even more fascinating, Paul uses that word for both kinds of people: those who are trusting in their works for their righteousness, (verse 4) *and* those who are trusting in God for their righteousness. (verses 5-8)

That Greek verb is used to describe the process of surveying the facts (to reckon, count, compute, calculate) and coming to a conclusion. In this case, God is discerning the truth and passing sentence. The word is translated thus:

- V4 - is...not reckoned
- V5 - counted
- V6 - imputeth
- V8 - impute

I believe what Paul is saying is that the reward to each person is based on God's conclusion after reviewing all that a person has in their "righteousness account." For the one trusting in God, He fills their righteousness account just as He has promised. However, for the one trusting in his own works, God will give what is owed, paying a debt. (verse 4) The problem becomes startlingly clear when we understand what our own righteousness is worth: "But we are all as an unclean thing, and all our righteousnesses are as filthy rags;" (Isaiah 64:6a)

Then what is the solution? We find it in verse 5: "But to him that **worketh not**, but **believeth on him** that justifieth the ungodly, his faith is counted for righteousness." (emphasis mine)

Now obviously, good works are a good thing and are expected of those who trust God for their imputed righteousness; (Ephesians 2:8-10) However, true good works are a *result* of God's imputed righteousness, not the cause.

I encourage you to go back to the beginning of this Musing and read those verses again with an understanding of that word. It makes all the difference in the world. And in the *next* world too.

13
Only the Blind Can See

Romans 4:4 "Now to him that worketh is the reward not reckoned of grace, but of debt. 5. But to him that worketh not, but believeth on him that justifieth the ungodly, his faith is counted for righteousness."

Yesterday we looked at the way God justifies us. Today's verses were part of that reading, and we looked at the word translated "reckoned" in verse 4 and "counted" in verse 5. We saw that faith justifies, but works do not.

Today let's look at another idea that tells us something is backwards to our mortal reasoning. If you ask the average person on the street, "Who is in right standing with God?" they might name some religious figure or mention people who are doing good—the kind, the generous, and the gentle. Some religious leaders and doers of good *are* right with God, but not all of them, because being "religious" or "good" is not God's basis for justifying us.

Verse 5 describes God as "Him that justifieth the ungodly." That's right; God only justifies the ungodly. John reinforces that position in his first letter: "If we say that we have no sin, we deceive ourselves, and the truth is not in us. If we confess our sins, he is faithful and just to forgive us our sins, and to cleanse us from all unrighteousness." (1 John 1:8-9)

Jesus also reiterated this truth when He addressed the religious elites of His day just after healing the man who was born blind. "And Jesus said, For judgment I am come into this world, that they which see not might see; and that they which see might be made blind. And some of the Pharisees which were with him heard these words, and said unto him, Are we blind also? Jesus said unto them, If ye were blind, ye should have no sin: but now ye say, We see; therefore your sin remaineth." (John 9:39-41)

These thoughts blend well with our Musing last time. The religious elites of Christ's day were convinced their "good works" were "good enough." They trusted in their works for their spiritual sight, and Jesus told them they were blind. However, those who believe in Christ, such as the blind man that He healed, are made whole. The blind man is a picture of the justification God gives to those who trust in Him.

14
Real Strength

1 Samuel 17:45 "Then said David to the Philistine, Thou comest to me with a sword, and with a spear, and with a shield: but I come to thee in the name of the LORD of hosts, the God of the armies of Israel, whom thou hast defied."

Several years ago, I wrote three devotionals similar to these except they were for a younger audience. An acquaintance published a children's devotional with daily readings from a number of different authors. It is aimed at fourth grade and above. One of the verses I chose to write on is today's verse. I am not repeating that devotional here; instead, I am writing about something I saw recently that reminded me of this passage.

A giant Philistine named Goliath had challenged Israel to send someone to fight him in a winner-take-all battle. He ranted in the valley like a wild bull and frightened the men of Israel's army. Finally, David, a teenager, wearied of the boasting and blasphemy, went down the hill to face the braggart. Goliath threatened to kill the young shepherd boy, but today's passage records David's confident reply: "Thou comest to me with a sword, and with a spear, and with a shield: but I come to thee in the name of the LORD …"

What prompted today's Musing was a picture of the silhouette of a huge giant with a spear and the smaller silhouette of young David with his sling. The caption is what struck me: "David didn't need to know how strong Goliath was because he already knew how strong God was."

When our focus is on ourselves, we can easily become sidetracked by our frailties; when our focus is on our problems, we see our inadequacies; when our focus is on our enemies, our weaknesses become enlarged. However, when our focus is on God, everything changes.

I am not talking about who we *think* God is and not even who we wish He was. Our confidence is lifted and our faith is strengthened when we focus on who God *says* He is, for then we will know that our fretting is in vain because "the battle is the LORD's." (1 Samuel 17:47)

15

The Magnificent Mending or The Righteous Repair

Psalm 40:6-8 "Sacrifice and offering thou didst not desire; mine ears hast thou opened: burnt offering and sin offering hast thou not required. Then said I, Lo, I come: in the volume of the book it is written of me, I delight to do thy will, O my God: yea, thy law is within my heart."

Of all the disasters the world has ever experienced, arguably *none* of them has been as devastating as the one recorded in Genesis 3. God created a perfect world, but Adam and Eve essentially declared, "That's not good enough." By their actions, they replaced God's living perfection with destruction and death.

Many years later, under the guidance of the Holy Spirit, one of their descendants, King David, penned the beautiful words we read in today's verses. Then, many more years later, another descendant attributed David's prophetic words to Christ: "Wherefore when he cometh into the world, he saith, Sacrifice and offering thou wouldest not, but a body hast thou prepared me: In burnt offerings and sacrifices for sin thou hast had no pleasure. Then said I, Lo, I come (in the volume of the book it is written of me,) to do thy will, O God." (Hebrews 10:5-7)

The sacrifices David mentioned are the requirements of the Law. (Hebrews 10:8) David lived **under** the Law and tried to live **by** it; however, he knew that there was something ineffective about it. To be clear, the problem is not with the Law, it's with us. The Law itself is **good**, however, we are not. As much as we might **want** to declare with David, "I delight to do thy will, O my God: yea, thy law is within my heart," we find that there is something else there too: "another law in my members, warring against the law of my mind, and bringing me into captivity to the law of sin which is in my members." (Romans 7:23)

Since God's perfect righteousness demands that we keep the **whole** Law, (Galatians 5:3) we need another way—a way that does not rely on our keeping the Law. God has provided just such a way, for as surely as Adam and Eve took away God's original design, establishing chaos and death in its place, God has taken away the schoolmaster-Law and established the Gospel of His grace. (Hebrews 10:9)

"Praise Him, all ye people." (Psalm 117:1b)

16

Can't Buy Me Love

1 Thessalonians 5:21 "Prove all things; hold fast that which is good."

On this date in 1964, the British musical group, The Beatles. released the hit single, "Can't Buy Me Love" in the United States. In it, an individual offers to buy expensive gifts for his friend as long as it "makes you feel alright." He states his reason as being that "money can't buy me love," and since it can't buy love, he might as well spend it on something like creating some happiness for a friend.

It is true that money can't buy love, but that is not the **only** thing money cannot buy. In fact, I suspect that the only things money **can** buy are things that are necessary for survival (food, clothing, shelter, medical care), things that bring pleasure or comfort (air conditioning, cars, literature, entertainment), and investments that we hope will increase in monetary value. Everything else—the things of true value such as love, kindness, and principles—cannot be bought. Oh sure, we can buy **imitations** of that which has intrinsic worth, but the real article? Not really.

We find an example in the life of author Kivi Bernhard, who studied the hunting habits and techniques of leopards and wrote a book on how his discoveries can be used to improve personal and business success. His insight won him an invitation to be the keynote speaker at a Microsoft conference designed around his book. The trouble arose when Mr. Bernhard, an Orthodox Jew, found out he was scheduled to speak on Saturday, the Jewish holy day. He told the schedulers that he could not participate, and when an offer to double his speaking fee did not change his mind, the Microsoft people rescheduled his event so that he did not have to speak on the Sabbath. When Bill Gates found out about Mr. Bernhard's stance, it is reported that he said, "There are some things that just cannot be bought with money." A different report quoted him as saying, "That's what happens when you have something that money can't buy."

Is there anything in your life that you would refuse to give up for money? Anything? "Prove all things; hold fast that which is good."

17
What Is Memory?

Mark 4:37- 40 "And there arose a great storm of wind, and the waves beat into the ship, so that it was now full. And he was in the hinder part of the ship, asleep on a pillow: and they awake him, and say unto him, Master, carest thou not that we perish? And he arose, and rebuked the wind, and said unto the sea, Peace, be still. And the wind ceased, and there was a great calm. And he said unto them, Why are ye so fearful? how is it that ye have no faith?"

My wife and I went to a dinner theater the other day. Without even asking for it, we ended up seated at the very same table—even in the very same seats—as our first time there twenty years ago. The same exact seating brought back fond memories; we reminisced about the first play we saw and the funny conversation one of the actresses drew me into during the interactive comedy.

All of my grandparents died before I was born. The last to die was my maternal grandfather, Fred Hope. Fred and my grandmother Roberta were missionaries to Cameroon. Since we never knew them, my cousin Edward Guthmann researched and created a beautiful documentary telling the story of their time among their African friends. You can find out more by searching for "*Return to Cameroun*" (the old spelling).

In the documentary, Edward asked the question, "What is memory? Is it something we gain, or something we lose?" That is thought provoking, isn't it? We gain memories by living, but sadly, as we age, some of those memories fade or perhaps slip from our minds completely.

That brings us to today's verse. Memory loss is sad; there are so many good things to keep in mind, but one of the most important things to remember is that God is sovereign. In spite of all appearances, He is in complete control of our lives and the whole universe. If we forget that—as I fear our world has mostly done—we find ourselves adrift in a dark and turbulent sea. On the other hand, if God is the center of our mindset, then whatever trials and tribulations come our way, we can be at rest even as Jesus was in the midst of a storm.

18
Truly Happy

Matthew 5:2, 4, 10-11 "And he opened his mouth, and taught them, saying, ... Blessed are they that mourn: for they shall be comforted. ... Blessed are they which are persecuted for righteousness' sake: for theirs is the kingdom of heaven. Blessed are ye, when men shall revile you, and persecute you, and shall say all manner of evil against you falsely, for my sake."

In this passage known as the Sermon on the Mount, Jesus pronounces a series of blessings; however, they are not blessings as we often think of in 21st-century Western culture. We hear "blessings" and often assume houses, cars, significant bank accounts, and attractive marriage partners. That misconception is enhanced when we find that the same Greek word is translated "blessed" in all nine verses (Matthew 5:3-11) and means "blessed or happy."

Now, someone might say, "You see there? God wants us to be happy!" Then they use that claim to justify doing whatever they please.

I'm not pointing fingers, dear friends; we all face that mindset. We are all bombarded with ads and enticements for "all the finer things in life." However, those "finer things," though some are nice, cannot be what Jesus was speaking of, because the blessedness He told us about sometimes involves mourning, as well as being reviled, persecuted, and defamed.

The late David Martyn Lloyd-Jones gave some perspective in his book, *Studies in the Sermon on the Mount*: "Happiness is the great question confronting mankind. The whole world is longing for happiness, and it is tragic to observe the ways in which people are seeking it. The vast majority, alas, are doing so in a way that is bound to produce misery. Anything which, by evading the difficulties, merely makes people happy for the time being, is ultimately going to add to their misery and problems. That is where the utter deceitfulness of sin comes in; it is always offering happiness, and it always leads to unhappiness and to final misery and wretchedness. The Sermon on the Mount says, however, that if you really want to be happy, here is the way. This and this alone is the type of person who is truly happy, who is really blessed. This is the sort of person who is to be congratulated."

> Trust and obey,
> For there's no other way
> To be happy in Jesus,
> But to trust and obey.
> ~ John H. Sammis

19

Two Different Payment Plans

Acts 17: 30 "And the times of this ignorance God winked at; but now commandeth all men every where to repent:"

Many people use plastic cards instead of cash to buy things. There are several different kinds of cards; I will mention two that are appropriate for today's thoughts:

- A *credit card* is issued by a bank. The bank pays the merchant when you buy something and then sends you a monthly bill for your total purchases.
- You can purchase a *prepaid card* for a specific dollar amount. When you buy something, some of the money you paid for the card is given to the merchant.

As a loose example, we can think of the credit card as a picture of how God dealt with the sins of people in the Old Testament. Sure they offered sacrifices, but God ordained those as a picture of what was to come. Remember, "It is not possible that the blood of bulls and of goats should take away sins." (Hebrews 10:4) Since the sacrifices didn't actually take away sin, the Lord "winked at" (meaning "overlooked") their sins, considering their sins to be like a credit purchase that would be paid for later. That "later payment" was at the cross of Christ. All the sins of the Old Testament saints (believers) were put on an account that would be paid in full at Calvary.

You probably already realize what the prepaid card represents; it pictures we who have been born since Calvary. The death and resurrection of the Lord Jesus Christ—along with paying for all the debt accumulated by the Old Testament believers—created a "credit" if you will, a positive balance, to pay for everyone who will ever come to God through Christ.

Also, according to Romans 8:22, the whole creation groans and travails in pain, awaiting the redemption. I am not sure how that is going to work, but in the end, sin will be purged, not just from believers, but also from the whole creation. That too has been prepaid by the Savior in His victory on the cross.

The only exception I know of is The Lake of Fire and all who go there. Don't go there. Come to God now; He offers forgiveness for sins, based on Christ's sacrifice two thousand years ago.

20

This Will Last Me the Rest of My Life

John 10:27-28 "My sheep hear my voice, and I know them, and they follow me: And I give unto them eternal life; and they shall never perish, neither shall any man pluck them out of my hand. My Father, which gave them me, is greater than all; and no man is able to pluck them out of my Father's hand."

If I recall correctly, starting somewhere in my dad's 60s, we knew exactly what he was going to say about any birthday or Christmas gift he got. Whatever it was, whether clothing or something else, he would say, "Oh, this will last me the rest of my life." The family joke became the fact that he had no idea he was going to live another thirty years and that those gifts would *not* last him the rest of his life. They would wear out, and he would need another one. He died in 2010 at age 93.

Sadly, that is the way with this fallen world; things wear out and things break. Additionally, sometimes we get tired of things even before they outlive their usefulness.

However, there is one gift my dad got that never wore out, never broke, and of which he never wearied. You see, Dad was a good man, but he was also a sinner. As a result, he was only good in the biblical sense because he had been made righteous by faith in Christ's sacrifice. That righteousness, that gift of salvation, lasted my dad from the time he trusted in Christ to the end of his life, and by God's tender mercy and grace, it will last him forever.

That same gift of forgiveness of sins and righteousness before a holy God is available to all who repent of their sin and trust in Christ, for "whosoever shall call on the name of the Lord shall be saved." (Acts 2:21) However, as they say, this is a limited-time offer; it expires upon your death, and possibly before. Since none of us knows when our time is over, the best advice is, "Behold, now is the accepted time; behold, now is the day of salvation." (2 Corinthians 6:2) The reason for that is because *now* is the only time you *know* for sure you will ever have.

Don't play with your forever. Trust in Christ. Now.

21

Define Good

2 Corinthians 5:21 "For he hath made him to be sin for us, who knew no sin; that we might be made the righteousness of God in him."

I realize there are some who argue about which day of the week The Crucifixion occurred. For this Musing, rather than engage that debate, I prefer to rejoice that Christ died for unworthy sinners and to acknowledge that I am one of them.

For today's thoughts, I borrow from cartoonist Johnny Hart, creator of the B.C. comic strip. One of his entries on a Good Friday featured two of his caveman characters, the first man sitting, the other standing. The conversation went as follows:

Seated man: "I hate the term 'Good Friday.' "
Standing man: "Why?"
Seated man: "My Lord was hanged on a tree that day."
Standing man: "If you were going to be hanged on that day, and
      He volunteered to take your place, how would you feel?"
Seated man: "Good."
Standing man, walking away: "Have a nice day."

As bleak and as dark as it was during that night-in-the-middle-of-the-day, God used that terrible event to restore to Himself all who believe. That was the best bad Friday any of us ever had. Indeed, it was a Good Friday.

In this season, may we prayerfully and thankfully meditate on what the Lord has done for us.

22
The Interposer

Ephesians 2:12-13 "That at that time ye were without Christ, being aliens from the commonwealth of Israel, and strangers from the covenants of promise, having no hope, and without God in the world: But now in Christ Jesus ye who sometimes were far off are made nigh by the blood of Christ."

Almost everyone likes a "superhero," someone who can stop evil and right wrongs. Superman has an interesting superpower; his body is impenetrable. Thus, if someone is in danger of being shot, Superman can simply step in the way. He absorbs the impact of the bullets, and they never reach the intended victim.

I thought of this when considering these lines from the Robert Robinson hymn, "Come, Thou Fount of Every Blessing:"

> Jesus sought me when a stranger,
> Wandering from the fold of God;
> He, to rescue me from danger,
> Interposed His precious blood.

I don't feel particularly comfortable comparing the incomparable Christ to an imaginary figure, but I thought of the imperfect Superman illustration because the word interpose means "to get in the way." As I have mentioned before, we tend to think of God as loving and kind, but a realistic understanding of Him must also include His holiness and His abhorrence of sin. As a result of what He is like—and what I am like—His wrath against me and my sin is huge; it is looming, and it is proper.

That is where the idea of interposing comes in. On the cross, Jesus Christ who had no sin stepped in the way of the just wrath against me. He interposed His precious blood between me and the holy God who had every right to be angry with me.

No wonder Robinson began his song:

> Come, Thou fount of every blessing,
> Tune my heart to sing Thy grace;
> Streams of mercy, never ceasing,
> Call for songs of loudest praise.

Let us praise Him with joyful hearts, for "He, to rescue us from danger, interposed His precious blood." In the words of another hymn, "Hallelujah, What a Savior!" (Philip Bliss)

23

Suffer Little Children to Come unto Me

Luke 18:15-17 "They brought unto him also infants, that he would touch them: but when his disciples saw it, they rebuked them. But Jesus called them unto him, and said, Suffer [allow] little children to come unto me, and forbid them not: for of such is the kingdom of God. Verily I say unto you, Whosoever shall not receive the kingdom of God as a little child shall in no wise enter therein."

Wow, what a passage. The disciples wouldn't allow parents to bring their little children to Jesus, but Jesus corrected them saying that the little ones are the only ones with the proper mindset. It was almost as if all the disciples were having a Philip-moment. Do you remember the time Jesus said to him, "Have I been so long time with you, and yet hast thou not known me, Philip?" (John 14:9) The disciples had spent three years with God in the flesh and yet still had trouble grasping even the simplest concepts about eternity.

However, before I start criticizing the disciples, I must remember that I have walked with the Lord for fifteen *times* that long, and I *still* imagine Him saying, "Bill, what are you thinking?"

I was reminded of this just hours ago as I sat in a restaurant. A family walked in with a one-year-old riding in his father's arms. The little guy had a rather carefree look on his face as if he was thinking, "I don't have any idea where we are going, but Dad seems to know, so I am sure everything is going to be all right."

That is what Jesus was talking about. The writer to the Hebrews tells us that without faith it is impossible to please God. (11:6) Children have their problems and their moods; remember, they are sinners just like the rest of us. Nevertheless, children are often simple and innocent in their thinking, especially if their past experience has been good.

The Lord doesn't always give us what we want; that is when one of our childish moods comes out. However, He has never mistreated us or given us cause to distrust Him.

Let us not be childish, but let us always be childlike in our approach to our Heavenly Father.

24

The Very First Commandment

Genesis 2:16-17 "And the LORD God commanded the man, saying, Of every tree of the garden thou mayest freely eat: But of the tree of the knowledge of good and evil, thou shalt not eat of it: for in the day that thou eatest thereof thou shalt surely die."

A lot is said about the Ten Commandments as well as the other laws God gave through Moses. Some say we must keep all the laws in order to enter Heaven. Dear friends, reading Leviticus through one time will make it sadly clear that *none* of us keep all the laws, including the rich ruler of Luke 18:18-23, who said "All these have I kept from my youth up." (verse 21) He didn't even keep the *first* of the Ten Commandments because he put his riches before God.

I recently heard a preacher mention the event presented in today's verses, pointing out that Adam and Eve only had *one* law, and they didn't even keep that. Additionally, they weren't sinners until *after* their disobedience! If *perfect* man can't even keep *one* law, are we sure we sinful mortals can keep more than 600 Mosaic laws and all the other commands God has given?

Now, you might ask why God give us the Law, and the Lord graciously answers that question in Galatians 3:24-25 where He says that the law is a schoolmaster—a teacher—to bring us to Christ. So then, if the law is our teacher, what does it teach us? The law certainly does not teach us to be lawless; rather it teaches us that our inability to keep the law requires us to rely completely on Christ for our salvation. "But after that faith is come, we are no longer under a schoolmaster. For ye are all the children of God by faith in Christ Jesus." (Galatians 3:25-26)

God had a reason for giving us the Law as a teacher. As with any teacher, we students must pay attention to what it is teaching us.

25

Don't Confuse the Trip with the Destination

John 20:1-2 "The first day of the week cometh Mary Magdalene early, when it was yet dark, unto the sepulchre, and seeth the stone taken away from the sepulchre. Then she runneth, and cometh to Simon Peter, and to the other disciple, whom Jesus loved, and saith unto them, They have taken away the Lord out of the sepulchre, and we know not where they have laid him."

While reading today's verses, five words jumped out at me: "Then she runneth, and cometh."

Mary Magdalene had gone out to Jesus' tomb "early, when it was yet dark." Why did Mary go out that early? Note that it doesn't even say she **awoke** to go to the tomb, just that she went. Remember, this is the woman out of whom Jesus cast seven devils, (Mark 16:9) and her rescuer—her Savior—had been murdered before her very eyes. (John 19:25) She was probably not getting much sleep at all.

When she arrived at the tomb, she found that someone had rolled the stone away and the Lord's body was missing. The next thing it says is that she started running. Note however, that she didn't run for the sake of running; she ran in order to arrive at a destination: "she runneth, and cometh to Simon Peter." She wanted Peter and John to know that the Lord's body was missing, so she hastened to tell them.

Do we believers major on motion and lose sight of the goal? Do we allow the flurry—the running—to become the purpose rather than the avenue to the destination? Are we satisfied with a lot of activity even if it doesn't accomplish much spiritual fruit?

Here are two examples:

- We have a glorious message. There are many ways to tell that message—by a life well lived, by writing, by speaking, by performing arts, etc. However, is our destination to put on a good show, or is our goal to effectively convey that message to other human beings?
- We are running a race and fighting the good fight. (1 Timothy 6:12; Hebrews 12:1) Are we doing that to show our ability to run and fight in our own strength, or are we doing so to glorify our Savior and cooperate with the Holy Spirit in our sanctification?

Don't just run. Run to arrive at a worthy destination!

26

A Troublesome Remembrance or There IS a Reason

Psalm 77:3 "I remembered God, and was troubled: I complained, and my spirit was overwhelmed. Selah."

The word translated "complained" is a Hebrew word that is elsewhere translated "ponder, mediate, and muse." That is what we try to do in these Musings, to ponder and meditate on God, His Word, and His activities. However, sometimes, when we compare two attributes of God that are seemingly opposite—for example, His love and His wrath—we become confused. We see His various dealings with different people at diverse times, and we don't understand.

Perhaps you have seen on television or in a movie, a circumstance in which a robot is given a command that violates its programmed ethical code or a computer is given an impossible mathematical equation. The electromechanical device locked up and was unable to continue until the request was rescinded.

British Bible teacher Alun McNabb read today's verse in a sermon he gave some years ago. When he finished speaking, a young student who did not have a Bible with him asked Brother McNabb, "Did you read, 'I remembered God, and was troubled?'" When McNabb answered yes, the young man said, "I thought you remembered God and were helped."

That is often our thinking too, isn't it? We expect that when we go to God and ponder His Word, we will obtain peace and tranquility; when that doesn't happen, we are not sure which direction to go—like a computer that has been asked to divide a number by zero. God has been our strength and rock, but now we don't know where to turn.

The problem is not in God; instead, our ability to fathom His purpose is hindered, partly because we don't have enough information. Timothy Keller expressed this point well when he said, "God will either give us what we ask for in prayer or give us what we would have asked for if we knew everything he knows."

Lord willing, tomorrow we shall see some examples of things that we or other mortals might miss in God's plan. For now, though, let us remember that God is good, kind, holy, just, gracious and so much more, all the time, all at the same time. As Charles Spurgeon said, "God is too good to be unkind and He is too wise to be mistaken. When we cannot trace His hand, we must trust His heart."

27

A Troublesome Remembrance, Part 2

Habakkuk 2:20 "The LORD is in his holy temple: let all the earth keep silence before him."

Last time, we saw that the Bible tells us incomprehensible things, some of which make us uncomfortable. I intended today to look at two striking events that demonstrate God's command over His creation; however, we will better understand God's actions and commands if we first understand Him, at least several things about Him.

We are accustomed to working on a horizontal plane; that is what I call the "Golden Rule" level. At this level, we expect certain behavior from others, and they expect the same from us. At least in some sense, we understand ourselves, and consequently, we understand others who are like us. However, though God works within the "Golden Rule" level for His own purposes, He dwells in an entirely different realm, a domain unique to Him alone. We rightly expect certain behavior from fellow mortals and resent when they move outside those parameters, so when God "violates our rules," we may think we are right to hold Him to our standards and feel justified in "judging" God.

As tempting as that may be, it is a gross distortion of reality. As the psalmist said, "Know ye that the LORD he is God: it is he that hath made us, and not we ourselves; we are his people, and the sheep of his pasture." (100:3) We are HIS creation, not the other way around; we must live according to HIS pronouncements, not insist that He live according to ours.

As we saw last time, God is good, gracious, loving, and kind, and we can have confidence He will act in a manner consistent with those attributes. However, He is also righteous, holy, and just, and we must expect Him to behave in ways that are consistent with *those* attributes too.

God is God in all of His being; nothing other than who He is would be God.

Finally, sometimes God explains His thoughts, as He does in the event we shall look at tomorrow, and sometimes He does **not** give reasons, as I plan to show in two days. However, the explanations He **does** give should assure us that He is trustworthy, even during the times when He does **not** explain His actions—at times when He is silent about His purposes.

28

A Troublesome Remembrance, Part 3

Jonah 4:1-2 "But it displeased Jonah exceedingly, and he was very angry. And he prayed unto the LORD, and said, I pray thee, O LORD, was not this my saying, when I was yet in my country? Therefore I fled before unto Tarshish: for I knew that thou art a gracious God, and merciful, slow to anger, and of great kindness, and repentest thee of the evil."

We have been looking at things God does that we do not understand. God commanded Jonah to go to Nineveh, a vile, wicked city, but Jonah ran away rather than go. God forced his hand, and Jonah finally went. It made Jonah livid when the people of Nineveh repented. Someone once suggested that the murderous Ninevites might have hurt or killed some of Jonah's family or friends. It is as if Jonah said, 'God, I *knew* you would be kind to them if they repented, and I ***don't like it!***'

God asked the prophet a sobering question in the closing verse of the book of Jonah: "Should not I spare Nineveh, that great city, wherein are more than sixscore thousand persons that cannot discern between their right hand and their left hand?" (Jonah 4:11) One hundred twenty thousand people were entrenched in their own evil traditions with consciences so ruined they didn't even know they were doing evil, and God shouldn't warn them?

Jonah knew they deserved God's judgment. God knew they deserved God's judgment. Yet, God purposed to send a prophet to them so that *they* knew they deserved God's judgment. Once they understood God's truth, they repented of their evil, and God spared one hundred twenty thousand people from a judgment that they richly deserved. *That* is who God is! He is of ***great*** mercy to those who will stop fighting against Him and humble themselves in repentance and faith.

Interestingly, this account of God's great kindness to Nineveh is recorded in the Old Testament, where God is supposedly some "angry ogre." Instead, in a staggering display of mercy, He spares a whole nation of wicked people who repented. God *is* good, and He is *very* patient.

Tomorrow, we shall see a chillingly different series of events, incidents in which God was just as patient, perhaps even more so, but which turned out frighteningly different because those groups insisted on rejecting God and His ways.

29

A Troublesome Remembrance, Part 4

Deuteronomy 7:1-2 "When the LORD thy God shall bring thee into the land whither thou goest to possess it, and hath cast out many nations before thee, the Hittites, and the Girgashites, and the Amorites, and the Canaanites, and the Perizzites, and the Hivites, and the Jebusites, seven nations greater and mightier than thou; And when the LORD thy God shall deliver them before thee; thou shalt smite them, and utterly destroy them; thou shalt make no covenant with them, nor shew mercy unto them."

During the last three days, we have considered a few thoughts about acts of God that are different than we might expect. We saw that God graciously spared repentant Nineveh, even though they had committed atrocities on a level with today's terrorists.

In today's verses, God commands the Israelites to "utterly destroy" seven nations that were in the land God had promised to Abraham and his descendants. The words God uses—"utterly destroy"— are chilling. What is not clear in the English is that the words "utterly" and "destroy" are translations of the *same Greek word*. The word used once means to "utterly destroy" or "completely destroy," but by using the word twice together God seems to be creating an emphatic command. It is as if the Righteous Judge of the Universe is saying, "Utterly, completely, destructively destroy them."

We see that as extremely intense, and the *apparent* overreaction can easily send our hearts staggering backward. However, we see God's command differently when we understand two things that are not clear in this section, but which we discover through other Scripture passages as well as historical sources. Briefly, those two things are: [1] In a sense, these nations were worse than Nineveh because the blood on their hands was the blood of their own children. They sacrificed their children to their heathen gods in horrific ways I will not describe here. [2] The indications are that God gave them about 400 years to repent, and they would not.

Faith in the true and living God is not some metaphysical sensation that gives a momentary tingle. Genuine faith in the true and living God is the confidence that He is the same when we cannot see Him, as He is when we can—that if He does something we cannot understand, it is because, as Timothy Keller said, we simply don't know everything He knows.

Tomorrow, Lord willing, a few final thoughts.

30
A Troublesome Remembrance, Part 5

Hebrews 11:1-2, 6 "Now faith is the substance of things hoped for, the evidence of things not seen. For by it the elders obtained a good report. … But without faith it is impossible to please him: for he that cometh to God must believe that he is, and that he is a rewarder of them that diligently seek him."

Some of these Musings are easy to write; sometimes the thoughts and words come to me faster than I can type them. However, some are harder to write, demanding that I labor over nearly every word. This series on "A Troublesome Remembrance" is the latter kind.

One of the things I have dreaded is that I might unduly frighten someone. Though we have surely seen that rebelling against the King of the Universe *should* frighten us, we *must* also understand that He is gracious and tenderhearted to those who turn to Him from their wicked ways. That creates in us a reverential *awe* of who He is and of the salvation and eternity He has bought for us with His precious blood.

One of our mortal shortcomings is the tendency to think of ourselves as autonomous—as sovereign in what we say and do: 'No one should *dare* challenge my speech or criticize my actions.' However, Isaiah pictures us as clay on the potter's wheel: "Surely your turning of things upside down shall be esteemed as the potter's clay: for shall the work say of him that made it, He made me not? or shall the thing framed say of him that framed it, He had no understanding?" (Isaiah 29:16) One of the most dangerous things about human pride is how easy it is for us to dismiss it, and sometimes, not even recognize it in the first place. It almost destroyed Nineveh, and it has cast multitudes of arrogant cultures onto the trash heap of history.

The conclusion of the whole matter is what we glean from Timothy Keller's quote; if we were like God and knew everything He knows, we would do exactly what He does. Let us not disdain the Potter for His marvelous, albeit perplexing, designs; rather let us lay aside our defiant thinking, saying as Thomas did, "My Lord and my God." (John 20:28) Then, and only then, we shall stand on solid ground, whether in tranquility or through trials.

31

Praises and Pejoratives

Luke 7:31-34 "And the Lord said, Whereunto then shall I liken the men of this generation? and to what are they like? They are like unto children sitting in the marketplace, and calling one to another, and saying, We have piped unto you, and ye have not danced; we have mourned to you, and ye have not wept. For John the Baptist came neither eating bread nor drinking wine; and ye say, He hath a devil. The Son of man is come eating and drinking; and ye say, Behold a gluttonous man, and a winebibber, a friend of publicans and sinners!"

Musings

There are words and phrases we use that can be a compliment, but which can also be used as a criticism—a statement meant to embarrass or cause shame. The former would be praise; the latter is called a pejorative.

For example, if someone is truly funny and able to make people laugh, "What a clown!" would be a positive statement of their comedic ability. However, for someone presenting comedy poorly or doing something to gain attention and doing it in a way that displeased those looking on, "What a clown!" would be derogatory.

Such is the case in today's verses in which Jesus is talking about the fickleness of His detractors. He said they were like children complaining that someone would not dance to their tune, nor cry over their sad tales. The Savior goes on to display their childish inconsistency, saying they criticized John for his behavior, but when Jesus came acting just the opposite, they weren't happy with Him either.

It was then they threw verbal mud at Jesus, calling Him "a friend of publicans and sinners!" Publicans were the IRS agents of the day, Jewish people who collected money for the Roman government, and they were despised.

The critics also used the term "a friend of sinners" in a negative sense, but I consider that to be such a precious title. "A friend of sinners!" I guess if I thought I was a pretty good guy, like they seemed to have thought they were, I might believe being a friend of sinners to be uncomplimentary too. On the other hand, since I *am* a sinner, I am glad He has purposed to make me His friend instead of condemning me.

APRIL

1

Praise in the Midst of Problems

Psalm 43:1-5 "Judge me, O God, and plead my cause against an ungodly nation: O deliver me from the deceitful and unjust man. For thou art the God of my strength: why dost thou cast me off? why go I mourning because of the oppression of the enemy? O send out thy light and thy truth: let them lead me; let them bring me unto thy holy hill, and to thy tabernacles. Then will I go unto the altar of God, unto God my exceeding joy: yea, upon the harp will I praise thee, O God my God. Why art thou cast down, O my soul? and why art thou disquieted within me? hope in God: for I shall yet praise him, who is the health of my countenance, and my God."

Here the psalmist expresses angst about the injustice of ungodly people. However, in the end, he asks, "Why art thou cast down, O my soul? and why art thou disquieted within me? hope in God: for I shall yet praise him, who is the health of my countenance, and my God."

Sure, we have problems in this world. When Job was facing his darkest hours he said, "Man that is born of a woman is of few days, and full of trouble." (Job 14:1)

We should use the resources God has given us to resolve any troubles we can. However, even during tribulations and sorrows, there is still one sanctuary for the troubled soul, and that is in intimate communion with God. "I go unto the altar of God, unto God my exceeding joy: yea, upon the harp will I praise thee, O God my God ... I shall yet praise him."

> O what peace we often forfeit,
> O what needless pain we bear,
> All because we do not carry
> Everything to God in prayer!
> ~ Joseph Scriven

In addition, let us not just bring our troubles to Him, for he says, "Be careful [anxious] for nothing; but in every thing by prayer and supplication *with thanksgiving* let your requests be made known unto God. And the peace of God, which passeth all understanding, shall keep your hearts and minds through Christ Jesus." (Philippians 4:6-7, note and emphasis mine)

Bowing before God, praying for needs with thanksgiving, and doing so from a heart of praise, now, *that* is a worthy occupation.

2

Atonement

Romans 5:6-11 "For when we were yet without strength, in due time Christ died for the ungodly. For scarcely for a righteous man will one die: yet peradventure for a good man some would even dare to die. But God commendeth his love toward us, in that, while we were yet sinners, Christ died for us. Much more then, being now justified by his blood, we shall be saved from wrath through him. For if, when we were enemies, we were reconciled to God by the death of his Son, much more, being reconciled, we shall be saved by his life. And not only so, but we also joy in God through our Lord Jesus Christ, by whom we have now received the atonement."

What a rich passage this is. When we could do *nothing* about our sinful condition, Christ died for us. As a result, we are justified (no longer guilty); saved from wrath; reconciled to God; and saved by Christ's life. Not only all *that*, but we also have received the atonement.

Let's look at that word "atonement." In the Old Testament, the Hebrew word has a strong feeling of covering over. The word is used in the account of Noah when God tells him to cover the ark inside and out with pitch. This is consistent with the animal sacrifices year after year that actually did not take away sin, but instead, covered it until it could be dealt with later. (Hebrews 10:4, 11)

However, the flavor in the New Testament is different. The Greek word has the sense of an exchange. In the marketplace, you expect a fair trade, a value of cash for an equal value of goods or services. But there is another sense to the word in which an adjustment is made, creating an *un*-equal deal. The marketplace example is when the buyer doesn't have enough money and the seller adjusts the price and suffers the loss so the buyer can make the purchase.

That my friends, is what God did for us through the work of the Lord Jesus! "While we were yet sinners"—while we were spiritually bankrupt, while we had ***zero*** spiritual capital—"Christ died for us." As a result, God can make the ultimate, infinite adjustment to our accounts so that the staggering debt is paid in full.

John Newton rightly called that, "Amazing Grace."

3
Two Kinds of People

John 15:17 These things I command you, that ye love one another. 18 If the world hate you, ye know that it hated me before it hated you. 19 If ye were of the world, the world would love his own: but because ye are not of the world, but I have chosen you out of the world, therefore the world hateth you. 20 Remember the word that I said unto you, The servant is not greater than his lord. If they have persecuted me, they will also persecute you; if they have kept my saying, they will keep yours also.

"There are two kinds of people." That phrase is often followed by a humorous comparison, such as, "There are two kinds of people: people who divide people into two groups and people who do not." But, sometimes the second half is more caustic or biting, such as an ethnic derision or ad hominem attack.

Jesus gives us an insightful declaration in today's verses. He sees a distinction between those who follow Him and those who do not. Of that distinction He makes at least four points:

- His followers are to love each other. (v17)
- We should not be surprised if the world has the same attitude toward us as it had toward Christ. (v18)
- The world is hostile toward us who have been chosen in Christ, even though we are no more worthy than they are. (v19)
- The way we know whether people love or hate Jesus is how they treat His followers. (v20)

God tells those who love Him to love each other as well. What does He think when his followers separate themselves from other believers? Perhaps it's because their skin is a different color? or because they have less (or more) money? or because they have a different opinion than we do?

C. S. Lewis said, "Christianity, if false, is of no importance, and if true, of infinite importance. The only thing it cannot be is moderately important."

Really trusting in Christ causes us to follow Him. Following Him means, among other things, loving His people. We do that by identifying with them as members of His family, our brothers and sisters in the faith.

Do we? Do I? Do you?

4

Games, Moons, and the Light of the World

John 8:12 "Then spake Jesus again unto them, saying, I am the light of the world: he that followeth me shall not walk in darkness, but shall have the light of life."

Matthew 5:14-16 "Ye are the light of the world. A city that is set on a hill cannot be hid. Neither do men light a candle, and put it under a bushel, but on a candlestick; and it giveth light unto all that are in the house. Let your light so shine before men, that they may see your good works, and glorify your Father which is in heaven."

Skeptics tell us that there are mistakes in the Bible. I imagine today's verses are on their list. Jesus tells His disciples, "I am the light of the world," but He also tells them, "Ye are the light of the world." Is that really a mistake?

I was reminded of this last night when my wife and I were playing a game. It is played with tiles marked with numbers 1 through 13, and each tile is one of four different colors. However, there are also two wild tiles. These wild tiles have no value or specific color of their own. They can be used as if they were *any* other tile in the game, and when they are put into play, they take on the value and color of the tile they represent.

In the same way, the moon does not "shine" in and of itself; instead it reflects the light of the Sun. In doing so, it gives light to the night without actually having any light of its own.

I believe that is what Jesus means here: He is the true light of the world; however, as we learn of Him and become more conformed to His image, (Romans 8:29) we reflect His glory. One result is that some will see our good works and glorify our Father who is in Heaven.

> The whole world was lost in the darkness of sin,
> The Light of the world is Jesus!
> Like sunshine at noonday, His glory shone in;

The Light of the world is Jesus!

Come to the light, 'tis shining for thee;
Sweetly the light has dawned upon me;
Once I was blind, but now I can see:
The Light of the world is Jesus!
~ Philip P. Bliss

5

Even the Weeds

Matthew 5:44-48 "But I say unto you, Love your enemies, bless them that curse you, do good to them that hate you, and pray for them which despitefully use you, and persecute you; That ye may be the children of your Father which is in heaven: for he maketh his sun to rise on the evil and on the good, and sendeth rain on the just and on the unjust. For if ye love them which love you, what reward have ye? do not even the publicans the same? And if ye salute your brethren only, what do ye more than others? do not even the publicans so? Be ye therefore perfect, even as your Father which is in heaven is perfect."

'Perfect' here does not mean sinless, it means complete or mature.

As we were driving home from our shopping trip recently, the view in front of us was cloudy but light, and the sky we could see was blue. However, I glanced in the rearview mirror, and the sky was the darkest gray I had ever seen it. We unpacked the car, and as I came out to the porch to retrieve the last items, the storm that had followed us home began soaking everything that was not under a roof.

As I sat on our front porch enjoying a significant spring shower, I noticed a tree just a few yards away. There are weeds that keep growing around the base of the tree too close for the riding mower to cut. I do cut them by hand occasionally, but they keep coming back. The thing that I noticed as I watched the rain fall was that it fell on the tree, and it also fell on the weeds.

God gives unique blessings to those who love and trust in Him; however, in His tender and loving kindness, He "sendeth rain on the just and on the unjust." He is especially good to those who love Him, but He is also good to those who do not love Him. In fact, He uses that very goodness to bring the lost to Himself. "Despisest thou the riches of his goodness and forbearance and longsuffering; not knowing that the goodness of God leadeth thee to repentance?" (Romans 2:4)

Lord, thank You for the goodness that You splash across this world like falling rain. Help us to be more grateful.

6

A Hot Mess

Genesis 1:31 "And God saw every thing that he had made, and, behold, it was very good. And the evening and the morning were the sixth day."

One day my wife was talking to our four-year-old granddaughter Sophie about the chaotic condition of her toy-scattered bedroom. Sophie agreed with Nana and called it a "hot mess."

This world is a "hot mess" too. Oh, for sure, there is beauty in the mess, but it is a mess nevertheless. In the beginning, God made everything and declared that it was very good; however, it only remained that way briefly, for the third chapter of Genesis records mankind's change from follower of God to rebel against Him.

Some of God's original beauty remains, but that tragic mutiny exacted an ugly toll from God's once pristine creation. Even with the aesthetic splendor we still enjoy, there is a pall over this world. Moreover, the events that occur daily in every major city, and with discouraging regularity in smaller communities, remind us of the scars upon our world.

One of the scars is that we must put locks on everything. In a world that is very good, we wouldn't need locks, but since this world is no longer very good, we lock our houses, cars and businesses, and must carry a pocket full of keys to enter our buildings and access our belongings.

However, there is good news in this fallen world. Jesus said, "I am he that liveth, and was dead; and, behold, I am alive for evermore, Amen; and have the keys of hell and of death." (Revelation 1:18) A friend of mine once called keys "the emblems of authority." The fact that Jesus has the keys of Hell and death is evidence that He has rightful authority over them, but to secure that authority, the Lord of glory "became obedient unto death, even the death of the cross." (Philippians 2:8) In so doing, Jesus paid the debt for all who acknowledge their sin and trust in God's forgiveness on Christ's merit.

We can rest in Christ's finished work on the cross for our eternal future and rest in this "hot mess" of our world because He has said, "These things I have spoken unto you, that in me ye might have peace. In the world ye shall have tribulation: but be of good cheer; I have overcome the world." (John 16:33)

7
Plan B

John 14:2-6 "In my Father's house are many mansions: if it were not so, I would have told you. I go to prepare a place for you. And if I go and prepare a place for you, I will come again, and receive you unto myself; that where I am, there ye may be also. And whither I go ye know, and the way ye know. Thomas saith unto him, Lord, we know not whither thou goest; and how can we know the way? Jesus saith unto him, I am the way, the truth, and the life: no man cometh unto the Father, but by me."

Contingency plans are important. Business and military leaders, and even individuals have backup plans for when our initial plans run into trouble—a Plan B, if you will. In human experience, this is often beneficial and can be the difference between success and failure.

However, there is one circumstance in which we must not count on an alternative; Jesus says it plainly in today's verses. Thomas objects to the claim Jesus made that His followers knew where He was going and how to get there. In His response to Thomas, the Lord tells the disciple, "I AM the way."

Some argue that the Greek does not contain the definite article "the" as it appears in the English translation ("the way, the truth, and the life.") However, Jesus seems to have anticipated a misunderstanding, for He completes His reply with an unambiguous statement: "No man cometh unto the Father, but by me." That *shouts* exclusivity.

For all my friends who are counting on an alternate plan, please let me remind you of something else Jesus said: "Verily, verily, I say unto you, He that entereth not by the door into the sheepfold, but climbeth up some other way, the same is a thief and a robber." (John 10:1)

Please think carefully and understand what I am saying. I am not trying to be divisive, and I am not trying to be argumentative. Neither am I trying to sway you with my own opinions. Instead, I am pleading with you to respond to God's offer of salvation, for there is no other way. If you refuse to come to God on His terms—by grace through faith in Christ—there is no Plan B.

That is a stark and sobering reality.

8

Management Styles

Romans 3:24-26 "Being justified freely by his grace through the redemption that is in Christ Jesus: Whom God hath set forth to be a propitiation through faith in his blood, to declare his righteousness for the remission of sins that are past, through the forbearance of God; To declare, I say, at this time his righteousness: that he might be just, and the justifier of him which believeth in Jesus."

The old adage is, "If you want the job done right, you have to do it yourself." A friend used to say, "If it's got to be, it's up to me." I once worked for a man with that philosophy. He regularly checked up on his employees to make sure they were getting their work done and that they were doing it the way he wanted it done. That is called "micromanaging" because the leader doesn't trust people with the small details.

The opposite management style involves delegating. The boss hires qualified, trustworthy people, tells them clearly what he wants them to do, and then expects them to do it.

I suppose there is a place and time for both styles. If you micromanage competent workers, they feel unappreciated and belittled, but if you simply delegate to people who don't care about doing a good job—or don't know how to—the job will be poorly done, if it gets done at all.

Paul uses an unusual word in today's verses; he says that God sent Christ "to be a propitiation." ***Strong's Concordance*** says that word is "relating to an appeasing or expiating." It describes someone who has the ability to take charge of an explosive situation and do what must be done to restore peace.

Without Christ, we abide (present tense) under God's wrath, (John 3:36) and He is "angry with the wicked every day." (Psalm 7:11) However, when it was the exact right time, a willing and gracious Father sent His willing and gracious Son to do what no one else could do. Jesus was the *only* one the Father could trust—the *only* one qualified—"to be a propitiation through faith in his blood ... that he [the Father] might be just, and the justifier of him which believeth in Jesus."

"O praise the LORD, all ye nations: praise him, all ye people." (Psalm 117:1)

9
Changing Worlds

2 Corinthians 5:4-9 "For we that are in this tabernacle [our bodies] do groan, being burdened: not for that we would be unclothed, but clothed upon, that mortality might be swallowed up of life. Now he that hath wrought us for the selfsame thing is God, who also hath given unto us the earnest of the Spirit. Therefore we are always confident, knowing that, whilst we are at home in the body, we are absent from the Lord: (For we walk by faith, not by sight:) We are confident, I say, and willing rather to be absent from the body, and to be present with the Lord. Wherefore we labour, that, whether present or absent, we may be accepted of him."

Chief Seattle was one of the leaders of the Duwamish tribe that lived in what is now the western state of Washington in the United States of America. The city of Seattle is located in the area where he and his people lived and is named after him.

Chief Seattle, like his people, was a believer in the Great Spirit; however, sometime during his life, he came into contact with Christian missionaries, and some think he may have become a genuine Christian. I recently saw a quote attributed to him; regardless of his own personal beliefs, he was right in what he said, "There is no death, only a change of worlds."

As strange as it may sound, death does not end life; it only forces a move to another world. The Bible clearly declares that a human being's spirit is everlasting—it never ceases to exist. When our spirit leaves this temporary home we call the body, it will go to one of two very different worlds.

Today's verses teach us a little bit about the eternal home of those who have placed their faith in God and have had their sins forgiven through the finished work of Christ. When we cease to be here, we begin to be there with Him.

There is also another world, the eternal home of those who reject God's mercy, love, and grace. I urge you to consider seriously the world to which you are heading, for whichever world we choose will be our home forever.

10

Gravesite or Delight

John 20:10-16 "Then the disciples went away again unto their own home. But Mary stood without at the sepulchre weeping: and as she wept, she stooped down, and looked into the sepulchre, And seeth two angels in white sitting, the one at the head, and the other at the feet, where the body of Jesus had lain. And they say unto her, Woman, why weepest thou? She saith unto them, Because they have taken away my Lord, and I know not where they have laid him. And when she had thus said, she turned herself back, and saw Jesus standing, and knew not that it was Jesus. Jesus saith unto her, Woman, why weepest thou? whom seekest thou? She, supposing him to be the gardener, saith unto him, Sir, if thou have borne him hence, tell me where thou hast laid him, and I will take him away. Jesus saith unto her, Mary. She turned herself, and saith unto him, Rabboni; which is to say, Master."

Imagine that you have just buried a dear friend. Several days later, you take flowers, only to find that the body is not there anymore and no one will tell you where your friend has been moved. You still have your memories, but you no longer have a special place to go to relive those fond times.

What an upsetting event for Mary that she would have no place to visit as she reflected on all Jesus had done for her and been to her. Now ask yourself this question. How long did Mary's disappointment last when she realized that Jesus was not in the tomb because He was standing there speaking to her?

Which is better: a gravesite to visit or a risen Savior with whom you can commune and fellowship? A gravesite to visit or a living Lord who you can worship?

I am sure Mary preferred the risen Savior and living Lord. The delightful truth is that the Lord we worship today is not dead, but alive. Alfred Ackley said it this way:

> I serve a risen Savior; He's in the world today.
> I know that He is living, Whatever men may say.
> I see His hand of mercy; I hear His voice of cheer;
> And just the time I need Him He's always near.

Hallelujah, what a Savior!

11
He Shall See

Isaiah 53:11 "He shall see of the travail of his soul, and shall be satisfied: by his knowledge shall my righteous servant justify many; for he shall bear their iniquities."

It has been awhile since I have seen the commercials, but one of the baking companies used to advertise that their English muffins had "nooks and crannies." They were speaking of the tiny holes left by air bubbles in the dough as it baked, suggesting those little holes would absorb the butter as it melted into the warm pastry.

Isaiah 53 is one of those Scripture passages with "nooks and crannies." It is filled with little pockets of truth and wonder, which strike awe into the awakened human heart. By "awe," I don't mean, "Oh, that's neat." By awe, I mean something like what happened in Martin Luther's heart as he sat contemplating the words of Jesus on the cross: "My God, my God, why hast thou forsaken me?" (Mark 15:34) I am told that Luther sat almost motionless for a long time contemplating those words; then he finally stood, mind filled with awe and wonder, and said, "God forsaken by God! Who can understand that?"

Today's verse makes just that kind of awe-filled statement: "He shall see of the travail of his soul, and shall be satisfied." Is it speaking of the work Jesus accomplished on the cross? Or perhaps, it is speaking of us poor sinners whom He has won by that work. Either way, we mortals—weak in ourselves on our best day—are part of what He won on that tree. To be sure, that was not all: He also glorified His Father, redeemed creation, and more. Nevertheless, part of His victory through the "travail of His soul" was that He won us. Truly awesome!

> Jesus, Savior, precious friend, You tell me in Your Word
> So many great and special things I do not understand;
> But if, dear Lord, You said to me,
>   "What one thing would you know?"
> I'd ask you as I held Your nail-scarred hand,
>
> "Why do you love me? Why do you care?
> It says You'll see, and You'll be satisfied.

You tell me that You love me,
>   and You proved it when You died,
But my question, precious Savior, is simply, "Why?"
~ W.F. Powers, early 1990s

I am continuously awestruck. I am also eternally grateful.

12

The Sparrows of Civilla Martin

Luke 12:6-7 "Are not five sparrows sold for two farthings, and not one of them is forgotten before God? But even the very hairs of your head are all numbered. Fear not therefore: ye are of more value than many sparrows."

The other day, I was talking to a dear friend who has had difficulties recently and has become fearful and apprehensive of the future. I understand that angst and even struggle with it myself sometimes; however, in the last few years, God has helped my feeble heart to focus, not just on His flawless plan, but also on His own glorious being. Oh, I wish I knew Him better and that I trusted Him more, but slowly, I am learning the sweet truth of Jean Sophia Pigott's sweet hymn:

>   Jesus, I am resting, resting
>   In the joy of what Thou art;
>   I am finding out the greatness
>   Of Thy loving heart.

In early 1905, Civilla Martin had an experience that prompted her to write another inspiring song of hope:

>   Why should I feel discouraged,
>   >   why should the shadows come,
>   Why should my heart be lonely,
>   >   and long for heav'n and home,
>   When Jesus is my portion?
>   >   My constant Friend is He:
>   His eye is on the sparrow,
>   >   and I know He watches me.

In today's verses, Jesus is speaking to His disciples, telling them that the same God who notices the sparrow watches over them. He goes on to tell them God values His followers more than a multitude of those little creatures and that God even knows the very number of hairs on our head. If God takes note of the little bird and is detailed enough that He can count the hairs on our head, surely Jesus is implying to His disciples that God is involved in the most minuscule details of our lives.

I am told that the Bible tells us 365 times "Fear not" or some other admonition toward restful faith. In fact, later in the same passage, the Lord Jesus tells His followers, "Fear not, little flock; for it is your Father's good pleasure to give you the kingdom." (Luke 12:32) Notice that giving them the kingdom is not something God must be coerced into doing; it is His *good pleasure!*

Trust God's love. It is real; it is strong; and it is good.

13

The Great Miscalculation

Psalm 49:11-13 "Their inward thought is, that their houses shall continue for ever, and their dwelling places to all generations; they call their lands after their own names. Nevertheless man being in honour abideth not: he is like the beasts that perish. This their way is their folly: yet their posterity approve their sayings. Selah."

The psalmist is identifying a problem in his time that has survived even to our day. The problem is the mindset that we and our legacies are immortal; however, our time in these earthly bodies is actually very limited. Even our memories among those we leave behind will fade over time, possibly rapidly depending on the relationship we had with them.

On the other hand, our *spirits* are eternal; that is true whether we believe in God or not. Our eternal *destination* is different depending on our relationship to God, but each of us will be somewhere forever. That is why it is so important to focus on the eternal even if our minds tend toward focusing on the temporal.

Elsewhere, the psalmist said, "The days of our years are threescore years and ten [70 years]; and if by reason of strength they be fourscore years [80 years], yet is their strength labour and sorrow; for it is soon cut off, and we fly away." (Psalm 90:10)

As much as our culture likes to glorify youth and appearance, both fade quickly; however, one thing that does *not* fade is the reality that one day we will pass over that line between this life and the next. In light of that, one question pleads for an answer: "Are you ready?" You can be, in Christ. I encourage you to trust Him now.

14
In His Image

Genesis 1:26-27 "And God said, Let us make man in our image, after our likeness: and let them have dominion over the fish of the sea, and over the fowl of the air, and over the cattle, and over all the earth, and over every creeping thing that creepeth upon the earth. So God created man in his own image, in the image of God created he him; male and female created he them."

What would it have been like to be in the Garden of Eden and watch The Almighty God gather dust together, breathe life into it, and see Adam abruptly open his eyes and gasp in his first breath? Then what would it be like to watch as He put Adam into a deep sleep, removed a rib, and from it make Eve? What an astonishing sight Creation must have been: from nothing to dirt; from dirt to man; from man's rib to woman! "And God saw every thing that he had made, and, behold, it was very good." (Genesis 1:31)

Soon after that, Adam and Eve withdrew their faith in God, placing it in themselves. In doing so, the first two humans became the first two mortals! Their bodies began to die, and as God had warned, their spirits died that very day. Suddenly, Creation was not "very good" anymore.

Even in all this, something I find comforting is a proper understanding of God. The behavior of God's creation did not catch Him off guard. Nothing—not even the destruction caused by The Fall—was a surprise to Him who knows all.

Additionally, God had a purpose and a plan that transcends human reasoning. Stop and consider this: God made humans in His image and told them to have faith in Him and His words; they didn't, and as a result, they fell away from Him, and His image in them was distorted. Since that tragic rebellion, God has been calling fallen mortals to have faith in Him and His words. In those who do, He is restoring His image, "For whom he did foreknow, he also did predestinate to be conformed to the image of his Son, that he might be the firstborn among many brethren." (Romans 8:29)

In summary:
- Faith withdrawn; image distorted.

- Faith regained by grace; image restored.

What grace! What a Savior! What a God!

15

Robbery, Riches, and the Mercies of God

Psalm 62:10 "Trust not in oppression, and become not vain in robbery: if riches increase, set not your heart upon them. 11 God hath spoken once; twice have I heard this; that power belongeth unto God. 12 Also unto thee, O Lord, belongeth mercy: for thou renderest to every man according to his work."

David tells us a lot in these three verses:
- Don't depend on robbery or oppressing others to get ahead. (verse 10) To all but thieves and oppressors, it is usually unnecessary to say this; however, we always do well to examine *our* motives too. Am I seeking the best for my fellow mortal, or am I just looking out for me? Am I a servant or a selfish person? Am I a giver or a taker?
- If your wealth *does* increase through valid means, don't think of it as a replacement for the security you have in the Lord. (verse 10) Instead, use it as a good steward of God's provision. Don't be a pool to collect God's mercies; be a thoughtful, diligent channel through which He blesses others.
- Always be aware that your life—and everyone and everything in it—is a gift from the Almighty God, which He bestows upon you by His powerful hand. (verse 11)
- Finally, we must *also* be aware that power is not the Lord's only attribute; among the many greatnesses of our God is His mercy. (verse 12) He is merciful in ways we cannot imagine; (Isaiah 55:8-9) His mercies are new every morning; (Lamentations 3:22-23) and His mercies endure forever. (Psalms 106:1, 107:1, 118:1-4, 29)

16

The Lord of the Personal Pronoun

Revelation 3:15-21 " **I** know thy works, that thou art neither cold nor hot: **I** would thou wert cold or hot. So then because thou art lukewarm, and neither cold nor hot, **I** will spue thee out of my mouth. Because thou sayest, I am rich, and increased with goods, and have need of nothing; and knowest not that thou art wretched, and miserable, and poor, and blind, and naked: **I** counsel thee to buy of me gold tried in the fire, that thou mayest be rich; and white raiment, that thou mayest be clothed, and that the shame of thy nakedness do not appear; and anoint thine eyes with eyesalve, that thou mayest see. As many as **I** love, **I** rebuke and chasten: be zealous therefore, and repent. Behold, **I** stand at the door, and knock: if any man hear my voice, and open the door, **I** will come in to him, and will sup with him, and he with me. To him that overcometh will **I** grant to sit with me in my throne, even as **I** also overcame, and am set down with my Father in his throne." (emphasis mine)

In these verses from the letter to the Laodiceans, Jesus refers to Himself with the personal pronoun "I" ten times:

- I know – you are lukewarm.
- I would – you were cold or hot, not weak and indecisive.
- I will spue – because you are displeasing to me.
- I counsel – you to acquire things that are truly valuable.
- I love – and that is why I want the best for you.
- I rebuke and chasten – because that *is* what is best for you in your condition.
- I stand – because I purpose to have you.
- I will – come to be your Savior and friend.
- I grant – you to sit with Me.
- I also overcame – and am set down with my Father.

Many scholars believe the Laodicean church, though an actual church in Asia Minor, also pictures the apathetic church that exists near the close of the church age. It *seems* that we are in that time. Wouldn't it be good if we rekindle our passion for Him—that we draw close to the One who loves us enough to speak truthfully to us about our weaknesses and our need for Him?

17
God's Thoughts

Jeremiah 29:11 "For I know the thoughts that I think toward you, saith the LORD, thoughts of peace, and not of evil, to give you an expected end."

God has purposes that we don't fully understand. Generally, we are not even aware of His purposes unless He tells us what they are. We have an example here in Jeremiah 29.

Today's verse is a wonderful promise in a not-so-wonderful setting. It is like a beautiful picture mounted in an ugly frame. Here God tells some of the Jews that He has good plans for them, but what we don't see if we take this verse out of context is that those same people were at a discouraging time in their lives. They had been carried off to Babylon by Nebuchadnezzar. God even told them that He had a hand in their captivity. (verses 4, 7, 14, and 20)

Let that sink in: ***God*** had purpose in ***causing*** their captivity; however, he gave them today's verse to assure them that He had not abandoned them and that their plight was not permanent—His plans included their restoration. (verse 14)

God also told them several other things:
- Until He restored them, they should live their lives in captivity as normally as possible. They were to build homes, plant gardens, (v5) and bear children to continue their lineage. (v6)
- They were not to rebel against their captors, but rather to promote peace in their cities because the peace of the city would mean peace for them. (v7)
- Some of the "prophets" among them were false prophets and were making predictions and statements that God never authorized. (v8-9)

How does this apply to Christians today? Here are several applications:
- God has promised an expected end to us too. We don't know all the details as to how we will get home, but we ***do*** know that the end will be a good one. (John 14: 2-3)
- Until he comes to take us home, we are to "occupy till I come" as Jesus implied in His parable. (Luke 19:13) Live

your life to the glory of God, being as peaceable and helpful as possible. (Romans 12:18; Hebrews 12:14)

- Some "spiritual truths" we hear are not true at all. Stay in the Bible and check things out for yourself .(Acts 17:11)

18
An Expected End

Last time we looked at today's verse: Jeremiah 29:11 "For I know the thoughts that I think toward you, saith the LORD, thoughts of peace, and not of evil, to give you an expected end."

Today I want to look at the same verse, but just the last two words: "expected end." When I was studying this verse for yesterday's Musing, I looked at these words and was struck with the beauty of what God is saying here.

The Greek word translated "end" means exactly that. It suggests a time in the future when what is happening now will be completed; however, it also has the flavor of a reward. How encouraging!

However, the word translated "expected" is the one that caught my attention. It literally means "a cord" or an attachment, implying something that is secure and will not drift away. Elsewhere in the Old Testament, it is translated "hope" (23 times) and "expectation" (7 times).

As I looked further at this word, I found that Job used it when he was in the depths of his despair: "Oh that I might have my request; and that God would grant me the thing that I long for!" (Job 6:8) The same Hebrew word that is translated "expected" in Jeremiah 29:11 is translated in Job as "the thing that I long for." I believe the Almighty God is assuring the Jews of Jeremiah's day, and by extension, Christians today, that the end that we long for—the glory of God in the restoration of that which is just, righteous, and good—is as sure as if it was tied to our wrist by a strong cord. It will *not* drift away!

Throughout the Scriptures, God has given us His word that His promises are sure; we cannot have a stronger bond than the promise of the Almighty. We must understand that struggles, even struggles of Job's magnitude, are temporary. As a result, when we endure the trials and struggles of this life, we can be comforted in knowing that the Sovereign God is in control and He promises us a sure and "expected end."

19
Can We Put It Off until Tomorrow?

Hebrews 9:27-28 "And as it is appointed unto men once to die, but after this the judgment: So Christ was once offered to bear the sins of many; and unto them that look for him shall he appear the second time without sin unto salvation."

In one of the episodes of an Old West television series, one of the characters was talking to the town doctor about death. He said, "When it comes to dying, I reckon everybody feels about the same way." The doctor asked, "What would that be?" to which the man replied, "They'd just rather do it tomorrow."

That probably fits most of us today; a little more time is what we want. However, as the first of today's verses says, all of us have two appointments: one with that great gateway into eternity, and the second one with the Judge.

The first of today's verses seems daunting, but it is actually just part of a larger truth. The word "as" in verse 27 connects to the word "so" in verse 28, making the latter verse a continuation of the earlier one. It is as if the writer is saying, "Death and judgment are sure, but so is the fact that Christ has saved believers from our sins by His death."

In other words, death and judgment are in our future, but Christ's death and judgment in the past remove the fear of our death and future judgment.

Death can be frightening in several ways. There is serious change accompanied by the uncertainty of the unknown. However, God promises that even though this passageway into the unknown brings change and uncertainty, we can rest in the assurance that on the other side of that great door is a gracious Savior who loves us and has purchased our pardon at great cost to Himself.

Horatio Spafford said it this way:

> Though Satan should buffet, though trials should come,
> Let this blest assurance control,
> That Christ has regarded my helpless estate,
> And hath shed His own blood for my soul."

Poets Dawn Rodgers and Eric Wyse call Jesus, "Wonderful, Merciful Savior, Precious Redeemer and Friend." To that I add, "Amen."

20
I Was Almost As Bad

Psalm 73:22-24 "So foolish was I, and ignorant: I was as a beast before thee. Nevertheless I am continually with thee: thou hast holden me by my right hand. Thou shalt guide me with thy counsel, and afterward receive me to glory."

Asaph was one of the psalmists, and he wrote today's verses. What did he mean by saying that he was foolish, ignorant, and beastly? The Hebrew words are similar to the English translation, suggesting stupidity (foolish), lacking knowledge (ignorant), and animal-like, perhaps regarding wisdom (as a beast).

Ouch! He was pretty hard on himself, wasn't he? We might well wonder why he wrote these things about himself. Well, we can't take today's verses in isolation; we often do great injustice to God's Word by not understanding verses in the framework of the whole passage. I remember hearing someone say, "A text without a context is a pretext." In other words, reading isolated verses without understanding the circumstances surrounding them often leads to a false conclusion.

So then, why did the psalmist write this self-rebuke? Early in the psalm he said, "My steps had well nigh slipped." (v2) Asaph realized he had almost fallen into a trap. What was that trap? It was the psalmist's envy of evildoers. They were doing well, prospering beyond reason, and Asaph wondered whether his attempt to live a godly life was worth the effort. However, as he pondered this dilemma, the answer came: "I went into the sanctuary of God; then understood I their end." (v17) Not only were things not going to end well for them, their destruction would be sudden, "as in a moment!" (v19)

The wicked and evildoers may have a lot now, but their time will end. Additionally, those who have much, especially if it is ill gotten, are often not very happy. No, they are not to be envied; they are to be pitied. (I don't say that as a pejorative, but as a tenderhearted reality.) Moreover, we should pray for them in meekness "if God peradventure will give them repentance to the acknowledging of the truth," (2 Timothy 2:25) just as He has graciously done for us.

Their error is greed and wickedness. Let us not allow envy to become ***our*** error, and thereby we follow them into misery and ruin.

21
Immortal, Invisible, God Only Wise

1 Timothy 1:17 "Now unto the King eternal, immortal, invisible, the only wise God, be honour and glory for ever and ever. Amen."

In 1876, Walter Smith, the nineteenth-century Scottish preacher, published ***Hymns of Christ and the Christian Life***. Among the hymns was one he himself wrote, a hymn that borrows from Paul's thoughts in today's verse. The first stanza reads:

> Immortal, invisible, God only wise,
> In light inaccessible hid from our eyes,
> Most blessed, most glorious, the Ancient of Days,
> Almighty, victorious, Thy great Name we praise.

I don't know about you, but when I see the words of a hymn, my brain replays the tune, and I start to sing the song in my mind. If I am not careful, I risk losing the words in the melody.

Stop a minute and think of that first word: "Immortal." ***Pow***, what a grand and glorious thought. Merriam-Webster's online dictionary defines immortal as "not capable of dying; living forever." God is immortal; we need have no fear of Him passing from the scene, leaving us to fend for ourselves.

Now, the dictionary notwithstanding, ponder this line from a Charles Wesley hymn:

> 'Tis mystery all: the Immortal dies:

This is indeed a mystery! How can the Immortal die? Yet, God tells us it is true. (Romans 5:6-8; 1 Corinthians 15:3) Let us follow Wesley's thought:

> 'Tis mystery all: the Immortal dies:
> Who can explore His strange design?
> In vain the firstborn seraph tries
> To sound the depths of love divine.
>
> He left His Father's throne above
> So free, so infinite His grace—
> Emptied Himself of all but love,

107

And bled for Adam's helpless race:

Now that the Immortal has died for our sins, He forgives us by grace through faith. Through His work on the cross, we will never come into condemnation because we have been justified by Christ's sacrifice. Wesley concludes:

> No condemnation now I dread;
> Jesus, and all in Him, is mine;
> Alive in Him, my living Head,
> And clothed in righteousness divine,
> Bold I approach th' eternal throne,
> And claim the crown, through Christ my own.

The Immortal died. For **us**! **Wow**! Let that captivate your mind today.

22
There Is a Difference

Psalm 43:4 "Then will I go unto the altar of God, unto God my exceeding joy: yea, upon the harp will I praise thee, O God my God."

Recently this verse caught my eye. As I saw it, my mind read the first "unto" as "onto." That certainly changes the meaning of the verse, doesn't it? "Then will I go *onto* the altar of God ...."

My misreading is obviously not what that verse means, but did you know that it *is* the message God presents to us in the New Testament? "I beseech you therefore, brethren, by the mercies of God, that ye present your bodies a living sacrifice, holy, acceptable unto God, which is your reasonable service." (Romans 12:1)

God's call to us is that we give ourselves to Him sacrificially, but not as a dead animal, consumed in the flame of an ancient altar. No, God calls us to be a "living sacrifice"—someone whose life He can use and direct to glorify Himself and bless others.

The verse in Romans is rich with spiritual truth, but let me point out just two other thoughts. Paul tells us to "present your bodies." This is not something that God does for us, it is something we must deliberately do ourselves: "present your body."

The second idea I see is that presenting ourselves to God is a "reasonable service." Much of our 21st-century Western culture has become about doing for ourselves: acquiring things and experiencing pleasure. There are good experiences we can rightly enjoy, and there are things that legitimately make our time on this Earth more pleasant, more efficient, and humanly speaking, even of a longer duration. However, what God is saying through the inspired writer is that those pleasures and experiences should not be the focus of life.

John, the cousin of Jesus, pronounced that proper focus: "He must increase, but I must decrease." (John 3:30) That is the gist of going "onto" the altar of God. Not all pleasant things and experiences are wrong in and of themselves, but I must guard against anything in my life that hinders my allegiance and usefulness to God.

My dear reader, I beseech us all by the mercies of God, that we joyfully present our bodies as living sacrifices, holy, acceptable unto God, which is our reasonable service.

23

Can't Nobody Fool God

Job 7:17 "What is man, that thou shouldest magnify him? and that thou shouldest set thine heart upon him?"

Psalm 8:4 "What is man, that thou art mindful of him? and the son of man, that thou visitest him?"

Psalm 144:3 "Lord, what is man, that thou takest knowledge of him! or the son of man, that thou makest account of him!"

My wife and I sometimes watch the old television shows. We especially like to figure out "who done it" before the guilty party is actually revealed. In one episode we watched recently, a lawyer's client had not been completely forthcoming. The other day, my wife commented that she did not remember movie lines very well, but she remembered the lawyer's advice to his client on that occasion: "Two people you should never lie to are your doctor and your lawyer; both can be fatal." After recalling that advice, my wife said, "And don't lie to God either." To that, I added, "Yes, for when you lie to God, you are really only lying to yourself because God knows everything anyway." Then I deliberately slipped in a little childish grammar and said, "Can't nobody fool God."

It is staggeringly wondrous to contemplate a Being who actually knows everything there is to know. As an example, God knows how many grains of sand there are, where each one is located, and exactly how much each one weighs. As useless as that might seem to us, I am just making the point that there is nothing—no person, no object, no action, and no thought—of which God is not *fully* aware in every intimate detail.

God is truly that vast. It was probably their consideration of something that overwhelming that caused Job and David to ask the questions in today's verses: "What is man, that Thou …."

God is infinite, yet He purposes to enter into a merciful, gracious, and saving relationship with sinful mortals who turn to Him in repentance and faith. No wonder Charles Gabriel marveled with words similar to those of David and Job:

> I stand amazed in the presence
> Of Jesus the Nazarene,
> And wonder how he could love me,
> A sinner, condemned, unclean.
>
> How marvelous! How wonderful!
> And my song shall ever be:
> How marvelous! How wonderful
> Is my Savior's love for me!

24
The Old and the New

2 Corinthians 5:17-18 "Therefore if any man be in Christ, he is a new creature: old things are passed away; behold, all things are become new. And all things are of God, who hath reconciled us to himself by Jesus Christ, and hath given to us the ministry of reconciliation;"

Several years ago, I came across a bouncy jazz piece that I found to be a fun little song. It tells the story of a man who became infatuated with a women he met, and he decided he would do anything she asked of him in order to make her his wife. As time progressed however, though he admitted the changes she made in him were good changes, they became increasingly burdensome. A repeated phrase throughout the song is, "You made me a better man, but I like the old me better."

I like the rhythm of the song, and the fun the vocalist and other musicians inject into it. Additionally, I can imagine the frustration of trying to meet someone else's expectations. However, as I recently contemplated the words of that song, I started thinking about my relationship to the Lord and the changes He is making in my life.

Similar to the expressions in that jazz number, some of the changes God is making in me cause discomfort. They are different from what I am accustomed to, they are contrary to my old nature, and the "old me" does not like them. Although my old nature bristles at some changes, to rephrase the song, "I like the new me better." As uncomfortable as some of these changes are, I know they are good for me and good for those around me. Most importantly, they bring glory to God as he demonstrates His power by changing an old, selfish, stubborn sinner into someone who is beginning to resemble His Son. (Romans 8:29)

We should already be amazed at what God is doing in us; if we are not, one day we shall be. God gives us one of the reasons in Ecclesiastes 3:14: "I know that, whatsoever God doeth, it shall be for ever: nothing can be put to it, nor any thing taken from it: and God doeth it, that men should fear before him."

25

Wisdom and Sovereignty

2 Timothy 1:9 "[God] hath saved us, and called us with an holy calling, not according to our works, but according to his own purpose and grace, which was given us in Christ Jesus before the world began …."

The Greek word translated "purpose" means to "set forth." A similar word is used twice in Hebrews 12. In verse 1, the word is translated "*set before*." It reads, "Wherefore seeing we also are compassed about with so great a cloud of witnesses, let us lay aside every weight, and the sin which doth so easily beset us, and let us run with patience the race that is set before us."

We often think that our lives are a series of random, disconnected events, but that is not true. The familiar passage in Romans 8:28 tells us we are "called according to his purpose." The word translated "purpose" here is the same Greek word in today's verse. It is God's purpose to set a race before us, and He tells us to run that race. We are not to run the race God has set before our neighbor; we are to run the race He has set before us. That includes all of the struggles, delights, and tests that He has purposed for us to encounter. The psalmist said, "The steps of a good man are ordered by the LORD." (Psalm 37:23a)

Frustration comes from being unaware that the sovereign God of the universe has set a specific path before us. American poet, writer, and speaker Jackie Hill Perry said it this way: "Discontentment is what happens when you believe that where God has you right now isn't where you should be. As if He's either not as sovereign as He says He is or as wise as He's revealed Himself to be." God has an eternal purpose for bringing particular people and circumstances into our lives.

Now, how can we best run our race? By following the "Lead Runner" who set the pace by running His race, keeping His focus on the prize *set before* Him. (same Greek Word as Hebrews 12:1) "Looking unto Jesus the author and finisher of our faith; who for the joy that was set before him endured the cross, despising the shame, and is set down at the right hand of the throne of God." (Hebrews 12:2)

26
Crossing the Red Sea

Exodus 14:15-18 "And the LORD said unto Moses, Wherefore criest thou unto me? speak unto the children of Israel, that they go forward: But lift thou up thy rod`, and stretch out thine hand over the sea, and divide it: and the children of Israel shall go on dry ground through the midst of the sea. And I, behold, I will harden the hearts of the Egyptians, and they shall follow them: and I will get me honour upon Pharaoh, and upon all his host, upon his chariots, and upon his horsemen. And the Egyptians shall know that I am the LORD, when I have gotten me honour upon Pharaoh, upon his chariots, and upon his horsemen."

Several hundred years after the Israelites moved into Egypt, God brought them out. During their exodus, a huge multitude of people left Egypt forever. At some point, Pharaoh regretted letting the people go and led his army in a chase to bring them back to the slavery from which he had freed them.

As the event unfolded, the fleeing Israelites were halted by the shores of the Red Sea and feared the onslaught of Pharaoh's approaching army. God then told Moses to raise his staff over the sea, and He promised the waters would part so the people could cross over to safety on dry ground.

In Romans 15:4, we are told that the things recorded in the Old Testament "were written for our learning, that we through patience and comfort of the scriptures might have hope." This certainly is one of those passages.

I have never stood on the shore of a body of water with a large, well-trained military contingent breathing down my neck. However, I *can* tell you this: I *have* been in impossible situations and have seen God demonstrate His sovereign power over those situations. On more than a few occasions, I have been anxious about something, and the Lord has proven my anxiety to be not only useless, but unnecessary.

Here is something else that was written for our learning: "Be careful [anxious] for nothing; but in every thing by prayer and supplication with thanksgiving let your requests be made known unto God." (Philippians 4:6)

Friend, if we want to have the peace of God which passes all understanding, then being anxious for nothing is our **only** option. (Philippians 4:6-7)

27
The Three Fs of Rejecting God

Psalm 14:1 "The fool hath said in his heart, There is no God. They are corrupt, they have done abominable works, there is none that doeth good."

Many things may be said about rejecting God and rebelling against Him. Today's verse tells us one of those things is *Foolishness*. Psalm 53:1 tells us the same thing almost word for word. It is the epitome of human folly to reject the clear evidence for the existence of God, for He has strewn that evidence across the sky. "The heavens declare the glory of God; and the firmament sheweth his handywork." (Psalm 19:1)

Not only is it foolish to reject God, but it is also *Futile*. After an unsuccessful bout with arrogant pride and a season of judgments wherein he ate grass and lived like a beast of the field, Nebuchadnezzar finally realized who really is in control when God finally returned him to a sound mind. Then Nebuchadnezzar declared, "All the inhabitants of the earth are reputed as nothing: and he [God] doeth according to his will in the army of heaven, and among the inhabitants of the earth: and none can stay his hand, or say unto him, What doest thou?" (Daniel 4:35)

Finally, dismissing, rejecting, or rebelling against God is ultimately *Fatal*, "For the wages of sin is death." (Romans 6:23a) Those who reject Christ's mercy and grace until their dying breath will find that they have fallen short of the glory of God. (Romans 3:23)

Note that death is not so much something that God gives us, but rather it is a wage—something we earn! Note also that the good news is that Romans 6:23 does not end where I paused, for the whole verse reads, "For the wages of sin is death; *but* the gift of God is eternal life through Jesus Christ our Lord."

It is not too late, but one day it will be. *No* mortal knows when that time will come. The *only* safe time to repent and willingly bow before the Lord Jesus is now, for *now* is the only time you can be sure of.

Know this, however: One day *every* knee shall bow and *every* tongue shall confess that Jesus Christ is Lord, to the glory of God the Father. (Philippians 2:10-11) Better to do that willingly now, than be made to do so when there is no hope.

28

Something about the Cross

Revelation 22:2 "In the midst of the street of it, and on either side of the river, was there the tree of life, which bare twelve manner of fruits, and yielded her fruit every month: and the leaves of the tree were for the healing of the nations."

The book of Revelation is powerful, but much of it is very bleak and foreboding; however, toward the end, reading it is like exiting a long, dark tunnel and finding yourself awash in glorious sunlight.

The setting for today's verse is the throne of God. I find the description of the tree to be beautiful for it says that the "leaves of the tree were for the healing of the nations." There will be no more curse; there will be no more darkness; there will be no more sin. All the results of human disobedience—all the things that have pitted people against God and each other—will be gone.

Friends, the same "healing of the nations" is in another tree. The cross has a post, resting on Earth and pointing into the heavens. When Jesus died on the cross, He paid for our sins and brought reconciliation between God and man, a vertical, up-and-down healing if you will. However, there is also a horizontal crossbeam, depicting a healing in our relationship with other human beings and particularly with other believers.

Though the two beams of the cross create a subjective picture, that truth is clearly explained in Scripture. "For he [Jesus] is our peace, who hath made both one, and hath broken down the middle wall of partition between us; Having abolished in his flesh the enmity, even the law of commandments contained in ordinances; for to make in himself of twain one new man, so making peace; And that he might reconcile both unto God in one body by the cross, having slain the enmity thereby." (Ephesians 2:14-16)

On the cross, the Lord Jesus healed the terrible enmity between God and all the mortals who come to Him by faith. However, He also healed the conflict among humans; in context, it is between Jews and Gentiles, but figuratively, among all people. We as Christians really should practice that reality better than we do today; however, in that final time, the leaves of the tree will truly be for the healing of the nations.

Hallelujah! What a Savior!

29
What Then?

Psalm 90:10 "The days of our years are threescore years and ten; and if by reason of strength they be fourscore years, yet is their strength labour and sorrow; for it is soon cut off, and we fly away."

Since a score is twenty, "threescore years and ten" is seventy years, and "fourscore" is eighty years. Some people live more than eighty years, but many don't even make it to "threescore years and ten;" two of my sisters and a number of other relatives and friends passed from this life before they reached that age.

Psalm 90 is attributed to Moses. Something he points out in today's verse is that whether we reach seventy years or not, or even if we make it to eighty years or more, a time comes when we are "cut off, and we fly away." Moreover, Moses says it is "soon" that the end approaches. I can tell you from experience, the closer I get to my final day in this world, the faster the other days seem to go by.

One thing I want to point out that is not clear in our English translation: God uses two different words that are translated "strength." The first ("by reason of strength") is what we normally think of as strength; it means "strength or might." However, the second one ("strength labour and sorrow") means arrogance or pride. I think the second "strength" is speaking of the haughty attitude by which we assume invincibility. We actually know better, but our self-sufficient pride allows us to push that thought into the back of our mind so we can ignore its haunting call.

The fantasy of escaping the inevitable end to this life robs us of two very precious things. First, we tend not to prepare for the next life if we cling to the fanciful notion that we may never leave this one. That is an eternally disastrous mistake, for life is followed by death, and then judgment. (Hebrews 9:27)

The second thing we lose by the foolish notion of our permanence in this world is the possibility of living our entire lives without producing anything of eternal value. As Moses tells us in verse 12 of this same psalm,

"So teach us to number our days, that we may apply our hearts unto wisdom."

30
Good Fun and Bad Fun

Psalm 84:9-12 "Behold, O God our shield, and look upon the face of thine anointed. For a day in thy courts is better than a thousand. I had rather be a doorkeeper in the house of my God, than to dwell in the tents of wickedness. For the LORD God is a sun and shield: the LORD will give grace and glory: no good thing will he withhold from them that walk uprightly. O LORD of hosts, blessed is the man that trusteth in thee."

The writer of this psalm is encouraged by the Lord's goodness. Notice his exclamation: "No good thing will he withhold from them that walk uprightly." What an assurance the psalmist had in God's provision! However, we must conclude something from that statement. It is not so much in what the psalmist says as in what he does not say. What he **says** is that God will not withhold anything that is **good**; what he does **not** say is that God will not withhold anything that is **fun**.

To be clear, I am **not** saying that God disproves of **everything** that we mortals enjoy, but I **am** saying that some things that are fun are **not** good. We even see that in the life of Moses who decided to suffer affliction with the people of God, rather than to enjoy the pleasures of sin for a season. (Hebrews 11:25) We need to understand that sin can be fun; fun and pleasure, though they **can** be good, are not **always** good. The wicked one wants to trick us into thinking that if it is fun it must be good. Therein is the danger, my friend.

Everything that God **says** is good is good, even if it is "fun"; however, if it violates what God says, then even if it is fun, it is not good. Let us ask God for wisdom to know the difference between what is good and the fun that isn't good. Let's also ask Him to help us walk according to that wisdom.

MAY

1

Lessons from Our Grammar Studies

Psalm 150:1-6 "Praise ye the LORD. Praise God in his sanctuary: praise him in the firmament of his power. Praise him for his mighty acts: praise him according to his excellent greatness. Praise him with the sound of the trumpet: praise him with the psaltery and harp. Praise him with the timbrel and dance: praise him with stringed instruments and organs. Praise him upon the loud cymbals: praise him upon the high sounding cymbals. Let every thing that hath breath praise the LORD. Praise ye the LORD."

This is the last of the psalms. Like the four psalms preceding it, Psalm 150 begins and ends with the same phrase: "Praise ye the LORD."

I recently came across this psalm in one of the Bibles I haven't used in awhile. While reading, I saw the notes I had written, and they prompted me to recall one of my school lessons from many years ago. Perhaps you too might recall the five questions to be answered in an announcement: Who, What, Where, When and Why. However, in this psalm, the questions are What, Where, Why, How, and Who.

WHAT? Praise ye the Lord. (v 1)

WHERE? Praise God in his sanctuary: praise him in the firmament of his power. (v 1)

WHY? Praise him for his mighty acts: praise him according to his excellent greatness. (v 2)

HOW? Praise him with the sound of the trumpet: praise him with the psaltery and harp. Praise him with the timbrel and dance: praise him with stringed instruments and organs. Praise him upon the loud cymbals: praise him upon the high sounding cymbals. (vs 3-5)

WHO? Let every thing that hath breath praise the Lord. (v 6)

Perhaps verse 6 also answers the question "When." As long as we have breath in us, we are to praise the Lord.

Oh, and one last thing … don't forget to Praise ye the Lord!

2

The Second Birth and the Best Berth

John 3:7 "Marvel not that I said unto thee, Ye must be born again."

Here Jesus was talking to Nicodemus, a Jewish ruler. Jesus told Nicodemus that he needed to be born again, but like all of us in our natural condition, the religious leader didn't understand. It may have helped him if he had known what Paul would later tell the Ephesians (2:2): "You hath he quickened [made alive], who were **dead** in trespasses and sins." (Comment and emphasis mine.)

Regardless of our physical and mental health, we all came into this world spiritually dead. We need a second birth, one that will give life to our dead spirits in the same way that our first birth gave life to our bodies and minds.

I also mentioned berth in our title. The term "give berth" is not used very much anymore, but it means to move back, to give space, as a doctor might ask so he can examine an injured person. The same word, berth, is use for the private area a sailor has aboard a ship, a place with his bunk that he can consider his own space.

The reason I mention berth today is that Jesus promised those who have experienced the new birth will have a special place in Heaven—a place to call home. "In my Father's house are many mansions: if it were not so, I would have told you. I go to prepare a place for you." (John 14:2) Jesus is preparing a "berth"—a unique personal place—for those who have experienced the second "birth."

Christ's promise continues in the next verse: "And if I go and prepare a place for you, I will come again, and receive you unto myself; that where I am, there ye may be also." (v3) Not only is Jesus preparing a place, that place is especially wonderful for it is where He is! There isn't any place more wonderful than that! Moreover, He promises to come back to take us to that place.

That berth, our own place in Heaven, is ours by the second birth, and the second birth is ours by grace, through faith in the great atonement, which was made by "the Son of God, who loved me, and gave himself for me." (Galatians 2:20)

Hallelujah. What a Savior!

3

Healed by a Heretic

John 9:24-25 "Then again called they the man that was blind, and said unto him, Give God the praise: we know that this man is a sinner. He answered and said, Whether he be a sinner or no, I know not: one thing I know, that, whereas I was blind, now I see."

John 9 tells of a blind man's encounter with Jesus. The disciples asked an interesting question: "Master, who did sin, this man, or his parents, that he was born blind?" (verse 2) They assumed the blindness resulted from some sin by the parents or something God knew he the man would do during his life. Being judgmental like that is nothing new; it is a sad part of the fallen human heart.

Jesus put some mud on the man's eyes and told him to wash it off in the pool of Siloam. When he did that, the blind man saw for the first time in his life. What a breathtaking experience that must have been!

Unfortunately, the disciples were not the only judgmental people that day; the incident came to the attention of the Pharisees. Some of them belittled the man and told him to renounced Jesus as a sinner. This man was raised in the traditions of his parents and was facing the possibility of being cast out of his religion. Still his response was firm; he who was born blind told them he could *not* comment on what he did *not* know, but he *could* comment on the one thing of which he was *sure*. "Whether he be a sinner or no, I know not: one thing I know, that, whereas I was blind, now I see."

Interestingly, the man's statement was similar to the way the disciples would respond several years later as they stood before another self-righteous committee: "We cannot but speak the things which we have seen and heard." (Acts 4:20)

At the end of John 9, the Pharisees confronted Jesus. He told them if they had recognized their sinful condition, their sins would have been forgiven; but since they thought they were already acceptable, their sins remained.

Because of the work of Christ on the cross, God forgives those who acknowledge their sins and turn to Him in faith; however, He rejects those who think they are good enough, even if they are religious leaders.

That is sobering. And humbling. And praiseworthy.

4

Show Us the Father

John 14:8-9 "Philip saith unto him, Lord, shew us the Father, and it sufficeth us. Jesus saith unto him, Have I been so long time with you, and yet hast thou not known me, Philip? he that hath seen me hath seen the Father; and how sayest thou then, Shew us the Father?"

Just days before His crucifixion, Jesus was talking with His disciples, and they were asking Him questions. He had just spoken of the Father, prompting Philip's request for Jesus to show the Father to them. Jesus' response to Philip is profound: "He that hath seen me hath seen the Father."

Philip wanted to know what the Father was like, and Jesus told him, I'm it! As He had told them previously, "I and my Father are one." (John 10:30) Jesus and the Father are of the same essence. When you have seen Jesus—when you know what He is like, when you know how He responds to situations—then you know what the Father is like and how He responds to those same situations.

It is unfortunate that our culture has come to think of the God of the Old Testament as mean and judgmental, while the God of the New Testament is thought of as loving. Yet, Jesus said that the Father was the same as He, Jesus, was.

Now, what was Jesus like? He was both loving and compassionate, and also firm and resistant. For example, He scolded the Pharisees and Sadducees for their hypocrisy (Mark 12:38-39) and drove the moneychangers out of the temple, (Matthew 21:12-13) but He was not hostile to Nicodemus, another religious leader. (John 3:1-21) What was the difference? The former had set up their own system of religious activity and resented Jesus' teaching, whereas Nicodemus had come with a seeking heart. It is true that Nicodemus questioned Jesus, but he did so to learn, not to challenge Jesus' authority.

The difference was the attitude: Were people "superior" to Jesus and therefore authorized to "correct Him," or were they humble, willing to learn from the King of the Universe?

Question: Do we come to God, demanding of Him as if we know best and He is just our servant, or do we humbly present our requests to Someone we trust for the best answer?

5

The Leper, the Centurion, and the Will of God

Matthew 8:2-3 "And, behold, there came a leper and worshipped him, saying, Lord, if thou wilt, thou canst make me clean. And Jesus put forth his hand, and touched him, saying, I will; be thou clean. And immediately his leprosy was cleansed."

Last year, my son Mark commented on today's verses, "In Matthew 8, we see that the leper actually teaches us how to pray. He does not approach Jesus asking to be healed, but rather says 'Lord, if you will, you can make me clean.' This demonstrates complete faith in both Jesus' power as well as sovereignty. The Bible tells us to go to the Father with our needs, but we should make sure we are approaching Him the right way."

Matthew 7 ends with people being startled at the teachings of Jesus "as one having authority." (v28-29) Now in chapter 8, a leper comes, confident in the authority and ability of Jesus, acknowledging it is *only* Christ's *will* that would decide his destiny.

Next, a Roman soldier came to the Lord and spoke of his ailing servant; Jesus said, "I *will*" go to the servant and heal him. The centurion said he was not even worthy for Jesus to enter his house, but then said something profound. As a centurion, he could order his men and servants to do something, and they had to do it. He acknowledged that Jesus had that same kind of authority and said, "Speak the word only, and my servant shall be healed," (v8) even though the suffering servant was not present.

This should be a great comfort to us. We must have all confidence that He has the absolute authority and the sovereign power to do *anything* He wills to do. However, God has purposes we do not comprehend, "For my thoughts are not your thoughts, neither are your ways my ways, saith the LORD. For as the heavens are higher than the earth, so are my ways higher than your ways, and my thoughts than your thoughts." (Isaiah 55:8-9)

We must not assume that just because we want something that God wants the same thing. He *may* want the same thing, and He definitely has the authority and power to accomplish it if that is His will. However, our faith must be in *Him* and in *His* authority and will, not just in His ability to do *our* will.

6

To Save Much People Alive

Genesis 50:19-20 "And Joseph said unto them, Fear not: for am I in the place of God? But as for you, ye thought evil against me; but God meant it unto good, to bring to pass, as it is this day, to save much people alive."

The maturity and wisdom that Joseph shows here is breathtaking. Joseph's brothers sold him into slavery. He ended up in Egypt, falsely accused, in prison, and forsaken; however, later, he saved Egypt and the region from starvation. (Genesis 37-50)

After Joseph's father died, his brothers feared that Joseph had only been kind for their father's sake and would now seek revenge. They pled with him for mercy; today's verses display Joseph's understanding of God's purposes. Joseph's brothers had an evil purpose in their actions; however, God *also* had a purpose in permitting their evil plan. The difference was that God's purpose was *good*—"to save much people alive."

As Christians, we should not do evil, but there are times when evil is done to us, even by those who are close to us, and even by those who claim to be Christians. It is sad that even genuine believers do wrong; for evidence, we only need to look into our own hearts. However, what makes today's verses so startling is that Joseph doesn't see his brothers' wrong against him; instead, he sees God's gracious and merciful hand. Joseph tells them they wanted to hurt him, but God wanted to save untold multitudes from starvation and ruin.

Again, we as followers of Christ should not do wrong. Even though we do, we should be growing in our relationship with Christ so that we disobey Him less as time goes by. The lesson from Joseph's words to his brothers is this: God is behind the scenes, working all things after the counsel of his own will. (Ephesians 1:11) We may see the evils perpetrated on others—and on us—and we don't like or understand it all; however, we *know* that God is working all things together for our good. (Roman's 8:28)

God's glory does not depend on me having a wonderful life with minimal problems. Instead, we glorify God when we trust Him *regardless* of our circumstances. It is *then* that we demonstrate our confidence in His goodness, and our faith pleases Him. He even assigns righteousness on its basis. (Romans 4:3)

7

The King's Ambassadors

2 Corinthians 5:20-21 "Now then we are ambassadors for Christ, as though God did beseech you by us: we pray you in Christ's stead, be ye reconciled to God. For he hath made him to be sin for us, who knew no sin; that we might be made the righteousness of God in him."

Ambassadors were useful throughout history, and they are useful today. An ambassador or emissary is someone sent on a mission on behalf of a king or nation. In today's verses, Paul says we are ambassadors for Christ; when we trust God to save us from our sins, He commissions us to tell others about His grace and mercy. Not all will believe because we cannot force Christ on them. Still, we are to share with anyone who will listen to God's offer.

Did you notice the word "pray"? We often think that means a religious activity where a person bows their head, closes their eyes, and folds their hands; however, that does not give us a clear picture of the word's meaning here. The word translated in this verse means to beseech, plead, or make a request. We go before God to praise Him, to worship Him, and to adore Him. We use the word prayer for all those activities, but it most properly describes the act of asking or pleading for something you want.

In today's verses, Paul uses that word to describe his attempt to encourage unbelievers to reconsider. As a representative of Christ and His Kingdom, he pleads, "Be ye reconciled to God." Paul is pleading with his readers as a representative of Christ for them to trust that God is telling the truth. We, as sinners, are in grave danger of God's just and righteous wrath, but for a limited time, God offers us forgiveness for our sins—the sins Christ died to pay for.

Many of my readers trust in God already; however, to those for whom Christianity is just a religious "thing" or not really important, I say with the apostle Paul, "Now then we are ambassadors for Christ, as though God did beseech you by us: we pray you in Christ's stead, '*be ye reconciled to God*.' For he hath made him to be sin for us, who knew no sin; that we might be made the righteousness of God in him." (emphasis mine)

8

A Type and an Antitype

Hebrews 9:27 "It is appointed unto men once to die, but after this the judgment:"

If I were giving a quiz on today's verse, could you tell me what is wrong with that quote? Go ahead; look at it again.

Do you see it? I omitted the first two words. "**And as** it is appointed unto men once to die, but after this the judgment:" Also note that the verse ends with a colon. Verse 27 is not a standalone statement, as we often quote it, but a picture or foretelling, a "type" of the contrasting "antitype" in verse 28.

27 And as it is appointed unto men once to die, but after this the judgment:
28 So Christ was once offered to bear the sins of many; and unto them that look for him shall he appear the second time without sin unto salvation."

Notice also the word "so" at the beginning of verse 28; it means "in the same way," and elsewhere in Scripture, it is translated "thus," "even so," and "on this wise." Well, what then does the picture in verse 27 tell us? How does "as it is appointed" fit together with "thus" or "even so"? The answer lies in a close look at the two statements.

The picture presented by verse 27 shows that man dies one time and that death sets the stage for judgment. Elsewhere, Scripture is clear that man's death and pending judgment are the results of sin. (Romans 3:23-24; Romans 5:12-11)

The type in verse 27 is compared to the antitype in verse 28. "So," or "in the same way," Christ died too, but instead of dying because of His *own* sins, He died for the sins of others. Also unlike man's death that sets the stage for judgment, *Christ's* death sets the stage for salvation!

Those verses are both bleak and glorious. Let's read them again: "And as it is appointed unto men once to die, but after this the judgment: So Christ was once offered to bear the sins of many; and unto them that look for him shall he appear the second time without sin unto salvation."

All Praise to Him who reigns above,
In majesty supreme,

Who gave His Son for man to die,
That He might man redeem.

Blessed be the name, blessed be the name,
Blessed be the name of the Lord.
~ S. Trevor Francis

9

Truth or Consequences

John 18:36-38a "Jesus answered, My kingdom is not of this world: if my kingdom were of this world, then would my servants fight, that I should not be delivered to the Jews: but now is my kingdom not from hence. Pilate therefore said unto him, Art thou a king then? Jesus answered, Thou sayest that I am a king. To this end was I born, and for this cause came I into the world, that I should bear witness unto the truth. Every one that is of the truth heareth my voice. Pilate saith unto him, What is truth?"

In 1940, a radio game show began airing called "Truth or Consequences." Contestants were required to answer a question, usually something silly that they were not likely to know. If they failed to do so, they would have to perform some stunt, usually something as silly as the question. It was all meant in good fun.

Today's verses remind us of another "truth or consequences," one that does have a pleasant side, but it also has a very serious side.

Pilate asked Jesus, "What is truth?" He probably had no idea that less than a week before, Jesus had told Thomas, "I AM the truth." (John 14:6) Something else Pilate did not know was that a time would come when he would stand before the one who stood before him that day—that the Man upon whom he passed judgment that day would one day pass judgment on him.

Something else that is misunderstood—not just by Pilate, but by many even today—is that we don't have to do something as serious as condemning an innocent man to death in order to go to Hell; all we need to do is ignore God's declaration that we have rebelled against Him and need His forgiveness and mercy. "I am good enough" we think, and on we go, headlong into the consequences of our rebellion and arrogant pride.

The pressing truth all of us must face today is our desperate and immediate need for a Savior, "For he saith, I have heard thee in a time accepted, and in the day of salvation have I helped thee: behold, now is the accepted time; behold, now is the day of salvation." (2 Corinthians 6:2)

We should also note that the keyword is "now"!

10

Forsaken

Isaiah 54:7-10 "For a small moment have I forsaken thee; but with great mercies will I gather thee. In a little wrath I hid my face from thee for a moment; but with everlasting kindness will I have mercy on thee, saith the LORD thy Redeemer. For this is as the waters of Noah unto me: for as I have sworn that the waters of Noah should no more go over the earth; so have I sworn that I would not be wroth with thee, nor rebuke thee. For the mountains shall depart, and the hills be removed; but my kindness shall not depart from thee, neither shall the covenant of my peace be removed, saith the LORD that hath mercy on thee."

Through Isaiah, God promises that He will not abandon His people. This is a message to Israel; however, "whatsoever things were written aforetime were written for our learning, that we through patience and comfort of the scriptures might have hope." (Romans 15:4) This and other passages like Matthew 28:20 and Hebrews 13:5 teach us that God will not forsake us either.

At times, God withdraws from us to teach, to test, or to correct, but He never abandons us. Everything He does is to display His majesty and bring glory to Himself (Psalm 19:1, Psalm 97:6) and to bring good to those who love Him. (Romans 8:28)

What is startling is that the reason He will **not** abandon us is that He **did** withdraw from the Lord Jesus on the cross. From the cross, Jesus cried, "My God, my God, why hast thou forsaken me?" (Mark 15:34)

Philippians 2:9-11 tells us that one day every knee shall bow and every tongue shall honor the Lord Jesus. Believers do not have to wait for "one day." We have the delightful privilege to praise and worship Him every day, all the time.

> All creatures of our God and King
> Lift up your voice and with us sing,
> Alleluia! Alleluia!
> Thou burning sun with golden beam,
> Thou silver moon with softer gleam!

And all ye men of tender heart,
Forgiving others, take your part,
O sing ye! Alleluia!
Ye who long pain and sorrow bear,
Praise God and on Him cast your care!

O praise Him! O praise Him!
Alleluia! Alleluia! Alleluia!
~ Francis of Assisi

11

Praise the Lord for His Goodness

Psalm 107:1, 8 "O give thanks unto the LORD, for he is good: for his mercy endureth for ever. … Oh that men would praise the LORD for his goodness, and for his wonderful works to the children of men!"

I see Psalm 107 as divided into several sections:
Verse 1 declares thanksgiving as the theme of the psalm.
Verses 2-9 speak of those whom God has redeemed; they were wandering in hunger and thirst, and were near despair. "Then they cried unto the LORD in their trouble, and he delivered them." (v6)
Verses 10-16 focus on those who end up in trouble because they rebel against God and ignore his counsel. Perhaps this is a believer in God who wanders away. "Then they cried unto the LORD in their trouble, and he saved them out of their distresses." (v16)
Verses 17-22 mention fools who thought they knew best and reject God. (Also see Psalm 14:1, 53:1.) Perhaps the fool, unlike the rebel, is someone who had not yet trusted in the Lord. In any event, "then they cried unto the LORD in their trouble, and he saved them out of their distresses." (v19)
Verses 23-32 discuss those who trust God and have seen His power. However, in their everyday activities they find themselves overwhelmed, in distress, or in danger. "Then they cry unto the LORD in their trouble, and he bringeth them out of their distresses. (v28)

The psalmist makes this plea to the members of each group: "Oh that men would praise the LORD for his goodness, and for his wonderful works to the children of men!" (verses 8, 15, 21 and 31)
The psalm goes on to declare the limitless power of Almighty God who turns rivers into a dry wilderness and fruitful land into barren land.

However, it also says His power can reverse those judgments and give great blessing, in His wisdom and in His time.

The psalm closes with this: "Whoso is wise, and will observe these things, even they shall understand the lovingkindness of the LORD." (v43) The wise and attentive will understand, not just the love of God, not just the kindness of God, but both stirred together in a sweet mixture.

"Oh that men would praise the LORD for his goodness, and for his wonderful works to the children of men!"

12
They Handed Him the Scroll

Luke 4:17-21: "And there was delivered unto him [Jesus] the book of the prophet Isaiah. And when he had opened the book, he found the place where it was written, The Spirit of the Lord is upon me, because he hath anointed me to preach the gospel to the poor; he hath sent me to heal the brokenhearted, to preach deliverance to the captives, and recovering of sight to the blind, to set at liberty them that are bruised, To preach the acceptable year of the Lord. And he closed the book, and he gave it again to the minister, and sat down. And the eyes of all them that were in the synagogue were fastened on him. And he began to say unto them, This day is this Scripture fulfilled in your ears."

I noticed two points in this passage. One was that "there was delivered unto him the book of the prophet Isaiah." It does not say whether Jesus asked for that particular section of the Scriptures or if it "just happened" that they gave Him Isaiah. If He didn't ask for that particular scroll, how amazing was the leading of God that they handed Him the specific passage from which He was to read. However, the primary thing I noticed was that here He was, reading to them from His own Word, in which Isaiah spoke of Him—that He was the fulfillment of that passage.

The reality is that His Word is just as valid for us today as it was for those in that day. To be clear, not everything in the Bible is a direct promise to me. For example, I don't believe I can march around a piece of property in the Middle East and claim it, as He told the Israelites to do. Nor do I expect God to raise me from the grave four days after I die, as He did for Lazarus. But I *do* need to be confident that the Bible is God's Word and everything He says *shall* come to pass just as He said it would, even the "impossible things" that I doubt.

Oh, dear reader, we desperately need two things today: One is to rightly divide God's Word—to *know* what it says to us today—and the other is to boldly *believe* what He says.

13

Idle Idols and the Glorious God

Psalm 96:2 Sing unto the LORD, bless his name; shew forth his salvation from day to day. 3 Declare his glory among the heathen, his wonders among all people. 4 For the LORD is great, and greatly to be praised: he is to be feared above all gods. 5 For all the gods of the nations are idols: but the LORD made the heavens."

I find it interesting that the English words "idol" (meaning false god) and "idle" (meaning not active) are pronounced the same. Another interesting point is what the Scriptures say about those two ideas. Psalm 115:3-7 tells us:

3 But our God is in the heavens: he hath done whatsoever he hath pleased.

4 Their idols are silver and gold, the work of men's hands.

5 They have mouths, but they speak not: eyes have they, but they see not:

6 They have ears, but they hear not: noses have they, but they smell not:

7 They have hands, but they handle not: feet have they, but they walk not: neither speak they through their throat."

These passages and others in Psalms tell us that false gods are mere idols. (96:5) They are the works of human hands made out of inanimate material, (115:4) and even though they look like they have senses and abilities, they neither speak, see, hear, smell, handle or walk. (115:5-7) A similar passage tells us that the mouths that cannot speak cannot even breathe. (135:17) You may also recall that Dagon, the god of the Philistines, fell over twice; the second time it broke into pieces. (1 Samuel 5:3-4)

Now notice the contrast between the idle idols and the true and living God who actively works in time and space. God saves; (96:2) He is glorious and wondrous; (96:3) and He is great, praiseworthy, and fearful. (96:4) He is also the Creator (96:5) who abides in the heavens and does whatever He pleases. (115:3)

On the one hand, there are gods who not only cannot help us; they cannot even help themselves. On the other hand is a God of great power and wisdom, holiness and grace, righteousness and mercy who calls us to repent of our self-centered ways and trust in Him.

"Choose you this day whom ye will serve;" (Joshua 24:15)

14

Faith, Mocking, and a Fly on the Wall

Matthew 9:23-25 "And when Jesus came into the ruler's house, and saw the minstrels and the people making a noise, He said unto them, Give place: for the maid is not dead, but sleepeth. And they laughed him to scorn. But when the people were put forth, he went in, and took her by the hand, and the maid arose."

A ruler had come to the Lord with both great grief and great faith. His grief was that his daughter had died, but the faith came in the man's certainty that Jesus could change that. Imagine the embarrassment the ruler experienced when they entered the house and the musicians and mourners began to mock the ruler's only hope. I imagine the poor father winced at the idea of chiding his *old* friends, but he knew that without his *new* Friend, his daughter was gone forever.

"I wish I had been a fly on the wall." That is an English expression for wishing you could have secretly witnessed a private event that only a few saw. In other words, you would like to have witnessed the event without anyone noticing that you were there.

The father and perhaps a few family members and friends stayed while the mockers were put out of the house. Then the fly-on-the-wall event took place—the King of *life* touched a victim of *death*, and His condition overpowered hers. Imagine being there when a warm hand touched a cold hand. Imagine hearing a gasp of breath drawn into what had been a lifeless body. Imagine the relief of the parents that they had not let the minstrels and friends dissuade them from their faith.

God still does miracles today. I've seen some, and I've been one. I am careful not to assume that God will always work the way I want Him to; He is not a genie in a bottle whom I summon at my will. However, we can bow humbly before Him with full assurance that everything He purposes to do for His glory, He *can* do. That includes miracles, if He so wills.

The Master comes, and the foolish crowd
Never can quite understand

The worth of a soul and the change that's wrought
By the touch of the Master's hand.
~ Myra Brooks Welch

15
What is Your Name?

Genesis 32:24-30 "And Jacob was left alone; and there wrestled a man with him until the breaking of the day. And when he saw that he prevailed not against him, he touched the hollow of his thigh; and the hollow of Jacob's thigh was out of joint, as he wrestled with him. And he said, Let me go, for the day breaketh. And he said, I will not let thee go, except thou bless me. And he said unto him, What is thy name? And he said, Jacob. And he said, Thy name shall be called no more Jacob, but Israel: for as a prince hast thou power with God and with men, and hast prevailed. And Jacob asked him, and said, Tell me, I pray thee, thy name. And he said, Wherefore is it that thou dost ask after my name? And he blessed him there. And Jacob called the name of the place Peniel: for I have seen God face to face, and my life is preserved."

Why did God ask Jacob what his name was? I believe the answer is back in chapter 27. Jacob had lied to his poor-sighted father, telling him that he was Esau in order to steal the blessing and birthright that rightfully belonged to his older brother. During the years that followed, Jacob never corrected that deception as evidenced by the fact that he feared a reunion with his brother. (chapters 32-33) However, much more ominous than lying to his father or facing a confrontation with his defrauded brother, suddenly Jacob was in the presence of the all-seeing, all-knowing God; he could not get away with lies now. Instead, the patriarch admitted that his name was Jacob rather than pretending to be someone else. By doing that, he started to be honest with God, and it was then that God blessed Jacob with the power his lies had hindered.

One of our desperate needs today is transparent honesty with God, but we will never be honest with God if we are not honest with ourselves. Anyone who will lie to themselves will also lie to God.

My friend, don't try to hide **anything** from God. You won't succeed because He knows everything anyway, and it will just hinder your closeness to Him.

Now, in light of God's infinite knowledge, tell Him who you *really* are. What is *your* name?

16
Finding God in the Dark

Isaiah 50:10 "Who is among you that feareth the LORD, that obeyeth the voice of his servant, that walketh in darkness, and hath no light? let him trust in the name of the LORD, and stay upon his God."

In one of his sermons on the subject of Christian assurance, British Bible teacher Alan McNabb said that one of the most difficult tasks a councilor faces is trying to encourage a believer who is in a dark place in their life and can't find God. Their theology whispers to them that He is there, but their experience shouts that He is not. They are calling out to God, but He doesn't seem to hear them or help in their distress.

Some people think true believers who have a vital relationship with God should never be in distress and darkness; however, I point you to the Psalms. David and Asaph were men of God, and yet many of their writings drip with stress of soul. True, that was the Old Testament, but the Scriptures assure us "whatsoever things were written aforetime were written for our learning, that we through patience and comfort of the scriptures might have hope." (Romans 15:4)

For the genuine believer who is in darkness, McNabb suggested today's verse, "Who is among you that feareth the LORD, that obeyeth the voice of his servant, that walketh in darkness, and hath no light? let him trust in the name of the LORD, and stay upon his God."

It is easier to hold onto God and find our stability in Him when we are in the light. However, when we are in the dark, His charge is the same: we must hold onto God and find our stability in Him until He—in His good timing—restores the light. As Peter said, "Lord, to whom shall we go? thou hast the words of eternal life." (John 6:68)

So then, whether we are basking in the blazing light of God's majesty, glory, and goodness or are in a dark place in our lives, we will always do well to yield to His Holy Spirit as He leads us to praise God, worship Him, and trust Him in every facet of our being. We must never forget that faith in God is the very essence of the Christian life.

17
I Don't Have To

Genesis 2:15-17 "And the LORD God took the man, and put him into the Garden of Eden to dress it and to keep it. And the LORD God commanded the man, saying, Of every tree of the garden thou mayest freely eat: But of the tree of the knowledge of good and evil, thou shalt not eat of it: for in the day that thou eatest thereof thou shalt surely die."

Some years ago, our Western culture began tossing around the phrase, "You are not the boss of me." The phrase even worked its way into the lyrics of a song and the title of a book.

That phrase is sometimes said in jest, but often it is said in defiance. Defiance is the way our first parents said it. Well, they didn't actually use those words, but those words surely were consistent with their actions. God told Adam not to eat fruit from the tree of the knowledge of good and evil; by disobeying, Adam declared that God could not tell him what to do. Ever since then, mankind has been telling the Almighty Creator, "You are not the boss of me."

I heard a story of some intellectual scientists who decided mankind had all the answers and that we no longer need God. One of them went to the Creator to give Him the news, and God suggested a contest. He and the scientists would each make a man to decide who would be best at being god. During the contest, the Creator began to form the dust of the ground, as He did in Eden. When the scientists did the same, the Lord said, "No, you go make your own dirt."

How drastically broken we mortals must be to think so highly of ourselves. Without meaning to be unkind, why do we assume we can live in God's world, breathe His air, and eat the many foods He provides, and then walk away from Him to do our own will? I cannot understand why a perfect Adam in a perfect world did that, but mortals do that today because we are born encased in a coffin of sin and are in desperate need of being raised from spiritual death.

We need spiritual life; we need mercy, grace, and forgiveness; we need a Savior. Thank God for the Lord Jesus, our Almighty Savior.

18

Posted, No Trespassing

Micah 7:19 "He will turn again, he will have compassion upon us; he will subdue our iniquities; and thou wilt cast all their sins into the depths of the sea."

On my drive home the other day, I saw a sign on an old car that had several other old cars behind it. The sign read, "Posted, No

Trespassing." The owner of the cars was telling all who saw the sign that they were not allowed in that area.

That reminded me of two other "No Trespassing" messages. The first one was just after the first couple violated God's instructions not to eat the fruit of the Tree of the Knowledge of Good and Evil in the Garden of Eden. To prevent them from eating from The Tree of Life after the fall, and I say this reverently, God posted a type of a no trespassing sign: "So he drove out the man; and he placed at the east of the garden of Eden Cherubims, and a flaming sword which turned every way, to keep the way of the tree of life." (Genesis 3:24)

Thus began a terrible stage in human history that includes disobedience and evil and violence and death. Not until one of their sons murdered his brother did Adam and Eve fully grasp the horror they had unleashed that day.

Remember I mentioned two "no trespassing" signs; the second one is hinted at in today's verse where the prophet Micah says, "Thou wilt cast all their sins into the depths of the sea." Not just into the sea, but into the *depths* of the sea.

Corrie ten Boom, World War II German prison camp survivor, made a keen observation of this truth when she said, "God takes our sins— the past, present, and future—and dumps them in the sea and puts up a sign that says *No Fishing Allowed*."

The writer to the Hebrews said, "For I will be merciful to their unrighteousness, and their sins and their iniquities will I remember no more." (8:12) If God casts our sins into the depths of the sea and remembers them no more, than what right do we have to dredge them up, continuously languish over them, and act as if He has not forgiven them?

In other words: "Posted, No Trespassing." Embrace His gracious forgiveness!

19

Endued with Power from on High

Luke 24:45-49 "Then opened he their understanding, that they might understand the Scriptures, And said unto them, Thus it is written, and thus it behoved Christ to suffer, and to rise from the dead the third day: And that repentance and remission of sins should be preached in his name among all nations, beginning at Jerusalem. And ye are witnesses of these things. And, behold, I send the promise of my Father upon you: but tarry ye in the city of Jerusalem, until ye be endued with power from on high."

Early portable electrical cells, what we usually call batteries, were made out of carbon, zinc, and other materials. Later, the alkaline cell was invented using different materials, but with a similar function. Later came the nickel-cadmium cells, and more recently, lithium-ion units. You have probably heard of lithium-ion batteries; many of today's rechargeable electronic devices use them.

That is obviously not a complete history of batteries, but it is sufficient to allow me to make this observation. The first two—carbon/zinc cells and the alkaline units—actually create electricity by a chemical reaction. When the chemical process is complete, the battery is pretty much dead. There are some exceptions, but they are not very satisfactory.

The other two designs—nickel-cadmium and lithium-ion—operate differently; they are charged by an external source. Something outside of the battery charges it so the power it delivers to the phone, tablet, or other devices actually comes from a different source. The cell or battery is not the supply of the power, only the delivery system.

Similarly, the Lord Jesus told the disciples to wait in Jerusalem because when He went back to Heaven, the Holy Spirit would come and take up residence in those who trusted in Christ. Why did they have to wait? Because without the Holy Spirit, they had nothing but natural human power. That was not enough to live the life to which God called them; they needed an outside power—divine power from on high.

We no longer need to await the coming of the Holy Spirit, for He is already here, living in every believer. (Romans 8:9) However, we *do* need to wait *upon* Him for His guidance and power, else we too will operate in the natural realm. That is sure to be futile if not disastrous.

20

Now He is a Great Preacher

Psalm 51:15-17 "O Lord, open thou my lips; and my mouth shall shew forth thy praise. For thou desirest not sacrifice; else would I give it: thou delightest not in burnt offering. The sacrifices of God are a broken spirit: a broken and a contrite heart, O God, thou wilt not despise."

David wrote Psalm 51 after Nathaniel confronted him about his sins concerning Bathsheba and Uriah. The earthly consequences of those sins followed David to his grave, but God forgave his broken and contrite heart. Even elegant sacrifices and expensive burnt offerings—such as were appropriate for David's sins—were only acceptable when offered in humility.

A friend recently posted that God does not need human wisdom to use a man or woman. In my reply, I mentioned the broken and a contrite heart of verse 17. I went on to say, "I heard once of a brother (perhaps Tozer, but I am not sure) who visited a church with his wife to hear a young man preach. On the way home, his wife asked what he thought of the young speaker and he said, 'He will be a great preacher some day, after God has broken him.' Before the next time they heard him speak, the young preacher had lost his wife to illness. On the way home, Tozer's (?) wife asked the same question, and the reply was, 'Now he is a great preacher.' "

I pointed out that God does not allow struggling without purpose, and that there is nothing wrong with knowledge in and of itself. However, a contrite heart is worth a thousand theological degrees. Then I posited several possibilities:

- If we humble ourselves, (1 Peter 5:6; James 4:10) He will exalt us and use us for His glory in His time.
- If we refuse to humble ourselves, He may *do* something to humble us, and *then* use us for His glory in His time.
- However, if we refuse to humble ourselves, and He does *not* do something to humble us, there are two possible scenarios here also, and neither of them is good:
  o He may just put us on a shelf to gather dust and become useless.
  o We may just be religious, but lost.

Both of those last possibilities should cause us to reflect very carefully.

21

The Perplexing Balance between Mercy and Wrath

Lamentations 3:21-23 "This I recall to my mind, therefore have I hope. It is of the LORD's mercies that we are not consumed, because his compassions fail not. They are new every morning: great is thy faithfulness."

Insomuch as it is humanly possible to comprehend God, any attempt to do so would be horribly imbalanced if it did not include a clear understanding of His just wrath. That said, our understanding of God would be equally warped if we did not have a clear understanding of His mercy.

However, to grasp God's mercy properly, we must *first* understand His just and righteous wrath. We tend to think of wrath as an excessive tantrum by someone who is overreacting to some offense unworthy of such a response. This is not true of God. God does not overreact to anything. His actions are perfectly just and rational, and we would be compelled to agree with Him if we fully comprehended how completely holy He is and how completely we are not.

Without a clear understanding of God's wrath, we can only partially envision the staggering scope of Jeremiah's amazing proclamation: "It is of the LORD'S mercies that we are not consumed." Without that understanding of righteous wrath, our comprehension of mercy is distorted, for in some sense, we feel like we are partially worthy of it. What we do not understand is that we are not.

Someone once said that grace is God giving us what we *do not* deserve, and mercy is God *not* giving us what we *do* deserve. I have not yet studied these two thoughts in detail, but I *can* say that they ring true in *my* life. God gives me so much grace and mercy that I do *not* deserve and withholds so much wrath that I *would* deserve were it not for Christ. He has also promised me more of the same in the forever to come.

Someone else once said of this passage, "The fact that we are not consumed says infinitely more about God than it ever says about us." Truly, "it is of the LORD'S mercies that we are not consumed, because his compassions fail not. They are new every morning: great is thy faithfulness."

Glory to God. Amen!

22
He Does; You Don't

2 Peter 1:2-4 "Grace and peace be multiplied unto you through the knowledge of God, and of Jesus our Lord, According as his divine power hath given unto us all things that pertain unto life and godliness, through the knowledge of him that hath called us to glory and virtue: Whereby are given unto us exceeding great and precious promises: that by these ye might be partakers of the divine nature, having escaped the corruption that is in the world through lust."

One episode in an Old Western television series told the story of a woman with an unsavory past who moved into town. She set up an honest business and gained the confidence and friendship of the townspeople, but later, a group of her former "friends" found out where she had moved and threatened to reveal her past if she didn't let them "partner" with her and turn her new business into the same old business she had fled. The hero of the series figured out what was going on and confronted and defeated the main antagonist. As the wounded bully crept out into the night, the woman spewed angry words after him. Just then, the hero called her back saying, "He has to live with his past; you don't."

I thought that story painted a beautiful picture. The woman lived in fear of being found out, and yet the hero and the other people in town stood with her, rejecting the smear tactics of her accusers.

Revelation 12:9-10 says that Satan accuses us before God day and night, but it also says God will cast him down one day. In the meantime, however, God sides with those who trust in Him, "For God hath not given us the spirit of fear; but of power, and of love, and of a sound mind." (2 Timothy 1:7) That power, love, and sound mind come to us because God saved us from our past and called us to "glory and virtue" in Christ.

Let us live carefully before the Lord. Our walk as believers should be one of gratitude and obedience; however, let's not shrink in fear of the shame and guilt of our past.

Peter says, "Grace and peace be multiplied unto you." How? "Through the knowledge of God, and of Jesus our Lord." Let us study to know God, and His grace and peace will surely be ours.

23
I Can Do Whatever I Want or A Breakdown in Society

Judges 21:25 "In those days there was no king in Israel: every man did that which was right in his own eyes."

This verse speaks of a time about fourteen hundred years before Christ, but the same is true even today. Just like the first couple in the Garden of Eden, many mortals refuse God's wisdom and leadership, and by doing so, bring about great tragedy.

One thing that people corrupt today is the gospel of Christ.

1 Corinthians 15:1-8 clearly defines the gospel:
- "Christ died for our sins according to the scriptures," thus solving our sin problem.
- "He was buried," proving His death actually happened.
- "He rose again the third day according to the scriptures," proving God's acceptance of His sacrificial work on Calvary. (Romans 4:25)

- He was seen by a multitude of eyewitnesses, proving His literal, bodily resurrection.

Sadly, we have lost something in our society. Many people think that whatever we speak or believe magically turns into truth. A part of that mindset is that many today change the gospel itself into something soft, warm, and fuzzy: "You're OK. God loves everybody and won't actually send anyone to Hell."

If I *earn* something by honest labor, it belongs to me. I can use it, loan it, or give it away. It is my possession to use to the glory of God, and that is *good*. However, if I *take* what someone else has earned with their labor, I have stolen it; that is *not* good no matter what I do with it.

I say all that to set up this thought: The gospel is *not* ours to do with as we please; the gospel is God's property, purchased by Him at His own expense. Therefore, we have absolutely no authority to change it in any way. In fact, the only two things we can rightly do with the gospel are believe and obey it ourselves, and preach it to others.

We *do* have the authority to *believe* and *spread* the gospel message because the One who rightly owns the gospel has commanded us to do so; however, we do not have *any* authority to *change* that message. God takes a very dim view of tampering with His words; He even pronounces grave judgments for doing that. (Revelation 22:18-19)

Let's respect what isn't ours, especially God's Word.

24
It Depends on How You Look at It

James 4:7-8 "Submit yourselves therefore to God. Resist the devil, and he will flee from you. Draw nigh to God, and he will draw nigh to you. Cleanse your hands, ye sinners; and purify your hearts, ye double minded."

Before there were motors, ships were wind-driven. To catch as much wind as possible, they raised canvas sails on tall poles or masts. Over time, they discovered another use for the mast. They put a small enclosure called a "crow's nest" near the top; an observer could stand up high and see land or other ships from farther away than if he was down on the deck.

Changing where you are standing changes what you can see. That is true on a ship, but it is also true in life. Approaching circumstances differently gives you a fresh outlook you may not have considered. My missionary friend Rick Bell recently said it this way. "Your trials can be

distractions causing you to stumble, or they can be **goads** prodding you on to greater faith, looking to God."

God does not purpose the trials of His people to defeat us. He gives trials to teach us truth, but in order to learn those truths we must change our viewpoint. By standing in the "crow's nest" of God's Word—a higher place—we can stop being distracted by the trial itself and focus on God's **purpose** in the trial.

What does God teach us in these trials? He may be teaching us to be more patient. (James 1:3) He may be challenging us to be more loving. (John 15:12; Romans 12:10) He may be urging us to greater confidence in Him. (Proverbs 3:5-6) Whatever the purpose of each individual trial, there are two ultimate goals for all of them.

One ultimate goal is to make us more like the Lord Jesus. "For whom he did foreknow, he also did predestinate to be conformed to the image of his Son, that he might be the firstborn among many brethren." (Romans 8:29)

Today's verses remind us of the other ultimate goal—to draw us closer to God. Hebrews 10:22 tells us the same thing: "Let us draw near with a true heart in full assurance of faith, having our hearts sprinkled from an evil conscience, and our bodies washed with pure water."

25

Grafted In

Romans 11:16-18 "For if the firstfruit be holy, the lump is also holy: and if the root be holy, so are the branches. And if some of the branches be broken off, and thou, being a wild olive tree, wert graffed in among them, and with them partakest of the root and fatness of the olive tree; Boast not against the branches. But if thou boast, thou bearest not the root, but the root thee."

I was raised in the big city, so it was not until science classes in school that I learned about grafting. For those who have forgotten or not learned yet, grafting is connecting the branch from one tree (or plant) into the trunk (stem) of another. Slits are cut in the host trunk, and the flared end of the new branch is slid into place. The joint is then bound up for support and cleanliness. In doing this, a new type of fruit can be grown from the host plant. The new branch is foreign—it doesn't naturally belong there—but by grafting, the new branch is able to survive, to thrive, and to bear fruit to its new host plant.

Paul uses grafting as a picture of people who are not Jewish but who come to trust in the God of Abraham. He says we are "graffed in." As a result, we have fellowship with Abraham's God and enjoy the same mercies and grace that Abraham enjoyed.

There are some differences, of course. Some examples: God didn't give Christians a piece of land in the Middle East, but instead a home in Heaven. We don't have a Levitical priesthood, but rather a Messianic priesthood. The Law is not our hope; instead, we trust in the work of Christ on the cross.

The Almighty God has purposed to save the Jews who believe, even though currently, many Jews do not trust in Him; however, God's purposes include saving many non-Jews, making us heirs of many of the same eternal blessings.

The keyword for both Jew and Gentile (non-Jew) is "believe," for Jews who do not believe and Gentiles who do not believe are equally lost and separated from God. Jews who *do* believe, rest in the God of Abraham by faith, and Gentiles who *do* believe, also rest in Abraham's God by faith and are part of God's family. We are grafted in!

26
What Faith Cannot Do

Habakkuk 2:4b "The just shall live by his faith."

I heard the story of a little girl who was sitting in her Sunday School class when the teacher asked, "What is faith?" The little girl stood up and boldly announced, "Faith is believing what you know ain't so."

That is cute and is the kind of comment we might expect out of a little child. However, that little girl's definition is partially correct—it is possible to believe "what ain't so."

For example, when I was in school I was taught, or at least I got the impression, that in the days of Christopher Columbus, the majority view was that the Earth was flat. I have since learned that by the time of Columbus, the flat-earth idea was starting to fade out, even though there were some who still held that belief. Let me use that flawed, "flat-earth" belief to give you one of my favorite illustrations about faith.

First, two questions. Did the "flat people," thinking the Earth was flat, make the Earth flat? The obvious answer is an obvious no. Now the second question: Did the "round people" thinking the Earth was round (actually spherical), make the Earth round? The answer here is *also* no. You might say, "But Bill, the Earth *is* round," to which I would reply, "Yes it is, but it is not round as a *result* of the "round people" *believing* it was round. In other words, the belief or faith of the "flats" did not make the Earth flat, and the belief or faith of the "rounds" did not make the Earth round. The Earth was round because that is the way it was made, and belief did not change that in any way.

Now, if faith is not about our belief making something true, then what *is* faith all about? Faith is about discovering and embracing the truth regardless of our preconceived notions. The "rounds" were right because they believed reality; the "flats" trusted their own flawed perception of reality and were wrong.

Read God's Word, dear friend. You can safely trust Him and what He says—for your life and for your forever.

27

Another Thought about Faith

Isaiah 55:8-9 "My thoughts are not your thoughts, neither are your ways my ways, saith the LORD. For as the heavens are higher than the earth, so are my ways higher than your ways, and my thoughts than your thoughts."

Last time, we considered that faith cannot change reality; instead, faith should align itself *with* reality. We may want our desires to come true, and we may set our "faith" upon them, only to be crushed when they are not realized. Whether we desire health for an ailing friend, attaining our dream job, or being able to afford some longed-for purchase, sometimes our faith presses up against a door that will not open, and the things we wish for may even dissolve before our very eyes.

Those events try us, and sometimes they try us to our very core. However, some questions may help us step back a little and examine where we have placed our faith. Have we placed our hopes in the things we want and in our assumption that God will automatically do whatever we ask Him to do? Or have we placed our faith in God Himself and what *His* purposes are? This is the level at which we really must grapple with today's verses, for God's thoughts and ways are far above (superior) to ours. Does God have a better purpose for my life that can only be fulfilled by making me walk down a path that is different from the one I plan?

Consider Abraham's long wait for the son of promise, Daniel's briefer but more terrifying wait in a den full of lions, or Hosea's heartache with an unfaithful wife. None of these saints could find comfort in their circumstances. Their *only* hope for a sense of well-being was to abandon their faith in their situation and place it fully on the One whose thoughts and ways were always higher and better than theirs.

Someone once said, "Faith is not about everything turning out okay. Faith is about being okay no matter how things turn out." That can only happen when our focus is on the Lord and we understand that His plans will always work out better than ours will anyway. (Romans 8:28-29)

28

Picking Our Battles Boldly

2 Corinthians 4:5-7 "For we preach not ourselves, but Christ Jesus the Lord; and ourselves your servants for Jesus' sake. For God, who commanded the light to shine out of darkness, hath shined in our hearts, to give the light of the knowledge of the glory of God in the face of Jesus Christ. But we have this treasure in earthen vessels, that the excellency of the power may be of God, and not of us."

A little while ago, a friend of mine posted 1 Peter 3:15: "But sanctify the Lord God in your hearts: and be ready always to give an answer to every man that asketh you a reason of the hope that is in you with meekness and fear." The context is that of suffering for our faith, and Peter says that even when we are persecuted, we should be open to giving a reason for our hope to those who are interested.

The very next post I saw that day was from another friend who posted a verse they seem to interpret as limiting believers' interaction with unbelievers. My friend then said, "There are some questions I do not get to ask. There are some conversations I do not get to join." My friend may be trying to avoid fruitless friction, even as Paul warned Timothy, (2 Timothy 2:23) and that is commendable.

However, Peter suggests, we are in the marketplace of ideas. The Old Testament image is that of sitting at the gate and "making one's case." Paul also seems to like that notion and regularly engages anyone who will listen, even if they eventually reject his teaching.

These two positions—one of openness and the other more isolated—form an interesting juxtaposition. Picking our opportunities may save us some friction, but it may also cause us to lose opportunities. J. Gresham Machen said, "A Christianity that avoids argument is not the Christianity of the New Testament."

Let's not debate merely for the sake of debating. We don't want to win the argument but lose the heart; however, let's not be timid either. We can be bold in our faith and in our witness, knowing that we serve the Lord

Christ, the King of Glory. Having *that* knowledge should encourage us with great boldness.

29

Remembering and Forgetting

Psalm 25:6-7 "Remember, O LORD, thy tender mercies and thy lovingkindnesses; for they have been ever of old. Remember not the sins of my youth, nor my transgressions: according to thy mercy remember thou me for thy goodness' sake, O LORD."

In these two verses, David makes three requests of God. First, he asks the Lord to remember His tender mercies and loving kindnesses. The king even reminds God (as if God needs reminding) that God's tender mercy and loving kindness are the ways He has *always* been: "for they have been ever of old."

The last request is also a plea for God to remember. This time it is not His tender mercies and loving kindnesses, but David himself: "according to thy mercy remember thou *me* for thy goodness' sake, O LORD." (emphasis mine.)

In between these two requests to remember, David makes a request that the Lord forget something: "Remember not the sins of my youth, nor my transgressions."

Aren't those the same requests we would make today? Lord, remember your mercy and loving kindness, remember me, and forget the things I have done against you. This combination of the Lord's remembering and forgetting can be done only because by His mercy, grace, and loving kindness, the Lord Jesus paid the penalty for our sins. Christ laid down His life to pay for the sins of our youth and our transgressions. In so doing, He has redeemed us to God and made us able to stand justified before Him.

The last Monday in May is the day we in the United States of America set aside to remember the brave and selfless women and men who have lost their lives in the defense of our land and other countries. I would not do anything to diminish that, for the Lord Jesus Himself told us, "Greater love hath no man than this, that a man lay down his life for his friends." (John 15:13) However, for Christians, let us *also* be mindful of the one who died to buy for us, not just freedom or safety, but freedom, safety, *and* eternal life.

30
Remembering

1 John 3:16 "Hereby perceive we the love of God, because he laid down his life for us: and we ought to lay down our lives for the brethren."

During Memorial Day weekend here in the United States, Americans remember and honor the men and women who died in active military service to our country. The various branches of the media cover this remembrance in one form or another, reminding us of the men and women who laid down their lives for their families, friends, and fellow citizens.

Winston Churchill gave a speech during the Second World War as the Royal Air Force was engaged in what we now call the Battle of Britain. He said, "Never in the field of human conflict was so much owed by so many to so few." However, in light of all the Memorial weekend coverage, a sad but realistic truth remains. We *won't* hear much publicly this weekend about the One who laid down His life for His enemies.

I am truly grateful for those who have paid so high a price to gain and preserve our national freedoms, but above all, I am eternally grateful to the King of Glory, who laid down His own divine life so that I might have His forgiveness for my rebellious sins against Him.

Thank you, my fellow Americans.

Thank you, my dear, dear Savior.

31
Sold for a Farthing

Matthew 10:29 "Are not two sparrows sold for a farthing? and one of them shall not fall on the ground without your Father."

Luke 12:6 "Are not five sparrows sold for two farthings, and not one of them is forgotten before God?"

Little birds were cheap during the time the Lord Jesus walked on this Earth. People used sparrows for their sacrifices if they were so poor they could not afford anything else. You could buy two of them for a farthing, the equivalent of about one half cent in today's money; however, if you had a whole penny, they gave you an extra one free. No wonder people gave them so little thought; they were almost worthless.

The other day, a friend posted the story of a preacher who moved several states away to take a job as pastor of a small church. One day his car was in the shop so he took a bus to church to do some studying. When he sat down, he noticed that the bus driver had given him a quarter too much in his change. It was just a small amount so he debated with himself whether to give it back or just keep it as a "gift from God." As he got off the bus, he told the driver about the mistake and returned the quarter. It turned out the driver had recognized the man as the new preacher in town. He was looking for a church to go to and gave the preacher the extra money to test his integrity. When the preacher gave the money back, the driver told him his motive and then said, "I'll see you Sunday." After the bus pulled away, the preacher steadied his shaking body against a telephone pole and prayed, "God, forgive me; I almost sold Your Son for a quarter."

How easy it is to become so preoccupied with our lives that our thoughts of God fade into the background. We sometimes devalue or discount things that are truly valuable; how tragic that we might allow our busy minds to discount the Lord of glory who is of infinite worth. Let us be careful not to "sell Jesus for a quarter" or for a billion quarters. He is of more worth than even our very lives.

JUNE

1
The Clash of the Titans

Romans 3:21-26 "But now the righteousness of God without the law is manifested, being witnessed by the law and the prophets; Even the righteousness of God which is by faith of Jesus Christ unto all and upon all them that believe: for there is no difference: For all have sinned, and come short of the glory of God; Being justified freely by his grace through the redemption that is in Christ Jesus: Whom God hath set forth to be a propitiation through faith in his blood, to declare his righteousness for the remission of sins that are past, through the forbearance of God; To declare, I say, at this time his righteousness: that he might be just, and the justifier of him which believeth in Jesus."

According to Greek mythology, the Titans were demigods (the children of gods). In the movie *Clash of the Titans*, one of these offspring, Perseus, had to fight underworld characters who were determined to rule both Heaven and Earth.

I was reminded of that epic story today as I was reading the words of the hymn, "Beneath the Cross of Jesus." In the five stanzas, Elizabeth Clephane gives a vivid description of the shadow of that cross that she has taken as a refuge for her weary soul. She wrote:

> Oh, safe and happy shelter!
> Oh, refuge tried and sweet!
> Oh, trysting place where Heaven's love
> And Heaven's justice meet.

The 21st century Western mind often thinks of God primarily in terms of His love and kindness. "Of course, He will be judgmental to really bad people," we imagine, "but not to people like me." However, Miss Clephane struck a profound and biblical chord when she evoked the image of a violent collision between God's love and His justice. God's immeasurable love beams bright with His kindness, but His incomprehensible passion for justice demands righteous vengeance. Those

147

two giants of divine reality met at the cross in the most spectacular clash to ever occur. That eternal event made the Greek myth seem like a fairytale.

To those who trust Him, God can be both "just AND the justifier" because of the cross.

Ellis Crum wrote, "He paid a debt He did not owe, for I owed a debt I could not pay."

Well said, Mr. Crum. Well said, Miss Clephane. And if I may say it reverently, well done, dear Lord Jesus!

2

Solely and Wholly

Ephesians 2: 8-10 "For by grace are ye saved through faith; and that not of yourselves: it is the gift of God: Not of works, lest any man should boast. For we are his workmanship, created in Christ Jesus unto good works, which God hath before ordained that we should walk in them."

One of the saddest misunderstandings I have ever encountered in my Christian life is the confusion between grace and works. I suppose it stems from the fact that both are legitimate biblical words and both are important within their own context. The problem occurs when one is confused for the other, and that problem can go either way.

On the one hand, someone might believe that once they utter a certain prayer, those "magic words" invoke some sort of get-out-of-hell insurance. They assume they have no responsibility to learn of God and begin to follow the guidance of the Holy Spirit who lives within true believers. They might think that all is well and they can live any way they please, but Paul rejects that assumption in verse 10, telling us that God saves us with the predetermined intent that our lives would change for the good.

On the other hand, someone might think they need God's grace to **help** them, but that grace is not enough by itself. They might assume that they must **add** the Mosaic Law or some other traditions or actions to **assist** God in saving or keeping them. Paul rejects that assumption too. (See verses 8-9.) We are saved entirely by grace, and we are saved by grace entirely.

Let us not to be unkind to those who don't understand this clearly. Each of us is at a different stage in our walk with God, and we each grow and mature at different rates on different subjects. I have been a Christian for almost 50 years and have learned many things about the Lord; however,

I know some people much younger than I am who are advanced beyond me in understanding some things about God, His Word, and walking in His ways.

Let us pray for one another that we would trust in God's mercy and saving grace. Additionally, let us be resolved *not* to trust our own feeble efforts to do what *only* the Almighty God can do, for by grace are we saved through faith, and that not of ourselves.

3

Volcanoes and Anxiety

1 Peter 5:7 "Casting all your care upon him; for he careth for you."

On June 3, 2018, there was a significant volcanic eruption in Guatemala that left more than 100 people dead. I read a post about that story with sorrow at the grief and pain there is in this broken world today. The next post I saw featured today's verse: "Casting all your care upon him; for he careth for you."

That verse was just a general post; the timing had nothing to do with the Guatemalan tragedy. Some would say it is insensitive to place the two in the same context; however, let me ask you this question: when is there ever a better time to contemplate the tenderness with which God cares for His people than when we are going through inconceivable heartbreak? I need God *always*; I need His mercy *always*; I need His tender care *always*. But when could I possibly sense that need more than when my world has been shaken to its core and a loved one has slipped out of my life?

To be sure, it probably isn't the best thing to go up to a grief-stricken person and just blurt out that verse; we need to be sensitive to the leading of the Holy Spirit in every situation. Nevertheless, we live in a fallen, broken world, and having that nugget of truth hidden in our hearts will go a long way toward comforting our own selves when we face our own volcanoes. Moreover, if we listen carefully to the Holy Spirit, that verse may also give us the gentle and soothing word someone else needs at the appropriate time.

Know Him. Trust Him. Be sensitive to Him. Share Him.

4

The Bounty of God

Psalm 13:5-6 "But I have trusted in thy mercy; my heart shall rejoice in thy salvation. I will sing unto the LORD, because he hath dealt bountifully with me."

Have you ever spent time thinking about the goodness of God? I suppose we all have done that in moments of gratitude, but I am asking if you have ever sat quietly—for ten or fifteen minutes or perhaps a half hour or more—reflecting on and marveling at the goodness of God by which He treats you kindly.

One of my joys is to wake up in the morning, turn my heart to God, and thank Him for giving me another day. I don't just do that as a habit; rather it is a genuine delight to marvel at His kindness to me.

This morning, as I sat basking in the remembrance of His tender mercies, He gave me this thought: "God woke me up this morning and gave me another day. When He is finished giving me new days, He will wake me up in Heaven."

It is no wonder that David said that the Lord had dealt bountifully with him. How marvelously gracious God is to those who love Him! Surely, "I have trusted in thy mercy; my heart shall rejoice in thy salvation. I will sing unto the LORD, because he hath dealt bountifully with me."

5

The Hidden Things

Philippians 4:6-7 "Be careful [full of care, anxious] for nothing; but in every thing by prayer and supplication with thanksgiving let your requests be made known unto God. And the peace of God, which passeth all understanding, shall keep your hearts and minds through Christ Jesus."

The gospel song "Just As I Am" has been an encouragement to many since its writing. The words were penned by Charlotte Elliott who lived to age 82, and the music was composed by William B. Bradbury who lived to 51.

Charlotte Elliott lived about 30 years longer than Mr. Bradbury did. I know of people younger than me who have passed from this life; you probably know of similar disparities in your experience. Why does God allow things like that?

Our reflections on such seeming inequalities plead for answers. I never have found an answer that satisfies my mind, but I have found one that satisfies my spirit. That answer is what God calls the "hidden things;" (Isaiah 48:6) they are the things that pose the question Nebuchadnezzar said we are not qualified to ask, namely, "What doest thou?" (Daniel 4:34-35)

Pastor and author Tim Keller said, "God will either give us what we ask for in prayer or give us what we would have asked for if we knew everything He knows." We must understand that God is good; only then can we rest in the comfort that if we knew what God knows, then what He does would make perfect sense.

Anxious days and sleepless nights will be our constant companions until we realize that we are not qualified to pass judgment on God. However, when we trust in Him and His sovereign wisdom, we are comforted with the peace He promises in today's verses, as well as in Proverbs 3:5-6, "Trust in the LORD with all thine heart; and lean not unto thine own understanding. In all thy ways acknowledge him, and he shall direct thy paths."

6

The Ugliness and the Beauty of the Cross

Psalm 85:10 "Mercy and truth are met together; righteousness and peace have kissed each other."

Sadly, much of current teaching implies that God is only loving and kind; however, the truth is that God is also holy and rightfully angry at sin. Our disobedience to His just standards is a rebellion against His righteous governance. The main reason we do not understand the rightness of God's anger is that we do not clearly understand the sinfulness of our sin. If we could grasp the vile, ugly, wickedness of our insurrection against our Creator, then we might understand His revulsion to it.

If we are brave enough to look honestly, the cross of Christ gives us a dreadful view of that anger, for it was on the cross that God poured out His wrath—that was rightfully due to us—upon His holy Son. The violence with which the Father came against Christ says volumes about the wrath that WE rightly deserved.

However, there is more to what we see on the cross, for it is the setting in which the Almighty God showed the truth of His holiness *and* the tenderness of His mercy—the righteousness of His anger and wrath *and* the beauty of His grace and peace.

151

Musings

The cross of Christ is the focal point of the history of the universe. At that precise place and time, God mingled the truth about the ravages of sin with the mercy by which He forgives repentant sinners. On the cross of Christ, God's righteousness and His peace kissed each other.

> When I survey the wondrous cross
> On which the Prince of glory died,
> My richest gain I count but loss,
> And pour contempt on all my pride.
>
> Forbid it, Lord, that I should boast,
> Save in the death of Christ my God!
> All the vain things that charm me most,
> I sacrifice them to His blood.
>
> See from His head, His hands, His feet,
> Sorrow and love flow mingled down!
> Did e'er such love and sorrow meet,
> Or thorns compose so rich a crown?
>
> Were the whole realm of nature mine,
> That were a present far too small;
> Love so amazing, so divine,
> Demands my soul, my life, my all.
> ~ Isaac Watts

7

How Shall We Answer?

Exodus 14:12 "Is not this the word that we did tell thee in Egypt, saying, Let us alone, that we may serve the Egyptians? For it had been better for us to serve the Egyptians, than that we should die in the wilderness."

Moses led the children of Israel out of slavery in Egypt, but you might recall that they stalled at the shores of the Red Sea. God moved in to resolve that crisis, but just before He did, the people threw verse 12 into Moses' face. In essence, they told him, "Didn't we tell you to leave us alone? Everything was fine in Egypt."

But was it? The Pharaoh decided the Israelites were a danger to his people and made things hard for them. Exodus 2:23 says, "The children of

Israel sighed by reason of the bondage, and they cried, and their cry came up unto God by reason of the bondage." And yet, here they are telling Moses that they would rather be back in Egyptian bondage. ***Really?***

Now, in all fairness, their plight did look dire, even life threatening. It is easy to criticize them from the comfort of our easy chairs; however, as difficult as it is, we must look closely at the challenge this presents to us today.

There are times when we as Christians in America are called upon to face uncomfortable situations, even hardships and loss of businesses and property. In some parts of the world, our fellow believers face worse, even death. As time goes on, the struggles each of us face could be increasingly difficult.

Even thinking about this is uncomfortable, and I don't bring this up to frighten us, but rather to focus us. Whether things become more difficult or not, we are—and will be—faced with choices, sometimes with serious consequences.

I have never been called on to face a life-and-death situation because of my faith, but it is a very real possibility, even here in the United States. We know of people who, during school shootings and other attacks, were slaughtered simply for their Christian faith.

My point is that it would be wise to make our decision now, before the trial comes. Will I trust God and stand in His strength for the truth, or will I deny Him and slouch back toward Egypt? We must each answer that question carefully and honestly.

8

When We Finally Make It Home, Part 1

Revelation 21:3-5a "And I heard a great voice out of heaven saying, Behold, the tabernacle of God is with men, and he will dwell with them, and they shall be his people, and God himself shall be with them, and be their God. And God shall wipe away all tears from their eyes; and there shall be no more death, neither sorrow, nor crying, neither shall there be any more pain: for the former things are passed away. And he that sat upon the throne said, Behold, I make all things new."

This life is a mixture of pleasure and pain, of strength and struggle, of vitality and vulnerability. What will it be like to move from this existence into one with no death, no tears, and no sorrow, where all things are made new?

My health is not what it was when I was younger: back pain, cataracts, not to mention my knees. I laughed the other day at the realization that my knees are as old as the rest of me! God promises believers that one day all that shall be gone.

Disappointments and sorrows are with us more often than we wish. God promises believers that one day all that shall be gone.

My mom and dad are home already. So are two sisters and other relatives and friends. In similar passages, God promises believers that one day we shall be reunited with them.

And sin—the cause of *all* of this heartache—has already been dealt with and shall one day be removed from our presence forever.

Some things about this life are hard, and some things about this life are wonderful; however, *nothing* in this life can be compared to what it will be like when we finally make it Home. By death or rapture, one day the joys and delights of Heaven will be a reality for believers.

Please note that these are promises for believers who trust in Jesus Christ and His completed work on the cross. That is not necessarily bad news for unbelievers, but it is devastating news for unbelievers who are still unbelievers when they die. The trouble is…we never know when that time will be.

Everyone will believe on the other side of the grave; there is no way around that. However, for those who wait until then, it will be too late. Trust Him today, my friend, while you still have time.

9

When We Finally Make It Home, Part 2

Revelation 21:3-5a "And I heard a great voice out of heaven saying, Behold, the tabernacle of God is with men, and he will dwell with them, and they shall be his people, and God himself shall be with them, and be their God. And God shall wipe away all tears from their eyes; and there shall be no more death, neither sorrow, nor crying, neither shall there be any more pain: for the former things are passed away. And he that sat upon the throne said, Behold, I make all things new."

Last time in verses 4 and 5a, we saw some of what awaits us when we finally make it home, things that will be missing but which we will not miss: tears, death, sorrow, crying, pain and everything old. However, everything in verses 4 and 5a depend on verse 3, which says, "Behold, the tabernacle of God is with men."

The word translated "tabernacle" is also translated "habitation" and "dwelling place." In other words, Moses' edifice of gold, silver, fine linen, and animal skins was the Old Testament symbol of the presence of God. John is announcing God's plan to dwell **with** us. We shall be His people—in His presence—and He shall be our God!

The Lord Jesus Christ purchased our redemption on the cross. As a result, God has forgiven our sins and made us "heirs of the righteousness which is by faith." (Hebrews 11:7) Now, because Christ's breathtaking sacrifice makes us right with God, He has purposed to dwell with us as His people and He as our God. Not only **that**, but He is going to dwell with us in a land where there is neither crying nor tears, neither death nor sorrow, neither pain nor damage, for everything is going to be new.

To comprehend this fully while we remain here in mortal flesh is beyond us. If the word "inconceivable" has any meaning, surely it applies here; however, by faith we can bask in the glory of what God says. As the songwriter penned,

> What a day that will be,
> When my Jesus I shall see,
> And I look upon His face,
> The One who saved me by His grace;
>
> When He takes me by the hand,
> And leads me through the Promised Land,
> What a day, glorious day that will be.
> ~ Jim Hill

10
The Friend at the Grave Site

John 11:39-44 "Jesus said, Take ye away the stone. Martha, the sister of him that was dead, saith unto him, Lord, by this time he stinketh: for he hath been dead four days. Jesus saith unto her, Said I not unto thee, that, if thou wouldest believe, thou shouldest see the glory of God? Then they took away the stone from the place where the dead was laid. And Jesus lifted up his eyes, and said, Father, I thank thee that thou hast heard me. And I knew that thou hearest me always: but because of the people which stand by I said it, that they may believe that thou hast sent me. And when he thus had spoken, he cried with a loud voice, Lazarus, come forth. And he that was dead came forth, bound hand and foot with graveclothes: and his face was bound about with a napkin. Jesus saith unto them, Loose him, and let him go."

Several weeks ago, my wife and I had the sad and precious privilege of visiting with some friends. They are a dear couple, and the wife had just lost her father, Bert. We saw them at the funeral home; they were strong, confident that they will see him again in Heaven. We continue to pray for them and their family.

As I was writing this, I got an email informing me that Pat, a friend I knew while I lived in South Carolina, went to be with the Lord. I am praying for them also.

I find comfort in today's verses in the light of these two events. Not that I expected Jesus to raise Bert from the dead at his viewing, nor to resurrect Pat now, even though He could. What is comforting in these verses is that Jesus demonstrated His *power* to override death and the grave, removing both their victory and their sting. (1 Corinthians 15:55) Additionally, He has not only proven He *can* raise the dead, He has promised that one day, He *shall* raise all who trust in Him.

We were born rebels, with hearts opposed to The Almighty and His ways. However, God not only redeemed us and forgave our sins, but he also made us his children. Let me repeat that. We were *rebels*, who—by grace through faith—God made into His *children*!

Amazing grace, indeed.

11

A While in a Whale or
The Plaintive Plea of the Moody Messenger

Jonah 2:7-9 "When my soul fainted within me I remembered the LORD: and my prayer came in unto thee, into thine holy temple. They that observe lying vanities forsake their own mercy. But I will sacrifice unto thee with the voice of thanksgiving; I will pay that that I have vowed. Salvation is of the LORD."

God gave Jonah a mission, and the prophet tried to run away from the One who is everywhere. How silly.

Why did Jonah run away? Because he hated the Ninevites and knew if they repented of their wickedness, God would forgive them. Jonah didn't want that. (Jonah 4)

The moody prophet ended up in a large sea creature that God had prepared for the occasion: a "great fish" in Jonah 1:17 and a "whale" in Matthew 12:40. Today's verses tell us what happened after spending time in the whale. He thought about what he had done and finally realized he had no hope except to confess his rebellion to God. He concluded that:

- His own lying selfishness had blocked God's mercy to him.
- Even in his mess, he could still turn back to God.
- He was thankful that he could do so.
- He promised to do what he said he would do.
- His only hope was in the Lord.

Once freed from his fishy prison, Jonah did what God told him to do. Did he mention his watery adventure in his message? If he did, the Ninevites may have thought, "If God can do that to people who won't listen to Him, we better listen to Him." Nineveh *did* repent, and God *did* save them.

Poor, angry Jonah was outraged; he sat outside the city and sulked. Jonah was a "messenger", but I wonder if he wasn't more of a "mess-anger," an "angry mess."

There is a lesson here for us: God has a plan for us, but he also has a plan for others. We must do what God commands *us* to do and not try to judge or control everyone else. Remember the Lord's reproof when He was instructing Peter, and the apostle shifted the attention to John. Peter said, "Lord, and what shall this man do? Jesus saith unto him … What is that to thee? follow thou me." (John 21:21b-22)

Let us also recall, "to obey is better than sacrifice." (1 Samuel 15:22)

12
In My Father's House

John 14:5-9 "Thomas saith unto him, Lord, we know not whither thou goest; and how can we know the way? Jesus saith unto him, I am the way, the truth, and the life: no man cometh unto the Father, but by me. If ye had known me, ye should have known my Father also: and from henceforth ye know him, and have seen him. Philip saith unto him, Lord, shew us the Father, and it sufficeth us. Jesus saith unto him, Have I been so long time with you, and yet hast thou not known me, Philip? He that hath seen me hath seen the Father; and how sayest thou then, Shew us the Father?"

These verses are a rather sad section of the Scriptures. Just days before His crucifixion, Jesus was talking with His disciples, and they were asking Him questions. He had just spoken of Heaven and said He was going away to prepare a place for them. (John 14:1-4) Then Thomas said they didn't know where He was going, and worse yet, they wouldn't know how to get there.

Do we have selective hearing like that? Jesus told them He was going to Heaven to prepare a place for them, and Thomas replied that he didn't know where Jesus was going or how to get there.

Jesus went on to tell them that **He was** the way to the Father, and that by knowing and seeing Him, they had known and seen an exact representation of what the Father was like. Then Philip demonstrated **his** selective hearing and requested Jesus to show them the Father.

In so many words, Jesus asked them if they were even listening to Him. I wonder if He doesn't ask the same question about me sometimes.

As my life has unfolded, I believe I have grown. I have had my ups and downs, but I believe that where I am today is further along the path than when I started this Christian journey almost 50 years ago. However, the further along I go, the more I realize that I battle with selective hearing too.

Charles Spurgeon once said, "Cast yourself simply on Jesus; let nothing but faith be in your soul towards Jesus; believe him, and trust in him, and you shall never be made ashamed of your confidence."

To that end, help me, Lord.

13
Two Thrones

2 Corinthians 5:10 "For we must all appear before the judgment seat of Christ; that every one may receive the things done in his body, according to that he hath done, whether it be good or bad."

Revelation 20:11 "And I saw a great white throne, and him that sat on it, from whose face the earth and the heaven fled away; and there was found no place for them."

Today's verses tell us about two judgment thrones, the Judgment Seat of Christ and The Great White Throne. Every human being who has ever lived will stand before one, but **only** one, of those thrones.

Some people think that God will decide **at the throne** whether to permit them into Heaven or send them to Hell, but that is false. We will appear before the Judgment Seat of Christ if we are **already** destined for Heaven, or we will appear before the Great White Throne if we are **already** destined for Hell. Our destination is determined before we die, and we can know what that destination is by whether we believe the gospel message.

You might ask, "Then what are the two judgments all about?" Two things come to mind.

- The Vindication of God: The dictionary defines vindicate as "to clear, as from an accusation, imputation, suspicion, or the like." Mortals, in our fallen condition, might think God is unfair or that He might judge wrongly; however, that is an error. At the Great White Throne, unbelievers will be made to understand the holiness and righteousness of God; they will know that God is right and that they have no excuse for rejecting His grace. (Romans 1:20) At the Judgment Seat of Christ, believers will be rewarded for their faith and faithfulness.

- Judgments Determine Reward: For the Christian believer, reward is based on deeds. For unbelievers, although *all* who reject the gospel of grace will be eternally lost, the punishment will be different for a kind, moral person than for a Hitler or a Stalin. (Mark 12:38-40) In any case, the "best" place in Hell will be horrible.

If you are a Christian, rejoice in His grace. If you are not, I plead with you; please stop your rebellion and seek God's mercy thru Christ before it is eternally too late.

14

A Feeling of Despair

Habakkuk 2:4b "The just shall live by his faith."

Some time ago I was in the hospital and rehab for a knee injury. My church friend Tom stopped by to encourage me. During the visit, he read a psalm, as he had done on previous visits. Before leaving, he laughingly mentioned that he had to be careful which psalm he read, that some psalms are not encouraging, mentioning Psalm 74 as an example.

Psalm 74 is dark and bleak. In it, Asaph said he knows that God is *able* to do certain things on his behalf, but the entire psalm is almost a continual lamenting that the Lord is *not* doing those things.

Have you ever been in Asaph's predicament? I have. For reasons best known to the Almighty, He allows us to go through valleys and experience cold shadows. Sometimes it is for discipline and sometimes for growth. Sometimes it's to test our faith and sometimes just to draw us close to Himself.

The Scriptures teach us that God is good, but just like Asaph, our experiences may imply that He is not. However, something we need to remember is that bleak feelings and a sense of despair do not give us an accurate picture of God's overall purposes. That is why the Lord does not tell us to have *feelings* about our relationship to Him; His command is always to have *faith* in Him.

In today's brief passage, Habakkuk reminds us of that point, assuring us that it is not an option: "The just shall live by his faith." The New Testament repeats that truth three times: Romans 1:17; Galatians 3:11; Hebrews 10:38.

Someone once said, "If God says something once, it is important, but if He says the same thing twice, we better pay very close attention." God not only put this statement in His Word four times, He said the same thing hundreds of times in different words. Why? Because we must have faith, not just in Him as God, but also in what He *does*. He says, "All things work together for good to them that love God, to them who are the called according to his purpose." (Romans 8:28) Denying that truth calls God a liar, but embracing that truth glorifies Him, for He says, "The just shall live by his faith."

15

The Life Is in the Blood

Romans 5:12-15 "Wherefore, as by one man sin entered into the world, and death by sin; and so death passed upon all men, for that all have sinned: (For until the law sin was in the world: but sin is not imputed when there is no law. Nevertheless, death reigned from Adam to Moses, even over them that had not sinned after the similitude of Adam's transgression, who is the figure of him that was to come. But not as the offence, so also is the free gift. For if through the offence of one many be dead, much more the grace of God, and the gift by grace, which is by one man, Jesus Christ, hath abounded unto many."

The first man, Adam, yielded to temptation in the garden. As a result, by that one act, the world was plunged into the vast darkness of sin. Indeed, Romans 8:22 says, "For we know that the whole creation groaneth and travaileth in pain together until now." In some sense, that evil rebellion has permeated "the *whole creation*," but in another sense, it has had a particular impact on the human race.

The late Martin DeHaan, a medical doctor during the first half of the 20th century, founded the "Radio Bible Class" and co-edited the devotional guide "Our Daily Bread." In his book, *The Chemistry of the Blood*, he makes a compelling argument that the sin nature is transmitted not through the body itself but through the blood. Furthermore, Dr. DeHaan says it has been established that the ability of the body to form blood comes from the father, not the mother. If that is so, through his tainted blood, Adam passed his sinful nature to the next generation; then, each succeeding generation passed it on to the next. As a result, all sinned, and all die. (Romans 5:12)

Now then, 1 Corinthians 15:47 makes a profound statement: "The first man is of the earth, earthy: the second man is the Lord from heaven." Who was the father of Jesus, the "second Adam?" Not Joseph; he was a stepfather. Mary's pregnancy was not from a son of Adam, but by the Holy Spirit. Jesus' blood was pure, and the shedding of the pure blood of the Lamb of God takes away the sin of the world. (John 1:29)

Who can fully understand the elaborate plans of Almighty God?

16

If The Son Shall Make You Free

John 8:32-36 "And ye shall know the truth, and the truth shall make you free. They answered him, We be Abraham's seed, and were never in bondage to any man: how sayest thou, Ye shall be made free? Jesus answered them, Verily, verily, I say unto you, Whosoever committeth sin is the servant of sin. And the servant abideth not in the house for ever: but the Son abideth ever. If the Son therefore shall make you free, ye shall be free indeed."

During the American Civil War, also called the War Between the States, Harriet Tubman, who escaped slavery on the Underground Railroad in 1851, helped a number of runaway slaves to find freedom. Modern sources doubt the authenticity of the quote, but she is attributed with saying, "I freed a thousand slaves. I could have freed a thousand more if only they knew they were slaves."

Whether the quote was from Mrs. Tubman or not, there is a glaring reality rising from it, and that streaming beacon shines right in our own faces today. In order for people to seek freedom, they must first realize they are *not* free. The prospect of change can be frightening, so there is little incentive to seek something else until we understand there *is* something different and better than what we have.

Jesus demonstrated that very thing in today's passage. He told men of his day that the truth would make them free, but they argued that they were Abraham's descendants and had never been slaves to anyone. Jesus then reminded them that when they sinned, they were slaves to sin, but if He, being the very personification of truth, made them free, they would truly be free.

The men to whom Jesus spoke were sure they didn't have a problem. It was that very attitude which caused them to turn away from the only One who could provide the solution they needed.

That same pride, that self-sufficiency, will hinder all us if we are not careful. May we acknowledge our spiritual inadequacy and turn to Christ, who to know is life eternal (John 17:3) *and* true freedom.

17

Darkness and Light

Romans 1:22-25 "Professing themselves to be wise, they became fools, And changed the glory of the uncorruptible God into an image made like to corruptible man, and to birds, and fourfooted beasts, and creeping things. Wherefore God also gave them up to uncleanness through the lusts of their own hearts, to dishonour their own bodies between themselves: Who changed the truth of God into a lie, and worshipped and served the creature more than the Creator, who is blessed for ever. Amen."

Yesterday, I mentioned the tragedy of the human heart that is so arrogant and self-sufficient that it cannot recognize its need for a Savior. I spoke to a friend on that subject; he forwarded to me part of a study in Romans, from Bible teacher Louis Voyer, which follows a similar theme.

In his study, Mr. Voyer commented on the spiritual darkness of the natural man as mentioned in Romans 1: "The darkness is appalling. It is the very darkness of death. There is *only one hope* in the midst of this dismal picture: the gospel 'the light of the knowledge of the glory of God in the face of Jesus Christ.' " (2 Corinthians 4:6)

The "darkness of death" that Mr. Voyer mentions is staggering in its certainty. It blinds us to the reality of God, of truth, and of life, death, and eternity. It causes us to grope in spiritual darkness, grasping at whatever we find. However, regardless of what we find, it will be empty until we find "the glory of God in the face of Jesus Christ." (2 Corinthians 4:6)

There is a cure to this stark blindness, and a cure is what we most desperately need, for this blindness leaves us in our sinful selves and can only lead to a dreadful end. Charles Spurgeon said it this way: "Sin and Hell are married unless repentance proclaims the divorce."

The true and living God, who is righteously angry at sin, has made a way for us by paying for our sins Himself. When we stop proclaiming our innocence, when we stop justifying ourselves and turn to Him from our wicked ways (repentance), then "He is faithful and just to forgive us our sins, and to cleanse us from all unrighteousness." (1 John 1:9)

18

Amazing Grace and Progressive Assurance

1 Corinthians 15:10 "But by the grace of God I am what I am: and his grace which was bestowed upon me was not in vain; but I laboured more abundantly than they all: yet not I, but the grace of God which was with me."

The apostle Paul was complicit in murder if not outright guilty of it; however, a time came when God broke through to his religious but stony heart and wrote words of grace in indelible ink.

By the way, it is that same startling grace by which He still saves today.

God's grace has broken through hard hearts throughout the history of His creation. Another example was about seventeen-hundred years after Paul's conversion on the road to Damascus. This time, during a terrible storm at sea, God broke through again and wrote his marvelous grace on the sacrilegious, stony heart of a wretched sailor named John Newton.

It doesn't make any difference if we are religious, sacrilegious, or just don't care at all. The fact is that *all* of us come into this world lost and separated from God, and *all* of us will pass out of this life in the same condition if not for the amazing, breathtaking grace of God.

When we first meet the incomparable Christ, there is often great elation. Over time, the wicked one takes every opportunity to put doubts into our minds, robbing us of the joy we have in the Lord; however, our salvation—our standing with God—is not the same thing as our assurance, for we can be secure in Christ and still find doubts and discouragements that shake us.

Sometime after Newton came to know the Lord, he wrote on the subject. "Assurance grows by repeated conflict, by our repeated experimental proof of the Lord's power and goodness to save; when we have been brought very low and helped, sorely wounded and healed, cast down and raised again, have given up all hope, and been suddenly snatched from danger, and placed in safety; and when these things have been repeated to us and in us a thousand times over, we begin to learn to trust simply to the word and power of God, beyond and against appearances: and this trust, when habitual and strong, bears the name of assurance; for even assurance has degrees."

Thank God for assurance, even if it requires trials to obtain.

19

Him with Whom We Have to Do

Hebrews 4:13 "Neither is there any creature that is not manifest in his sight: but all things are naked and opened unto the eyes of him with whom we have to do."

People who claim that they are not accountable to their Creator are just as accountable to Him as we who do not make that claim. We *all* are responsible to the Lord God our Maker for our actions, speech, and yes, our very thoughts.

The crucial difference is that He firmly commands us—and graciously invites us—to bow before Him *now* while we still live and breathe. By so doing, in the end, we shall appear before God, our Redeemer and Savior. If we continue to rebel and remain stiff-necked against Him, we *still* shall bow before Him one day; however, we will not appear before the Lord our Savior, but before the Lord, our Righteous Judge.

"For he saith, I have heard thee in a time accepted, and in the day of salvation have I helped thee: behold, now is the accepted time; behold, now is the day of salvation." (2 Corinthians 6:2)

20

He Shall Direct thy Paths

Proverbs 3:5-6 "Trust in the LORD with all thine heart; and lean not unto thine own understanding. In all thy ways acknowledge him, and he shall direct thy paths."

In this hectic world in which we can hardly take a breath between one activity and another, it is sometimes considered "unspiritual" not to be busy. There is always something to do, and we find ourselves running "from pillar to post" as the saying goes. That is true whether it is in business, sports, school, or social obligations. It is even true in our spiritual lives; church activities, mixed in with everything else, can drive us to endless, and sometimes useless distraction.

Is it wrong to be busy? No, but it can be a waste of energy, both spiritually and otherwise, to run ourselves to exhaustion. After all, even Jesus withdrew Himself from the crowd to spend time with the Father.

God did not make human beings to be Going, Going, Going all the time. That is why he made us to need periods of sleep each day, and gave us a day of rest each week. Remember, "The sabbath was made for man, and not man for the sabbath." (Mark 2:27)

Twentieth-century preacher and writer, G. Campbell Morgan, said it this way: "Waiting for God is not laziness. Waiting for God is not the abandonment of effort. Waiting for God means, first, activity under command; second, readiness for any new command that may come; third, the ability to do nothing until the command is given."

Those points are worth reconsidering:

- Waiting for God is not being lazy or negligent.
- We are to be doing what God has given us to do.
- We should always be ready for new direction from God.
- We should be willing to wait patiently between assignments.

That last one is what runs most counter to our Western sensibilities. However, we must remember that Paul spent three days in Damascus waiting for Ananias, and three more years with God before he began his ministry. In addition, Moses spent forty years awaiting his greatest assignment, and even Jesus was thirty years old before He began His public ministry.

Let us never shirk our God-given responsibilities, but let us never think of ourselves as self-sufficient operatives on a level above Moses or Paul—or the Lord Jesus Himself.

21

I've Got This

Psalm 116:5 "Gracious is the LORD, and righteous; yea, our God is merciful. 6 The LORD preserveth the simple: I was brought low, and he helped me. 7 Return unto thy rest, O my soul; for the LORD hath dealt bountifully with thee. 8 For thou hast delivered my soul from death, mine eyes from tears, and my feet from falling. 9 I will walk before the LORD in the land of the living."

Recently I worked on an intense project, and my involvement was a delight and a pleasure. However, when the task was complete, I experienced some discouragement. Being a little down is not unusual for me after a sustained effort, even if I feel like the endeavor was honoring to the Lord.

I usually read a passage of Scripture before getting out of bed in the morning, and after several days of my pensive mood, I sat up in bed and asked the Lord to make the passage particularly meaningful to me. I had been going through the psalms, and that day I came to Psalm 116. My heart did a double-take when I got to verse 7; I had to go back and reread it. "Return unto thy rest, O my soul; for the LORD hath dealt bountifully with thee."

How sweet and kind it was for the Lord to give me such an encouraging answer as quickly as He did. I fully recognize that His timing is often not the same as ours, and sometimes it serves His perfect purpose to answer us after our timing has already come and gone. However, that morning His answer was quick, it was sweet, and it was precious. It was as if He was saying, "I've got this. Everything is okay."

It is always appropriate for us to trust in the Lord, but it is especially so when there is something that seems out of balance. In fact, when things seem to be less than they should be, who **better** to go to than the very One who **made** us?

A car comes with a manual that instructs us on its proper use and care. We have a manual also—the Bible. In it, God gives us wisdom for our lives and assurance that He is in control and all is well.

22

The Master of the Sea

Mark 4:37-41 "And there arose a great storm of wind, and the waves beat into the ship, so that it was now full. And he was in the hinder part of the ship, asleep on a pillow: and they awake him, and say unto him, Master, carest thou not that we perish? And he arose, and rebuked the wind, and said unto the sea, Peace, be still. And the wind ceased, and there was a great calm. And he said unto them, Why are ye so fearful? how is it that ye have no faith? And they feared exceedingly, and said one to another, What manner of man is this, that even the wind and the sea obey him?"

I want to look at this passage over the next few days. Jesus and the disciples are in a boat. A great storm comes up and frightens the disciples.

166

They awaken Jesus. He stands and rebukes the storm, and the water becomes calm.

The point I want to make today is that the disciples could have saved themselves a great deal of worry if they had studied the Scriptures a little better. Had they done so, they would have come upon Psalm 107: "They that go down to the sea in ships, that do business in great waters; These see the works of the LORD, and his wonders in the deep. For he commandeth, and raiseth the stormy wind, which lifteth up the waves thereof. They mount up to the heaven, they go down again to the depths: their soul is melted because of trouble. They reel to and fro, and stagger like a drunken man, and are at their wits' end. Then they cry unto the LORD in their trouble, and he bringeth them out of their distresses. He maketh the storm a calm, so that the waves thereof are still. Then are they glad because they be quiet; so he bringeth them unto their desired haven." (Psalm 107:23-30)

Notice in Psalm 107 that it is the Lord who commands the storms to come! We might not feel comfortable with that, but it is true nonetheless. However, it also says He brings us into our desired haven.

Fear not, believer! His storms have purpose, and they do not interfere with His ultimate plan. Instead, they are actually part of it. He is taking us safely home *His* way—and in *His* time.

23

Does God Care?

Mark 4:37-41 "And there arose a great storm of wind, and the waves beat into the ship, so that it was now full. And he was in the hinder part of the ship, asleep on a pillow: and they awake him, and say unto him, Master, carest thou not that we perish? And he arose, and rebuked the wind, and said unto the sea, Peace, be still. And the wind ceased, and there was a great calm. And he said unto them, Why are ye so fearful? how is it that ye have no faith? And they feared exceedingly, and said one to another, What manner of man is this, that even the wind and the sea obey him?"

Today, let's look at this passage from another angle. Verse 38 says, "And he was in the hinder part of the ship, asleep on a pillow: and they awake him, and say unto him, Master, carest thou not that we perish?"

Jesus had told His disciples, "Let us pass over unto the other side." (v35) What was Jesus saying? He was telling them they were going to go over to the opposite shore. This was not something that the Lord hoped would happen but maybe wouldn't happen. Jesus said that is what they were going to do and ***that*** is what they were ***going*** to do. He was so sure of it that He went into the back of the boat and fell asleep!

However, to the disciples, going over to the other shore was not what ***looked*** like was going to happen. Even to the experienced fishermen among them, a sudden storm rising up and filling their boat with water was terrifying. "Carest thou not that we perish?" they asked.

Oh, if they had only understood His earlier words, "Let us pass over unto the other side." If they had only understood who Jesus really was! Once awakened, Jesus ***showed*** them His power, and they finally started to understand: "What manner of man is this, that even the wind and the sea obey him?"

Do you have storms in your life? Do what you can; use the resources God has given to you. But don't fail to go to the Master, "casting all your care upon him; for he careth for you." (1Peter 5:7) He really does care, and He is in full control.

24

Why Are Ye So Fearful?

Mark 4:40-41 "And he said unto them, Why are ye so fearful? how is it that ye have no faith? And they feared exceedingly, and said one to another, What manner of man is this, that even the wind and the sea obey him?"

For our third look at Mark 4:37-41, I want to concentrate on the last two verses. The Lord was asleep in a boat and had just been awakened in the middle of a violent storm that terrified His disciples. He stood up in the boat, rebuked the weather, and the storm melted into a great calm. Then He turned to His followers and asked them why they were fearful and why they had no faith.

That might sound a little harsh to us; after all, the storm had filled the boat with water. However, the Greek word translated fearful means literally that, but it comes from another Greek word that carries with it the thought of dread. In other words, the disciples were not only frightened, but they had likely lost heart and were sure there was no way out.

That fear caused them to focus on the wind and the sea and the sinking vessel and the water in it. In fact, it caused them to concentrate on everything except their only hope—the One who was their only hope even ***before*** the storm came along.

Now notice that Jesus linked that fear with their lack of faith. He had performed miracles before; why did they assume He could no longer do so?

By this time, however, they were looking at Jesus, probably wide-eyed and with mouths half open, for it says, "they feared exceedingly." The two words translated "feared exceedingly" are different from the earlier "fearful." Both these consecutive words are accurately translated "feared exceedingly," and together it might be said they convey a "fearful fear!" However, though these words convey a sense of dread, they include a distinct sense of reverence, amazement, and awe. Try to imagine what it was like for the disciples suddenly to realize they were in the presence of Someone who could command the elements of creation with His voice!

Now understand this—you *are* in His presence! You step every step, breathe every breath, and think every thought in the presence of your Creator. Honor Him with your breath, with your life, and with your whole being.

25

The Difference

Mark 4:37- 41 "And there arose a great storm of wind, and the waves beat into the ship, so that it was now full. And he was in the hinder part of the ship, asleep on a pillow: and they awake him, and say unto him, Master, carest thou not that we perish? And he arose, and rebuked the wind, and said unto the sea, Peace, be still. And the wind ceased, and there was a great calm. And he said unto them, Why are ye so fearful? how is it that ye have no faith? And they feared exceedingly, and said one to another, What manner of man is this, that even the wind and the sea obey him?"

In our final consideration of this passage, we will compare two different storms featuring two different people. I am speaking of Jesus in this account and the Old Testament prophet Jonah. There is a vast difference between them, but there are also similarities as to how God worked in those two events.

Jonah rebelled against God, but God didn't let that stop Him from working His purposes. Jonah paid a price for his stubbornness, yet through it all, God demonstrated His power to Jonah's traveling companions, lavished mercy on Nineveh, and taught Jonah some valuable lessons. In a similar way, God also worked powerfully through His Son and brought the disciples to greater faith. The contrast is that in the New Testament account, Jesus submitted to His Father, whereas Jonah was obstinate and childish.

God works all things after the counsel of his own will, (Ephesians 1:11) which Paul discovered on the road to Damascus. Peter found that out when Jesus died in spite of Peter's protests. Jacob learned that lesson and had a limp the rest of his life as a reminder.

The lesson *we* must learn—and it is a lesson to our own benefit—is that *no one* can thwart God's purposes, and He *will* be glorified in all that He does. However, we save ourselves a lot of suffering and heartache when we submit to His will and work *with* Him instead of striving against Him. We also receive more blessings when we trust God.

"O taste and see that the LORD is good: blessed is the man that trusteth in him." (Psalm 34:8)

26

A Beautiful Picture

Galatians 4:4-5 "But when the fulness of the time was come, God sent forth his Son, made of a woman, made under the law, To redeem them that were under the law, that we might receive the adoption of sons."

One of the greatest personal tragedies in human history is the account of Naomi and Ruth. In the book of Ruth chapter 1, an Israelite named Elimelech moved his wife Naomi and their two sons to the country of Moab. While they were there, Elimelech died; then the two sons married Moabite women, and finally, the sons died. I cannot imagine what frightful and overwhelming grief Naomi must have experienced, but that was her story.

As we read further, we find that the famine ended, and Naomi and Ruth—one of her daughters-in-law—moved back to Bethlehem with broken hearts and little else. Naomi told the women of Bethlehem no longer to call her Naomi (which means "my delight") but to call her Mara ("bitterness") "for the Almighty hath dealt very bitterly with me," she said. (Ruth 1:20)

In chapter 2, with no other means of food, Naomi sent Ruth out to engage in gleaning, the ancient practice of recovering the grain that was missed during harvesting. Ruth ended up in the field belonging to Boaz, a wealthy relative who, according to another ancient custom, was second in line to be the kinsman redeemer—someone to purchase Elimelech's land and redeem his name and family. The man who was first in line declined, so Boaz bought the land from Naomi and took Ruth as his wife.

Chapter 4 tells us that Boaz and Ruth had a son; the women who had heard Naomi change her name came to rejoice with her for God's grand provision even during her deepest sorrows.

Naomi's situation was desperate and frightening. Today's verses remind us that until the time was right, our situation was the same; however, "when the fulness of the time was come, God sent forth his Son … To redeem them that were under the law, that we might receive the adoption of sons." My friends, Ruth's story started out very badly and ended up very well. Our story started out desperately worse, but by God's amazing grace, through faith, it shall end infinitely better.

Let us say with the psalmist, "O praise the Lord, all ye nations: praise him, all ye people." (117:1)

27

The Good, the Bad, and the Unforgiven

Matthew 22:8-10 "Then saith he to his servants, The wedding is ready, but they which were bidden were not worthy. Go ye therefore into the highways, and as many as ye shall find, bid to the marriage. So those servants went out into the highways, and gathered together all as many as they found, both bad and good: and the wedding was furnished with guests."

Here, the Lord gives a parable about a king who prepared a wedding for his son. He sent his servants to bid the invited guests to come, but everyone made excuses and refused to attend. Then the king sent the servants into the streets to invite everyone they found. In they came, as today's verses say, "both bad and good." I think the Lord used this as a picture of those who will be in Heaven. Some are "good" in the eyes of man, and some are "bad." Though *all* are bad in the eyes of God, He makes believers worthy of Heaven by grace through faith. (Ephesians 2:8-10)

Matthew 22 mentions two other groups of people besides the ones who came to the wedding. The first group was the invited guests who not only refused to come, but mistreated and even murdered the servants the king sent to them. (vv3-6) The king rose up in anger and unleashed inconceivable fury upon them. (v7) We might understand this as a picture of the just wrath God will one day visit on those who refuse His invitation to grace.

The second group is represented by the man who was there without a wedding garment. (vv11-12) In those days, a king would provide robes for his guests. The king told the servants to invite everyone, and they could come in any condition—good or bad; however, when they came in, they had to put on the garment that the king provided. This man did not, and he was cast out. I believe this represents those who are religious but never really bow before God, accepting His forgiveness in Christ.

Just like the "good man" in John chapter 3 and the "bad woman" in John chapter 4, we all—good and bad—need a Savior.

On the cross, Christ purchased our right standing with God. Don't leave this life without His robe of righteousness; you will not like how things turn out. (See Matthew 22:13.)

28

Don't Become Distracted

Philippians 3:13-14 "Brethren, I count not myself to have apprehended: but this one thing I do, forgetting those things which are behind, and reaching forth unto those things which are before, I press toward the mark for the prize of the high calling of God in Christ Jesus."

Here are two related thoughts:
- All of us have seen times in a movie or TV show, or even real life, when a person is doing one thing, then suddenly becomes distracted and abandons the original purpose in order to follow the interruption.
- Many times, cars driving behind me follow too closely, creating an unsafe condition. The trouble is that I cannot control that very well, but I *can* control the traffic ahead of me by setting my speed to allow a safe stopping distance between the car ahead and me.

How are those two things related? Well, in a way, life is like those two scenarios—distraction and control. Think about our past and our future; we have absolutely no control over the past, whereas we *can* do things that will affect our future.

A problem arises when the past haunts and distracts us. We cannot change or control the past. It is like the car that follows too closely; it distracts us, but we can do very little about it. The future is different though. Regardless of our past, we *can* make good decisions today that shape our future in godly ways.

I believe this is what the apostle is telling the believers at Philippi. We will never be free from the distractions of past sins and mistakes until we deliberately "forget those things which are behind." Additionally, until we are free of the past we will never be able to "reach forth unto those things which are before (future) and press toward the mark for the prize." We cannot do anything about the "cars behind us" (sins, poor decisions, mistakes) except forget them. After all, God forgets the sins Christ paid for. (Jeremiah 31:31-34; Hebrews 8:12, 10:17) Do we have the right to remember and beat ourselves up over what God says He forgave and forgot?

"As far as the east is from the west, so far hath he removed our transgressions from us." (Ps 103:12)

29
What Were You Thinking?

Ephesians 2:8-10 "For by grace are ye saved through faith; and that not of yourselves: it is the gift of God: Not of works, lest any man should boast. For we are his workmanship, created in Christ Jesus unto good works, which God hath before ordained that we should walk in them."

These verses came to mind as I thought of an episode of the Monk television series. Adrian Monk was a police officer with a peculiar childhood. He was annoyingly analytical, meticulous to a fault, and painfully self-effacing. As an adult, these behaviors were somewhat softened by his marriage to his college sweetheart Trudy. She passed away before the series begins, making his oddities flourish, which is a major theme in the show.

Throughout the series, Adrian has flashbacks and apparitions of the now-deceased love of his life. In one recollection of his time with Trudy, Adrian says to her, "Thank you for marrying me." Then in a moment that was typical of Monk's damaged self-confidence, he asked, "What were you thinking?"

With due respect to God, the Lover of my soul, that same question arises in my own mind when I think of His startling mercy to me. I contemplate the vastness and Holiness of God, then contrast it with the lostness into which I was born and the sinfulness with which I still struggle. And when I think, not just of God's grace in saving and forgiving me, but also of the incomprehensible price He had to pay to do so, Monk's question echoes in my mind: What was in the heart of God that He thought of me?

Musings

"He [Jesus] shall see of the travail of his soul, and shall be satisfied: by his knowledge shall my righteous servant justify many; for he shall bear their iniquities." (Isaiah 53:11)

> Jesus, Savior, precious Friend, You tell me in your Word,
> So many great and precious things I do not understand;
> But if, dear Lord, You said to me
> "What one thing would you know?"
> I'd ask You as I held Your nail-scarred hand,
>
> "Why do you love me? Why do you care?
> It says you'll see, and you'll be satisfied.
> You tell me that you love me
> And you proved it when you died,
> But my question, precious Savior,
> Is simply, why?"
> ~ W.F. Powers

"What is man, that thou art mindful of him? and the son of man, that thou visitest him?" (Psalm 8:4)

30

Broken Worlds and Gardeners

Philippians 3:12-14 Not as though I had already attained, either were already perfect: but I follow after, if that I may apprehend that for which also I am apprehended of Christ Jesus. Brethren, I count not myself to have apprehended: but this one thing I do, forgetting those things which are behind, and reaching forth unto those things which are before, I press toward the mark for the prize of the high calling of God in Christ Jesus.

While we were driving last week, my wife and I discussed the drug culture in our country. There has been a particularly sad rash of deaths recently, prompting a renewed interest in ending the tragedy that haunts so many.

As we drove, we came upon a field of crops and noticed a farmer nearby. We live in a rural area and such sights are common to us, but what a refreshing contrast to the discouraging topic we were considering just moments before.

Many folks are stuck in a battle with drugs, a battle which many of them wish they could escape. Thankfully, some finally see a chance for change and press toward the light like a young plant pushing through the soil, seeking the light and warmth of the Son. Instead of the despair that once covered them, they now see the Gardener of their souls standing nearby. God is pruning and weeding, digging and raking, tending His tender plants, and bringing them to growth and maturity.

Have any of us arrived yet? We might think of those who have gone before, those who have graduated from the school of this life. But for those of us who are still among the "undergraduates," we press on toward the high calling to which God has appointed us.

"Now we see through a glass, darkly," the apostle Paul explains to us. (1 Corinthians 13:12) At this time in our schooling, the heavenly Schoolmaster has more to teach us. At this point in life, the Vineyard Keeper is still pruning the vine. Until He is finished, let us continue in hope, "confident of this very thing, that he which hath begun a good work in you will perform it until the day of Jesus Christ." (Philippians 1:6)

JULY

1

Human Reasoning and Biblical Authority

Genesis 3:1-4 "Now the serpent was more subtil than any beast of the field which the LORD God had made. And he said unto the woman, Yea, hath God said, Ye shall not eat of every tree of the garden? And the woman said unto the serpent, We may eat of the fruit of the trees of the garden: But of the fruit of the tree which is in the midst of the garden, God hath said, Ye shall not eat of it, neither shall ye touch it, lest ye die. And the serpent said unto the woman, Ye shall not surely die:"

I write these Musings to inspire believers in their faith. I hope they also encourage non-Christians to trust the Savior. A problem exists though, in that our culture is drifting away from our Christian heritage and becoming hostile to God and His Word.

As an example, a little while ago, I saw an article that claimed that churches should not depend on the Bible as a moral guide. I do not know if the writer insists that other belief systems forsake their revered writings, but he seems comfortable in demanding that of Christians.

Writer, speaker, and radio host Michael Brown published an insightful counterargument. He correctly claimed that the Bible is a valid source of Divine moral wisdom and asks why anyone would find comfort in it if it weren't. In Brown's closing, he succinctly defined the problem: "What is lacking is not the inspiration of Scripture or the wisdom of Scripture or the moral authority of Scripture. What is lacking is the understanding of human beings. That's exactly why we need God's Word."

As Christians, we should be kind; we should be gracious with unbelievers, even as Brown was. At the same time though, we must bear witness to God and His truth. As Billy Graham once said, "Courage is contagious. When a brave man takes a stand, the spines of others are often stiffened." We must expose uninformed and erroneous arguments. (1 Timothy 1:4; 2 Timothy 4:4) The claim that the Bible is not a valid moral authority surely is one such uninformed and erroneous argument.

2

She Judged Him Faithful

Hebrews 11:11 "Through faith also Sara herself received strength to conceive seed, and was delivered of a child when she was past age, because she judged him faithful who had promised."

In Genesis 17, God told Abraham he would have a son. Chapter 18 records Sarah overhearing that promise and laughing at the idea of a hundred-year-old man and a ninety-year-old woman having a child.

We are often reminded of Sarah's laughter, but Genesis 17:17 says that Abraham laughed also. I do not know whether Abraham's laugh was a laugh of mocking, uncertainty, or anticipation, and the same with Sarah's laughter. In any case, "Abraham believed God, and it was counted unto him for righteousness," (Romans 4:3) and Sarah "judged him faithful who had promised."

There are times when we laugh too. I don't mean at a joke or funny story, but at the circumstances, we face. Sometimes, we laugh because we see God's kind hand and bubble over with excitement in watching Him work in our lives. At other times, we may give in to nervous laughter because we can't imagine that God can—or will—actually do what He says He will do. However, we must believe God and judge Him faithful, remembering that "without faith it is impossible to please him." (Hebrews 11:6)

One other thing to consider: Sarah "judged him faithful *who had promised*." Even though the couple wanted a son, their confidence was not in their desires, circumstances, or plans. Their confidence, their assurance, their *faith* was in the Almighty God, and that confidence was because God *said* he was going to give them a child.

Let us trust in God; what He says is true. He is good, and He is faithful who has promised.

3

Freedom

John 8:32-36 "And ye shall know the truth, and the truth shall make you free. They answered him, We be Abraham's seed, and were never in bondage to any man: how sayest thou, Ye shall be made free? Jesus answered them, Verily, verily, I say unto you, Whosoever committeth sin is the servant of sin. And the servant abideth not in the house for ever: but the Son abideth ever. If the Son therefore shall make you free, ye shall be free indeed."

The religious leaders of His day really disliked Jesus. As a result, they argued with Him incessantly. If the Lord had stated that grass was green, even then they may have disagreed. Instead, Jesus told them that the truth would make them free. Here He was, the Truth in person, standing in front of them, and they did not recognize Him, even as Pilate would not just before he condemned the Truth to hang on a cross. (John 18:38)

Jesus said He is "the way, the truth, and the life." (John 14:6) Many today still refuse to accept His claim; nevertheless, Jesus was right.

When we claim to know more than He does—when we claim that we are right no matter what He says about Himself, life, or truth—then our blindness to truth leads us into slavery. Sometimes we are slaves to possessions, other times to lust, and still other times to power or hate. However, ultimately it is slavery to the lack of the truth. Only the truth of God can rescue us from the addictions that enslave us.

Tomorrow is the day that marks the American declaration that freed us from servitude to a British monarch an ocean away. Several months ago, Americans commemorated the end in 1865 of a war that finally started to unravel the imposition of slavery perpetrated on *this* side of the Atlantic. And yet many of us today, people of a vast number of skin shades, occupations, and backgrounds, are still servants to sin.

May this be the day that we become serious with the Lord Jesus. May this be the season we declare our independence from sin in the only way possible, and that is in humble repentance, taking Christ at His word, and declaring our dependence upon Him.

4
How Much Does It Cost to Be Free?

2 Peter 2:17-19: "These are wells without water, clouds that are carried with a tempest; to whom the mist of darkness is reserved for ever. For when they speak great swelling words of vanity, they allure through the lusts of the flesh, through much wantonness, those that were clean escaped from them who live in error. While they promise them liberty, they themselves are the servants of corruption: for of whom a man is overcome, of the same is he brought in bondage."

On July 4, 1776, representatives of the American colonies, then British subjects, began signing a document declaring their break from

England's King George III. They had concluded that the king was not acting in their best interest and therefore decided to break from the king and start a new and separate nation. Ironically, on June 23, 2016, almost 240 years later, the British people voted to break from the European Union for essentially the same reason.

Understandably, the decree of the colonies did not sit well with King George, and the citizens of the colonies had to fight a war to affect their freedom. Thankfully, even though there was some friction and discomfort in the recent Brexit vote, our British friends did not have to fight a war. As I write this, although there have been economic ripples and verbal expressions of displeasure, they have been relatively minor and seem to be working themselves out.

These two events tell us something: Whether by armed conflict or mere commotion, there is a cost for change—there is a price for freedom.

That is true in the spiritual world as well. In today's verses, Peter speaks of those who promise freedom to others but fail to deliver; instead, they lead others into the bondage of their own lusts. Not so with Jesus who promised freedom and then delivered it personally at great cost to Himself. The price He gave was His life!

Peter describes those who promise liberty but do not follow through. In contrast, God "hath given us an understanding, that we may know him that is true, and we are in him that is true, even in his Son Jesus Christ. This is the true God, and eternal life." (1 John 5:20)

Now, *that* is *freedom*. That is good news.

5

No Room

Matthew 22:35-40 "Then one of them, which was a lawyer, asked him a question, tempting him, and saying, Master, which is the great commandment in the law? Jesus said unto him, Thou shalt love the Lord thy God with all thy heart, and with all thy soul, and with all thy mind. This is the first and great commandment. And the second is like unto it, Thou shalt love thy neighbour as thyself. On these two commandments hang all the law and the prophets."

To us, a lawyer is someone who represents another person in court; however, in the Bible, a lawyer is a person who is an expert in interpreting and teaching Jewish Law. The passage says this lawyer tempted Jesus. Perhaps he was hoping Jesus might give an explanation that would upset the Pharisees or Sadducees, or even the people, thereby damaging Christ's image and message. Whatever the reason, Jesus tells this lawyer to love God with his all and to love his neighbor in the same way he loves himself.

It was then that Jesus added one more sentence: "On these two commandments hang all the law and the prophets."

You may be like me. I tend to read things very quickly, especially if I am familiar with the words. I think, "That's nice," and then go on reading. But what did Jesus mean when He said all the Law and the prophets hang on those two commands?

If I truly love God with all my heart, soul, and mind and my neighbor as myself, would I murder my neighbor who God made in His image? Would I steal from them? Would I commit adultery with my neighbor's spouse? When I disobey God, I am placing my desires above God's instructions and above my neighbor's wellbeing. God did not give the Law and the prophets to focus us on the Law and the prophets; God gave the Law and the prophets to stir our hearts toward faith in Him, for His glory, and for the good of people, including ourselves.

The old nature wants to be the center of attention, and Satan is always delighted to tempt us away from God. Perhaps what Jesus is saying is that in a heart focused on loving God and loving man, there will be no room for focusing on theft, adultery, and murder.

6

Good Plans in Hard Times

Jeremiah 29:11 "For I know the thoughts that I think toward you, saith the LORD, thoughts of peace, and not of evil, to give you an expected end."

Here God promises He has a plan; His purposes are not for evil, but for an "expected end." The Hebrew word "expected" does not just mean something we know is coming; something bad can be expected too. Instead, this word has a sense of something longed for—something good.

Most of us know that verse; perhaps you've claimed it for yourself. However, back away and look at the context. Jeremiah is proclaiming this message from God to those whom Nebuchadnezzar has taken captive. Before that, God sent the prophet to warn his rebellious people, (chapter 26) and then told them He would turn them over to Nebuchadnezzar, king of Babylon. (chapter 27)

This sounds dire, and it was. This also sounds permanent, but it wasn't. Today's verse in context says, "For thus saith the LORD, That after seventy years be accomplished at Babylon I will visit you, and perform my good word toward you, in causing you to return to this place. For I know the thoughts that I think toward you, saith the LORD, thoughts of peace, and not of evil, to give you an expected end. Then shall ye call upon me, and ye shall go and pray unto me, and I will hearken unto you. And ye shall seek me, and find me, when ye shall search for me with all your heart." (Jeremiah 29:10-13)

Often we claim Old Testament promises for our own, as if God made them to us. We need to take care to understand God's Word in context. However, those things ***were*** written for our learning, (Romans 15:4) and we should not miss the lessons they teach us.

Now, what lessons do we learn from this passage? For one thing, God does indeed purpose good for His people today. Nevertheless, if we insist on exercising our stiff necks and hard hearts, we may end up in trouble for a season. It is always best if we live lives of humble obedience, but if we ***do*** find ourselves to be in a mess—whether by our own stubbornness or otherwise—we should humble ourselves under God's wise hand and trust Him to show us His good end in His good time.

7

The Majesty of the King

Proverbs 25:6-7 "Put not forth thyself in the presence of the king, and stand not in the place of great men: For better it is that it be said unto thee, Come up hither; than that thou shouldest be put lower in the presence of the prince whom thine eyes have seen."

The casual attitude toward God today concerns me. For sure, there is also downright contempt, which has been around for virtually all of mortal history. However, today there is an alarming lack of reverence and awe for God, even in the Christian community.

We must not think of God as our buddy. He is the uncreated Creator of the heavens, the Earth, and everything else that exists. Moreover, He has called us to trust in Him. Though we are not "buddies," He ***has*** made us His children by faith in His Son! (Galatians 3:26) We must never lose the grandeur of that.

My readers live under different forms of government all around the world; however, imagine that you live in a land ruled by the most powerful king ever to reign. His kingdom covers vast territories that he has conquered, and his power is limitless. Now imagine that one day this king calls you to appear before him. You tremble as you enter his presence. As you bow before him, he rises from his throne, takes you by the arm, and leads you out onto the balcony. You stand there quivering as you wonder what he is going to do. Imagine now what goes through your mind as he raises his hands for silence from the throng below and then announces for all to hear, "My loyal subjects, I want you all to know that this person standing here with me is my friend."

That is what the Almighty God has done. Through inconceivable grace, by the precious blood of His only-begotten Son, the Almighty Creator has befriended us. We should love Him and adore Him, and we must always trust Him as our friend. However, we should never carelessly or casually presume upon God or take lightly the glory of His majestic being.

We must remember that even though God is always good and always our friend, He also is always God!

> Majestic sweetness sits enthroned
> Upon the Savior's brow;
> His head with radiant glories crowned,
> His lips with grace o'erflow.
> ~ Samuel Stennett

8

The Priests and the Priest

Exodus 25:1-2, 8-9 "And the LORD spake unto Moses, saying, Speak unto the children of Israel, that they bring me an offering: of every man that giveth it willingly with his heart ye shall take my offering. ... And let them make me a sanctuary; that I may dwell among them. According to all that I shew thee, after the pattern of the tabernacle, and the pattern of all the instruments thereof, even so shall ye make it."

The word "tabernacle" means "a dwelling place," a place where God dwelt and met His people in Old Testament times.

In today's verses, God commanded Moses to collect materials to build a tabernacle. Nothing was to be forced or demanded; the offerings were to be given willingly. In the following chapters, God gave the details of the tabernacle, even who should oversee its construction. Additionally, He also detailed the attire and consecration of the priests. These priests would offer sacrifices for the people year after year.

Later, when the people came into the Promised Land, the temporary, portable tabernacle was replaced with a more permanent structure, the Temple. This was the new place where God would dwell and where He would meet His people, but the same priests still offered the same sacrifices, year after year.

The tabernacle was portable, and the temple was stationary; however, the Ark of the Covenant was ever-present, first in one structure and then the other. The Ark was a symbol of God's promise; however, a time came when God made a new covenant. In doing so, He brought forth another Priest (Jesus) who would end the need for all other priests because, "this man, after he had offered one sacrifice for sins for ever, sat down on the right hand of God." (Hebrews 10:12) Why does it say Christ sat down? Because He had completed His work of being our sacrifice. Unlike the priests who offered sacrifices year after year, Jesus had finished His work, so He sat down.

One last thing: Just before he was murdered, Stephen saw Jesus *standing* on the right hand of God. (Acts 7:59-60) Perhaps *this* speaks of His unfinished, intervening work on our behalf, for we are told, "Wherefore he is able also to save them to the uttermost that come unto God by him, seeing he ever liveth to make intercession for them." (Hebrews 7:25)

9

From the Lesser to the Greater

James 3:3-6 "Behold, we put bits in the horses' mouths, that they may obey us; and we turn about their whole body. Behold also the ships, which though they be so great, and are driven of fierce winds, yet are they turned about with a very small helm, whithersoever the governor listeth. Even so the tongue is a little member, and boasteth great things. Behold, how great a matter a little fire kindleth! And the tongue is a fire, a world of iniquity: so is the tongue among our members, that it defileth the whole body, and setteth on fire the course of nature; and it is set on fire of hell."

James gives us three word pictures in these verses. The first is of controlling a large horse with a small bit, and the second is of controlling a large ship with a small rudder. James does not speak of the third one as being controlled by anything. In fact, he speaks of the tongue as being totally *out of control* and warns of the flaming fury it becomes when it is *not* controlled.

Today's verses give us pictures of sins in general. We might think they are "little sins," although if we are not careful, they will lead us to disastrous sins. The Holy Spirit uses God's Word like a bit or a rudder to direct and guide us; if we resist, our whole lives can end up in flames.

The English Puritan Thomas Manton said, "As little sticks set the great ones on fire, and a wisp of straw often enkindles a great block of wood, so we are drawn on by the lesser evils to greater, and by the just judgment of God allowed to fall into them, because we made no conscience of lesser. The lesser commandments are a rail about the greater, and no man grows downright wicked at first, but rises to it by degrees."

My father used to say that fire is a good servant but a bad master. That is, if you control fire, you can use it for many good things, but if it gets out of control, it can very suddenly do great damage. Our passions are the same. Let us, by God's power, use the "rudder" of God's Word (Psalm 119) to steer clear of even the "lesser sins."

10

Where Have You Been?

Luke 24:15-18 "And it came to pass, that, while they communed together and reasoned, Jesus himself drew near, and went with them. But their eyes were holden that they should not know him. And he said unto them, What manner of communications are these that ye have one to another, as ye walk, and are sad? And the one of them, whose name was Cleopas, answering said unto him, Art thou only a stranger in Jerusalem, and hast not known the things which are come to pass there in these days?"

Some years ago, the commercials for a vegetable juice drink showed someone choosing a soft drink or other beverage and then, on second thought, being surprised that they had not thought of the vegetable drink instead.

Perhaps you have had that kind of moment. Maybe not a drink choice, but have you ever had a conversation with a friend and later realized that the point they were making went right past you without you even noticing it?

Can you imagine what went through the minds of the two disciples on the road to Damascus when they realized they had asked, in effect, "Are you the only one in Jerusalem that doesn't know these things?" to the very person who was the center of those things? How silly they must have felt.

How often do we experience God's presence and completely miss it? An answered prayer; comfort in a storm; a reminder that we are His and that by His grace we "will dwell in the house of the LORD for ever." (Psalm 23:6) Moreover, how often do we experience God's grandeur and miss it? His creation; the beauty of music; the gift of sight; *life*! One of the things I like to do is get down on the ground and look closely at all the intricacies of some tiny lawn flower. How did God put all the details of that incredible design into a seed?

We live in the presence of the Almighty God, the Lord Jesus is at the right hand of the Father making intersession for us, and the Holy Spirit lives in us to comfort and direct us. May we never lose the wonder of who God is and what He has done!

11

Unfathomable Immensity

Psalm 147:4-5 "He telleth the number of the stars; he calleth them all by their names. Great is our Lord, and of great power: his understanding is infinite."

God's starry heavens fascinate me. Until recently, scientists believed there were between one hundred and two hundred billion galaxies in the universe, many of which are made up of one hundred billion stars or much more. Recently, by using more modern and more powerful equipment, they have come to believe there may be up to *ten times* that many galaxies. Numbers so large fit comfortably into the memory of a computer, but the human mind does not have the capacity to grasp them fully.

As amazing as that is, let me suggest another aspect to this. If you get in a space vehicle and travel one direction until you come to the edge of the universe—wherever that is—when you get there, God will be there waiting for you. Now get back into your rocket and go all the way over to the *opposite* edge of the universe, and again you will find God waiting for you. Now consider this: when you get to that second edge and find God waiting for you, you need to realize that He is still at the first edge.

God is present everywhere, all the time; theologians call that omnipresence. God has been everywhere, all the time, throughout all time. Trying to fully grasp that is like trying to comprehend hundreds of billions of galaxies, each filled with billions of stars. Yet it remains true.

Now, let me give you one final aspect. God made the moon, the sun and the other stars, and the planets, and He did so out of nothing. The Creator God speaks, and things that are not, become things that are. Then with that same voice, He tells us He loves us, and He proved it by personally paying for our sins with His own life.

> He left the Splendor of Heaven
> Knowing His destiny

Was the lonely hill of Golgotha
There to lay down His life for me.

If that isn't love
The ocean is dry,
There're no stars in the sky,
And the sparrow can't fly.
~ Dottie Rambo

Truly, "Great is our Lord, and of great power: his understanding is infinite." So is His love for us.

12

Are You Praying or Singing?

James 5:13 "Is any among you afflicted? let him pray. Is any merry? let him sing psalms."

James gives us a lot of practical advice, as we see in today's verse. Let's look first at the second point James makes. "Is any merry? let him sing psalms." This should almost be automatic to the Lord's people; all is going well, so we sing. Whether we sing out loud or our hearts just overflow with praise and adoration, we should be in an attitude of worship, praise, and song.

But what if things are *not* going well? James also has some encouragement in this situation. "Is any among you afflicted? let him pray." We might read this as, "Are you sick? Ask God to remove it." However, James actually covers illness in the next verse so this is a different situation. There are two key words James uses here, "afflicted" and "pray." Let's take a closer look at them:

The word that is translated "afflicted" means to experience painful hardship. That *might* be illness, but it could be so much more. It might be the loss of a job, the death of a loved one, or the betrayal of a friend. These life experiences and others tear at our souls and afflict us. The good news is that God, through James, tells us what to do next.

Pray. That too makes sense; we are tormented, so we come to God for help. According to *Strong's* Greek definition, the flavor of the word includes supplication—asking for assistance and relief, and even includes a sense of urgency. But the meaning also includes the idea of worship! In other words, we don't just come to God to ask; we also come to give—to worship, praise, and adore.

What wonderful advice the Lord gives us in this verse. Supplication is in order whenever we or others have need; praise, worship, and adoration are in order all the time. Think about it this way: since the Lord is our spiritual Bridegroom, we should be loving Him "in sickness and in health, for richer or poorer, for better or for worse." And why not? Truly He is the Redeemer and Lover of our souls.

"A thousand, a thousand thanksgivings, I bring Blessed Savior, to Thee." (Ernst C. Homburg; Trans. Mrs. Frances Bevan)

13

The Eclipse

Acts 26:24-28 "And as he thus spake for himself, Festus said with a loud voice, Paul, thou art beside thyself; much learning doth make thee mad. But he said, I am not mad, most noble Festus; but speak forth the words of truth and soberness. For the king knoweth of these things, before whom also I speak freely: for I am persuaded that none of these things are hidden from him; for this thing was not done in a corner. King Agrippa, believest thou the prophets? I know that thou believest. Then Agrippa said unto Paul, Almost thou persuadest me to be a Christian."

We are all aware of occasional eclipses that bring darkness to various places on Earth. However, there are also troubles that constantly plague our world; hatred, violence, rebellion, and wickedness come from the depths of the soul and bring a different kind of darkness.

Several chapters before today's reading, religious leaders brought charges against the apostle Paul to Felix the governor. In chapter 25, Felix set up a meeting between Paul and King Agrippa and outlined the charges to the king. Acts 26 records Paul's defense to King Agrippa as he detailed his conversion and laid out the Christian message Jesus sent him to proclaim. Incidentally, in Acts 26:18, the apostle said Jesus sent him to open people's eyes and to turn them from *darkness* to *light*, from Satan to God, so they could have the forgiveness of sins.

In today's verses, Felix interrupted and told Paul he was crazy. The apostle assured the governor he was not crazy; instead, the incredible things he was saying had occurred in public, not in secret. Then he asked Agrippa if *he* believed, and in one of the saddest comments ever uttered Agrippa said, "*almost* thou persuadest me to be a Christian."

Therein lays the problem. Paul longed that Agrippa was not only *almost*, but instead completely, convinced and obedient to the gospel of Christ. If all of us were, that creeping darkness of hate, violence, rebellion, and wickedness that is settling over the world even now would soften into the light of love, gentleness, obedience, and righteousness.

To my knowledge Agrippa never believed, thus remaining part of the problem instead of part of the solution. Don't be an Agrippa; be a Paul.

14

Toggles

Hebrews 11:6 "But without faith it is impossible to please him [God]: for he that cometh to God must believe that he is, and that he is a rewarder of them that diligently seek him."

Fifty years ago, my parents moved our family into a house two doors down from an electrician and his family. My sister Betsie became friends with one of the daughters.

After a while, we discovered that my sister's new friend, though she was the daughter of an electrician, did not know what a toggle switch was. We gave her the nickname "Toggles."

A toggle switch is a type of electrical switch that was commonly used in homes to control ceiling lights. Many of us do not know how a toggle switch works or any other type of switch for that matter. Additionally, most of us don't have anymore than a very basic understanding of automobile engines, air conditioners, and computers. However, we do not have to understand *how* those things *work* in order to *enjoy* their benefits; we know that they work, and so we confidently use them.

Faith is like that in a way. We cannot possibly comprehend the grand scope of such a deep matter as faith; nevertheless, that does not prevent us from trusting God. But how does that faith affect everyday life? To answer that question, we must consider a contrast between faith in ourselves and faith in God. On one side, Adam's disobedience implied that God wasn't being truthful and that Adam would have to watch out for himself. That was a slap in the Creator's face and an affront to His character. In contrast, faith in God is an expression of confidence in God's faithfulness; by it, a person rejects Adam's conclusion and declares that God is truthful after all.

As with toggle switches, cars, and electronic gadgets, we do not need to know every intricate detail of how faith works, but what we absolutely *must* know is that God is worthy of our trust and that "He is a rewarder of them that diligently seek Him." Even as the Scriptures say of

Abraham, he "believed God, and it [faith] was counted unto him for righteousness." (Romans 4:3)

15
Full or Empty

Ephesians 5:17-18 "Wherefore be ye not unwise, but understanding what the will of the Lord is. And be not drunk with wine, wherein is excess; but be filled with the Spirit;"

There is an old saying, "As a moth is drawn to a flame, even so...." It is used to compare the moth's irresistible attraction to light—even the light of a dangerous flame—to a person who gravitates toward poor choices that might well ruin him or her.

Pride is like a flame in that sense. Humans are easily drawn to believe we are better than others are and that we deserve more money, prestige, power, or stuff than someone else does. Someone who lets pride become a driving force in his life is said to be "full of himself." Today's verse says we should be filled with the Holy Spirit; however, we cannot be filled with the Spirit while we are filled with ourselves, our desires, and our ambitions, which Paul says is not wise.

Today's verses create an interesting contrast; they compare being drunk with being filled with the Spirit. What happens when you are under the influence of wine? You **behave** as if you are under the influence of wine, with delayed reactions, poor judgment, etc. What happens when you are under the influence of the Holy Spirit? You **behave** as if you are under the influence of the Spirit, exhibiting love, joy, peace, longsuffering, kindness, goodness, faithfulness, gentleness, self-control, etc. (Galatians 5:22-23)

When we are full of ourselves, we exhibit self-centered behavior; when we are full of the Spirit, we honor God by doing as Christ taught us in Matthew 5:16: "Let your light so shine before men, that they may see your good works, and glorify your Father which is in heaven."

I can be full of myself but empty of God, or I can be empty of myself and full of the Spirit of Christ. I cannot be both; that option is not available.

"Choose you this day whom ye will serve." (Joshua 24:15)

16

Ladies and Gentlemen

Philippians 2:2-4 "Fulfil ye my joy, that ye be likeminded, having the same love, being of one accord, of one mind. Let nothing be done through strife or vainglory; but in lowliness of mind let each esteem other better than themselves. Look not every man on his own things, but every man also on the things of others."

My wife and I were watching a TV comedy awhile back. One of the women on the program was rather promiscuous, and one of the men was snobbish and judgmental. When the woman was invited to a British gala, her friend suggested she might meet a nobleman, and said, "Some lord may make you a lady." The man quietly quipped, "It would actually take the real Lord to make *her* a lady."

The fall of this world—and all the sin and death that has resulted—is a terrible thing. However, the problems are compounded when we think, "*That* person *really* needs God, but me? Not *that* much. I'm not *that* bad."

We mortals like to put on airs. Our competitive pride, our sense of self-importance cause us to see ourselves as better than others. That is what causes us to be rude or demand priority treatment ahead of others. Sometimes emergencies and special circumstances *do* require special priorities, but to wake up every day thinking we are better or more important than others is just selfish sin.

Lest you think I am singling you out, I am not. *All* of us are subject to the arrogance the man in that comedy displayed, just as we are all subject to temptation like the woman.

In the passage that follows today's verses, Paul describes Christ's willing submission to death on the cross to redeem us from our sins. He tells us to let that same attitude control us too, for the glory of God and the good of people, including ourselves.

The only way any of us can have right standing with God in the first place is by believing what He says and trusting in His grace through Christ. In like manner, the only way we can overcome our selfish tendencies is by believing what He says and yielding to the Holy Spirit's leading so that we follow Christ in His gracious humility.

17

Christian Believers

Acts 11:25-26 "Then departed Barnabas to Tarsus, for to seek Saul: And when he had found him, he brought him unto Antioch. And it came to pass, that a whole year they assembled themselves with the church, and taught much people. And the disciples were called Christians first in Antioch."

I find it very interesting that the word Christian only appears three times in the whole Bible. It is plural in today's verse and singular in Acts 26:28 and 1 Peter 4:16. Other terms used more often are saint, follower, believer, etc.

Max Harold Powers, my late father, was a humble, gracious giant of a man. Six feet and 2 inches tall in his prime, he stood out in almost any crowd. Whenever my dad spoke of those who trust in the Lord, he called them "Christian believers." I don't remember asking him about the term, but I suspect he started using it when it became clear to him that the word Christian was becoming less meaningful. People started associating it with being born in a Western nation. It was as if they might say, "Of course I am a Christian; I was born in America. I'm not a heathen, you know."

Yet, being born in a country that might be considered civilized doesn't make anyone a Christian. As someone said, "Going to church doesn't make you Christian any more than going into a garage makes you an automobile." The same goes for the other things we might associate with being a Christian or even just being a "good" person.

At this point, I anticipate someone asking, "Okay then, if being born in a 'Christian nation' or going to church, etc. does not make me a Christian, then what do I have to do?" Jesus answered that very question when people asked Him what they should do to please God. "Then said they unto him, What shall we do, that we might work the works of God? Jesus answered and said unto them, This is the work of God, that ye believe on him whom he hath sent." (John 6:28-29)

In other words, the only way to become a Christian is to abandon all hope of anything other than Christ. As He said in another place, "I am the way, the truth, and the life: no man [no person] cometh unto the Father, but by me." (John 14:6)

18

The Things They Did

1 Corinthians 13:11-13 "When I was a child, I spake as a child, I understood as a child, I thought as a child: but when I became a man, I put away childish things. For now we see through a glass, darkly; but then face to face: now I know in part; but then shall I know even as also I am known. And now abideth faith, hope, charity, these three; but the greatest of these is charity."

The word translated "charity" in this passage is the Greek word "agape" (uh-gop'-a). which is also translated "love" in many other verses.

Have you ever read a passage in Scripture over the years and then one day, as you read it again, you see something new—something fresh that you never saw before? That happened to me yesterday. I was reading in 1 Thessalonians 1:2-3 which says: "We give thanks to God always for you all, making mention of you in our prayers; Remembering without ceasing your work of faith, and labour of love, and patience of hope in our Lord Jesus Christ, in the sight of God and our Father."

One thing that struck me was the three things Paul recalled about the believers at Thessalonica: their work of faith, their labor of love, and their patience of hope. That is, they made their efforts because they had confidence it was what God wanted them to do; they made those efforts not grudgingly, but lovingly; and they were patient during their efforts because they had a sure hope in Christ.

A second thing struck me as I was writing this Musing. Those are the same three things Paul mentioned to the Corinthian church when he was teaching them about faith, hope, and charity (love). (1 Corinthians 13:13)

Paul's words are a good reminder to us also. We should do what God has gifted, enabled and directed us to do; we should do so lovingly; and we should rest in the solid hope we have in the Lord Jesus "who gave himself for us, that he might redeem us from all iniquity, and purify unto himself a peculiar people, zealous of good works." (Titus 2:14)

19
Mine, All Mine

Titus 2:11-15 "For the grace of God that bringeth salvation hath appeared to all men, Teaching us that, denying ungodliness and worldly lusts, we should live soberly, righteously, and godly, in this present world; Looking for that blessed hope, and the glorious appearing of the great God and our Saviour Jesus Christ; Who gave himself for us, that he might redeem us from all iniquity, and purify unto himself a peculiar people, zealous of good works. These things speak, and exhort, and rebuke with all authority. Let no man despise thee."

Yesterday, we looked at faith, hope and love and their relationship to our works and actions. We closed that Musing with a citation from today's verses, "Who (Christ) gave himself for us, that he might redeem us from all iniquity, and purify unto himself a peculiar people, zealous of good works." (Titus 2:14) Paul was instructing his young student Titus in the purposes of God in redeeming people to Himself.

In this verse, we see a word that seems to be out of place. God is refining what He calls "a peculiar people." To the twenty-first-century mind, the word peculiar means odd or strange—something that might cause a sideways glance from a suspicious observer. Now, in all honesty, those adjectives fit to some extent, in that non-Christians often see Christian believers as odd, strange, or suspicious. They particularly view us that way the more Christ-like we become. That may sound odd in itself, but remember, Jesus was *completely* Christ-like, and they crucified Him. The world thinking of us as misfits may be somewhat disconcerting to us, but the Lord Jesus Himself said, "If the world hate you, ye know that it hated me before it hated you." (John 15:18)

However, as harsh as is the world's reaction to us "peculiar people", the word translated "peculiar" has a much more precious meaning. According to *Strong's Concordance*, the word is periousios (per-ee-OO-see-os) and means "that which is one's own, belonging to one's possessions." I find it endearing that the things that cause the world to look askance at us are the very things God is doing in us to refine us as His personal possession. We are His, all His; and He is ours!

God is good! May His people always rejoice in His goodness, and praise Him for it.

20

Jehovah Rapha

Exodus 15:26 "If thou wilt diligently hearken to the voice of the LORD thy God, and wilt do that which is right in his sight, and wilt give ear to his commandments, and keep all his statutes, I will put none of these diseases upon thee, which I have brought upon the Egyptians: for I am the LORD that healeth thee."

I was in my early 60s before I began to use regular maintenance prescriptions. Ever since then, I have come upon an illness here, and another there, and my doctors have been able to help me, sometimes with therapy, other times with a pill or a shot.

I love my fellow believers who think we must depend only on God for our healing. Indeed, "Jehovah Rapha" means "the LORD that healeth thee." That is what God calls Himself in today's verse. I *do* trust in God for my provisions, including my health and life. However, I believe God *also* uses physicians like Doctor Luke who wrote the gospel bearing his name in the same way that He uses police, firefighters, and others to protect us from various dangers and harms.

Having said that, I have a confession to make: I am fairly diligent in following doctors' instructions, but if I trust mortal doctors and others to provide advice, counsel, and protection, why do I not *completely* trust God to do *all* that HE says He will do?

Sometimes our faith is strong, and sometimes, in the words of songwriter Rich Mullins, "We are not as strong as we think we are." May we all learn more of the wisdom, power, and grace of the King, May we all trust Him and rejoice in our life eternal, which comes from Him, the only true God, and Jesus Christ, whom He has sent. (John 17:3)

21

Worthy is the Lamb

My mentor, Wayne Schlichter, writes a weekly devotional. With his permission, today I share one of his posts:

~~~~~

July

Revelation 4:11 "Thou art worthy O Lord, to receive glory and honor and power: for Thou hast created all things, and for Thy pleasure they are, and were created".

Some years ago, Hollywood produced a movie starring Tom Hanks entitled **Forrest Gump**. One of the lines in the movie was "Stupid is as stupid does." Forrest was a rather simple man who was quoting a saying of his mother. The point being, the action of a person revealed their character or perhaps their lack of character. What a person does often reveals what a person is. The Bible is a more accurate gauge of what a person is. The Bible is "inerrant" in all it reveals.

That same Bible reveals that Jesus is worthy! In Revelation chapters four and five, The Lord is twice said to be worthy and sung to be worthy twice by those around the throne. There are other occasions where He is revealed as worthy. In contrast, we are told there was none worthy to open the judgment seals, except Christ. A search was made of all mankind and none was found worthy. (Revelation 5:4)

We may ask, "Why was it so important that one should be worthy?" It is because all the rest had sinned in life; there had to be someone sinless who could open the books from which the final judgments would come. You and I would never be worthy in our own selves to pass judgment upon the world. One must be perfectly righteous to pass that judgment. Any righteousness that we have is imputed righteousness. It is Christ's righteousness imputed to us. (Romans 4:5-6 & 22) His righteousness in us makes us acceptable in the eyes of God. His sacrifice at Calvary cleanses the repentant believer from all sin—past, present, and future. That is the only basis for our forgiveness and acceptance to God.

The Son of God came to Earth as the Son of man. He is the eternal Son of God, coming to be the son of man, born of a virgin. Therefore He did not inherit the nature of sin in His human flesh, as the sin nature is inherited through the man, Adam. (Romans 5:12) Satan tempted Eve, but Eve crushes the Serpent's head by her seed, the Lord Jesus Christ.

"And I will put enmity between thee (Satan the Serpent) and the woman, and between thy seed and her seed (Christ); it (the enmity) shall bruise thy head, and thou shalt bruise his heel" (Genesis 3:15).

Christ crushed the head of Satan; in that act, His "heel was bruised". In other words, Christ was "bruised for our iniquity" when He crushed the power of Satan. His wounds at the cross were not eternally fatal. He conquered death and the grave. Worthy is as worthy does.

Hallelujah!

22

I'm Not the Man I Used to Be

Mark 10:46-52 "And they came to Jericho: and as he went out of Jericho with his disciples and a great number of people, blind Bartimaeus, the son of Timaeus, sat by the highway side begging. And when he heard that it was Jesus of Nazareth, he began to cry out, and say, Jesus, thou son of David, have mercy on me. And many charged him that he should hold his peace: but he cried the more a great deal, Thou son of David, have mercy on me. And Jesus stood still, and commanded him to be called. And they call the blind man, saying unto him, Be of good comfort, rise; he calleth thee. And he, casting away his garment, rose, and came to Jesus. And Jesus answered and said unto him, What wilt thou that I should do unto thee? The blind man said unto him, Lord, that I might receive my sight. And Jesus said unto him, Go thy way; thy faith hath made thee whole. And immediately he received his sight, and followed Jesus in the way."

Bartimaeus (bart-uh-MAY-us) was blind. What do you think went through his mind when he began seeing colors, motions, things that caused the sounds he had known for years, and the faces of people he had only heard? Imagine the wonder of that moment and the moments that followed.

That experience changed Bartimaeus forever. Jesus told him, "Go thy way," but as soon as he received his sight, he "followed Jesus in the way." While he was still blind, his "way" was sitting by the roadside, begging. Not anymore! His new way was to follow the Master.

Have you had a Bartimaeus moment, one when you realized what God has done for you? Did it change you? I'm not asking if you're perfect (none of us are), but I'm asking if you are following the Master. The blind man left behind his garment—probably little more than rags and tatters— and came to Jesus. Giving up the old life is easier when you understand it was worthless compared to where you are headed.

Was Bartimaeus among the disciples present when Jesus passed through the walls into the upper room? I don't know, but if he was there, it sure was a special bonus for simply following someone who had done so much already.

23

Passports and Visas

Romans 5:19 "For as by one man's disobedience many were made sinners, so by the obedience of one shall many be made righteous."

A while ago, my wife and I went on a cruise. Since we were leaving the U.S. and visiting other countries, we needed passports. Often, countries require a visa to enter, especially for extended stays; visas are not required to briefly visit some foreign tourist areas.

A passport is a small booklet with a photograph and other personal information that proves you are who you claim to be. The visa is a stamp or some other marking in your passport placed there by a representative of the country you want to visit, showing that you have permission to enter their country.

I would like to use the passport and visa as illustrations of something else. The passport typifies you. God sees you, and He knows who you are. As amazing as it may seem, God knows every human being—past, present, and future. In some sense, you yourself are your passport; God doesn't need a booklet to know that you are you.

But what about the visa? For the purposes of today's discussion, the visa represents God's approval for you to enter His country, a place we know as Heaven. Regardless of your "passport" (you being truly you), without a visa, you cannot enter His Kingdom. The passport is worthless without the visa, the stamp of approval.

You might wonder who assigns that personal visa? And how? The answers to those two questions are both simple and vastly complex, and at the same time, free and exorbitantly expensive. The **complex** and **expensive** part is that God's permission to enter Heaven took an amazing plan whereby Jesus Christ would pay the staggering penalty for our sin by His own death on the cross. The **simple** and **free** part is that God freely offers us the forgiveness of sins, a right standing with Himself, and His stamp of approval guaranteeing our right to enter His country when our time in this world is done.

Dear friend, do not be satisfied with your "personal passport" alone; it is only valid if it has God's visa, His stamp of approval that your sins are forgiven by the sacrifice of Christ. Ask for that heavenly visa—God's forgiveness—today! Only then are you ready to enter God's country.

24

Rescued Milk

Colossians 1:12-13 "Giving thanks unto the Father, which hath made us meet to be partakers of the inheritance of the saints in light: Who hath delivered us from the power of darkness, and hath translated us into the kingdom of his dear Son:"

The other day, upon returning home from the store, I dropped a one-gallon jug of milk while getting it out of the car. It seemed to be all right, so I picked it up and carried it into the house. When I set it on the counter, I noticed a small puddle begin to form around the base of the container. The fall to the ground had created a very small crack. Thankfully, we had just finished with a one-gallon jug of distilled water, so I was able to rescue most of the white liquid.

Word pictures are never fully adequate to represent profound truth, but in some way—some gloriously wonderful way—God has done the same for us as I was able to do with that milk. That old container was damaged and incapable of holding milk. In a similar way, we were broken by sin and thus were unable to hold anything spiritually good. As little as we like to acknowledge that reality, we were bankrupt in our spiritual being; we were dead in trespasses and sins. (Ephesians 2:1)

Furthermore, even the law—God's good and perfect law—was not able to fix our problem. It could point out that the problem was there, but it could not fix it.

What then was the solution? What was God to do? Like in the simple and imperfect picture of my pouring the milk from a broken container to a good one, God rescued us by taking us out of the kingdom of darkness and putting us into the Kingdom of His dear Son. By sheer grace, solely through Christ's work of redemption, God took us out of an impossible, unfixable, fatal disaster, and moved us into a realm of light, loving kindness, and eternal life.

> I stand amazed in the presence
> Of Jesus the Nazarene,
> And wonder how He could love me,
> A sinner, condemned, unclean.
>
> How marvelous! How wonderful!
> And my song shall ever be:

How marvelous! How wonderful!
Is my Savior's love for me!
~ Charles H. Gabriel

Thank Him with all your heart. He is worthy!

25

Being Wiser than the Wise

Psalm 119:97 "O how love I thy law! it is my meditation all the day. 98 Thou through thy commandments hast made me wiser than mine enemies: for they are ever with me. 99 I have more understanding than all my teachers: for thy testimonies are my meditation. 100 I understand more than the ancients, because I keep thy precepts."

Although there are a number of things we can learn from today's verses, I want to concentrate on two in particular. First, notice the progression the psalmist unfolds:

- I love God's law. (v97)
- That makes me wiser than my enemies. (v98)
- That makes me wiser than my teachers. (v99)
- That even makes me wiser than the wisest people in the past. (v100)

Now, it is important that we distinguish between arrogant bragging and stating the facts as they are. The psalmist sounds like he is a narcissistic braggart, but is he? I suggest that he is not, and my reason for that conclusion is the second thing that I noticed about these verses:

Just as the writer does in all but four verses of this entire Psalm, in today's passage he mentions God's words of instruction.

- Law (v97)
- Commandments (v98)
- Testimonies (v99)
- Precepts (v100)

The reason I don't think of the psalmist's attitude as conceited is that in each statement, the psalmist ties his wisdom to his relationship to God's Word.

- Thy law is my meditation. (v97)
- Through thy commandments (v98)

- Thy testimonies are my meditation. (v99)
- Because I keep thy precepts (v100)

Please understand me here. The writer is not saying that we can live independent of ancient wisdom and godly teachers. If we were to do that, we would open ourselves to pride and expose ourselves to danger. However, what the psalmist *is* saying is that there is no one wiser than the person who learns, meditates on, and obeys the laws, commands, testimonies, and precepts of God.

> Leaning on the Living God,
> Trusting in His written way,
> Makes me wise in all I do,
> In all I think and say.
> ~ W.F. Powers

26

Failure and Success

Joshua 1:8 "This book of the law shall not depart out of thy mouth; but thou shalt meditate therein day and night, that thou mayest observe to do according to all that is written therein: for then thou shalt make thy way prosperous, and then thou shalt have good success."

Joshua was a faithful assistant to Moses for a number of years. When Moses died, the Lord appointed Joshua to take Moses' place and lead the people into the Promised Land.

Today's verse is part of God's personal instruction to Joshua. In it, the Lord tells the new leader to follow the commands He gave to Moses, words that Moses had written down—"this book of the law." If Joshua did that, the Lord promised he would prosper and have "good success."

The human definition of failure was summarized in a Chinese fortune cookie I got the other day: "There is but one cause of human failure. And that is man's lack of faith in his true self." Now, it is true that we should diligently apply our talents and skills to our daily activities, but God's remedy for failure is *not* placing our faith in ourselves, but in Him and His words.

The 21st-century, Western mind tends to think about "prosper" and "success" as houses, cars, and bank accounts; however, the words God used convey deeper meanings.

The word translated "prosper" means to advance—to become profitable. At first, that seems to fit with our idea of prosper and success; however, by using that word together with the word translated "success" God refines His intended meaning.

Based on the word God used, success is "to be prudent, be circumspect, wisely understand, prosper." Success by God's standard is to live a life of wisdom and understanding. In other words, "success" is behaving as God tells us to in His Word, for when we do that, we begin to act like Him. Since we were made in His image for the purpose of reflecting His Glory, we are *most* successful when we do exactly that.

To encourage Joshua on this path, God gave him a promise. The Lord later gave that promise to us also, "I will not fail thee, nor forsake thee." (Joshua 1:5, Hebrews 13:5)

Trust in His Word, and follow His ways, "for then thou shalt make thy way prosperous, and then thou shalt have good success."

27

The Flaming Tongue

James 3:3-6 "Behold, we put bits in the horses' mouths, that they may obey us; and we turn about their whole body. Behold also the ships, which though they be so great, and are driven of fierce winds, yet are they turned about with a very small helm, whithersoever the governor listeth. Even so the tongue is a little member, and boasteth great things. Behold, how great a matter a little fire kindleth! And the tongue is a fire, a world of iniquity: so is the tongue among our members, that it defileth the whole body, and setteth on fire the course of nature; and it is set on fire of hell."

The Bible is a message from God to be read carefully, absorbed prayerfully, and obeyed willingly. In today's verses, James starts with two simple word pictures. Horses, both big and small, have one thing in common: a trainer can use a small bit and bridle to control it. Similarly, any ship regardless of size can be steered by a comparatively small rudder.

James applies those two illustrations to the tongue. That little muscle only weighs 60-70 grams—about 2-3 ounces—and yet it can start the verbal equivalent of a raging forest fire. The word translated "world" in verse 6 is the Greek word from which we get our English word, cosmos; it was used to describe the vast universe. The tongue is an inconceivably destructive force of iniquity. Like a wild animal or an uncontrolled ship, it has almost limitless power to destroy. Additionally, I take the phrase "it is set on fire of hell" to mean that the wicked one and his followers are always looking for a tongue they can use to gossip, slander, harm, or destroy someone.

However, there is a boomerang effect; though the purpose of the speaker is to make a public spectacle of someone else, it also displays a clear image of what the speaker is really like inside. Radio Bible teacher Chuck Swindoll said, "We need to think of our tongue as a messenger that runs errands for our heart. Our words reveal our character."

Someone once said that just because something enters the mind doesn't mean it should exit the mouth. Let us remember, God tells us what to do **and** how to do it. "Speak the truth in love." (Ephesians 4:15)

28

All Is Right, Except What Isn't

Genesis 3:4-6 "And the serpent said unto the woman, Ye shall not surely die: For God doth know that in the day ye eat thereof, then your eyes shall be opened, and ye shall be as gods, knowing good and evil. And when the woman saw that the tree was good for food, and that it was pleasant to the eyes, and a tree to be desired to make one wise, she took of the fruit thereof, and did eat, and gave also unto her husband with her; and he did eat."

In the mid 1800s, Poet Robert Browning wrote a brief work titled "Pippa's Song":

> The year's at the spring,
> And day's at the morn;
> Morning's at seven;
> The hill-side's dew-pearl'd;
> The lark's on the wing;
> The snail's on the thorn;
> God's in His heaven—
> All's right with the world!

Mr. Browning was right, but he was also wrong. When he said, "All's right with the world," he was wrong because of all the evils we see in this world: murder and violence, stealing and corruption, bullying and intimidation, cheating and vengeance. All this has come about by the rebellion of our first parents. Sadly, all this did not stop with them, for it has been the practice of fallen man ever since.

However, when Browning said, "All's right with the world," he was also right in all the ways we see in the Scriptures. Mr. Browning's prose give us a vision of an orderly flow: the year, the day, the morning, the hillside, the lark and the snail are all behaving as they should. In a very real sense, there is a calm assurance in knowing that the true and living, sovereign God is in Heaven, and in spite of the terrible ravages that sin has visited upon His creation, God is still God; He is still sovereign; and He is still in control.

There is a place for human reason, but if we rely only on our own senses, we will find that some place down the road, there is no more road. When we come to the end of ourselves, God is there. In the midst of our confusion and turmoil, He is there with His wisdom and peace. In the sense in which I can trust God in all things, "God's in His heaven, All's right with the world!"

29

Something Faith Does Not Do

Philippians 2:5-8 "Let this mind be in you, which was also in Christ Jesus: Who, being in the form of God, thought it not robbery to be equal with God: But made himself of no reputation, and took upon him the form of a servant, and was made in the likeness of men: And being found in fashion as a man, he humbled himself, and became obedient unto death, even the death of the cross."

Notice that today's passage is a command, not a suggestion. It is telling us to observe Christ's humble obedience and embrace that attitude as our own. Kent Brantly is a doctor who did that very thing. He and others went to Liberia to help with an Ebola epidemic. In 2014, Dr. Brantly contracted Ebola himself, but thankfully, later recovered. I recently saw a quote from him: "Faith is not something that makes you safe."

Our 21st century Western culture often thinks of our faith as an impenetrable shield that makes us immune to the woes of this fallen world. Contrariwise, in the Scriptures, we see believers being persecuted and killed for their faith, and tradition tells us that all the apostles except John died a martyr's death.

Steven Curtis Chapman captured some of that zeal in his song:

> Nobody stood and applauded them,
> So they knew from the start this road
> would not lead to fame.
> All they really knew for sure
> was Jesus had called to them;

He said, "Come follow Me," and they came.
With reckless abandon, they came.

Empty nets lying there
at the water's edge,
Told a story that few could believe
and none could explain,
How some crazy fishermen
agreed to go where Jesus lead
With no thought to what they would gain
For Jesus had called them by name,

And they answered...
We will abandon it all for the sake of the call,
No other reason at all but the sake of the call;
Wholly devoted to live and to die
for the sake of the call.

This command was not exclusively for first-century Christians; it is for us as well. Do we all have to go to some foreign country and die as martyrs? Not necessarily, but *all* of us *are* to embrace that mindset so that regardless of where God places us, we are willing to do what He commands, regardless of the cost.

30

Seen and Unseen

1 Corinthians 12: 22-23 "Nay, much more those members of the body, which seem to be more feeble, are necessary: And those members of the body, which we think to be less honourable, upon these we bestow more abundant honour; and our uncomely parts have more abundant comeliness."

When we hear the phrase "seen and unseen," we often think of the physical world, which we see with our eyes, and the spiritual world, which we only see by faith. That is a legitimate use of those terms, but today's verses speak of a different kind of seen and unseen.

The church at Corinth was quite worldly; Paul had to lecture them on several things. One of the problems was their craving to be noticed—to be in the spotlight. They wanted to have the flashiest spiritual gifts that got everyone's attention so others would know how "spiritual" they were.

What they did not understand was that spiritual maturity is not demonstrated by which gift someone has, it is shown by faithfully exercising the gift that God in His wisdom gave them.

In previous verses, Paul asked them which body parts were important; he then listed hands, feet, eyes, ears, and smelling (nose). Just because their purposes are different doesn't mean one is better; the whole body suffers if *any* of its parts cannot or will not do its task. The same in the church: if I faithfully exercise my gift well, no matter how "small or insignificant" it is, the church will be better off for it. We don't need a "big" and "noticeable" gift, we need to do what the wise Creator has designed and gifted us to do.

One online video I like shows a group of high school or college students as they masterfully perform Maurice Ravel's classical composition, "Bolero." Afterward the conductor had a few individuals stand for applause, which is appropriate. However, that handful of young people who stood could not have created that majestic music by themselves, it took *all* the instrumentalists working together under the conductor's leadership to create that wonderful recording.

Do you feel your part in church life is "small and insignificant?" Don't look at the size or perceived importance of your gift. Instead, look at your Creator who gave you that gift and serve Him joyfully. (1 Thessalonians 2:4) If He gave you a spiritual gift, it is important.

31
Some, but Not All

Psalm 21:1-2 "The king shall joy in thy strength, O LORD; and in thy salvation how greatly shall he rejoice! Thou hast given him his heart's desire, and hast not withholden the request of his lips. Selah."

David, king of Israel, wrote these verses. David was a sinner. Why would God be kind to him and grant the requests of a sinner?

Those of you who read these Musings regularly know that God's peaceable kindness to David—or anyone else for that matter—is only by His grace through the completed work of Christ on the cross. For David, that work was yet future, and for us it is past, but for God it is all present before Him. He applies His grace to believers before the cross as easily as He does to us who live after the cross.

However, there are other people mentioned in Psalm 21—namely, there are sinners to whom God will *not* apply grace. Beginning in verse 8,

Musings

David mentions the enemies of God and describes what He will do to them instead of offering grace.

I was taught to read Scripture in the light of several questions, one of which is, "What does this passage tell me about God?" To answer that question, consider the following:

The true and living God, who created the heavens and the Earth, is majestic in His holiness and limitless in His power. We as mortals are, by nature, in rebellion against Him. Every sin we commit is an act of treasonous insurrection. Nevertheless, the Almighty God, in an act of inconceivable mercy, is gracious to those who stop fighting against Him and surrender. However, His anger is kindled against those who refuse to do so. (Psalm 7:11)

Which side are you on? Are you like David who bowed before God, acknowledging his sin and rebellion, (Psalm 51) or do you insist that you are good enough as you are?

Be very careful, my friend. You can safely come to God just as you are, but He will not accept you on your own terms. His mercy is to those who come to Him for forgiveness based only on the gospel of Christ. The truth is we have nothing to offer Him except surrender and faith.

AUGUST

1

Love and Hailstones

John 15:11-13 "These things have I spoken unto you, that my joy might remain in you, and that your joy might be full. This is my commandment, That ye love one another, as I have loved you. Greater love hath no man than this, that a man lay down his life for his friends."

Have you ever heard of Fiona Simpson? She lives in Kingaroy about 100 miles from Brisbane, Australia. One day she was driving with her baby in a car seat in the back when she encountered what others described as a "brutal supercell hailstorm." Suddenly two of the car windows were broken out and large hailstones began striking the little one. Fiona scrambled into the back seat and lay over baby Clara, shielding the infant with her own body.

For her heroism, Fiona was rewarded with a body full of cuts and deep bruising, including welts approaching the size of a tennis ball. In an interview, this loving woman said, "I'm just a mum…You do anything you can to protect your child, no matter what, even at your own expense, and I would do it again."

Wouldn't it be wonderful to have someone who loved you like that? Well, the precious truth is that Jesus not only told His disciples, "Greater love hath no man than this, that a man lay down his life for his friends," but He willingly did that Himself. "God commendeth his love toward us, in that, while we were yet sinners, Christ died for us." (Romans 5:8)

Fallen human beings have a tragic tendency to become numb and unfeeling to what we see or hear repeatedly. As inconceivable as it is, one of those things is the story of the God-man willingly surrendering to a painful, humiliating death in order to redeem people to Himself.

May we all be increasingly aware of—and thankful for—Christ's tender mercies and loving kindness, since "Hereby perceive we the love of God, because he laid down his life for us." (1 John 3:16a)

2

All but Forgotten

Psalm 16:5-6: "The LORD is the portion of mine inheritance and of my cup: thou maintainest my lot. The lines are fallen unto me in pleasant places; yea, I have a goodly heritage."

Some years ago, I had the most painful experience of my life. It was so painful that as I was going through it, I remember thinking that I would gladly go through *all* of my *other* painful experiences a second time rather than endure that new one.

A very good friend went through the same thing several years before I did and told me he has finally gotten to where there is no pain and the experience is so distant in his memory that it seemed as if it happened to someone else. Over time, I have found the same to be true. What once seemed like being run over by a fast moving truck—every day—has become a sad, but mostly distant, awareness.

As I write this, I am reminded of another verse: "Yea, though I walk through the valley of the shadow of death, I will fear no evil: for thou art with me; thy rod and thy staff they comfort me." (Psalm 23:4)

Regardless of my circumstances—no matter what difficulties God allows me to endure—I know I can trust God, because "the lines are fallen unto me in pleasant places," and in the end, "I will dwell in the house of the LORD forever." (Psalm 23:6)

"It is of the Lord's mercies that we are not consumed, because his compassions fail not. They are new every morning: great is Thy faithfulness." (Lamentations 3:22-23)

> Great is Thy faithfulness, O God my Father,
> There is no shadow of turning with Thee;
> Thou changest not, Thy compassions, they fail not
> As Thou hast been Thou forever wilt be.
>
> Great is Thy faithfulness! Great is Thy faithfulness!
> Morning by morning new mercies I see;
> All I have needed Thy hand hath provided—
> Great is Thy faithfulness, Lord, unto me!

3

Big Lessons in a Small Package

Proverbs 6:6-8 "Go to the ant, thou sluggard; consider her ways, and be wise: Which having no guide, overseer, or ruler, Provideth her meat in the summer, and gathereth her food in the harvest."

Today's verses tell us to learn industriousness from the ant. The passage goes on to say that if we don't learn that lesson—if we don't provide for ourselves and store up a little to carry us through lean times—we will end up in poverty.

Now, lest we misunderstand the passage, other Scriptures warn us not to be totally self-sufficient. We must recognize that even our ability to supply for ourselves comes from God, so our root-level confidence must be in Him. Another misapplication is if we assume that we are to hoard everything for ourselves and our immediate family and not share with others what God has given to us. We must guard against both of those mistakes.

However, by observation, I have learned two other lessons about the ant. One is its lack of awareness of much that is going on about him. I was outside an hour ago and observed several ants going about their business, seemingly unaware of my presence just a few feet away. The second point is his fear of man when he *does* sense our presence. When one is crawling on my workbench and I move something nearby, it scurries off as if I meant it harm, which I didn't.

Those two personal observations remind me of many people in their relationship to God. Many people are completely unaware of God's presence, and if they ever think about Him at all, they are sure He only wants to hurt them or make their lives miserable. How sad that they have such a pitiable, distorted view of God because "If God be for us, who can be against us? He that spared not his own Son, but delivered him up for us all, how shall he not with him also freely give us all things?" (Romans 8:31-32) "All things" there doesn't mean everything we want; good parents protect their child from things that would harm them.

So, along with industriousness, I suggest that we learn from the ants to be continually aware of God's presence and not to see Him as a cosmic killjoy but rather as an all-wise Provider who loves us.

4

Knights in Dented Armor

2 Corinthians 12:9 "And he said unto me, My grace is sufficient for thee: for my strength is made perfect in weakness. Most gladly therefore will I rather glory in my infirmities, that the power of Christ may rest upon me."

I usually limit these Musings to about 400 words or less, making them a 1 or 2-minute read. However, today's thoughts come from an article I wrote during a very broken time in my life. It is a little longer, but I thought it might be an encouragement:

> In days of yore
> When knights were bold,
> And ladies fair,
> And drag'n tales told …

Medieval days certainly brought us romantic images of life: fire-breathing dragons, damsels in distress, and men with nerves of steel to match their suits of armor. Now we have newer icons of excellence: Olympic athletes, Superman, and Wonder Woman to name a few. Somewhere in between the knights and Superman, we had George Washington, Molly Pitcher, Davy Crockett, Paul Bunyan, and others. In all these people, fictional or real, we find bigger-than-life characters who grab our attention and challenge us to be more and do more than we thought we could.

But what about the Olympian who stumbles? What about the hero who has shortcomings? What about the armor-wearing knight when some of the shiny perfections have given way to dents and rust?

If you were to ask those who seem to you to be almost "flawless," most would admit to times they wish they could return to some of the choices in their lives for a chance to do things over. Two of my heroes are my mom and dad. While they did not spend a lot of time regretting the past, several times they expressed disappointment in not having been better parents. (Just so you know, I couldn't imagine better parents.)

Sometimes, the dents and rust we imagine are just lies that others have said about us. Perhaps they misunderstood us, or maybe they were just being unkind or vicious. However, sometimes the blemishes are actual flaws we have: choices we make, things we do, or words we speak in anger. Those dents often cause our hearts to cringe.

However, we often overlook another angle—the angle from which God sees things. Oh, He sees the dents; He sees the rust; He sees the imperfections. None of the mistakes we make—accidental, careless, or otherwise—catch God by surprise or escape His notice. None of the things others say affect His thoughts about us. In fact, God tells us in today's verse, "My strength is made perfect in weakness." God is glorified when He uses broken people because then we know we cannot boast about the results. If I am always able to make the best choice and take the right path, I might just do things on my own and not trust in God for my strength and direction. However, when I yield to the Lord and follow His instructions, I am more likely to give God credit for the outcome because dented knights are less likely to boast than shiny ones. And though He graciously shares His love and mercy, He says He won't share His glory. (Isaiah. 42:8)

Now some might say, "Then I can do whatever I want because God is in control, and He can straighten out any mess I make." The Lord cautions us not to make that brash mistake. (Psalm 19:13, Romans 6: 1-4) Nevertheless, we need to understand that though the dents and rust are not good and sometimes there are things of which we should be humbly ashamed and repentant, they are not the end. The Lord knew about the dents before Calvary, and He still laid down His life for us. Rather than being discouraged or careless with our lives, we should yield to His goodness that leads us to repentance. (Romans 2:4) His grace should challenge us to higher levels of loving devotion and cause us to bow humbly before the One who loved us and gave Himself for us.

May we never stop trusting His forgiveness of our sins, and may we never stop praising Him for who He is and what He has done for us.

5

Salesmen and Representatives

2 Corinthians 5:17-21 "Therefore if any man be in Christ, he is a new creature: old things are passed away; behold, all things are become new. And all things are of God, who hath reconciled us to himself by Jesus Christ, and hath given to us the ministry of reconciliation; To wit, that God was in Christ, reconciling the world unto himself, not imputing their trespasses unto them; and hath committed unto us the word of reconciliation. Now then we are ambassadors for Christ, as though God did beseech you by us: we pray you in Christ's stead, be ye reconciled to God. For he hath made him to be sin for us, who knew no sin; that we might be made the righteousness of God in him."

Some people think Christians are judging when we witnesses to them, and honestly, sometimes we Christians are a little offensive in our witness. A few thoughts may help everyone.

We are not salesmen "closing a deal." It is not our job—or even within our capability—to save someone; we can only work with the Holy Spirit. He must open a person's understanding to the gospel; (Acts 16:14) if He does not, all our efforts and pressure will be in vain. Don't get ahead of God; be sensitive to His leading and cooperate with Him.

Two phrases Paul uses are, "We are ambassadors for Christ, as though God did beseech you by us," and "we pray you in Christ's stead." We do not witness on our own behalf; we must plead with people on Christ's behalf the way He would if He were standing before them. Christ is in Heaven, but He has commissioned us to go on *His* behalf, inviting other mortals to come to Him as the only source of grace, mercy, and forgiveness. If the Holy Spirit is not already working in someone, pressure may create friction and resentment, but not salvation. Witness lovingly; trust the Spirit for guidance and cooperate with Him.

Another phrase is, "be ye reconciled to God." It is God's message that we convey, not our own. Sin has destroyed the communion God once had with mankind, but God offers redemption and forgiveness through Christ to all who come to Him in humility and faith.

We pray you, be reconciled to God.

6

What Do We Know?

Romans 8:26-28 "Likewise the Spirit also helpeth our infirmities: for we know not what we should pray for as we ought: but the Spirit itself maketh intercession for us with groanings which cannot be uttered. And he that searcheth the hearts knoweth what is the mind of the Spirit, because he maketh intercession for the saints according to the will of God. And we know that all things work together for good to them that love God, to them who are the called according to his purpose."

Notice the word "know" in these verses; it is translated from a Greek word meaning to see and perceive through careful insight and even has a sense of knowing by experience. Let's look particularly at what they say in verses 26 and 28.

In verse 26, the word is negated: "we *know not* what we should pray for." (emphasis mine) In moments when our hearts are heaviest, we often do not know what to say to God. In those dark times, the Holy Spirit takes the unspeakable burdens of our hearts and presents them to the Father.

The same word, without negation, is used in verse 28: we *do know* that all things work together for the good of God's people. Since God is good, we can have confidence that all will turn out well, even when we can't see what He is doing.

Finally, let's look at one other word; it is at the end of verse 28. The word translated "purpose" is a Greek word; ***Strong's Concordance*** says it means "setting forth." God is good, He only does good, and His purpose is to *set before* us a good path. As He says in Hebrews, "Wherefore seeing we also are compassed about with so great a cloud of witnesses, let us lay aside every weight, and the sin which doth so easily beset us, and let us run with patience the race that is *set before us*, Looking unto Jesus the author and finisher of our faith; who for the joy that was *set before him* endured the cross, despising the shame, and is set down at the right hand of the throne of God." (12:1-2, emphasis mine)

Jesus endured the cross that was set before Him; let us run the race that is set before us, asking God's help to do so, even when we can't understand His reasons.

7

A Fool's Paradise

Psalm 14:1 "The fool hath said in his heart, There is no God. They are corrupt, they have done abominable works, there is none that doeth good."

Psalm 53:1 "The fool hath said in his heart, There is no God. Corrupt are they, and have done abominable iniquity: there is none that doeth good."

Those of you who read these Musings regularly know that I try to choose my words carefully as I seek to convey biblical truth. If someone is upset with something I say, I want it to be because they are uncomfortable with the truth, not because they are uncomfortable with the way I said it.

The Lord forbids us from calling people fools. (Matthew 5:22, Greek: μωρός [mo-ros'] "foolish, impious, godless") I believe that is because unlike God, we cannot know someone else's heart. However, God uses that very English word in today's verses for those who deny Him. (Hebrew נבל [naw-bawl'] "foolish, senseless, fool")

Why would God call someone a fool? Is He just being provocative? I believe the answer to those questions are found in the words

213

of the late Pennsylvania evangelist R.E. Rhodes, who said, "There are many things God will tolerate in the human heart, but second place doesn't happen to be one of them." Not only has the atheist said that God is not *first* in his life, he says that God is not even *last*! God calls that person a fool.

The Cambridge English Online Dictionary says that the term "fool's paradise" means, "to be happy because you do not know or will not accept how bad a situation really is." Without God, we are in indescribable peril. No matter how much our culture tells us otherwise, our lives are not an accident, there is a God, and to deny that is to *risk everything forever*.

God has great patience and great mercy, but His great judgment awaits mortals who refuse His mercy. My friend, turning your back on your only hope is a fool's paradise.

I plead with you on Christ's behalf, literally, don't be a fool.

8

No Weapon Formed against Thee

Psalm 91:1-7 "He that dwelleth in the secret place of the most High shall abide under the shadow of the Almighty. I will say of the LORD, He is my refuge and my fortress: my God; in him will I trust. Surely he shall deliver thee from the snare of the fowler, and from the noisome pestilence. He shall cover thee with his feathers, and under his wings shalt thou trust: his truth shall be thy shield and buckler. Thou shalt not be afraid for the terror by night; nor for the arrow that flieth by day; Nor for the pestilence that walketh in darkness; nor for the destruction that wasteth at noonday. A thousand shall fall at thy side, and ten thousand at thy right hand; but it shall not come nigh thee."

Look at these promises: dwelling under the shadow of the Almighty, no harm from night terrors or flying arrows, and more. Add to these that no weapon shall prosper against us, (Isaiah 54:17) and God heals all our diseases. (Psalm 103:3)

But what about the Christians around the world who are being persecuted and slaughtered for their faith every day? What about genuine believers who become sick and die "before their time," or are murdered, or die in accidents and disasters?

Did God make promises He cannot keep, or do we just misunderstand? Friends, the problem is not in God, it is in our weak, mortal understanding. It is *not* that weapons, illness, and accidents never affect Christians; it is that they only serve God's sovereign purposes regarding His children. Things that happen to us are safely under God's control. The King of Heaven is still working out His will in our lives, and we can trust Him not to fail, regardless of appearances.

The Lord has allowed me to suffer a crushing personal loss, to develop an illness I will have the rest of my life (unless, of course, He heals me, which He could do), and has healed my cancer. I don't fully understand God's ways, but I *do* understand that regardless of my feelings or circumstances, I can safely trust in the One who is all *powerful*, all *wise*, and all *good*.

"God is too good to be unkind, and He is too wise to be mistaken. And when we cannot trace His hand, we must trust His heart." - Charles Spurgeon

9

A Matter of Life and Death

Hebrews 2:14 "Forasmuch then as the children are partakers of flesh and blood, he also himself likewise took part of the same; that through death he might destroy him that had the power of death, that is, the devil."

We are told in today's verse that the devil has the power of death. Jesus told His disciples that "the thief cometh not, but for to steal, and to kill, and to destroy." (John 10:10a) That is his domain. That is what he does.

What a terrible existence to live only to damage what God has made. Even though we were ruined in the fall, and, according to Ephesians 2:1, our spirits actually died (the work of the devil), Satan insists on wreaking further havoc and destruction. As we read in today's verse, he has the power of death, and he delights to use it.

How precious, then, that there is Someone who has the power of life. This is born out in the rest of Jesus' words recorded in the John 10 passage: "The thief cometh not, but for to steal, and to kill, and to destroy: I am come that they might have life, and that they might have it more abundantly." It is further supported by Christ's high-priestly prayer: "These words spake Jesus, and lifted up his eyes to heaven, and said, Father, the hour is come; glorify thy Son, that thy Son also may glorify thee: As thou hast given him power over all flesh, that he should give eternal life to as many as thou hast given him. And this is life eternal, that they might know thee the only true God, and Jesus Christ, whom thou hast sent." (John 17:1-3)

This whole thing we call life is not about health, wealth, and happiness. It is about finding the truth as revealed in the person of Jesus Christ and glorifying God by yielding to that truth. The other option is to yield to the destroyer—the father of lies (John 8:44)—the one with the power of death.

So then, one has the power of death, and the other has the power of life. By God's kind grace, I will follow the King of Life. How about you?

10

The Humdrum of Life

Matthew 26:1- 4 "And it came to pass, when Jesus had finished all these sayings, he said unto his disciples, Ye know that after two days is the feast of the Passover, and the Son of man is betrayed to be crucified. Then assembled together the chief priests, and the scribes, and the elders of the people, unto the palace of the high priest, who was called Caiaphas, And consulted that they might take Jesus by subtilty, and kill him."

In today's verses, we see the Lord tell His disciples He was going to be crucified. A little later in verse 12, He implies it again, saying that the woman anointing Him with ointment was doing that for His burial. However, when the Lord died on the cross—just as He said He would—somehow they were surprised.

I sometimes find that I read passages in the Bible and my familiarity causes me to overlook details. I am not trying to make excuses, but the trouble is not just with me today; Jesus' disciples were right there with Him, and they had the same problem.

I don't want this Musing to be a scolding session, partially because I would have to be the first in line, but also because instead of pointing out weakness, I want to encourage godly strength and change. To that end, I offer two thoughts:

- When we read Scripture, especially familiar passages, let's watch closely what words God uses and how He uses them.
- Let's be more aware of what He is doing in us and what He purposes to do through us.

If we do that, I suggest our lives will be less humdrum, and that they will be more full, more interesting, and yes, even more challenging.

11

Distorted Glory, Restored Glory

Psalm 106:19-20: "They made a calf in Horeb, and worshiped the molten image. Thus they changed their glory into the similitude of an ox that eateth grass."

On day six of Creation, along with animals, God made humankind. (Genesis 1:24-31) He distinguished man from animals in that He made man "after his own image," (Genesis 1:26-27) and when God breathed life into Adam, he became a living soul. (Genesis 2:7)

God displayed startling creativity in the colors, sizes, and shapes of His creation. The more we learn of His intricate designs the more amazing they become. However, God's purpose for man has always been different from animals.

God created human beings in His image to reflect His glory in a way that none of His other creations do. That was destroyed in Genesis 3 when the serpent lied his lies and Eve and Adam disobeyed their Creator. Ever since then, our reflection of God has been warped and distorted.

Today's verses draw our attention to that fact. Imagine the insult as God's highest creation likens Him to a cow, implying that He is no more majestic or worthy of worship than an animal. How destructive and ruinous was Adam's fall; it is truly astounding that we can reflect the image of God at all.

However, God, in infinite wisdom, compassion, and design, purposed not to let that disaster stand. Some 4,000 years after the fall, on a hill outside Jerusalem, the Lord Jesus Christ—God in human flesh—allowed His own rebellious creation to jam a thorny wreath onto His head, hammer nails through his hands and feet, and hang Him in a shameful display for all to see. Even worse, in that vulnerable moment, the heavenly Father punished Christ, not for His own sins, but for ours. By doing that, God created a way that "as many as received him, to them gave he power to become the sons of God, even to them that believe on his name." (John 1:12)

God is restoring His image in those who trust in the finished work of Christ on the cross.

I stand amazed in the presence
Of Jesus the Nazarene,
And wonder how He could love me,
A sinner, condemned, unclean.

217

How marvelous! How wonderful!
And my song shall ever be:
How marvelous! How wonderful!
Is my Savior's love for me!
~ Charles Hutchinson Gabriel

12

Two Qualities of our Humanity

Psalm 70:4-5 "Let all those that seek thee rejoice and be glad in thee: and let such as love thy salvation say continually, Let God be magnified. But I am poor and needy: make haste unto me, O God: thou art my help and my deliverer; O Lord, make no tarrying."

One thing that I have noticed about the Psalms is that they are very human. I do not mean that they are not God's Word (2 Timothy 3:16), but rather that they speak to our mortal condition.

We sometimes think of people in the Bible as superhuman and that they "have it all together," as the saying goes; however, that is false. They sweated when they were hot and shivered when they were cold. They got hungry and thirsty. They rejoiced in triumphs and sorrowed in losses, and sinned just as we do.

Today's verses give a glimpse of two very human qualities. The first is in verse 5: "But I am poor and needy: make haste unto me, O God: thou art my help and my deliverer; O Lord, make no tarrying." This is also consistent with the first three verses, in which David displays very human emotions, pleading for the Lord's speedy help and deliverance. These verses reveal the human condition we know as fear or anxiety.

The second human quality is shown in verse 4 and is a deliberate choice as compared to the automatic fear-response David displays in the other verses: "Let all those that seek thee rejoice and be glad in thee: and let such as love thy salvation say continually, Let God be magnified."

Here David steps out of his sense of fear and into a sense of the majesty of his Savior. In the other four verses of this psalm, he is "poor and needy" (v5) and pleads for God to "make haste" (v1) and "make no tarrying" (v5) in delivering him from his fearful circumstances. However, in verse 4, he pauses in the midst of his fears and encourages all who seek God and love His salvation to rejoice in His goodness and desire that He receive the honor He is due.

That is part of our mission too, dear friends. God has purposed to leave us in a fallen world and calls us to magnify His name, even amid life's challenges. Let's all be about that calling.

13

At the End of Each Quarter

Jonah 4:9-11 "And God said to Jonah, Doest thou well to be angry for the gourd? And he said, I do well to be angry, even unto death. Then said the Lord, Thou hast had pity on the gourd, for the which thou hast not laboured, neither madest it grow; which came up in a night, and perished in a night: And should not I spare Nineveh, that great city, wherein are more than sixscore thousand persons that cannot discern between their right hand and their left hand; and also much cattle?"

My reference to the end of each quarter might cause some who read this to think of a sporting event; however, the quarters I am talking about are the divisions in the book of Jonah, which is divided into four chapters, with each chapter closing in a very powerful way.

The first three chapters end with specific events: chapter 1 closes with God preparing a great fish to swallow His runaway prophet; chapter 2 ends with God commanding the fish to deposit Jonah on the shore; chapter 3 ends with God showing great mercy to the wicked city of Nineveh when they repented.

In the fourth chapter, Jonah goes up on a hill and sulks. Today we might say he had a "pity party." For some reason, Jonah really hated the Ninevites; I have heard that perhaps his family or friends had been their victims in the past. Whatever the cause, God asks the prophet twice why he is upset. Finally, in angry and sarcastic words, Jonah tells God that he doesn't like Him being merciful to Nineveh. Today's verses describe the Lord's gentle reply. He reminds the angry prophet that he didn't like it when a simple shade plant perished; he then asked him why it was wrong to have mercy on 120,000 human beings.

Does it bother you when God shows mercy to someone you don't like? Isn't it good *anytime* that God shows mercy? Moreover, consider that person you don't want God being merciful to. What if God had the same amount of mercy for you as you want Him to have for them? That puts a different perspective on it, doesn't it?

Let us not be bitter like Jonah. Instead, let us rejoice that God was kind to Nineveh and that He is also kind to us and to others.

14

O Ye of Little Faith

Today we look at the only five verses in the Bible that contain the phrase, "O ye of little faith:"

1. Matthew 6:30 "Wherefore, if God so clothe the grass of the field, which to day is, and to morrow is cast into the oven, shall he not much more clothe you, O ye of little faith?" Here, in the context of the Lord teaching the disciples to pray, he asks them if God cared for temporary things like grass what made them think He would not provide for them?
2. Matthew 8:26 "And he saith unto them, Why are ye fearful, O ye of little faith? Then he arose, and rebuked the winds and the sea; and there was a great calm." Here the Lord calms the storm and asks, in so many words, why they doubted His care and ability to provide their needs.
3. Matthew 14:31 "And immediately Jesus stretched forth his hand, and caught him, and said unto him, O thou of little faith, wherefore didst thou doubt?" Here the *ye* (plural) is replaced with ***thou*** (singular) as Jesus chides Peter for doubting His ability to make Peter walk on water.
4. Matthew 16:8 "Which when Jesus perceived, he said unto them, O ye of little faith, why reason ye among yourselves, because ye have brought no bread?" Here Jesus was cautioning them about the "leaven of the Pharisees and of the Sadducees." (v11) Instead, they thought He was criticizing them for forgetting to bring bread for their journey; He reminds them He can feed thousands with almost nothing.
5. Luke 12:28 "If then God so clothe the grass, which is to day in the field, and to morrow is cast into the oven; how much more will he clothe you, O ye of little faith?" This is Luke's account of Christ's lesson in Matthew 6:30.

Note that each of today's verses is in the form of a question. What do we learn from these verses? The same thing Jesus taught us about God watching over sparrows: that we are more important to God than many sparrows. The Lord is teaching us that He provides for us (food and clothing) and protects us (life storms, etc.). If the great God can meet our needs and promises to do so, can we not trust Him? Let's not be "We of little faith."

15
Bigger and Smaller

John 3:30 "He must increase, but I must decrease."

Today's verse recounts John's testimony regarding the Lord Jesus. The baptizer is bearing witness to his need to become less before men so that the sweet fragrance of Christ would be more evident. He wanted those around him to see what is important about life, not what is comparatively unimportant.

Not to be unkind toward us mortals, but on the eternal scale, we have nothing to offer others except the Savior. Someone once said witnessing is just one beggar telling other beggars where to find bread. Someone else said it this way: "If you meet me and walk away, you have lost nothing, but if you meet Christ and walk away, you have lost everything." That is why it is so important for people to see Christ in us; in order to accomplish that, we must "shine" a little less.

As life speeds by, we find that we become a little weaker, our joints hurt a little more, and our memories become less reliable. As bad as that sounds, it is a perfect setting for us to become stronger spiritually—not strong in ourselves, but to yield ourselves to the Holy Spirit, whose task it is to glorify Christ in us. (John 7:37-39; 15:26-27)

Now, a word to those who are still strong in body and mind. Your struggle is more challenging because we mortals naturally tend to rely on our own wisdom and strength. As we age, we *must* depend more on God's strength, but for young people, yielding to the Holy Spirit seems less necessary. That is true if your goal is to display your own glory, but if you want to display Christ's glory, you must do so in the power of God's Spirit.

As I write this, I am looking at a picture of one of our grandchildren. The picture is set in a frame, but like all frames, the center is cut out. The frame *holds* the picture but does not get in the way of the picture. It is the same with us. If we want people to see Jesus through us, we must yield to the Holy Spirit, for He will make Christ prominent.

He must increase, but we must decrease.

16
David's Prayer for God's Glory

Psalm 72:17-20 "His name shall endure forever: his name shall be continued as long as the sun: and men shall be blessed in him: all nations shall call him blessed. Blessed be the LORD God, the God of Israel, who only doeth wondrous things. And blessed be his glorious name forever: and let the whole earth be filled with his glory; Amen, and Amen. The prayers of David the son of Jesse are ended."

Some of the psalms are considered messianic, that is, they prophesy something about the coming of Christ, the Messiah. Psalm 72 is such a psalm. For example, consider verse 2: "He shall judge thy people with righteousness, and thy poor with judgment." Also, verse 11: "Yea, all kings shall fall down before him: all nations shall serve him."

For sure, as with the other psalms, there is a historical setting to consider. This psalm is referred to as "A Psalm for Solomon," and therefore would be a prayer by David for his son, as the father/king leaves his throne to his son/successor.

That being said, there is much gold for our consideration in this passage. We are encouraged to take in the spectacle of who God is, what He has accomplished as God, and how His works benefit us. We are also encouraged to praise Him for His Being and His works and to tell others of Him so that they praise and bless Him too.

Matthew Henry, writing of these verses, said this: "We are taught to bless God in Christ, for all he has done for us by him. David is earnest in prayer for the fulfillment of this prophecy and promise. It is sad to think how empty the Earth is of the glory of God, how little service and honour he has from a world to which he is so bountiful. May we, like David, submit to Christ's authority, and partake of his righteousness and peace. May we bless him for the wonders of redeeming love. May we spend our days, and end our lives, praying for the spread of his gospel."

Well said, Mr. Henry. Well said.

17
I Know Not Any

Isaiah 44:6-8 "Thus saith the LORD the King of Israel, and his redeemer the LORD of hosts; I am the first, and I am the last; and beside me there is no God. And who, as I, shall call, and shall declare it, and set it in order for me, since I appointed the ancient people? and the things that are coming, and shall come, let them shew unto them. Fear ye not, neither be afraid: have not I told thee from that time, and have declared it? ye are even my witnesses. Is there a God beside me? yea, there is no God; I know not any."

Here, God is telling Israel that He is their Lord, King, and Redeemer; then He tells them that He is the *only* God. Notice He does not say that there are other gods, but Israel should not pursue them, He says there *isn't* any other god. In fact, His final phrase in today's reading is, "I know not any." Dear friends, if the Omniscient God does not know about it, it does not exist.

Many of you believe this. Not that we understand all there is to know about God—especially His triune nature—but we have read this and other passages and embrace the truth of God. However, there is something below the surface in the human heart that tends to supplant His ways. Oh, we don't brag that we are God, and in our conscience mind, we don't even think that we are, but our actions betray us. Let's look at one example:

God knows that at some level we all face the temptation to judge others based on what they look like, where they come from, the clothes they wear, or the amount of money they have; if we didn't have that tendency, He would not have bothered to tell us not to judge. (James 2:1-9) When we judge others anyway, we act as if we are not only wise enough to judge other people, but also to pass judgment on His instruction for us *not* to judge. Friends, that's not good.

Lord willing, we shall look more at judging next time. In the meantime, we should remember that God is a lot better at being God than we are. Let us trust Him and yield to Him gladly.

18

To Judge or Not to Judge

Matthew 7:1 "Judge not, that ye be not judged."

John 7:24 "Judge not according to the appearance, but judge righteous judgment."

During one election cycle, I saw a yard sign promoting the candidacy of "Judge Powers." I thought of posting a picture of the sign with the caption, "Well, maybe I *do* have the right to judge everyone." I didn't post that, but it might have been fun to see the comments.

The two verses above are the kinds of passages scoffers point to as "contradictions in the Bible." One verse says *not* to judge and the other says we *should* judge. What does that mean? Does the Bible really contradict itself? In the same way that a diamond has many facets, let's look at judging from several different angles.

It is important to understand that only God can see into a person's heart, so only God can judge righteously at that level. We cannot see into the heart, so we cannot accurately judge motive. We may have *some* insight into the heart if someone *tells* us why they committed some act, but beyond that, we don't know what is deep within. I think this is what Jesus was saying in Matthew 7:1.

However, in John 7, Jesus had just healed a man on the Sabbath day, and some people accused Him of breaking the law. This is more the area where we *can* judge, for we are not dealing with unseen intentions but with visible actions. Of course it is right for the Lord of the Sabbath to heal on the Sabbath, but it is wrong for someone to rob a bank. We don't fully understand motive, but we can say of certainty that it is wrong to do what God says not to do.

Also, my judgments are always clouded if there is something wrong in my own life. A beam in my eye makes it impossible to see a splinter in my neighbor's eye. (Matthew 7:3-5) When there *is* a proper need for clear judgment I must make sure I have no unconfessed sin or impure motive in my own life.

Lastly, our goal should *never* be to pretend we are superior. Rather, our judgments should always be in meekness with the goal to restore our friends to fellowship with God, with ourselves, and with others. (Galatians 6:1)

19

Servants and the King

Mark 9:35 "And he sat down, and called the twelve, and saith unto them, If any man desire to be first, the same shall be last of all, and servant of all."

Here Jesus was responding to the debate the disciples were having over which of them would be greatest in His kingdom. I don't think the Lord's comment was as much condemnation for their brashness as it was instruction on the *way* to be great in His kingdom. Unlike in this world, the highest, most elevated and glorified office in His kingdom is the position of servant. We must remember that the Lord was the greatest servant of all time, and He is instructing us so that we don't waste our lives merely on ourselves. The result of us being conformed to His image (Romans 8:29) is that we will become servants like He is.

If you want to be great in His kingdom, serve others. Indeed, what did He tell us is the second greatest of all the commandments? Wasn't it to love others the same way we love ourselves? (Matthew 22:39)

My heart literally aches for all the poverty and suffering in this fallen, broken world, but I cannot even begin to make any significant difference in the lives of so many people. But as someone once said, I may not be able to help the whole world, but I could be the whole world to one person.

Is there something you could do at your church or in your neighborhood that would make life better for someone? Do you know an elderly person whose life would be made easier if you mowed their lawn or drove them to an appointment or the store? How about a struggling family that could use help with buying groceries or a single mom who needs her car tuned up, her gas tank filled, or her children looked after while she runs errands or gets some rest?

Finally, whether you can do much or only a little, don't do *anything* in order to be noticed by others; do it humbly in front of the Lord who sees and judges rightly. Remember, He wasn't as impressed with those who gave a small percentage of their great wealth as He was with a widow who gave a great percentage of the little she had. (Mark 12:41-44)

20
Psalm 23:1

Psalm 23:1 "The LORD is my shepherd; I shall not want."

This psalm is filled with the blessings of God. Those blessings include:

- Security and assurance (v1)
- Rest and provision (v2)
- Refreshing and guidance (v3)
- Peace and comfort (v4)
- A testimony, abundance to overflowing (v5)
- Goodness, mercy, and an eternal home with God (v6)

However, at the very beginning, the Lord attaches a condition to those blessings: "The LORD is my shepherd." All of these gifts and promises are wonderful, even life sustaining, but they are only promised to the sheep who belong to the Shepherd who offers them.

I heard a Bible teacher tell of being in the Middle East. As he drove out into the countryside, he had to stop and wait for two shepherds who were talking in the middle of the road. All the while, the two flocks mingled together. When their visit was over, the two men went their way, and as they did, they each made what the teacher described as a chortling sound in their throats. The sheep separated out from the mass and followed their own shepherd.

Jesus, the Good Shepherd said, "My sheep hear my voice, and I know them, and they follow me:" (John 10:27) God showers His blessings on all mankind. (Matthew 5:45) However, the particular blessings of God belong to those who are His. Do you belong to the Shepherd, or are you still the lost sheep Jesus spoke of in Luke 15:1-7?

21

O Praise the Lord

Psalm 117:1-2 "O praise the LORD, all ye nations: praise him, all ye people. For his merciful kindness is great toward us: and the truth of the LORD endureth forever. Praise ye the LORD."

Psalm 117 has only two verses, making it the shortest of the Psalms and shorter than any chapter in the Bible; however, that doesn't mean that it is short on message, for its message is to praise God. That is even more interesting when you realize that this psalm is also the middle "chapter" of the Bible. I know the original writings were not in chapters and verses; the chapters were assigned in the 1200s and the verse divisions several hundred years later, so we should not make a huge item of this being the middle chapter. However, it is interesting that everything "worked out" so that the middle chapter calls us to engage our hearts in one of man's highest callings—praise to God.

Do you recall our school lessons about the questions to ask about a particular event: "Who, What, When, Where, Why, and How?" Today's psalm addresses three of those things: "What, Who, and Why."

What? - The first four words and the last four words give us that answer; we are to praise the Lord.

Who? - Are only the Jews to praise God? Is praise only for super saints? Or is it just for the church in general? No, *all* nations and *all* people are to praise Him. That is why we share the gospel with the lost so that the King of glory "peradventure will give them repentance," (2 Timothy 2:23-26) thus increasing the voices that are lifted up in praise.

Why? - "For his merciful kindness is great toward us: and the truth of the LORD endureth forever." That is a very good reason.

So, I remind us all, dear friends, today and *every* day, "O praise the LORD, all ye nations: praise him, all ye people. For his merciful kindness is great toward us: and the truth of the LORD endureth forever. Praise ye the LORD."

22
A Safe Place

Psalm 91:1- 4 "He that dwelleth in the secret place of the most High shall abide under the shadow of the Almighty. I will say of the LORD, He is my refuge and my fortress: my God; in him will I trust. Surely he shall deliver thee from the snare of the fowler, and from the noisome pestilence. He shall cover thee with his feathers, and under his wings shalt thou trust: his truth shall be thy shield and buckler."

Today's verses talk about a safe place—a place of refuge and protection. What I find particularly interesting is that this "safe psalm" is quoted in reference to the Lord Jesus. (See v12 and Matthew 4:6.) However, though God is the one who protects, Jesus *did* suffer. Why would this psalm suggest that God protects Messiah, and by implication protects us too, when He allowed great trauma in the life of the Lord Jesus and also allows trials and difficulty for us?

This is one of those seeming "contradictions" that perplex us and that scoffers like to point to as "proof" the Bible is flawed. However, what is actually flawed is our understanding. We live in a broken world that exists under the penalty of sin. We are subject to the same weaknesses and frailties as are common to the human experience.

Could God be saying in this psalm that He protects us so that the effects of this fallen world do not thwart His purposes for and through us? Things *will* and *do* happen that disrupt *our* plans, but God's ways are above our ways, (Isaiah 55:9) and He will protect us from the "noisome pestilence"—the destructive plague—that the enemy sends to sidetrack God's purposes.

Will God prevent every disruption to *our* plans? Frankly, that hasn't been true in *my* life; just like you, my troubles are real. However, even as in the case of Jesus coming into this world, God has purpose in the life of those who love Him, and He will not allow the enemy to prevail. He works all things after the counsel of his own will, (Ephesians 1:11) and ultimately His perfect will shall be done in Earth, as it is in Heaven. (Matthew 6:10)

Through all circumstances, our safe place is with God Himself. I am glad.

23
Every Which Way

Proverbs 14:12 "There is a way which seemeth right unto a man, but the end thereof are the ways of death."

Has someone you know said or done something that will follow them for the rest of their lives? Not something evil or bad, just some little thing that stuck with them—something that brings a chuckle or an embarrassed smile whenever it is brought up.

Pete, one of my best friends in the world, had a funny boyhood incident involving his dislike of strawberry ice cream. As a toddler, my sister Debbie used to make such a smeary mess on her highchair tray that bowls and utensils would stick to it; even into her adulthood, we teased about her being a human "glue pot."

One of *my* events occurred when a friend and I—both of us in our teens—were going to rebuild the valve body from his automatic transmission. For those who don't know, the valve body controls the shifting operation and involves many precision parts. Ken was apprehensive about all the valve pieces, and I said, "Don't worry; they can only go back together one way." I was right, but exactly *how* they went back together was the problem. My buddy ended up having to get the transmission service manual before we could finally reassemble everything.

Even with all its beauty, this world is a very broken place. Adam's fall plunged this world into a chaos that only seems to get worse with time. How? God gave Adam a simple but very specific command. He told him not to eat of that *one* tree, but Adam took the same cavalier attitude I had about the valve body. It was as if he thought, "I don't need to follow the rules. I can do whatever I want, and everything will be just fine."

Look at us now! Division, hatred, selfishness, rebellion, murder, and more—all just to get our own way. To paraphrase one TV personality, "How's that working for us?"

God gave wise council to Adam. He also gives wise council to us in His Word, the Bible. We must understand it in its context to be sure; we must rightly study His Word (2 Timothy 2:15) so that we don't misinterpret or wrongly apply. However, we must heed His godly guidance, for He says, "This is the way, walk ye in it." (Isaiah 30:21)

24

Bad Choices, Good Choices

Romans 6:23 "For the wages of sin is death; but the gift of God is eternal life through Jesus Christ our Lord."

Recently, my wife and I watched a Western in which a pretty young woman arrived on the stagecoach. She and a rugged-looking blacksmith had been writing each other, and she agreed to come to town to get to know him better with the possibility of marriage.

The kindly blacksmith was struck by her beauty and set out to win her heart. Trouble arose when a man showed up and accused her of swindling him out of a large amount of money. He wanted her to pay him back, or he would have her arrested. The blacksmith withdrew the money from the bank and paid the debt.

Later, a private scene between the accuser and the woman revealed that they were partners in a scheme to go from town to town, victimizing successful businessmen. However, several scenes showed that the woman had developed a tender heart for the blacksmith; she wanted to leave in shame and quit her dishonest lifestyle. Her partner threatened her with exposure, and she went along with one more extortion from the blacksmith before the swindlers left town together.

When the blacksmith heard that she was gone, he finally realized the truth. He caught up with the stagecoach, recovered his money from the man, removed the women from the coach, and made the coach driver leave. Then he got on his horse and told the woman she must walk several miles back to town to go to jail. When she protested that he was not making the man go to jail, he replied, "I didn't love him."

The two of them arrived back in town. The weary woman leaned against the horse, exhausted, and obviously dreading the future. The blacksmith dismounted the horse, nodded toward the marshal's office and said, "There's the jail." After a long pause, he nodded in a different direction and said, "And there's the church," indicating he still wanted to marry her. When she finally realized the forgiveness he was offering, she collapsed against him with tears of remorse and gratitude, for it was not the church building that offered her forgiveness, but the blacksmith himself.

In the same way, it is not the church that offers us forgiveness, but The Lord Jesus Himself. We have sinned against a kind, gracious God; He has died to pay for our transgressions and now offers us a loving union with Himself forever.

> Amazing grace, how sweet the sound
> That saved a wretch like me."
> ~ John Newton

25
Let That Soak In

Matthew 16:12 "Then understood they how that he bade them not beware of the leaven of bread, but of the doctrine of the Pharisees and of the Sadducees."

Depending on who we listen to, butter and margarine may not be very good for us. I don't use a lot of spreads, but when I do, I like it to be melted. When I butter toast, I like the toast to be warm enough that the butter doesn't just spread on top, but actually melts in. The same with a baked potato; I like for the butter to melt in and flavor each bite.

In a similar way, one of the things I am learning in my study of the Scriptures is the difference between gleaning facts and absorbing truth. Let me explain.

When I read the Bible and come upon some instruction, I have a choice. One option is to put it on a list of things I must or must not do. I think of this as spreading butter on cold toast. The spread lays there on top—in touch with the bread, but never really gets down deep into the toast. It will be eaten at the same time as the toast, and it will add to the flavor, but it will not be the same. If I put God's instructions on a do/don't do list, it may change my actions, but it will not have the same impact on who I am.

The other option is to absorb that truth like the warm toast absorbs the melted butter. We must embrace God's wisdom as reality, so that instead of looking at a list, we are looking at the Lord.

Early in my driving experience, I was taught that new drivers tend to look just beyond the hood to see if they are staying between the lines. The better way is to look some distance down the road—not just to see where you are, but to look where you are going.

Our goal is to be like Jesus. If we are always looking at a list, we are concentrating on ourselves and how we are performing. If instead, we look at the Savior and concentrate on Him, we began to become like Him and start to think like Him. When we do that, our behavior will be more like it should be.

26

By Grace, through Faith

Ephesians 2:8-10 "For by grace are ye saved through faith; and that not of yourselves: it is the gift of God: Not of works, lest any man should boast. For we are his workmanship, created in Christ Jesus unto good works, which God hath before ordained that we should walk in them."

You are probably familiar with today's verses. They tell us that our salvation is a gift from God. From these wonderful verses, we learn two things:

First, no amount of good works will earn God's grace. In fact, trying to be right with God by mixing His grace with our good works is, to use the old expression, like trying to mix oil and water. Paul warns us against that in Romans 11:6: "And if by grace, then is it no more of works: otherwise grace is no more grace. But if it be of works, then is it no more grace: otherwise work is no more work." (Also, see Galatians 5.)

Second, in these verses, God also tells us that good works will be the result of the free salvation He gives us by grace. Wayne Schlichter, one of the men who mentored me when I was a young Christian, says it this way, "Good works are the *fruit* of salvation, not the *root*." In other words, our works will not produce salvation in us, but our salvation will produce good works in us.

We must trust God completely for our salvation, knowing for sure that we cannot add to—or subtract from—what He has given us as a free gift. The Old Testament writer put it this way: "I know that, whatsoever God doeth, it shall be for ever: nothing can be put to it, nor any thing taken from it: and God doeth it, that men should fear before him." (Ecclesiastes 3:14)

With that assurance in our hearts, we are now free to honor God by yielding to Him as He makes us more like Christ. We can do so by witnessing to others of God's saving grace, by helping those in need, and by doing other good works. Thereby, we can express our thankfulness to God for His great kindness to us and give the world an example of a redeemed life.

27

For Thine Is the Power

Matthew 6:9-13 "After this manner therefore pray ye: Our Father which art in heaven, Hallowed be thy name. Thy kingdom come. Thy will be done in earth, as it is in heaven. Give us this day our daily bread. And forgive us our debts, as we forgive our debtors. And lead us not into temptation, but deliver us from evil: For thine is the kingdom, and the power, and the glory, for ever. Amen."

I had an unusual dream awhile back. I dreamed my phone was going off in church, and I could not turn it off. I even removed the battery, and it continued to alarm even with the battery out. It turned out I was sleeping through a wake-up alarm on my phone, and my wife had to wake me up turn it off.

Later I read this verse: "Thy kingdom is an everlasting kingdom, and thy dominion endureth throughout all generations." (Psalm 145:13) In this verse, God describes His kingdom as an "everlasting kingdom." Everlasting is not just future; everlasting includes *now*.

God invites fallen, broken human beings into His kingdom. He calls us to turn from our rebellious and self-centered ways, to trust Him for forgiveness through Christ, and to enjoy the privilege of being a child of The Eternal King. When we come to Him in faith, we are spiritually connected to God, and His power works in us and through us. However there are things that can interfere with that connection—selfishness, greed, and lust to name a few. Those things don't break the connection, only interfere with it. In Revelation 2:4, Jesus doesn't tell the Ephesians they have *lost* their first love, only that they have *left* it—that they have turned aside to pursue something else.

Back to my dream: How silly is a dream when a phone can continue to function when it is disconnected from its only source of power? In the same way, it is unrealistic to assume we can function on a spiritual level without God's power in us. We maintain that channel of power by reading His Word and by confessing and turning from the things that interrupt our fellowship with Him.

Read the Word, meditate on it, and always be in an attitude of prayer. His is the power, and by His power in us, we can live lives that honor Him.

28

The Battle of Chauncey Demon

Hebrews 12:1-3 "Wherefore seeing we also are compassed about with so great a cloud of witnesses, let us lay aside every weight, and the sin which doth so easily beset us, and let us run with patience the race that is set before us, Looking unto Jesus the author and finisher of our faith; who for the joy that was set before him endured the cross, despising the shame, and is set down at the right hand of the throne of God. For **consider him** that endured such contradiction of sinners against himself, **lest ye** be wearied and faint in **your** minds." (Emphasis mine)

In one episode of an American television western, the governor commissioned a marshal to secretly spy out a troubled town. While there, the marshal met his old friend, Chauncey Demon. Chauncey used to be a brave man and stood for right, but since he and the marshal last met, Demon's wife and son were killed, and he had become a heavy drinker. When the marshal tried to enlist his help in the Governor's task, Demon protests that he can't—that he is facing his own enemy that cannot be defeated with guns. He says of this battle, "It's me against me."

Have you been there? Are you there now? Are you fighting a battle that hardly gives you a moment's peace? Today's verses have a name for that: "the sin which doth so easily beset us." Or perhaps it is not a sin; maybe it is a decision that was morally neither good nor bad, but ended up being a huge error for which you cannot forgive yourself. Whether it was a moral failing or a genuine mistake, this passage has the remedy: "let us run with patience the race that is set before us, looking unto Jesus the author and finisher of our faith."

If your struggle is with a mistake, let it go. If your struggle is with a sin, confess it to the Lord; trust in His forgiveness; and turn from it. In either case, stop beating yourself up.

How can you do that? I can't give you an easy answer. Not because I don't want to, but because I haven't found one. However, I *can* tell you it involves confessing our sins to God, (1 John 1:9) embracing His forgiveness, and seeking His face every day. And sometimes, every moment.

29

I See the Light

Psalm 36:9 "For with thee is the fountain of life: in thy light shall we see light."

This verse speaks of light; however, the first verse of this psalm speaks of the darkness of a wicked heart. "The transgression of the wicked saith within my heart, that there is no fear of God before his eyes." David sees the deeds of the wicked, and his heart tells him the problem lies deeper than the acts of the wicked person; the trouble lies in their unabashed rebellion against God.

The Apostle John gives a similar insight: "And we know that we are of God, and the whole world lieth in wickedness." (1 John 5:19)

As I mentioned, today's verse speaks of light. I like how David says it: "in thy light shall we see light." That wording reminds me of something C.S. Lewis said: "I believe in Christianity as I believe that the sun has risen: not only because I see it, but because by it I see everything else." By Christianity, Lewis is not speaking of some mere religiousness, but rather, the truth that God has revealed to us in the gospel of Christ. Indeed, Jesus *is* that spiritual light which illuminates our understanding. *He* is the light by which we see light, and *He* is the light by which we see everything else.

The verse in 1 John that follows the one I quoted above says, "And we know that the Son of God is come, and hath given us an understanding [spiritual light], that we may know him that is true, and we are in him that is true, even in his Son Jesus Christ. This is the true God, and eternal life." (1 John 5:20) Earlier in his epistle, John tells us more: "This then is the message which we have heard of him, and declare unto you, that God is light, and in him is no darkness at all." (1 John 1:5)

We live in a spiritually dark world, and wickedness is all around us. Being *aware* of the darkness is good, but *focusing* on it is not. Instead, let us follow more advice from John: "But if we walk in the light, as he is in the light, we have fellowship one with another, and the blood of Jesus Christ his Son cleanseth us from all sin." (1 John 1:7)

30

Negotiating with Terrorists

Genesis 3:4-8 "And the serpent said unto the woman, Ye shall not surely die: For God doth know that in the day ye eat thereof, then your eyes shall be opened, and ye shall be as gods, knowing good and evil. And when the woman saw that the tree was good for food, and that it was pleasant to the eyes, and a tree to be desired to make one wise, she took of the fruit thereof, and did eat, and gave also unto her husband with her; and he did eat. And the eyes of them both were opened, and they knew that they were naked; and they sewed fig leaves together, and made themselves aprons. And they heard the voice of the LORD God walking in the garden in the cool of the day: and Adam and his wife hid themselves from the presence of the LORD God amongst the trees of the garden."

Many nations will not negotiate with terrorists. The fear is that if terrorists are successful by kidnappings or other threats, they will only do more of the same in the future, putting more lives at risk and costing more money.

In a sense though, we all have things in common with those terrorists. Thankfully, few of us go around killing others, but we all come into this world as rebels against God. Yes, family and society do help shape us into "civilized" people, but we are still a lot like our first parents who were convinced God was holding out on them—that He was not really interested in what was best for them. As a result, we as their offspring rebel against His Word as if God means us harm; however, "He that spared not his own Son, but delivered him up for us all, how shall he not with him also freely give us all things?" (Romans 8:32)

God promises good to them who come to Him in repentance and faith, but we *must* come on His terms. As A.W. Tozer put it, "God never negotiates with men. Jesus Christ's death on the cross put an end to any kind of negotiations. It is now Christ or nothing."

Come to Him *now*, my friend. You will find that God, who is righteously angry at sin and rebellion, is also full of loving kindness for those who humbly trust Him.

31
Corn in the Soybean Field

Ephesians 2:19-20 "Now therefore ye are no more strangers and foreigners, but fellow citizens with the saints, and of the household of God; And are built upon the foundation of the apostles and prophets, Jesus Christ himself being the chief corner stone;"

Farmers in our part of the United States grow a lot of soybeans, corn, and winter wheat. As we drive past soybean fields, I often see a few cornstalks poking up above the soybean bushes. The corn might be from kernels left in the field last year when the farmers planted corn there. Or perhaps, a few corn kernels were accidentally mixed into the soybean seeds before they were planted. I don't know how they get there. It is a beautiful sight to see acre after acre of soybean bushes; the sight is only marred by the presence of a few other plants that would fit perfectly well in a field of cornstalks, but are conspicuously out of place in a bean field.

That is what we are like. Paul tells us in today's verses that we are "no more strangers and foreigners, but fellow citizens with the saints, and of the household of God." Did you grasp what the apostle said there? We are not strangers and foreigners; instead, we are fellow citizens in the household of God. However, the problem is in that phrase, "household of God." Though we are fellow citizens with other believers, for now, we are living in a soybean world. We stick out here because we *are* strangers and foreigners in a sea of lostness.

Now, don't get me wrong. That is not a problem, but it could become a problem if we are uncomfortable being different and begin thinking that we need to "fit in" so that we don't "stand out."

Compromise is easy; I know. I have to fight it every day and usually many times each day. But if we Christians stand out, occasionally someone will see us and wonder what makes us different. They may even ask us why we are different. And, by the grace of God, some of them may want to become different too.

SEPTEMBER

1

Sonka Monka

Romans 8:26-27 "Likewise the Spirit also helpeth our infirmities: for we know not what we should pray for as we ought: but the Spirit itself maketh intercession for us with groanings which cannot be uttered. And he that searcheth the hearts knoweth what is the mind of the Spirit, because he maketh intercession for the saints according to the will of God."

Only a handful of Bible verses are better known than Romans 8:28: "And we know that all things work together for good to them that love God, to them who are the called according to his purpose." This verse reminds us that we *know* something. That something is that the events of our lives are not random and haphazard; they are part of a pattern that God oversees in order to bring about good for us. Not every event *seems* good, but all are ingredients of the whole.

However, have you ever noticed the contrast between Romans 8:28 and the two verses preceding it? Those two verses are our reading for today and tell us there is also something we do *not* know. The Holy Spirit helps us with our prayers for we do not know "what we should pray for as we ought." Sometimes we are at a *total* loss for words; we cannot even put our burdens into sounds—"cannot be uttered"—so the Spirit takes the burdens of our hearts and conveys them perfectly to the Father in Heaven.

I don't remember the event, but my mother told me when I was two or three years old, we were going somewhere. That was a different time than today, before seatbelts and children's car seats, and I was standing in the back seat of the car looking out the window. As we backed down the driveway, I suddenly gasped and said, "*Sonka monka*!" My mom told me that she didn't know what a "sonka monka" was, but that she was pretty sure she didn't want to back out in front of one. She stopped, and within moments, a motorcycle rode past. I didn't know what to say, but in her wisdom, Mom knew how to react.

God has purposed that all things work together for good, and that includes the Holy Spirit's help when we don't even know how—or what—to pray. God is *so* good! Praise Him for His goodness!

2

Driveways and Fences, Mailboxes and Lighthouses

"Wherewithal shall a young man cleanse his way? by taking heed thereto according to thy word" (Psalm 119:9) Later in the same Psalm, the writer gives us a companion verse: "Thy word is a lamp unto my feet, and a light unto my path." (Psalm 119:105)

We live out in the country. We are a ten-minute drive to three small municipalities, a half hour from two larger towns, and an hour from three major cities. As a cost-cutting measure, our township has turned off the street lamps at all but the most dangerous intersections. I say all that to say this: nights are *dark* out where we live. When there are no clouds, we have a breathtaking view of the stars, but on a cloudy night, especially when the moon is not out, it can be truly pitch black outside.

This darkness is especially evident when we attempt to back down our rather long driveway. If we have backed in, the headlights solve the problem, but when we must back out, the darkness of night seems to swallow whatever illumination our backup lights create. To make matters worse, until recently I had a decal promoting my children's book that covered my entire rear window; I had to rely completely on my side mirrors to navigate my way down the driveway, between two fence posts, and to the side of the mailbox.

Over time, I finally found one thing that makes the job quite easy. The backup lights are bright enough that they reflect a little off the fence posts and the mailbox. If I look in my driver's side mirror and maneuver the car so that it comes down alongside the mailbox, I know I will miss the posts and I will not hit anything else.

Before radar, GPS, and other advanced technologies, people erected lighthouses along dangerous seashores. These lighthouses cast strong beams of light out into the darkness. By that light—in a similar way to navigating my driveway by focusing on a landmark—seagoing vessels steered clear of danger.

However, as the psalmist asks, how shall a young man cleanse his own personal way? By lining up with the ancient landmark of the Bible. Why? Because God's Word illuminates the good path.

To stay on the good path, stay with The Book. To get *back* on the good path, get *back* into The Book.

238

3

Return Ye Now Every One

Jeremiah 18:7-11 "At what instant I shall speak concerning a nation, and concerning a kingdom, to pluck up, and to pull down, and to destroy it; If that nation, against whom I have pronounced, turn from their evil, I will repent of the evil that I thought to do unto them. And at what instant I shall speak concerning a nation, and concerning a kingdom, to build and to plant it; If it do evil in my sight, that it obey not my voice, then I will repent of the good, wherewith I said I would benefit them. Now therefore go to, speak to the men of Judah, and to the inhabitants of Jerusalem, saying, Thus saith the LORD; Behold, I frame evil against you, and devise a device against you: return ye now every one from his evil way, and make your ways and your doings good."

These verses are part of a message from God to the nation of Israel. However, the things in the Old Testament are for our learning, (Romans 15:4) and these proclamations virtually scream at 21st century America and much of today's world.

Condensed, it says, "If I declare judgment on a sinful nation and it turns from its wickedness, I will withhold my judgment. But if I purpose to bless a nation and it turns to evil, I will withdraw my blessing." Israel, Nineveh, and others found that to be true. Are we so naive as to think we are immune to God's righteous hand?

Disasters happen from time to time, but are the current abundance of floods, droughts, and wildfires the hand of God against us for our sins? Are injustices and terrorism, and predictions of earthquakes and volcanoes and floods, judgments from the Almighty for our transgressions? We don't know for sure, but we certainly cannot declare that they are not! Three things *are* sure:

1. We as a nation are presently in great rebellion against the revealed will of God.
2. He uses nature as He wills to judge mortal rebellion.
3. He even uses evil men to accomplish His purposes against evil people who think they are "not so evil."

I am not judging others, for I too am a sinner; however, it is well past time for all of us to repent of our sins and plead for His mercy. May we do so quickly before that option is gone.

4

Faith, Hope and Love

1 Corinthians 13:11-13 "When I was a child, I spake as a child, I understood as a child, I thought as a child: but when I became a man, I put away childish things. For now we see through a glass, darkly; but then face to face: now I know in part; but then shall I know even as also I am known. And now abideth faith, hope, charity, these three; but the greatest of these is charity."

We Westerners sometimes give from a distance. Charity might be putting food in a collection box at Christmas time, donating a garment to a clothing drive, or giving money to a relief organization. To be fair, that is proper; each of those things is an act of charity. We give something, and someone else benefits, even though we never meet those we help.

There is another aspect to charity, however, and that is when you personally sacrifice your time, your abilities, and yourself. It is then that you truly enter into the need and identify with it. It is then that you get close enough to see the tear hidden in the corner of the eye and hear the faint, whispered cry for help.

Are you aware that the word translated "charity" in today's verse is usually translated "love"? And it is not just any love; it is love in its highest form. The English language uses the single word love to cover many subjects, but the Greek language uses different words that we might try to cover with only one. The highest form of love in the Greek language is the word "agape" (ag-ah'-pay); it is that sacrificial love Jesus spoke of when He said, "Greater love hath no man than this, that a man lay down his life for his friends. (John 15:13) It is also the word He demonstrated when He died to save us.

That word, **agape**, is the word in 1 Corinthians 13. Paul says that great works without that kind of unselfish love do not benefit us. (verses 1-3) He then goes on to describe that love, saying it is patient and kind, it doesn't envy, misbehave or entertain evil thoughts, and it is not arrogant, proud, or temperamental.

The best part is that although faith and hope are good, when we no longer need them, we will still have love.

5
Double Entry

Colossians 1:12-13 "Giving thanks unto the Father, which hath made us meet to be partakers of the inheritance of the saints in light: Who hath delivered us from the power of darkness, and hath translated us into the kingdom of his dear Son:"

In the world of finance and accounting, one of the ways to make sure everything is tracked properly is a double-entry system whereby every transaction comes *from* one account and *to* another account. For example, a check may be given to the electric company. The double-entry system sees the check removing money from the bank account (minus), an also sees the money moved over to the electric company account (plus). I want to borrow the term "double entry" as an illustration of a different kind of operation.

Today's verse tells us that God has made a transaction; by grace through faith, He has moved us out of the "darkness kingdom" and into the "light kingdom" of His dear Son. However, the Lord uses another interesting "double." He uses two beautiful word images to describe this transaction.

My cousin and good friend Pete Sweemer pointed one of them out to me; God says He has *adopted* us. Ephesians 1:5 says, "Having predestinated us unto the adoption of children by Jesus Christ to himself, according to the good pleasure of his will." We find other mentions of adoption in Romans 8:15, 8:23, 9:4, and Galatians 4:5.

The second word image is that we are *born* into His family. 1 Peter 1:23 says we have been "born again, not of corruptible seed, but of incorruptible, by the word of God, which liveth and abideth for ever." Jesus used that same mental picture twice in His conversation with Nicodemus in John 3, saying, "Ye must be born again." (vs. 3)

How beautiful, that the Lord would use two different depictions of His mercy to us. We have been born into His family by grace. (Ephesians 2:8-10) As if that is not secure enough, He has also adopted us into His family. A double entry, if you will. Sort of a secure security we might call it.

> Praise God, from whom all blessings flow;
> Praise Him, all creatures here below;
> Praise Him above, ye heav'nly host;
> Praise Father, Son, and Holy Ghost!
> ~ Thomas Ken – 1674

6

Judging, Part 1

Matthew 7:1 "Judge not, that ye be not judged."

John 7:24 "Judge not according to the appearance, but judge righteous judgment."

Judging is serious business; let's take a closer look. We will look at *God's* judgments today; next time, we will look at the judgments *we* are supposed to make.

What is judging? It is discerning whether something is right or wrong. We see bumper stickers and posters saying, "Don't judge me" or "Only God can judge me." It is true that only God can judge us ultimately, but it may come as a surprise that God also tells us that *we* are to judge under certain circumstances. Today's verse from John's epistle tells us exactly that.

Now, "Don't judge" and "Do judge" sound like one of those supposed 'biblical contradictions,' but it isn't. First, let us look at God's judging, and then next time we will look closer at our obligations when we judge.

God tells us that He not only sees actions, but He can see the very "thoughts and intents of the heart." (Hebrews 4:12) In the next verse, He says, "All things are naked and opened unto the eyes of him with whom we have to do." God *knows* everything and *sees* everything. He has all the facts before Him. Additionally, He has no sinful influences to pollute His judgments. Therefore, He will only judge with *full* knowledge and only with absolute truth and righteousness.

This is the kind of judging we cannot do; therefore, God commands us not to. It requires full knowledge, not only of the event, but all motives involved, and a world full of other things we do *not* know or understand.

We will look at human judgment next time, but allow me to make one further comment on God's judgment. As I mentioned above, some people say, "Only God can judge me." I do not judge their intentions for I do not know their hearts. However, God not only *can* judge us, He *will* judge us. Someone who casually says "Only God can judge me"—without seriously contemplating the full impact of saying that—is playing with a fire they cannot possibly comprehend, for it burns hot and long.

My dear friend, carefully consider your standing with God and make it sure.

7

Judging, Part 2

John 7:24 "Judge not according to the appearance, but judge righteous judgment."

Previously, we looked at how God judges and why He forbids us to make those kinds of judgments. He knows all the details of every event and cannot yield to sinful emotions.

Today's verse reminds us that God sometimes calls us to judge too, sometimes even to judge ourselves; however, He commands us that we are **not** to judge based on sudden whims, personal feelings, or prejudices. We should always judge rightly. How can we do that? We don't know everything like God does, and our fallen natures may tempt us toward self-interests and revenge. These are the things we need to guard against if we are ever called upon to render judgment.

Let's look at a societal example. God tells us that theft is wrong. If we are serving on a jury and genuine evidence is presented (eyewitness accounts, forensic evidence, etc.), then it would be proper to render a guilty verdict. On the other hand, if we know the accused and dislike him or find his appearance to be shabby or distasteful, we **must** take great care that our emotions do not cloud our decision; we must stay with the facts as they are. The same caution is appropriate if we like the accused or find his appearance to be admirable. One other concern would be if we try to read someone's motive into the act—aren't we assuming we can see into another person's heart, which only God can do?

We are less likely in our personal lives to pass judgment on bank robbery, but we may be called to settle some dispute among friends, and it is equally important that we "judge not according to the appearance, but judge righteous judgment."

When we base righteous decisions on real facts, not hysterics or emotional manipulation, we are aligning our judgments with God's way of judging.

Micah 6:8 says, "He hath shewed thee, O man, what is good; and what doth the LORD require of thee, but to do justly, and to love mercy, and to walk humbly with thy God?"

First, always render righteous judgment.

Second, showing mercy is easier in a personal situation but may be possible within other settings too.

Third, walking humbly with God will protect us from our own pride, which is good since God forbids that too.

8

Introspection

1 Corinthians 11:30-32 "For this cause many are weak and sickly among you, and many sleep. For if we would judge ourselves, we should not be judged. But when we are judged, we are chastened of the Lord, that we should not be condemned with the world."

In the previous two Musings, we looked at judging. We first looked at the things only God can judge. Secondly, we looked at the times we might be called to judge right from wrong or guilty from not guilty. I did not title this writing "Judging, Part 3." Instead, I titled it "Introspection," which is the discipline of examining yourself; that is one legitimate and proper form of judging.

Today's verses come just after Paul criticizes the Corinthians for having a rather apathetic attitude towards the Lord's Supper. The apostle reminds the reader that sober self-examination is always in order when we come to the Remembrance Table. We should not be casual or flippant regarding our worship of the Savior, and the apostle Paul tells his readers that there are some who have become sick and even died as a result of their careless treatment of the Lord's Supper.

Other areas in our lives require introspection too. In chapter 2 of Paul's letter to Titus, he exhorts us to live careful and honorable lives. How can we know if we are doing that if we do not examine our lives? Additionally, in a very sobering passage, (2 Corinthians 13:5) we are even challenged to examine ourselves as to whether we are in the faith.

Now, if we are not careful, it can be easy to move out of the proper area of self-examination and into the area of self-absorption. Unfortunately, that just puts the focus on us rather than on the Lord Jesus and how well we are following Him.

In closing this final look at discerning and judging, I encourage each of us to occasionally look inwardly long enough to make sure we are following the Master; otherwise, let us always keep our eyes on Him.

9

Getting to Spring

Genesis 8:21-22 "And the LORD smelled a sweet savour; and the LORD said in his heart, I will not again curse the ground any more for man's sake; for the imagination of man's heart is evil from his youth;

neither will I again smite any more every thing living, as I have done. While the earth remaineth, seedtime and harvest, and cold and heat, and summer and winter, and day and night shall not cease."

Autumn has long been my favorite season of the year. I'm sure I have mentioned before, that when I was a child we did not have air conditioning. Therefore, it came as a great relief when Mr. Autumn started blowing his cool breeze through our windows. The problem is that Autumn is only three months long, and then comes Winter.

I used to like Winter too, but as the years continue to come and go, I find Winter to be less "fun in the snow" and more like the low-temperature version of a hot summer. As a result, I have also started to develop a special affinity to Spring.

However, as much as I like Spring, I was reminded of a simple fact recently when a friend posted a photo of a cardinal sitting on a branch as snow swirled around it; the caption was a quote by Susan Gale: "Hang on; the only way to get to Spring is through Winter."

That is true. I suppose that if you have the resources, you can travel to some place where the winter is nicer than wherever you live. However, you still are a slave to Winter because you cannot return home—and to your own, true Spring—until Winter takes his leave.

That is also true of some of the seasons during life that we looked at last time. There are things we can do to correct some uncomfortable situations; however, *some* of the seasons we find ourselves in are only resolved by holding on to God and waiting for His timing to end them.

Additionally, in the worst cases, when we find that we haven't even the strength to hold on to God, all we can do is trust Him to hold onto us. Friends, we can trust Him to hold us, for He loves His people and delights in our faith in His goodness.

10

Rivers and Men

Luke 12:15 "And he [Jesus] said unto them, Take heed, and beware of covetousness: for a man's life consisteth not in the abundance of the things which he possesseth."

Is life pleasant, or is it painful? Is it easy, or is it difficult? Is it a delight, or is it a chore? The answer to all those questions is, "Yes." Yes, life is all those things. Sometimes life is even more than one of those things at the same time.

As we live our lives, it is important to understand what life is. Our modern society leads us to believe that life is about climbing the ladder of success; about accumulating, earning, and buying.

However, if that is the actual meaning to our existence, why is it that when people reach some plateau of success, they are discontent and feel they need to get back on the ladder and keep climbing?

Furthermore, real life has nothing to do with the accumulation of things. That is what Jesus says in our verse today. Life is not about stuff. The Lord went on after this verse to tell of the farmer who had a good harvest one year and decided to build bigger barns to hold it all. He thought he was on easy street, that he was set for the rest of his life. The sad thing is that he **was** set for the rest of his life because that night he died.

There is nothing wrong with possessions as long as they don't possess us and lead us astray. By leading astray, I do not necessarily mean doing things we might call evil; sometimes it just means going with the flow and not deliberately keeping our hearts focused on God and His will for our life.

The late Adrian Rogers said, "Rivers and men both become crooked by following the path of least resistance." Our "successes" tempt us to take our ease, and that often leads us down the road to complacency or even worse.

> Wasted years, wasted years oh how foolish
> As you walk on in darkness and fear.
> Turn around, turn around, God is calling,
> He's calling you from a life of wasted years.
> ~ Wally Fowler

11

Not-So-Hidden Treasures

Luke 6:45: "A good man out of the good treasure of his heart bringeth forth that which is good; and an evil man out of the evil treasure of his heart bringeth forth that which is evil: for of the abundance of the heart his mouth speaketh."

In 1673, Richard Baxter published *A Christian Directory*, in which he advised parents not to allow their children to disrespect or be contemptuous toward them. Instead, he prescribes a clear parent/child distinction saying, "Too much familiarity breedeth contempt, and imboldeneth to disobedience." I would add that being loving and friendly toward your young child is a good thing, assuring them that you mean them well. However, Mr. Baxter is correct; trouble is very likely if the difference in authority is blurred.

I fear that familiarity also breeds contempt regarding the Scriptures, and if not contempt, at least dismissal. That is true with respect to a companion verse to today's passage: "For where your treasure is, there will your heart be also." (Luke 12:34)

We sometimes express shock and horror at some wicked act, wondering why someone would do such evil. We would be just as grieved, but perhaps less surprised, if we read these two verses carefully. A person's heart—their innermost passion—chases what it values most. (Luke 12:34) However, it not only chases what it values, it displays what it values for all to see. (Luke 6:45) That is why, even though we are **not** to judge **motives**, we **are** able to perceive a heart's attitude toward good and evil based on what manner of speech and actions that heart produces. "Wherefore by their fruits ye shall know them." (Matthew 7:20)

As much as we enjoy this life—and it is good to enjoy and share God's blessings—we should be more concerned that we "lay up for yourselves treasures in heaven, where neither moth nor rust doth corrupt, and where thieves do not break through nor steal." (Matthew 6:20) If Heaven is where our treasures are, our heart will be focused on God, and our hearts will bring forth good words and good works. If it is not focused on God, then sadly, that too will be evident in a person's talk and walk.

Heaven is my home, and it contains my treasure. I want my life to show that, and it will. Imperfectly, but surely.

12
Saying and Doing

2 Corinthians 5:17 "Therefore if any man be in Christ, he is a new creature: old things are passed away; behold, all things are become new."

The "ouch factor" will be rather high in today's thoughts—perhaps for you, but definitely for me. Someone once said that when you use your finger to point at someone, there are three other fingers pointing back at yourself. So today, you can just watch as I "preach" to myself. I will open my heart and let you see some of my struggles, for the bane of my life is the sin that remains.

I love my fellow Christians who believe today's verse teaches that when God saves us from our sins, the old nature is eradicated and we can no longer sin. However, I have not found that to be true in my life. I am *fully* aware that today's verse is absolutely true. What I am *not* so sure of is our understanding of that verse. Here's why.

Why would Peter tell believers to "abstain from fleshly lusts" (1 Peter 2:11) if it is not possible for us to sin? Why does Paul condemn the church at Corinth for tolerating sin in their midst? (1 Corinthians 5) If there is no danger of going astray, why does Jude warn us of ungodly men who have crept into the churches? People do not need to be warned not to do something they cannot do. Could it be that today's verse actually speaks of our perfect standing before God and that the truth of the verse needs to be worked out into our daily lives? (Philippians 2:12)

Having said that, there are several reasons why my sin grieves me. Primarily because I am dishonoring the One who loved me and gave His life to save me. That alone *should* grieve me.

However, there is another lesser but still important reason, and that is this. My sin—a harsh comment, insensitivity to someone's need, a selfish act—damages my testimony. It may give someone the excuse they seek to reject my Savior. Richard Baxter once wrote, "Take heed to yourselves, lest your example contradict your doctrine ... lest you unsay with your lives what you say with your tongues, and be the greatest hinderers of the success of your own labors."

Dear friends, that is good advice.

13

Good Morning

1 Thessalonians 4:16-18 "For the Lord himself shall descend from heaven with a shout, with the voice of the archangel, and with the trump of God: and the dead in Christ shall rise first: Then we which are alive and remain shall be caught up together with them in the clouds, to meet the Lord in the air: and so shall we ever be with the Lord. Wherefore comfort one another with these words."

Many years ago, a friend's father passed away. We took one of our sons with us to the visitation; I believe he was three or four at the time. We visited with our friend for a while, then I picked up my son and took him over to the casket. With words that I hoped would make sense to him, I explained that our friend's father had died. I told him that he used to live in this body, that it was just his temporary house, and that he had moved out and gone to live at Jesus' house. We visited our friend a few more minutes and then left. As we walked to the car, my son asked, "Dad, are we going to Jesus' house now?" What a precious thought that was just then.

In 1968, the southern gospel quartet, The Imperials, released an album that included the old spiritual, "Great Gettin' Up Morning." I had not heard that song for several years, but I was recently thinking about the Lord returning for His people when that phrase came to my mind. What a wonderful way of saying it: that "Great Gettin' Up Morning."

I like theology. The word simply means "the study of God," and it is about understanding what God says about Himself. However, I do not know a better and more encouraging theological term for the resurrection of God's people than that "great gettin' up morning."

Mahalia Jackson, the late gospel and blues singer, wrote another song with the same title and a few of the same lines. She once said something that I thought was appropriate to this line of thinking, "When you sing gospel, you have a feeling there is a cure for what's wrong." By God's grace, through Christ's sacrifice on the cross, we have a cure for what's wrong, and one result is going to be on that "great gettin' up morning."

14
Selah

Psalm 32 "1 Blessed is he whose transgression is forgiven, whose sin is covered. 2. Blessed is the man unto whom the LORD imputeth not iniquity, and in whose spirit there is no guile. 3. When I kept silence, my bones waxed old through my roaring all the day long. 4. For day and night thy hand was heavy upon me: my moisture is turned into the drought of summer. Selah. 5. I acknowledged my sin unto thee, and mine iniquity have I not hid. I said, I will confess my transgressions unto the LORD; and thou forgavest the iniquity of my sin. Selah. 6. For this shall every one that is godly pray unto thee in a time when thou mayest be found: surely in the floods of great waters they shall not come nigh unto him. 7. Thou art my hiding place; thou shalt preserve me from trouble; thou shalt compass me about with songs of deliverance. Selah."

According to the lexicon in *Strong's Concordance*, "selah" means to "lift up." Apparently, it was used to highlight or emphasize what is being said. Selah is used 3 times in this psalm, in verses 4, 5, and 7.

Verses 3 and 4 create a picture of desolation. David is "roaring," perhaps moaning or groaning, but he is also "silent." It seems he is lamenting but cannot bring himself to put his transgressions into words. Selah, think about that.

In verse 5, he finally verbalizes his sin, and God forgives him. Selah, think about that.

In verse 7, David recognizes God as his hiding place and deliverance. I wonder if he is also annoyed with all the anguish he caused himself by not confessing his sins sooner. Selah, think about that.

God's way is the best way. God goes on in the psalm to instruct us not to be like a horse or mule that must be controlled with a bit and bridle. Instead, we should willingly heed God's instruction, and thereby avoid sin in the first place. That too is something worth thinking about.

Selah.

15

The Internet Allows Me to See God's Amazing Designs

Psalm 19:1-3. "The heavens declare the glory of God; and the firmament sheweth his handywork. Day unto day uttereth speech, and night unto night sheweth knowledge. There is no speech nor language, where their voice is not heard."

My formal education, as well as my personal observations and experiences, have left me in awe of the Creator of the universe. That sense of God's majesty has only deepened as the internet allows me to find photos, videos, and articles that display or describe His glorious creativity.

For example, consider the human, animal, and plant life on Earth. Many plants require animal life for pollination (bees), seed distribution (birds and mammals), and carbon-dioxide (human and animal life in general). At the same time, directly or indirectly, humans and animals depend on plants for food and oxygen.

Next, do you remember seeing drawings depicting what an atom looks like? Isn't their similarity to a solar system interesting? There are clear differences, to be sure, but whether looking down through a microscope or up through a telescope, the similarities between the micro and the macro are striking.

The third illustration in our virtually inexhaustible list is the universe itself. Astronomers tell us that we know of 100 to 200-billion galaxies, each with up to a trillion stars. Furthermore, estimates suggest there are probably ten times as many galaxies as we thought previously— as many as 2-trillion galaxies. And who knows how big that number will become as telescopes become increasingly powerful? We have no idea where it ends.

Many of my internet evidences are written or recorded by people who do **not** see God in their discoveries, but He still shines through. I am in no way being condescending when I say that I feel truly sorry for people like that. For all who look for the truth, it is right there in the sky, as well as on top of the Earth, under the surface, and even in a drop of stream water, for "The heavens declare the glory of God; and the firmament sheweth his handywork."

16

Hems and Blood Sacrifices

Matthew 9:20-22 "And, behold, a woman, which was diseased with an issue of blood twelve years, came behind him, and touched the hem of his garment: For she said within herself, If I may but touch his garment, I shall be whole. But Jesus turned him about, and when he saw her, he said, Daughter, be of good comfort; thy faith hath made thee whole. And the woman was made whole from that hour."

The precious woman in today's verses had a blood disease for more than a decade. Think about that—sick for more than a decade! The doctors were unable to cure her illness, and in fact, her health got worse. Then she heard that Jesus was nearby and determined to touch his clothes in an act of faith.

That woman's faith restored her health, but only partially; she had another problem different from the first. By her touch, her faith fixed her body, but the other problem went much deeper. This problem was not with her blood; it was a problem with her heart.

It is the same with each of us, dear friends. Whether we have the body of an athlete in his mid-twenties or of a seventy-year-old cancer patient, we all came into this world with a damaged heart. By "heart" I am not speaking of the blood-pumping muscle in our chests; I am referring to the very innermost core of who we are. God even says that core is dead in its sinful condition. (Ephesians 2:1) Until a blood transaction occurs—one that is different from that of the woman in today's verses—then as Jesus told the Pharisees, "our sin remaineth." (John 9:41)

That "blood transaction" is an act of God whereby He applies the shed blood of Christ to the account of a lost soul who trusts in Him for His mercy and grace. When that happens, we have the forgiveness of our sins; we are made right with God; and our dead souls are alive with an everlasting life—a life that will last forever.

That is the result of the work of the mighty Lord of Heaven who loved us and gave Himself for us. "This is the LORD"s doing; it is marvellous in our eyes." (Psalm 118:23)

Hallelujah! What a Savior.

17

Streaming Thoughts

Psalm 19:14 "Let the words of my mouth, and the meditation of my heart, be acceptable in thy sight, O LORD, my strength, and my redeemer."

Streaming is a buzzword. Well, it is one of dozens of buzzwords. These days, it seems we have several new buzzwords every week. For my readers who are not familiar with the term, streaming is the technology that allows a viewer to watch live video over the internet.

Even though "streaming" is a technology term, it might also be useful to think of that word regarding our own speech. Speaking honestly and boldly is usually a good thing; however, it is possible for us to say things—even true things—that don't need to be said.

There is an interesting word usage in Psalm 17:4, which says, "Concerning the works of men, by the word of thy lips I have kept me from the paths of the destroyer." The primary thought is that David has obeyed God's Word, and he has thereby avoided doing evil. What I find interesting though is that the Hebrew word translated "lips"—along with meaning the feature on the face—is also used for a seashore or riverbank. In other words, it describes the place where the water stops, a barrier that prevents water from going any further and causing damage.

Our lips are like that seashore. Many thoughts come to our mind, but according to today's verse, we should only allow words that are acceptable to God to flow through our lips or even linger in our hearts, for that matter. In fact, a good way to safeguard our lips from *words* that are unacceptable to God is to guard our hearts from *thoughts* that are unacceptable to God.

According to 1 Corinthians 6:20, we Christians have been bought with a price and do not belong to ourselves. That includes our lips, which are the "shore" over which our thoughts pass. If He owns us, let us yield to Him and only allow those things that are acceptable to Him to flow through our lips—lips that He owns.

18

High above the Fray

Ephesians 1:3 "Blessed be the God and Father of our Lord Jesus Christ, who hath blessed us with all spiritual blessings in heavenly places in Christ:"

As an imaginative child, I dreamed about flying. I didn't even have to flap my arms. I just raised them up and ran, and I lifted off the ground.

Recently, I have seen advertisements for remote controlled flying toys called quad copters, the least-expensive of them costing just a few dozen dollars. For ten or twenty dollars more, there are units with video cameras that will record what you would see if you were sitting on the unit as it flies. However, if you want to spend a *lot* of money, there are even thousand-dollar models where the camera signal is sent back to electronic goggles you wear so you can see the camera image while you are flying the unit from down below. I have never used one of these gadgets, but I have seen video of what the goggles show, and I actually got the visual sensation of flying.

An interesting aspect of these camera toys is that you can see things in the distance and from angles that are impossible to view from the ground. I have resisted the temptation to buy one of the inexpensive camera units, but I still think how neat it would be to fly it over my house and see the replay of the front yard, then the roof, then the backyard in one smooth, continuous, hovering video.

Technology and imagination are wonderful things; however, are you aware that as Christians we are to seek those lofty and elevated "spiritual blessings in heavenly places" that God has for us? Colossians 3:1-3 says, "If ye then be risen with Christ, seek those things which are above, where Christ sitteth on the right hand of God. Set your affection on things above, not on things on the earth. For ye are dead, and your life is hid with Christ in God."

It would be fascinating to watch the video from a small camera as it hovers over lawns and trees, over houses and streets. However, that pales in significance to grasping the spectacular things God has done for us and the wonders He still has in store for those who trust in Him!

19

Temporary and Permanent

Acts 9:6a "And he trembling and astonished said, Lord, what wilt thou have me to do?" (Paul on the road to Damascus)

Hank Ketcham wrote a newspaper comic titled "Dennis the Menace." On weekdays, it was a single panel, and Dennis was usually involved in some mischief that caused annoyance for others in the cartoon and a chuckle for the reader. If I recall correctly, Mr. Ketcham repeated one Christmas panel several years; it showed Dennis sitting on the floor—completely surrounded by toys—saying something like, "Is that all there is?"

I recently had an unusual experience. As I left the house to run some errands, I saw a fresh grave being dug in a nearby cemetery. When I returned later, the grave was filled in. In just a few short hours, the remains of one of our fellow mortals had been laid to rest. I have been to funerals and burials before, but I have never witnessed the opening *and* closing of a grave within hours of each other.

The temptation might be to stand at the graveside of a friend or relative and ask, "Is that all there is?" Thankfully, the answer is no, there is more, and that answer applies to all. However, that answer is both good news for some and bad news for others. Why? Because almost everything that happens before the grave is temporary, but virtually everything that happens after the grave is permanent.

Death is like the screen mesh in a strainer that allows liquids to pass through but strains out the solids. All of our possessions—money, cars, houses, lands—*all* we have accumulated is filtered away from us by death. Even if we have gold, silver, and cash put into our grave with us, we do not have control over it, for it simply lies in the ground with our bodies while the "real us" is long gone.

There is nothing wrong with having money, as long as we earn it and use it to the glory of God. However, we cannot take *any* of this world's goods with us into the next world. We must understand that money is our temporary servant and not our master. We Christians already have a Master; let us therefore lay our servant, our riches—whether much or little—at the feet of our Master and ask Him, "Lord, what wilt thou have me to do?"

20
In the Image

Genesis 1:27 "So God created man in his own image, in the image of God created he him; male and female created he them."

Romans 1:22-23 "Professing themselves to be wise, they became fools, And changed the glory of the uncorruptible God into an image made like to corruptible man, and to birds, and fourfooted beasts, and creeping things."

Moses tells us that God created man in his own image. A few verses later, he tells us, "God saw every thing that he had made, and, behold, it was very good." (Genesis 1:31)

Then, the fall of mankind occurs. (Genesis 3)

Ever since then, mankind has been making his own god in the image *he* chooses. Sometimes we make our god in the form of "birds, and fourfooted beasts, and creeping things" (Does this remind you of nature worship?), and sometimes we get arrogant and unimaginative enough that we simply make our god in *our own* image. We may think of it as being in the *form* of "super men," but it is actually "corruptible man," nevertheless.

Ever since that great disaster of Genesis 3, we have had wickedness and evil, suffering and sorrow, and murder and death.

God's way was better.

And still is.

21
How to Be Forgiven for the Unforgivable

Jonah 3:4-5 "And Jonah began to enter into the city a day's journey, and he cried, and said, Yet forty days, and Nineveh shall be overthrown. So the people of Nineveh believed God, and proclaimed a fast, and put on sackcloth, from the greatest of them even to the least of them."

By God's command, Jonah escaped the great fish and went to that wicked city to warn them. Just a few verses later, the king declared that every one should repent of their violence and evil ways because "Who can tell if God will turn and repent, and turn away from his fierce anger, that we perish not? And God saw their works, that they turned from their evil way; and God repented of the evil, that he had said that he would do unto them; and he did it not." (verses 9-10)

I just read an article about Islam and the Qur'an; one thing in particular struck me as very sad. The article paraphrased Qur'an 4:116 as saying "all sins are forgivable except idol worship." Wanting to know the actual wording, I read the passage myself from the Sahih International Translation; it does indeed say that Allah will not forgive anyone who equates someone else with him. Another translation used the word "partner," adding the flavor that Allah will not forgive anyone who thinks he needs a helper, someone equal to him. It goes on to say Allah will forgive lesser sins if he chooses to do so, but he does not forgive those who place anything or anyone on his level.

I am so encouraged by this passage in Jonah. In His inexpressible kindness, the true and living God who created the heavens and the Earth, sent Jonah to warn Nineveh of His pending judgment, but when that wicked city, including the king, turned from their sinful ways and back to God, the Lord of all grace withdrew His judgment.

Sin is the cause of every evil in the universe, and we dare not dismiss it lightly; however, the mercies of God should captivate us in absolute awe, especially because at one time *all of us* were rebels against Him and placed something or someone above Him, often ourselves.

"Oh that men would praise the LORD for his goodness, and for his wonderful works to the children of men!" (Psalm 107:8) What wonderful advice.

22

Being Forever

Romans 3:21-26 "But now the righteousness of God without the law is manifested, being witnessed by the law and the prophets; Even the righteousness of God which is by faith of Jesus Christ unto all and upon all them that believe: for there is no difference: For all have sinned, and come short of the glory of God; Being justified freely by his grace through the redemption that is in Christ Jesus: Whom God hath set forth to be a propitiation [pleasing sacrifice] through faith in his blood, to declare his righteousness for the remission of sins that are past, through the forbearance of God; To declare, I say, at this time his righteousness: that he might be just, and the justifier of him which believeth in Jesus."

It is almost impossible for us mortals to conceive of forever. I think the reason is that we cannot see any examples. Plants and animals die; cars and cell phones quit working; even our friends and family slip away from us. We cannot imagine forever because everything we know ends.

That is almost true, but not exactly. Human beings are alive forever. Not our bodies, but our souls—the real us. That is true for everyone, great or small, rich or poor, good or bad. However, there is one difference. All will be alive forever; some will live eternal life, while others, as strange as it sounds, will live the anguish of eternal death. This is an unpleasant topic, but one that we must consider. Regardless of how much we would rather not face this reality, ignoring it will not change it or make it go away.

I was reminded of this truth when I saw a picture of a young lady wearing a tee shirt with the sobering words, "Live forever or die forever." Even as distasteful as that thought is, there is good news. God has provided eternal life through Christ Jesus who willingly suffered death as our substitute. He paid for our sin, the sin in us that caused death in the first place.

Yes, the good news is that we don't need to "die forever." God says it this way: "The wages of sin is death; but the gift of God is eternal life through Jesus Christ our Lord." (Romans 6:23)

Trust God for His forgiveness through Christ's sacrifice. By His grace, you can live life forever.

23
Being Forever, Part 2

1 Corinthians 15:51-53 "Behold, I shew you a mystery; We shall not all sleep, but we shall all be changed, In a moment, in the twinkling of an eye, at the last trump: for the trumpet shall sound, and the dead shall be raised incorruptible, and we shall be changed. For this corruptible must put on incorruption, and this mortal must put on immortality."

I deliberately limit the length of these devotionals so they are brief and to the point. As a result, I cannot always cover every angle of the subject. I was aware of that shortcoming about yesterday's Musing titled "Being Forever" in which we looked at the biblical reality that we humans shall actually exist forever, in either bliss or misery. We considered the eternality of our spirits, but time forbad me to account for the equally biblical reality that in eternity our spirits will be reunited with our bodies. Today's verses, and those that follow them, deal with that truth for those who trust in God for the forgiveness of their sins. It is the case of these Christian believers I wish to consider today.

I lost both my parents in 2010; my cousin Jim lost both of his in 2015. All four of them were Christians, so Jim and I have a vested interest in understanding what happens to our loved ones when they die. The same also applies to us when we, as Hamlet said it, "have shuffled off this mortal coil."

When we, as Christian believers, pass from this life, the spirit leaves the body and goes to be with the Lord (2 Corinthians 5:1-8) while the body decays and disintegrates. Now again I refer you to today's verses, for they proclaim the sure declaration of the unchangeable God of the Bible. In this passage, He makes it clear that He will not only restore our decayed body but will change it into a form like unto Christ's glorious, resurrected body! (Philippians 3:21)

"Behold, I shew you a mystery," Paul declares, and what a wonderful revelation God has given us through the apostle. "We shall not all sleep, but we shall all be changed … For this corruptible must put on incorruption, and this mortal must put on immortality."

"O death, where is thy sting? O grave, where is thy victory?" (1 Corinthians 15:55)

24

I Change Not

Daniel 12:4 "But thou, O Daniel, shut up the words, and seal the book, even to the time of the end: many shall run to and fro, and knowledge shall be increased."

In the early 1990s, I went to a conference where I learned that information was doubling every five years. However, in an article published in 2014, David Schilling noted that knowledge was then doubling every 13 months and quoted IBM as predicting that knowledge will eventually double every 12 hours.

About the same time, I purchased my first XT computer, an IBM clone running the DOS operating system. At that time, you had to buy the hard drive separately, and I paid $229.95 for a whopping 20-megabyte drive! Today, that is about twenty, medium-resolution digital photographs. Several months ago, I purchased a 2-terabyte drive (100,000 times more capacity than a 20-megabyte drive) for $60.00.

Times surely are changing, not only in matters of knowledge and technology, but in many other ways as well. Jesus told His followers of a time we would "hear of wars and rumours of wars." Then He said, "see that ye be not troubled: for all these things must come to pass, but the end is not yet. For nation shall rise against nation, and kingdom against kingdom: and there shall be famines, and pestilences, and earthquakes, in divers places." (Matthew 24:6-7) Those things are happening even now, as I write this.

How can we live in the midst of these overwhelming changes and unsettling events? We find one of the most stabilizing truths in this ever-changing world tucked away in Hebrews 13:8 that says, "Jesus Christ the same yesterday, and to day, and for ever." Did you notice Jesus' command in Matthew? "See that ye be not troubled." Why does He tell us we should not be troubled? "For all these things *must* come to pass." (emphasis mine) The Lord Jesus—who loved us and gave His life for us; who does not change and to whom all power has been given—(Matthew 28:18) says these things are part of His plan and purpose.

That, dear friend, is the reason it is both safe and good that we "be not troubled." God is in control.

25
The Importance of Knowing

Psalm 39:1-4 "I said, I will take heed to my ways, that I sin not with my tongue: I will keep my mouth with a bridle, while the wicked is before me. I was dumb with silence, I held my peace, even from good; and my sorrow was stirred. My heart was hot within me, while I was musing the fire burned: then spake I with my tongue, LORD, make me to know mine end, and the measure of my days, what it is; that I may know how frail I am."

I used to live in a rural community, where ever so often, I would see posters announcing a "Strongest Man Contest." I never attended one of the contests as a spectator, and I am certain I never qualified as a participant. I do enjoy watching people apply their skills in sports, but at my age, I am realizing that any such skills I ever had, even at lesser levels, are fading rapidly.

I use the word "Musings" as the title for these writings. Muse means to meditate, to ponder, to glean understanding by reflecting on an idea. Today's verses use that word. In them, David ponders his sinful condition, especially as it manifests itself through his tongue. As a result, he hesitates to talk, even for good. The more he thinks about it, the hotter the fire burns in his heart. Finally, in verse 4, he asks God to help him comprehend how truly feeble, limited, and temporal he is.

259

In our youthful exuberance, we think of ourselves as invincible. We may say with our lips, "Yes, one day I will die," but our mortality is always in the back of our thoughts. Nevertheless, young men in their forties have heart attacks, and men in their twenties have motorcycle accidents. And they are gone. These are not merely words for effect; these are actualities I learned of this very week.

I do not write this to *dis*courage, but rather to *en*courage along a good path. Let us live our lives fully, but let us temper that fullness with reality. Living an abundant life includes living it in a way that pleases our Creator knowing that our gifts and talents are from Him, that our days are limited, and that in the words of the Rich Mullins song, "We are not as strong as we think we are."

26

I Hate Buttermilk

Isaiah 55:8-9 "For my thoughts are not your thoughts, neither are your ways my ways, saith the LORD. For as the heavens are higher than the earth, so are my ways higher than your ways, and my thoughts than your thoughts."

The goals we mortals have may be laudable and good, or they may be selfish and corrupt. Either way, because we are damaged creatures, our efforts are often flawed and sometimes disastrous.

However, according to today's verses, God's ways are always above ours. There is another verse, one in Ecclesiastes, which tells us some details about His ways: "I know that, whatsoever God doeth, it shall be for ever:" (His ways are eternal.) "Nothing can be put to it, nor any thing taken from it:" (His ways are perfect; no additions or subtractions required.) "And God doeth it, that men should fear before him." (His ways always have purpose.) (3:14)

Since God's ways are so far above ours—and even past finding out, (Romans 11:33) we often do not understand what He is doing until after He has already done it. Such was the case when Joseph was sold into slavery, when Moses fled into a forty-year exile, when Paul was knocked off his horse and blinded, and when Jesus hung on the cross.

I read an interesting illustration the other day; I don't know who the author is. "One Sunday morning at a small Southern church, the new pastor called on one of his older deacons to lead in the opening prayer. The deacon stood up, bowed his head and said, 'Lord, I hate buttermilk.' The young pastor opened one eye and wondered where this was going. The deacon continued, 'Lord, I hate lard.' Now the pastor was totally perplexed. The deacon continued, 'Lord, I ain't too crazy about plain flour. But after you mix 'em all together and bake 'em in a hot oven, I just love biscuits. Lord, help us to realize when life gets hard, when things come up that we don't like, whenever we don't understand what You are doing, that we need to wait and see what You are making. After you get through mixing and baking, it'll probably be something even better than biscuits.' "

God is always good, but sometimes He tests our faith a little while before He shows us that goodness.

27

The Master Sin

Galatians 5:1-4 "Stand fast therefore in the liberty wherewith Christ hath made us free, and be not entangled again with the yoke of bondage. Behold, I Paul say unto you, that if ye be circumcised, Christ shall profit you nothing. For I testify again to every man that is circumcised, that he is a debtor to do the whole law. Christ is become of no effect unto you, whosoever of you are justified by the law; ye are fallen from grace."

Every day, we see the disastrous results of the Fall that occurred in the Garden of Eden. But God, by His inconceivable grace, gave His Son as a ransom to redeem us from our lost condition.

Sometimes people wonder if it is possible to fall from that grace. After all, the Bible does use that term in today's verses. By the way, that is the only place it is found in the Bible. However, seeing the words "fallen from grace" without looking at the whole of what God is saying here leads us to think that falling from grace is the result of some sin we commit.

Now, in one sense, that is true. However, as evil and base as sins are—murder, sexual sins, blasphemy, idolatry, covetousness, etc.—and they *are* evil and base, there is only one "master sin" that God connects to being "fallen from grace", and that is believing we must add something to that grace, thereby rejecting Christ's completed work on the cross.

We absolutely *should* be growing in our love for the Lord, and we *should* flee from those things that displease Him. However, in context, "the yoke of bondage" to which Paul refers is not the sins of the flesh, but the pride of the heart. It is as if we say, "God's grace is good but not good enough; however, I can add something of my own effort that will make it perfect." That speaks against the Lord Jesus who said of His work on the cross, "It is finished."

Circumcision, observance of days or foods or traditions—all of these may be perfectly fine in their place, and I am not trying to talk anyone out of them. ***However***, if we are ***depending*** on those things or ***anything*** other than Christ's sacrifice for our righteousness—whether laws or works—we are operating outside the boundaries of grace. (Romans 11:6)

Let us beware.

28

Lazarus and Fear

John 11:39-44: "Jesus said, Take ye away the stone. Martha, the sister of him that was dead, saith unto him, Lord, by this time he stinketh: for he hath been dead four days. Jesus saith unto her, Said I not unto thee, that, if thou wouldest believe, thou shouldest see the glory of God? Then they took away the stone from the place where the dead was laid. And Jesus lifted up his eyes, and said, Father, I thank thee that thou hast heard me. And I knew that thou hearest me always: but because of the people which stand by I said it, that they may believe that thou hast sent me. And when he thus had spoken, he cried with a loud voice, Lazarus, come forth. And he that was dead came forth, bound hand and foot with graveclothes: and his face was bound about with a napkin. Jesus saith unto them, Loose him, and let him go."

As I type this, I am sitting in the lobby of a Kentucky state park lodge. We have been here a number of times, and it is one of our favorite homes away from home. Tomorrow we will leave and head back to our house several hundred miles away. As much as we like it here, our house is more familiar; it is where we are at home.

The story of Lazarus in this passage is encouraging. There is great comfort in knowing that the Lord Jesus can raise the dead. However, let me ask you a question you may not have considered before: What was going through Lazarus' mind when he lay dying the ***second*** time?

Unlike almost every other mortal, Lazarus had a unique advantage in that he had already been on the other side; he already had been where he was going. In the same way that I know what to expect when I step into my house tomorrow, Lazarus knew what he would see when he opened his eyes after he died again. What anticipation he must have had! What fearlessness he had in knowing what to expect.

We don't have that experience; however, we ***do*** have the promise of God that He is there, and that He has prepared a place for us. (John

14:2-3) We can eagerly anticipate our new heavenly home even though we have not been there yet!

29

The Revelation of Paul

Romans 1 "20 For I am not ashamed of the gospel of Christ: for it is the power of God unto salvation to every one that believeth; to the Jew first, and also to the Greek. 17. For therein is the **righteousness** of God **revealed** from faith to faith: as it is written, The just shall live by faith. 18. For the **wrath** of God is **revealed** from heaven against all ungodliness and unrighteousness of men, who hold the truth in unrighteousness. 19. Because that which may be known of God is manifest in them; for God hath shewed it unto them. 20. For the invisible things of him from the creation of the world are clearly seen, being understood by the things that are made, even his eternal power and Godhead; so that they are without excuse:" (emphasis mine)

Yes, I know that the human author of the book of Revelation was John; however, God also revealed things through Paul. I am thinking particularly of two of those revelations in today's verses. God has revealed His *righteousness*, and He has revealed His *wrath*, but He has done these two things in different ways.

Speaking of God's righteousness, Paul uses the word "therein," (v17) referring back to the gospel. (v16) God is declaring that in His righteousness, He has purposed to send His only begotten Son to redeem all who have faith in Him. The gospel is part of *how* God displays His righteousness to man.

However, in contrast, this passage does not present *how* God reveals His wrath, but *why*. If you read all of Romans 1, you find Paul's list of the works of rebellion that reside in the ungodly and unrighteous human heart. In the end, he announces that "they which commit such things are worthy of death." (v32) That sounds harsh, but what we are talking about here is insurrection against the God of the universe! *Let that sink in!*

God calls us to live by faith, to believe what He says and live accordingly. On the contrary, rebellion is to deny either His wisdom or His authority,s and most likely, both.

So then, He places the choice before us: the wisdom of God or the foolishness of man; the gospel of salvation or the ways of death; the righteousness of God or the wrath of God.

"Choose you this day whom ye will serve." (Joshua 24:15)

30
Like a Flint

Isaiah 50:5-7 "The Lord GOD hath opened mine ear, and I was not rebellious, neither turned away back. I gave my back to the smiters, and my cheeks to them that plucked off the hair: I hid not my face from shame and spitting. For the Lord GOD will help me; therefore shall I not be confounded: therefore have I set my face like a flint, and I know that I shall not be ashamed."

Saying a person has done something with "reckless abandon" says they have embarked on some activity so aggressively that it seems they are willing to risk everything—including life itself—in order to complete the endeavor. Such a person believes that the cause is just and the outcome will be worth the cost.

The Lord Jesus was never reckless; however, with confidence in, and in agreement with, His Father, Jesus came to die for mortal rebels. Even as today's prophetic verses say, He "set His face like a flint," indicating a steely determination. He purposed that the cause was just and the outcome would be worth the cost, even though He knew what that cost would be.

> He left the splendor of heaven,
> Knowing His destiny
> Was the lonely hill of Golgotha,
> There to lay down His life for me.
> ~ Dottie Rambo

The late Tim Hansel, wrote, "One day, while my son Zac and I were out in the country, climbing around in some cliffs, I heard a voice from above me yell, 'Hey Dad! Catch me!' I turned around to see Zac joyfully jumping off a rock straight at me. ... I became an instant circus act, catching him. We both fell to the ground. For a moment after I caught him I could hardly talk. When I found my voice again, I gasped in exasperation: 'Zac! Can you give me one good reason why you did that???' He responded with remarkable calmness: 'Sure. Because you're my Dad.' His whole assurance was based on the fact that his father was trustworthy. He could live life to the hilt because I could be trusted. Isn't this even more true for a Christian?"

Jesus trusted His Father enough to abandon Himself to redemption's plan. Can we not trust the great God to save us and abandon ourselves to His strong and capable arms?

OCTOBER

1

Bad Connections and Good Connections

1 Thessalonians 5:16-18 "Rejoice evermore. Pray without ceasing. In every thing give thanks: for this is the will of God in Christ Jesus concerning you."

Several weeks ago, we went to a family reunion in a rural area on a small lake. The wooded area was wondrous, the temperature was pleasant, and the company was enjoyable. Additionally, knowing that the spectacular setting was the handiwork of God made everything delightful.

In this rustic setting, I had no cell phone service; however, a thought occurred to me while we were there. Even though I could not call anyone, I could still talk to God. On a number of occasions, I did just that; I spoke to the glorious God who had created our stunning surroundings. In addition, one brother gave thanks before we enjoyed the delicious meal.

God tells us in today's verses that we should always rejoice, pray, and give thanks. Isn't it wonderful that God has made this world in such a way that even when we are in the middle of nowhere, and even in the dark of night, we can still reach out to Him to offer praise and gratitude, and to make petition? It is our delight and privilege to be able to do so. It should always bring peace to our hearts to know that regardless of cell phones and radio towers, and even power failures, we can always talk to our God.

On the day of the reunion, that thought brought me even greater delight than enjoying family in God's spectacular creation.

2

Islamic State and the Grace of God

Psalm 2:1-3 "Why do the heathen rage, and the people imagine a vain thing? The kings of the earth set themselves, and the rulers take counsel together, against the LORD, and against his anointed, saying, Let us break their bands asunder, and cast away their cords from us."

That psalm goes on to say that God will laugh at their folly and deal with them in wrath, vexation, and sore displeasure. We do great injustice to the understanding of God when we downplay His holiness, justice, and righteousness; however, we do equal injustice when we overlook the staggering grace, mercy, and loving kindness that are just as much a part of His being.

Some years ago, while ISIS was fighting for control in Iraq, many Iraqis fled for their lives. Fatima was one of them. One evening, she was drawn to the sound of singing in a tent in a refugee camp. She approached cautiously, and though embarrassed when noticed by the Christians worshiping inside, she came closer and asked if she could enter and listen to what they were saying. By the time the meeting finished at 4 AM, she was on her way to embracing Christ as Savior and asked if she could bring friends and family to the next meeting.

Fatima, her husband, and three daughters put their trust in Jesus for their salvation, and according to an area ministry leader, within a few weeks, her involvement led to another 60 families making the same commitment. "Tent churches are going on everywhere," the leader said. "Last week we had 68 families openly surrender their lives to the Lord. With all their large needs and difficult situations that they are going through, they thank God for the indwelling of Christ in their hearts. A dozen of those families were Muslims."

We often have no idea what the True and Living God is doing, but this report is not unique. God has purposed out of the chaos and mayhem that ISIS unleashed to bring precious souls to Himself.

I never get used to what You do.
I never get used to watching You
Take a life beyond redemption,
Make it Yours, and make it new.

I never outgrow the miracle—
A heart that was empty, flowing full—
I never get used to what You do.
~ Twila Paris

3

Lost Lambs

Isaiah 53:6 "All we like sheep have gone astray; we have turned every one to his own way."

My late Aunt Winifred, speaking of her childhood, described herself as a "timid soul;" children like that don't venture far from the familiar. Others are more daring and wander out on their own. Whether timid or bold, from time to time, a child becomes separated from all they recognize. I remember watching my children wander to where they could not see me; I saw them, but when they realized they could not see me, a sudden panic came over their faces.

A little while back, I was writing and used a word I didn't remember using before. I suspected it was not original with me, but I didn't know how the word came into my mind. My spellchecker didn't even recognize it. The word was "lostness." A desperate sense befalls us when we realize we are lost. However, as bad as that is, it is starkly worst to be lost and not even know it. Our awareness of being lost prompts us to seek the familiar, but, when we don't even *know* we are lost, we continue to wander without seeking a solution because we don't even think there *is* a problem.

I deliberately left off the last part of today's verse because I wanted to emphasize what lostness is. In full, the verse says, "All we like sheep have gone astray; we have turned every one to his own way; and the LORD hath laid on him the iniquity of us all."

Long before we knew we were lost, God knew we were lost. Long before we knew we needed a solution, God knew we needed a solution. And He created that solution! In His wisdom, mercy, and loving kindness, God made a way to bring wandering people back to Himself. Only God can redeem us from our lostness, and He did so by paying the penalty for our sins. Twila Paris said it this way:

> "I was so lost, I should have died,
> But You have brought me to Your side
> To be led by Your staff and rod,
> And to be called a lamb of God
>
> Oh, Lamb of God, sweet Lamb of God;
> I love the holy Lamb of God.

Oh, wash me in His precious blood,
My Jesus Christ, the Lamb of God."
~ Twila Paris

The Lamb cures our lostness!

4

Unfeigned Faith

1 Timothy 1:5 "Now the end of the commandment is charity out of a pure heart, and of a good conscience, and of faith unfeigned."

Reputable pottery artisans would not lie to their buyers about flaws in their products. However, I am told there were some in Bible times—and perhaps even now—who would press wax into small cracks in clay pottery to conceal the imperfections. The dishonest craftsman would "feign" or pretend that he was selling a quality product. That is the meaning of the word used here. The older apostle Paul is challenging young Timothy not to have a pretend or flawed faith, but rather to have *un*feigned faith.

In a Hallmark movie titled *A Dream of Christmas*, a woman who is annoyed at her husband makes an offhand remark that she wishes she was not married anymore. The next morning, she awakes to finds out that she is single; that instead of the years she had been married, she has been climbing the corporate ladder; and that she is now a senior advertising executive at her company. Her entire life is different, but the premise of the story is that she finds out her new life is not what she thought it would be. As a result, she seeks out her husband who now has no idea who she is. As they enter into a professional relationship, they also begin to warm up to each other personally. The woman knows how impossible her story would seem to him, so without going into detail she starts hinting at her dissatisfaction with the way her life has turned out. Her now not-husband replies, "I ask myself all the time how did I end up here? The paths we take sometimes … I wonder if my life would be different if I had made other choices. And I feel like a fraud at some level. Right? Imposters? Like … we're not good enough? We keep pretending?"

Whether we are talking about faith or any other aspect of life, it is important that we guard against being a fraud, against feigning or pretending who and what we are. We need to be authentic and honest, with fellow travelers in this life, but especially with God.

As Paul says, "The end of the commandment is charity out of a pure heart, and of a good conscience, and of faith unfeigned."

5

Is There an App for THAT?

Several years ago, on this date, our daughter-in-law wrote a very encouraging article comparing life's problems to our smart phones. With her permission, I share it with you today.

Jennifer Powers
October 5, 2015

Is there an App for THAT???

No one seems to have come up with an App to fix life's problems.

We can't just make disappointment disappear like magic by flicking it off our screen. We can't click our way to freedom from insecurity, fear, tragedy, gripping pain, terminal illness, or sin.

We may be able to tap and drag and click and point our way through our mobile devices all day long, but at the end of the day, our trouble-filled lives still exist.

Jesus says to us in John 16:33, "I have told you these things, so that in me you may have peace. In this world you will have trouble. But take heart! I have overcome the world." Life's troubles have been overcome by our Savior and Lord Jesus Christ.

No, we don't get an "easy button" or a surefire way for our troubles to disappear; however, the *King of the universe* has overcome the world and the troubles contained therein.

Because of what He has *already* done, I say to you today...

- There's an App for that...God's Word.
- There's an App for that...God's grace.
- There's an App for that...God's healing.
- There's an App for that...God's strength made perfect in weakness.
- There's an App for that...God's peace in the storms of our lives.

He is *it*! He is *all* we need. Reverently, He's the "App" for *all* that!

6

Pray for the Peace of Jerusalem

Psalm 122:6-9 "Pray for the peace of Jerusalem: they shall prosper that love thee. Peace be within thy walls, and prosperity within thy palaces. For my brethren and companions' sakes, I will now say, Peace be within thee. Because of the house of the Lord our God I will seek thy good."

I love the Lord's people. Although there are different understandings among genuine believers, we must love and encourage one another. That notwithstanding, one of the different understandings that makes me saddest is the thought some people have that God is done with Israel.

There can be no doubt that ever since Israel's rejection of Christ, she has been set aside, but is that permanent or only for a time? You might recall that was not the first time Israel lost her testimony; there were other times during which Israel's disobedience became severe enough that the Lord brought significant judgment.

Isn't that somewhat like us? It grieves me that I sin. When I do, sometimes God nudges me, and other times He gives me a pretty hard smack. But does he disown me? How about His promise that "I will never leave thee, nor forsake thee?" (Hebrews 13:5) That's a promise from God. If he will not break that promise to us—and I trust in Him that He won't—why would He break His promise to Abraham and to His seed forever? (Exodus 32:13)

As a father, I had many shortcomings. That too grieves me. However, if I, as an imperfect father, never even considered disowning my children when they disobeyed me, would the perfect Heavenly Father break His promise and disown any of His people?

Dear saints in the Lord, there was a time when no one reading this Musing knew the Lord; however, in the fullness of our time, the precious Spirit convicted us of sin and brought us to a saving knowledge of Christ. In the same way, it is true that many of the Jewish people do not *yet* know the Lord Jesus as their Messiah, but that doesn't mean that He has abandoned them. A promise of God is a promise kept.

God still loves the children of Abraham. He tells us in today's verses to pray for the peace of Jerusalem, and by reasonable extension, all of Israel. Let us love His earthly people and pray for them as He commands us.

7

The Scope and Duration of Sovereignty

Romans 6:12-14 "Let not sin therefore reign in your mortal body, that ye should obey it in the lusts thereof. Neither yield ye your members as instruments of unrighteousness unto sin: but yield yourselves unto God, as those that are alive from the dead, and your members as instruments of righteousness unto God. For sin shall not have dominion over you: for ye are not under the law, but under grace."

I recently saw two completely different graphics; however, the more I considered their individual messages, the more I realized a connection.

I knew Methuselah died just before the flood (at age 969), and that the flood occurred more than 1,600 years after Adam fell. What one meme showed, that I initially overlooked, was that Methuselah was more than 200 years old when Adam died. Methuselah may well have told Noah things he learned directly from Adam.

The second meme named four women in the linage of Jesus:

Tamar, a woman embroiled in a scandal with her father-in-law.

Rahab, the Gentile harlot from Jericho who became the mother of Boaz and great, great grandmother to King David.

Ruth, the Moabite who endured great personal tragedy to become wife to the same Boaz and great grandmother to David.

Bathsheba, with whom King David committed adultery before he murdered her husband.

Four women, all different from each other: Israelites and Gentiles; participants in damage and pain, or innocent victims of damage and pain. Even David, a key figure in this linage, was tormented by his enemies, and yet later, he himself became the perpetrator of terrible injustice.

How do these two different thoughts come together? Neither time nor human weakness and suffering thwart the purposes of God. Adam and those of his day lived incredibly long lives, whereas mortals today do well just to make it to their 100th birthday. The lives of the women mentioned spanned more than 500 years and included tragedy and triumph. David's great sin—that haunted him the remainder of his life—did not prevent his repentant heart from humbling himself before the Lord.

Today's verses teach us to abstain from sin, a lesson we should take seriously. However, we should never let sins of the past—even our recent past—keep us from repenting, returning to the Lord, and trusting Him for His presence in our lives.

8

We Are All Damaged

Daniel 3:25 "He answered and said, Lo, I see four men loose, walking in the midst of the fire, and they have no hurt; and the form of the fourth is like the Son of God."

Daniel 6:22 "My God hath sent his angel, and hath shut the lions' mouths, that they have not hurt me: forasmuch as before him innocency was found in me; and also before thee, O king, have I done no hurt."

The first of today's verses records Nebuchadnezzar's words of astonishment after he had three Hebrews thrown into a hot furnace and no harm came to them. The second verse records Daniel's response to an inquiry by Darius, king of the Medes; Darius had been tricked into casting Daniel into a den of lions, and the next morning he called down to Daniel asking about his well-being.

Humans with power regularly hurt other humans who have less power. Lord Acton's familiar quote is, "Power tends to corrupt and absolute power corrupts absolutely." That is not always the case, but it happens all too often.

I recently saw a promotion for a novel. I have not read it, so I cannot comment on it, favorably or otherwise. The name of the book is, *We're All Damaged*. That title struck a chord with me. Do you remember the old saying, "There are two kinds of people," then it goes on to describe the difference between the two kinds? Well, there *are* two kinds of people: damaged people who admit they are damaged, and damaged people who do *not* admit they are damaged.

God says we all start out damaged, even to the point of being spiritually dead. (Ephesians 2:1) He also warns that the *wages* for our disobedience is *eternal* death. (Romans 6:23) However, by Christ's sacrifice on the cross, He made a way for us to escape that destiny. For sure, death at the end of *this* life will come if the Lord does not first return for His people; however, the *second* death—the hell we deserve by condition and conduct—is swallowed up in loving grace and tender mercy for those who bow before Him now in faith and repentance.

Turn to Him today, dear friend. Trust Him now while there is time. "Boast not thyself of to morrow; for thou knowest not what a day may bring forth." (Proverbs 27:1)

9

My Ways Are Not Your Ways

Job 38:4 "Where wast thou when I laid the foundations of the earth? declare, if thou hast understanding."

In the early days of my career as an electrical designer, before computers had advanced to where they are today, we used drafting boards and graphite pencils to draw on special paper-like sheets called vellum. After the design was complete, if someone complained that they actually had a different concept in mind, we would ask, "Where were you when the graphite was going down?" In other words, why didn't you speak up during the early stages of the project when your desired features could have been easily incorporated into the original design?

God poses a similar question to Job in today's verse. Job had endured great trial for much longer than I could have, but eventually Job started expressing his frustration and confusion. In Job 38, we see that after God accomplished His purposes, He finally spoke out and reminded Job that he was not by God's side "when the graphite was going down." In other words, Job was not involved in the Creator's design, but that didn't mean God did not have good and intelligent purposes in Job's suffering which Job simply could not comprehend.

Do you suffer? Is it starting to get you down? I understand; I have been there too. In fact, to one extent or another, *all* of us have been there. However, I don't say that to "preach" or point an accusing finger. Instead, I just want to come alongside and encourage you just like many have encouraged me in my trials. The fact that we don't understand God's designs does not mean that He has lost control or doesn't care about us. As Paul reminds us in Romans 11:33, "O the depth of the riches both of the wisdom and knowledge of God! how unsearchable are his judgments, and his ways past finding out!"

Please take heart. God is still good—like He has always been—and His purposes will ripen in our lives, even if He leads us through dark valleys to bring them to pass.

10

All We Like Sheep

Isaiah 53:6 "All we like sheep have gone astray; we have turned every one to his own way; and the LORD hath laid on him the iniquity of us all."

I recently saw a billboard that focused on the increase in deaths by the abuse of certain drugs and recommended carrying an antidote to use when someone has overdosed. That message gave me both joy and sorrow. The joy came in knowing some lives might be saved. The sorrow came from knowing some people would die as a *result* of that antidote because they would use dangerous drugs hoping someone would rescue them if anything went wrong. What they overlook is that the antidote may not be available, those nearby might not know how to administer it, or it may just be too late.

Did you know there is a similar but deeper problem, my friends? As today's verse explains, those who struggle with drugs are not the only ones in danger. *All* of us have gone the wrong way; we have gone our *own* way instead of God's way. The *good* news is that our plight has a second similarity to the billboard message. There is a remedy for our problem, an antidote if I may use that term. It is in the last part of today's verse: "the LORD hath laid on him the iniquity of us all." The Bible says, "The wages of sin is death; but the gift of God is eternal life through Jesus Christ our Lord." (Romans 6:23) Jesus came into this world to save sinners, and He did so by suffering death—our due punishment—on the cross.

There is one more similarity here. Many, like the addict, do not understand the seriousness of this danger. They feel that they can safely live as they wish without accountability or reckoning. They believe they do not need God's forgiveness. If that were so, why did God go to the extent of laying on Jesus the iniquity of us all? That doesn't make sense if we don't have a problem.

"For what is your life? It is even a vapour, that appeareth for a little time, and then vanisheth away. (James 4:14) Do not ignore the antidote, my friend. Please do not wait until it is too late.

11

At the End of It All

Psalm 26:1,3,5 "Judge me, O LORD; for I have walked in mine integrity: I have trusted also in the LORD; therefore I shall not slide. ... For thy lovingkindness is before mine eyes: and I have walked in thy truth. ... I have hated the congregation of evildoers; and will not sit with the wicked."

Many years ago, I heard someone say that if you have to tell others how wonderful you are, you probably aren't. I suppose there is a proper time and place to mention our good qualities to others, but a reasonable modesty probably constrains that most of the time.

This psalm is interesting, not only in its transparency, but also in its contrast. For some reason, David feels compelled to list his good qualities for God: he has walked in integrity; he has trusted the LORD; he has walked in God's truth; he has refused to keep company with evildoers and the wicked. All of this is indeed laudable.

The same sense permeates the whole psalm right up to the middle of verse 11; it is then that David writes, "redeem me, and be merciful unto me."

I do not understand the full impact of this psalm, and I suspect that it would take a great deal of study to draw out all its flavors. However, one thing I believe we can take away from this passage is that even though we try to follow the Lord and walk in His ways, at the end of it all, even the best of us would fall woefully short if it were not for His redeeming mercy.

> Mercy there was great, and grace was free;
> Pardon there was multiplied to me;
> There my burdened soul found liberty
> At Calvary.
> ~ William R. Newell

12

Paraclete Transport

Psalm 103:13-17 "Like as a father pitieth his children, so the LORD pitieth them that fear him. For he knoweth our frame; he remembereth that we are dust. As for man, his days are as grass: as a flower of the field, so he flourisheth. For the wind passeth over it, and it is gone; and the place thereof shall know it no more. But the mercy of the LORD is from everlasting to everlasting upon them that fear him, and his righteousness unto children's children;"

I live in the Midwestern United States. Recently, I saw a truck from Paraclete Transport. I had never heard of that company, so I looked them up. They are a Canadian business located about fifty miles west of Winnipeg, Manitoba.

What caught my attention was the name itself. Paraclete is a Greek word meaning to come alongside in order to help or represent. That company comes alongside other companies and supports them by moving their products to market.

The reason that name caught my eye is because I have seen a form of that word before. You probably have too or at least a translation of it. The apostle John uses it five times in the New Testament. It is translated "Comforter" four times in his gospel (John 14:16; 14:26; 15:26; and 16:7) and always refers to the Holy Spirit whom Jesus promised to send when He departed. The fifth use is in John's first epistle where he says, "My little children, these things write I unto you, that ye sin not. And if any man sin, we have an advocate with the Father, Jesus Christ the righteous:" (1 John 2:1) Here the word is translated "advocate." John urges us not to sin, but if we sin, we have a parakletos, an advocate who comes alongside as a representative. In this verse, the word includes the sense that *Strong's Concordance* describes as "one who pleads another's cause before a judge."

The gospel passages promise that the Holy Spirit will be with us as our helper. The verse in the epistle promises that if sin overtakes us, Jesus represents us before His Father and pleads our case.

God understands us fallen mortals well. He sends His Spirit as our helper and guide, and He—the righteous Judge—listens to Jesus as He petitions on our behalf.

Praise God for His amazing wisdom and mercy.

13
Turning over the Mic

Radio announcers occasionally yield to someone else to speak for a while. In radio jargon that is called "turning over the microphone to a guest speaker" or simply, "turning over the mic." My mentor Wayne Schlichter writes a weekly devotional similar to my Musings. They are always good, but the last two have been especially insightful. Today and tomorrow, I am "turning over the mic" to my friend. I am sure you will be encouraged:

~~~~~

Think on These Things

Exodus 3:10-11 Come now therefore, and I will send thee unto Pharaoh, that thou mayest bring forth my people the children of Israel out of Egypt. And Moses said unto God, Who am I, that I should go unto Pharaoh, and that I should bring forth the children of Israel out of Egypt?

Who am I?

After being retrieved from the Nile River, the first forty years of Moses' life was spent in Egypt in the household of Pharaoh the King. Pharaoh's daughter raised him. The next forty years was spent in the wilderness shepherding sheep for his father-in-law. It was then that the Lord appeared to him in a burning bush that caught his eye.

"And Moses said, I will now turn aside, and see this great sight, why the bush is not burnt." (vs. 3) This appearance of the Lord is called a "theophany.". There are a number of special appearances of the Lord in the Old Testament.

God was calling Moses to His service. He was calling Moses to deliver the children of Israel from four hundred years of bondage in Egypt. Moses' response was, "Who am I, that I should go unto Pharaoh, and that I should bring forth the children of Israel out of Egypt?" That would have been my response as well. Likely it would have been yours. But we never know; God may well call us to do some "special" thing for Him. Moses did not feel ready or think he was the right person for this great task, but considering his past history, he was exactly the right man for the job.

God's choices are perfect.

That leads me to say that God does not call people whom He has not already prepared. Your life is a preparation for "some kind" of service to the Lord. If your heart is being stirred about some need, do not put it aside thinking that you cannot do what God is prompting you to do. It may be teaching a Sunday school class. It may be a call for more personal study or training to teach and shepherd God's flock. Some have the gift of "helps", which can be put to use in the local church and among the people of God. There is also the gift of "mercy" which is a great blessing in visitation to the sick or needy. Most churches need people whom God has encouraged to serve in these things. Ministry to God does not have to be done by "professionals." You can be a great blessing to others if you will yield yourself to the Lord to do His will.

You may be thinking that you are not able. Moses thought that: "And Moses said unto the LORD, O my Lord, I am not eloquent, neither heretofore, nor since thou hast spoken unto thy servant: but I am slow of speech, and of a slow tongue." (Exodus 4:10) But God asked him, "Who made your tongue? I will be with your tongue." If God calls, He equips! If He wants you to get up and say something, do not hold back. He is your strength and help.

"God is my strength and power: and he maketh my way perfect." (2 Samuel 22:33)

14

The Three Tenses of Our Salvation

As I mentioned last time when radio announcers yield to someone else to speak for a while, it is called "turning over the mic." Today I am again turning over the mic—or actually the pen—to my mentor and friend. I am sure you will be encouraged:

~~~~~

2 Corinthians 1:9-10 "But we had the sentence of death in ourselves, that we should not trust in ourselves, but in God which raiseth the dead: Who delivered us from so great a death, and doth deliver: in whom we trust that he will yet deliver us."

What wonderful truths are found for us in these two verses. They begin with the fact that we were under condemnation for our sins. The next thought is that we cannot trust in our own natural abilities to do anything sufficient to atone for these transgressions. The third truth is that God is the One who raises the dead. In our natural state, we would never have anything that could somehow make us right with God. In the grave, we have no strength to raise ourselves from death's grasp. Without God, our destiny would be an eternity in Hell. And though many do not believe in such a place, the Bible assures us that Hell exists and is a place to be avoided.

But God has delivered the believer from the power of the grave! Our next verse tells us of the three tenses of this great deliverance. The first is in the past tense. He delivered us from—notice—"so great a death"!

Why so great? Because the outcome is final and unchangeable! Once death comes, it is too late to change the outcome. But God has delivered us!

The second truth tells us that He "doth deliver" us. That is present tense. That means that He keeps on delivering us. Living day by day can never take away your salvation. Ephesians 4:30 reminds us that we are "sealed unto the day of redemption"; that is the day of resurrection. Jesus as our High Priest "is able to save to the uttermost... seeing He ever liveth to make intercession for us" (Hebrews 7:25). Nothing can separate us from the love of God (Romans 8:39).

Then we have the third truth that we are looking at in verse 10c... "He will yet deliver us!" That is future tense! That is our great hope, which in Biblical terms means our assured expectation.

"And our hope of you is steadfast, knowing, that as ye are partakers of the sufferings, so shall ye be also of the consolation" (2 Corinthians 1:7).

Salvation is the gift of God through Christ's sacrifice on the cross and His rising again from the dead. We could never achieve that salvation ourselves: "It is the gift of God, not of works lest anyone should boast" (Ephesians 2:8-9).

Let us just thank Him and rest in His finished work giving us this wonderful gift.

Wayne Schlichter

15
That's Why

Psalm 23: "The Lord is my shepherd; I shall not want. He maketh me to lie down in green pastures: he leadeth me beside the still waters. He restoreth my soul: he leadeth me in the paths of righteousness for his name's sake. Yea, though I walk through the valley of the shadow of death, I will fear no evil: for thou art with me; thy rod and thy staff they comfort me. Thou preparest a table before me in the presence of mine enemies: thou anointest my head with oil; my cup runneth over. Surely goodness and mercy shall follow me all the days of my life: and I will dwell in the house of the Lord for ever."

This psalm is abundantly rich in expressions about God and how He deals with His people. Another favorite passage, Psalm 100:3, also uses the same imagery: "Know ye that the Lord he is God: it is he that hath made us, and not we ourselves; we are his people, and the sheep of his pasture."

It is interesting that God uses sheep to illustrate human beings. I am told that sheep are not particularly intelligent; as such, they need regular care and almost constant overseeing. Humans *are* intelligent and creative, but I believe the illustration here is in the realm of spiritual wisdom; whether or not we admit it, we do not naturally do well in that arena. Hence, we need a good shepherd, and thank God, we have one!

Even though I have read this psalm many times, just today I noticed the reason God gives for all of this. Yes, He leads us, He feeds us, and He protects us, only allowing those struggles He knows to be beneficial, but why? I think He reveals that in verse 3 of Psalm 23 when He tells us why he leads us in the paths of righteousness; it is "for his name's sake." God is glorified—His name is magnified—when His sheep follow Him in paths of righteousness. I think that reason also covers the whole psalm. God is glorified by demonstrating His faithfulness when He cares for His people, "the sheep of his pasture."

"Surely the righteous shall give thanks unto thy name: the upright shall dwell in thy presence." (Psalm 140:13)

I am very glad that the Lord is my shepherd!

16

Jerry, Jesus, and Justification

Mark 10:14 "But when Jesus saw it, he was much displeased, and said unto them, Suffer [permit] the little children to come unto me, and forbid them not: for of such is the kingdom of God."

On this date in 2018, my friend and former coworker Sherrie sent me an email about Jerry, another former coworker, telling me of his passing and informing me of the funeral arrangements. I am not sure if Sherrie lost my email address, but instead of a separate, dedicated email, she replied to a Musing email I sent two years ago. No problem; either way was fine. However, what caught my eye was the title of the Musing in that email: "Suffer Little Children to Come unto Me."

Jesus was annoyed with His disciples when they prevented the little children from coming to Him. "Look at them," He might have said; "This is what people in Heaven are like." Sometimes we see children as noisy and rambunctious, but what God sees is human beings who are trusting. Oh sure, they are sinners; they have tempers and at times become disobedient. However, they often let their parents carry or drive them somewhere without any awareness of where they are going. Sometimes they even fall asleep, an expression of absolute confidence that Mom or Dad know where they are going: "I don't have to worry because everything is going to be okay."

Do we have that kind of faith? That is what Jesus says we need. Jerry needed it, I need it, and you need it. Jesus said He came into this world to pay for our sins, and He tells us to trust Him for His forgiveness and the promised eternal home that comes with it.

Yes, we have uncertainties and doubts. However, although our hearts and minds struggle with what the songwriter called, "fightings and fears, within, without," the song continues by urging us to say, "Oh Lamb of God, I come. I come."

Dear friend, as someone once said, "Life is short, death is sure; sin the curse, Christ the cure." My friend Jerry has crossed over that bridge into eternity. One day I shall cross also, as will you. After we make that journey, there is no changing—no "do-overs." We must come to Him *now*, by faith.

"Behold, now is the accepted time; behold, now is the day of salvation." (2 Corinthians 6:2b)

17
Shaking My Head

Romans 8:31 "What shall we then say to these things? If God be for us, who can be against us? 32 He that spared not his own Son, but delivered him up for us all, how shall he not with him also freely give us all things?"

I am sure you have heard this passage before, perhaps even in these Musings. However, it is true that you can read a passage of Scripture many times and still get a fresh glimpse after your tenth or fiftieth reading. You can read and reread and reread again, and still come away shaking your head in awe of who God is and what He does.

Romans 8 is especially such a passage. This chapter begins with no condemnation (v1) and closes with no separation. (v39) In between these two verses are treasures that we could study for years and never fully grasp.

The thought I want to consider today is sandwiched after the two questions in verse 31: ("What shall we then say to these things? If God be for us, who can be against us?") and before the question at the end of verse 32: ("How shall he not with him also freely give us all things?")

That thought is this: "He that spared not his own Son, but delivered him up for us all … " (v32)

Jesus told us, "Greater love hath no man than this, that a man lay down his life for his friends," (John 15:13) but Paul later reminds us that, "God commendeth his love toward us, in that, while we were yet sinners [sinners, *not* friends], Christ died for us." (Romans 5:8 [comment mine]) The Heavenly Father purposed to deliver up His Son for our sins. Equally amazing is that the Son entered into that sacrifice of His own, loving will.

In this breathtaking display of selfless kindness, God—through Christ—"hath given unto us all things that pertain unto life and godliness, through the knowledge of him that hath called us to glory and virtue." (2 Peter 1:3)

May we sing with joy and appreciation the words of that precious song, "A wonderful Savior is Jesus my Lord, a wonderful Savior to me." ~ Fanny Crosby

18

As Far as the Eye Cannot See

Jeremiah 5:21 "Hear now this, O foolish people, and without understanding; which have eyes, and see not; which have ears, and hear not."

There is a saying that is used to describe a vast land mass or great distance: "As far as the eye can see."

The speed limit on the road past our house is 55 miles per hour. Within several hundred feet of our driveway, there is a hill and curve in one direction, and in the other direction a dip in the road deep enough that for a moment you cannot see a full-size car. Both make pulling out onto the road somewhat dangerous. Several days ago, as I turned in the direction of the hill and curve, I thought of it being "a blind spot as far as the eye *cannot* see."

There is a quote similar to today's verse: "There are none so blind as those who will not see." It means that if a person refuses to accept truth that is displayed right in front of them, then they are blind only because they choose to be.

As I pondered this, I marveled at the three-dimensional view of several layers of clouds above, each layer moving at a different rate as I drove along. Then the thought came to me: how could a system ever have formed by mere chance that waters most of the Earth simply by transforming hundreds of thousands of tons of water into vapor and then lazily floating them above the Earth for thousands of miles?

Someone might say that it is just the natural result of the way things are in this world, the result of natural laws. However, I would ask, how about the miracle of the human eye? Or the ear? Or the nerves that allow the sense of touch? Or the amazing heart? Or the brain? Or why does a common potato have one more set of chromosomes than a human being does? Or why does the Atlas blue butterfly have almost ten times as many chromosomes as we humans do? A *butterfly*!

Scientists "who will not see" the creation of God tell us that all these things just happened. They might say I am the one who "will not see." But really? All this is "coincidence?" I just don't have enough faith to believe that.

19

Staying with Plan A

John 6:62-67 "What and if ye shall see the Son of man ascend up where he was before? It is the spirit that quickeneth; the flesh profiteth nothing: the words that I speak unto you, they are spirit, and they are life. But there are some of you that believe not. For Jesus knew from the beginning who they were that believed not, and who should betray him. And he said, Therefore said I unto you, that no man can come unto me, except it were given unto him of my Father. From that time many of his disciples went back, and walked no more with him. Then said Jesus unto the twelve, Will ye also go away?"

Besides the twelve disciples, many people followed Jesus. Perhaps they liked the miracles; perhaps they enjoyed being in the presence of a famous person; perhaps they thought He was going to suddenly defy Rome and reestablish the Israelite kingdom.

Somewhere along the way, Jesus' popularity faded with many because He started teaching things they did not like. Those annoyed followers began to drift away, and it was then that Jesus turned to the twelve and asked if they were going to abandon Him too. In the next two verses, Peter spoke for the group: "Then Simon Peter answered him, Lord, to whom shall we go? thou hast the words of eternal life. And we believe and are sure that thou art that Christ, the Son of the living God." (John 6:68-69)

Peter was all in. He didn't understand everything, and he certainly didn't know what his faith would require of him. However, he knew there was no Plan B.

I wish I could remember who said this and give credit, but I just don't recall who it was. However, I heard someone say he wanted to have absolute faith in Jesus, so much so that when he reached Heaven, if he was told, "That is not enough, what have you done personally?" he would sadly turn and walk away because Christ was all he had—Jesus was his only hope.

We do not understand all that the Bible says; we don't have to. What we *do* have to grasp is that Jesus is who He said He is, has done what He said He would do, and that by His finished work He saves us.

That is enough.

20

Amazing Grace and Why We Need It

Ephesians 2:8-9 "For by grace are ye saved through faith; and that not of yourselves: it is the gift of God: Not of works, lest any man should boast."

Many years ago, there was a man who was complicit in murder if not outright guilty of it. His name was Saul, and he was from the city of Tarsus. We know him better as the apostle Paul. How deceived he was, thinking that persecuting Christians somehow honored God. He was angry at those terrible blasphemers and set out to make them pay for their sins. However, a time came when God broke through to that religious but stony heart and wrote words of grace with indelible ink. It was then that Paul suddenly realized that it was *he* who was a blasphemer, not the Christians. (1 Timothy 1:13)

How glorious was that grace in the life of the apostle! By the way, it is that same startling grace by which God still saves today. You see, the fact is that *all* of us come into this world lost and separated from God; *all* of us are *born* in insurrection against our Creator, regardless whether we are religious, sacrilegious, or just don't care one way or the other. You might say, "I was not born opposed to God," but that statement itself is rebellion because God says we *all* start out that way. (Romans 3:23) If we say we didn't, we are calling God a liar. (1 John 1:8)

That is quite brazen, isn't it? Yet, God tells us through the pen of the apostle Paul, "God commendeth his love toward us, in that, while we were yet sinners, Christ died for us." (Romans 5:8)

The extreme danger in this life is not from the fact that we are sinners and rebels; the danger comes from thinking that God is lying to us, that He is trying to frighten us unnecessarily, and that we really are not that bad. Passing into eternity with that attitude is the most serious, the most dangerous, and the most everlasting mistake we can possibly make. It is also the only mistake from which there is no hope of escape.

Turn to God now for the forgiveness of your sins, through faith in the sacrificial work of Christ. Only anguish and regret await those who refuse.

21

Corruptible Things like Silver and Gold

1 Peter 1:18-19 "Forasmuch as ye know that ye were not redeemed with corruptible things, as silver and gold, from your vain conversation received by tradition from your fathers; But with the precious blood of Christ, as of a lamb without blemish and without spot:"

Isn't Peter's word picture a little strange? Yes, silver will tarnish, so in that sense, it is corruptible. However, gold does *not* tarnish. Why would the apostle list both of them as corruptible? Well, what happens when something becomes corrupted? Forgetting precious metals for a moment, when an object becomes corrupted it becomes of lesser value and perhaps of no value at all. For example, think of spoiled food, a tainted drink, or expired medications. When these items become corrupted, they are unusable. They become worthless.

Now let's think again about Peter's precious metals. We can clean tarnished silver. Collectors of antiques caution against non-professionals cleaning silver, I suppose because a tiny amount of the valuable material may be removed by cleaning; however, gold does not tarnish. It does not oxidize like silver, iron, copper, and a number of other elements. Then the question arises again: Why did Peter include gold in his list of corruptible things?

I think the answer only shows up when we shine the light of eternity on it. Gold, and even silver, are valuable here in this world, but no matter how much of it we have, it becomes totally worthless—totally corrupt—as we slip into the cold river over which we cross to the other side.

Actually, it is not just silver and gold. No matter what earthly goods we perceive to be of value here, they are worthless to our eternal well-being. That is why Peter reminds us that we are not redeemed with corruptible things—whether silver, gold, or even our religious traditions. We have been redeemed by "the precious blood of Christ, as of a lamb without blemish and without spot." Our eternal destiny depends totally on the precious blood of Christ, "the Lamb of God, which taketh away the sin of the world." (John 1:29) He is The One who is ***incorruptible***. By Him, we are saved. Praise Him!

22
Surety and Stability

Psalm 11:1-4 "In the LORD put I my trust: how say ye to my soul, Flee as a bird to your mountain? For, lo, the wicked bend their bow, they make ready their arrow upon the string, that they may privily shoot at the upright in heart. If the foundations be destroyed, what can the righteous do? The LORD is in his holy temple, the LORD's throne is in heaven: his eyes behold, his eyelids try, the children of men."

In today's passage, the psalmist says the wicked are trying to destroy the upright; however, the Lord is in His holy temple, seated on His throne, and His eyes see what is going on. Furthermore, later in the psalm, David points out that God will bring judgment on those who walk in iniquity because He loves righteousness.

The Bible tells us of the trials and struggles of Paul and Peter. Though it is not specific about the ends of their lives, tradition suggests Paul was beheaded and Peter was crucified. Was God able to sustain them through their trials but unable to prevent their deaths? Is God's power limited by the strength and anger of unbelievers? *No!* Psalm 2 says that God laughs at such a silly idea.

What then? God has purpose in what he decrees, and He has purpose in what He permits. Satan and his followers may be the agents of our trials, but as we find in the first two chapters of Job, the wicked one can do ***nothing*** beyond the limits that God sets. Additionally, God is glorified in whatever He allows, including our tribulation and even our death that ushers us into His presence. He also is actively involved in seeing to it that these things work together for our good, (Romans 8:28) even when we can't understand how. It is exactly for this reason that he calls us to trust Him because "without faith it is impossible to please him." (Hebrews 11:6)

So then, "whether we live, we live unto the Lord; and whether we die, we die unto the Lord: whether we live therefore, or die, we are the

Lord's." (Romans 14:8) For this reason, we can rejoice in His goodness and rest in His wisdom.

23

Left Brain, Right Brain

Proverbs 3:5-8 "Trust in the LORD with all thine heart; and lean not unto thine own understanding. In all thy ways acknowledge him, and he shall direct thy paths. Be not wise in thine own eyes: fear the LORD, and depart from evil. It shall be health to thy navel, and marrow to thy bones."

I am left-handed and take some teasing for that fact. The other day, my wife posted a meme that included a left-hand joke, and one of the kids quickly reminded her that both of her children are left-handed. (For a moment, I felt vindicated. <smile>)

I have a favorite response to lefty jabs: Since the left half of the brain controls most of the functions on the right side of the body, and the right half of the brain controls most of the functions on the left side of the body, left-handed people are the only ones in their right mind. As you might imagine, that comment raises groans from the right-handed people who hear it.

Left-handed and right-handed people think differently too. They process information differently; for example, even though my teachers taught me to do addition from right to left, I often add two rows of numbers from left to right quicker than I could do in reverse. Lefties are often more creative while righties are usually more logical and analytical. Sure, there is plenty of overlap, and generalities are not always true. However, one thing we can know for sure: the *best* human mind will never be a match for the mind of God.

God has set forth some of His thoughts, the product of His mind, in written form—His Word. We are able to read it, study it, ponder it, learn from it, and practice it, all to our benefit. The trouble comes when we choose to rely on our own feeble wisdom and follow our own way. Eve did that, Adam did that, and their progeny have been doing that ever since. Sadly, we all know how that has worked out.

My friend, don't be so quick to follow your own path; trust in the LORD with *all* your heart and lean on Him for *His* wisdom. Your health and well-being, your safety and life, and even your eternity depend on Him.

24
The Icing on Top

Psalm 56:11 "In God have I put my trust: I will not be afraid what man can do unto me. 12. Thy vows are upon me, O God: I will render praises unto thee. 13. For thou hast delivered my soul from death: wilt not thou deliver my feet from falling, that I may walk before God in the light of the living?"

The phrase "the icing on top" is used to describe something that is better than expected. In other words, you didn't just get plain cake or some other sweet dessert, you also got "the icing on top."

In today's verses, David expresses his faith in God; (v11) states that he does not need to fear people; (also v11) and then says he is obligated to render praise to God. (v12) In the beginning of verse 13, he gives one of the reasons he will praise his God: "For thou hast delivered my soul from death." Here David is acknowledging that God has (past tense) taken care of his most essential need—that of his eternal soul.

So, David doesn't need to fear people, and he doesn't need to fear death. However, there is one thing that is nagging at him, and that is his own potential to sin. He asks God, "Wilt not thou deliver (future) my feet from falling?" (v13) And why does the psalmist crave this relief? "That I may walk before God in the light of the living." (Also v 13) This is the icing!

I am keenly aware that we can belittle ourselves so much that it becomes self-fulfilling. If we always focus on how bad we are, it will begin to influence us toward bad behavior. Nevertheless, in this passage, David recognizes the truth that the old sin nature is still with us, looking for opportunities to cause us to stumble. As always, we need a balance. We shouldn't flood our thoughts with condemnation, but we also must not think we are invincible.

The salvation of our souls was accomplished in the past by Christ on the cross; however, our daily walk—our practical holiness as we live in this world—is something for which we must constantly seek God's help. Oh Lord, "thou hast delivered my soul from death: wilt not thou deliver my feet from falling, that I may walk before God in the light of the living?"

25

Taking a Detour

Acts 16:6-9 "Now when they had gone throughout Phrygia and the region of Galatia, and were forbidden of the Holy Ghost to preach the word in Asia, After they were come to Mysia, they assayed to go into Bithynia: but the Spirit suffered them not. And they passing by Mysia came down to Troas. And a vision appeared to Paul in the night; There stood a man of Macedonia, and prayed him, saying, Come over into Macedonia, and help us."

Have you ever been moving happily through life, and then something interferes with your plans? That is especially aggravating if you love God and want to do His will, but these bumps and swerves in the road of your life keep messing things up.

A meme I saw recently said, "Sometimes the interruption is the assignment." In other words, the things that we see as disruptions may actually be God calling us to go in a different direction. The new path may be temporary such as when He calls us to help a friend, or it could be more life-altering like doing missions work, either locally or even in a foreign country.

I offer two cautions here: As is often the case, we can go to extremes in either direction. In this case, either we could let *everything* distract us from focusing on the work the Lord has purposed us to do, or we could be so focused and rigid on what we *think* He wants us to do that we miss His redirection.

Today's verses tell us of one of Paul's missionary journeys during which the Holy Spirit prevented him from going, first to Asia, and then to Bithynia. Why would God prevent the apostle from going to preach the gospel? Isn't that what he was supposed to do? Well, yes, but the Lord purposed that Paul should do that in Macedonia. God threw roadblocks in Paul's path to get him to change course. The Lord indeed wanted the apostle to carry the message of grace, but He wanted the message taken first to someplace other than where Paul was headed.

We must guard against the extremes. May we not be so easily distracted that we are blown around like a leaf in the wind, but let us also not be so set in our ways that we become insensitive to God's leading.

26
The Sufficiency of Christ

2 Corinthians 12:9 "And he said unto me, My grace is sufficient for thee: for my strength is made perfect in weakness. Most gladly therefore will I rather glory in my infirmities, that the power of Christ may rest upon me."

My dad once told me of a union leader who was interviewed on television during a contract dispute. The reporter asked what the leader would settle for; he replied, "Just a little bit more."

This Musing is not about unions and management; instead, it is about *all* of us. Whether it is finances, possessions, or personal relationships, there is often a hunger for a little bit better, a little bit bigger, a little bit more. But what do we actually need? Money? Stuff? Relationships? God knows *everything* we need, but He also knows our greatest need is more confidence in Him.

Recently in our church bulletin, there was a quote by the late Jerry Bridges. In his book, *Transforming Grace*, Mr. Bridges said this: "Before we can learn the sufficiency of God's grace, we must learn the insufficiency of ourselves. As I have said, the more we see our sinfulness, the more we appreciate grace in its basic meaning of God's undeserved favor. In a similar manner, the more we see our frailty, weakness, and dependence, the more we appreciate God's grace in its dimension of His divine assistance. Just as grace shines more brilliantly against the dark background of our sin, so it also shines more brilliantly against the background of our human weakness."

That same Sunday, our pastor mentioned something else about Mr. Bridges; it was a simple thought that he included in his daily prayers:

Lord, I am willing
To receive what You give,
To lack what You withhold,
To relinquish what You take,
To suffer what You inflict,
To be what you require.

The dynamic of that prayer is not in the "magic words" but in the submissive attitude of a humble heart. Even if we don't use those very words, may we always have a submissive attitude toward the Lord and His infinite wisdom.

291

Remember, we are broken, and God is not. Whether He gives or takes, whether He withholds or brings to pass, it is for His glory and for our good. (2 Corinthians 4:15)

27

Are All Religions the Same?

Psalm 115:1 "Not unto us, O LORD, not unto us, but unto thy name give glory, for thy mercy, and for thy truth's sake."

Some say that all religions are the same, that they all lead to the same god and that we all should respect each other's faith. Is that true? Well, yes and no. Let's take a closer look.

RESPECT – Our Lord teaches us as much as it is possible to "Live peaceably with all men" (Romans 12:18) and "Do good unto all men, especially unto them who are of the household of faith." (Galatians 6:10) The sentence structure and the word "especially" force us to conclude it also means unbelievers, those *not* of the household of faith. Yes, we should love and respect those who believe differently than we do.

SAME GOD – Do all religions lead to the same god? With all due respect, making this claim reveals a lack in understanding what various religions teach. For example, no mortal can fully comprehend the Triune God; nevertheless, Christianity teaches that the one true God consists of three persons. Jews, Muslims, and others reject that teaching. There are also religions that believe in many gods. At least one religion claims there is no god at all. Some teach that everything is god or that their members can become gods. No, by their own claims, there is no single god to which *all* religions lead.

SAME BELIEFS – Are all religions the same in essence? Well, some faiths teach that "converts" should be won by peacefully communicating truth, and others believe converts are to be made by any means necessary, including force and violence. Some have specific teachings while others are more ethereal. Some belief systems encourage a passionate faith where members long for others to find the same joy and peace they have; others have a more take-it-or-leave-it approach.

No, even though there are similarities on the surface, we cannot conclude that all "religions" are the same. This is certainly not an in-depth assessment of the subject; that is beyond the scope of this brief writing. However, this review does give solid reasons why Christians cannot agree that all religions are the same or that they lead to the same god. It also shows—with biblical authority—that we should be as respectful, gracious, and kind to others as we can.

28

The Terror of the Lord

2 Corinthians 5:11 "Knowing therefore the terror of the Lord, we persuade men; but we are made manifest unto God; and I trust also are made manifest in your consciences."

Wayne Schlichter, my friend and mentor, once drew my attention to a devotional reading about the rich man in Mark 10 who came to Jesus and asked Him, "Good Master, what shall I do that I may inherit eternal life?" The writer focused on the fact that the man seemed to be excited about the idea of living forever, but didn't seem to grasp the fact that he had sinned against God and needed to be made right with the One from whom he was seeking eternal life. (verses 17-22)

I replied to my friend, "The young man's question, 'What shall I do that I may inherit eternal life?' rather than 'What must I do to be saved?' reminded me of a rather staggering quote I recently read from Paul Washer: 'When a man gets saved, he gets saved from God. The justice of God was coming for you. God saved you from Himself.' It is overwhelming that God's mercy is such that though I was rightly under His just wrath, and though He would have been completely justified if He rained His just wrath down on me, He instead saved me *from* Himself by taking that just wrath *upon* Himself. With what mortal words can we adequately describe the grace of God?"

God can save us from His just wrath and give us eternal life because He first died to pay for that which caused our eternal death.

> Rock of Ages, cleft for me,
> Let me hide myself in thee;
> Let the water and the blood,
> From thy wounded side which flowed,
> Be of sin the double cure;
> Save from wrath and make me pure.
> ~ Augustus M. Toplady

29

What Do You Need?

Luke 4:4 "And Jesus answered him, saying, It is written, That man shall not live by bread alone, but by every word of God."

We mortals tend to think we know what we need. Sometimes we do, but many times what we *actually* "know" is not what we *need*, but what we *want*. I saw a meme recently that addressed this point; it said, "Sometimes God will give you exactly what you wanted just to show you it's not at all what you need." That goes well with today's verse.

One good question is, what *do* you need? Another good question is, how do you *find* what you need? Two people were disagreeing on how their plans got mixed up. They thought they had agreed on the subject, but it turned out that they were not even close to agreeing. Finally, one of them said, "What you thought you said was not what I thought I heard." What we "think" we need may not even come close to what we really need; it may be a *desire*, but not an actual *need*. The answer to both of those questions—what do we need and how do we find it—is available to us, but we must look in the right place.

What would you say to a fellow who thought it was a good idea to put thick grease in the crankcase of his car instead of oil? You could argue with him all day long, and he might argue back for just as long. However, the best way to end the argument would be to take out the owner's manual and show him exactly what the manufacturer *says* to put in the crankcase.

The same is true with us. Our Creator has given us a written document telling us what we need and where to go to find it. The Bible is so much more than an owner's manual—it is a love letter, a historical document, beautiful poetry, a book of wisdom and more. However, it is also a communication from our Creator telling us where to go to find the fulfillment of our greatest need, and that great need is for the Creator Himself.

God's offer of grace, mercy, love, and kindness is revealed in the Bible, and it can save us from a lifetime of regret as well as an eternity of much worse.

30
Yea Lord, Thou Knowest

John 21:15-17 "So when they had dined, Jesus saith to Simon Peter, Simon, son of Jonas, lovest thou me more than these? He saith unto him, Yea, Lord; thou knowest that I love thee. He saith unto him, Feed my lambs. He saith to him again the second time, Simon, son of Jonas, lovest thou me? He saith unto him, Yea, Lord; thou knowest that I love thee. He saith unto him, Feed my sheep. He saith unto him the third time, Simon, son of Jonas, lovest thou me? Peter was grieved because he said unto him the third time, Lovest thou me? And he said unto him, Lord, thou knowest all things; thou knowest that I love thee. Jesus saith unto him, Feed my sheep."

Three times during the trial of Jesus, Peter denied knowing Him; however, Jesus heard him the third time and looked at him. There was Jesus in His hour of greatest need, and Peter—one of His closest followers—denied Him in His presence. When he realized Jesus had heard him do that, "Peter went out, and wept bitterly." (Luke 22:62)

In today's verses, Jesus meets some of His disciples after His resurrection. Imagine Peter's discomfort being around Jesus just days after publicly denying Him. What shame and guilt. Peter probably could hardly look Jesus in the eye.

The first two times Jesus asks Peter if he loves Him using the Greek word "agapao," the highest form of sacrificial love; Peter responds both times with the word "phileo," a lesser, friendship love. However, the third time Jesus asks the question, He uses Peter's word, "phileo." It is at this point that Peter breaks down: "Lord, thou knowest all things; thou knowest that I love (phileo) thee."

Peter was grieved, but was it because Jesus asked three times, or was it because *in* the third question, Jesus changed the word down to Peter's level? Did using Peter's word make Peter realize he didn't love Christ the way Christ deserves? Would that grieve you? I know it grieves me.

I find it interesting that the Lord's instruction all three times was to feed His sheep and lambs. We should be careful with our lives, but it was as if the Lord was saying to Peter, and to us, "Instead of concentrating on your past, let Me help you help others in your future."

31

How is Your Eyesight?

Revelation 3:17-19 "Because thou sayest, I am rich, and increased with goods, and have need of nothing; and knowest not that thou art wretched, and miserable, and poor, and blind, and naked: I counsel thee to buy of me gold tried in the fire, that thou mayest be rich; and white raiment, that thou mayest be clothed, and that the shame of thy nakedness do not appear; and anoint thine eyes with eyesalve, that thou mayest see. As many as I love, I rebuke and chasten: be zealous therefore, and repent."

Today's verses contain the advice the risen Lord Jesus gave to the church at Laodicea, and by implication, to us today. Notice the reference to the "eyes."

Why would Jesus make these remarks? After all, we're all good people, aren't we? Well, it is true that most of us do not behave as badly as the worst of us do, but the trouble goes deeper than conduct. There is something within our fallen natures that cannot accept the truth about the very brokenness that prevents us from seeing that brokenness. Today's verses point to the fact that there is something wrong with our spiritual eyes; they were damaged in the Fall and are unable to see spiritual truth. We see ourselves as "not too bad," but God says, "Yes, you really are sinful, unwise, and broken." Paul even says in Ephesians 2:1 that before God saved us from our sins, we were spiritually dead, and friends, "dead" is seriously broken.

Not all is lost; God has purposed to redeem a people from the fall, and by His grace, He is doing just that. Jesus loved the Laodiceans (verse 19), even as He loves His people today. The reason Jesus gives for counseling them to get good from Him is "Because thou sayest..." (verse 17) In other words, Christ directed those He loved because they were sure they didn't **need** any direction. He didn't just counsel them to take advantage of His resources because their resources were insufficient; He counseled them because their spiritual eyes were so damaged they couldn't even *see* that their resources were insufficient.

Christ's wise counsel is to those He loves; (verse 19) let's not let our pride trick us into thinking we can see better than He sees—that we know better than He knows.

NOVEMBER

1

A Longing Heart and a Balanced Life

2 Corinthians 5:6-9. "Therefore we are always confident, knowing that, whilst we are at home in the body, we are absent from the Lord: (For we walk by faith, not by sight:) We are confident, I say, and willing rather to be absent from the body, and to be present with the Lord. Wherefore we labour, that, whether present or absent, we may be accepted of him."

One of the things I find precious in these verses is Paul's use of the word that is translated "confident." The Greek word means to exercise bold courage. The apostle says that this confidence expresses itself in a person who chooses to live boldly, knowing for a fact that when life in this world ends, life in the next world begins.

I was listening to a Christian radio station several days ago. The station was some distance away, and the weak signal interfered with the programming. Though it was difficult to make out the words of the song, I was able to hear this refrain: "I'm happy and free, but inside of me, I'm longing for home."

So, how do we balance these two worlds: the one in which I am happy and free, and the other one for which I long? The answer is in the last verse of today's passage: "Wherefore we labour, that, whether present or absent, we may be accepted of him." This verse has two more words that are interesting.

The first, translated "labor," doesn't just mean work; it means work that we are eager or earnest to do. The second word is translated "accepted," and it means "fully agreeable;" another phrase for "accepted" might be "in tune" or "in harmony." The same Greek word, translated "well pleasing" in Philippians 4:18 and Hebrews 13:21, suggests that the way to be well pleasing to God while we are in this world is to seek to be in harmony with the Lord, living out His will for our lives. When we are laboring in that kind of close harmony with God, life down here will start being a lot more like the life we look forward to at home with Him.

297

2

The Pending Ending

Revelation 22:1-5 "And he shewed me a pure river of water of life, clear as crystal, proceeding out of the throne of God and of the Lamb. In the midst of the street of it, and on either side of the river, was there the tree of life, which bare twelve manner of fruits, and yielded her fruit every month: and the leaves of the tree were for the healing of the nations. And there shall be no more curse: but the throne of God and of the Lamb shall be in it; and his servants shall serve him: And they shall see his face; and his name shall be in their foreheads. And there shall be no night there; and they need no candle, neither light of the sun; for the Lord God giveth them light: and they shall reign for ever and ever."

The late Orson Wells was thrust into prominence by his 1938 radio production *War of the Worlds*, which depicted fears of global calamity from a Martian invasion. There is a certain trepidation in the phrase "the end of the world," and that angst is well warranted for those who refuse the salvation of God through Christ.

However, "the end" also has a startling bright side for those who *do* trust in God for the forgiveness of their sins. Read today's verses again, and imagine the absolute bliss it reveals. Arriving at this passage, the universal rebellion against the Almighty Creator has been quelled, and the final chapter opens with this glorious picture of light and goodness, of wellness and peace—all of it "for ever and ever."

God is not petty as some people think. His anger at sin is a righteous anger. We must remember that the human race—all of us in some form or another—have disobeyed Him. To compound the problem, when He offers forgiveness at great personal sacrifice, some call God a liar saying they don't need forgiveness, that they are good enough. The earlier chapters of Revelation dispel that myth very quickly.

If we want to participate in the glories of Revelation 22, we must abandon our notions of self-righteousness and take God at His word, for He tells us not only that we *are* as bad as He says we are, but that we will be made perfect, by grace, through faith in Christ.

3

Healthy, Wealthy, and Wise

3 John 1:1-4 "The elder unto the wellbeloved Gaius, whom I love in the truth. Beloved, I wish above all things that thou mayest prosper and be in health, even as thy soul prospereth. For I rejoiced greatly, when the brethren came and testified of the truth that is in thee, even as thou walkest in the truth. I have no greater joy than to hear that my children walk in truth."

"Early to bed and early to rise, makes a man healthy, wealthy, and wise." That was first published by John Clarke in 1639, and later by Benjamin Franklin in his Almanac. At first glance, it appears that the apostle John is wishing the same for his friend, Gaius: "Wealth, health, and a prosperous soul." However, I don't believe that is the focus of this passage.

We often read Bible verses as a complete thought; that is occasionally a proper understanding, as in the Proverbs, but not always. Verses 2-4 in today's passage are an example of verses which must be read together to be properly understood.

In verses 3 and 4, John expresses his delight that Gaius is walking in the truth. This is the prosperity of the soul that John mentions in verse 2, and the apostle is wishing that the rest of Gaius's life was doing that well.

The Bible is not clear about how Gaius was doing in the matter of health and material goods. Romans 16:23 mentions someone by that name who was a host to Paul, but even if it were the same person, hospitality does not require great wealth or perfect wellbeing. Still, the fact that John wishes prosperity and health at the same level as the soul suggests that was not the case in the life of Gaius.

In either event, John was placing emphasis on the immaterial rather than the material. Why is that important? Jesus said, "For what shall it profit a man, if he shall gain the whole world, and lose his own soul?" (Mark 8:36)

The Scriptures teach us to chase after God and His righteousness, and to pray for His provision of the lesser things. If instead, we seek health or wealth as the first priority, the most important things will soon suffer neglect.

May God spare us that careless choice.

4

Don't Let Yourself Get in the Way

3 John 1:1, 9, 12 "The elder unto the wellbeloved Gaius, whom I love in the truth. ...I wrote unto the church: but Diotrephes, who loveth to have the preeminence among them, receiveth us not. ...Demetrius hath good report of all men, and of the truth itself: yea, and we also bear record; and ye know that our record is true."

Last time we looked at verses 1-4 of this letter John wrote to his friend, Gaius. Today we look at more of that letter where John mentions two other people.

We already looked at John's praise to Gaius, but John continues through verse 8 delighting that his friend is walking in the truth and that he is conducting his life in such a way that it is evident that the truth is shaping his actions. In verse 12, John expresses the same kind of encouragement about Demetrius whom others also praise for his godly life. The problem comes in the middle where John mentions another man named Diotrephes; he was not like Gaius and Demetrius. Instead, Diotrephes loved to "have the preeminence." He loved being at center stage. You see, Diotrephes had the problem of pride.

Pride is a very ugly thing, but it doesn't alarm us at first because it starts in the heart where we think we can keep it hidden. We may not even notice when it starts to release its poison into our souls, but it soon finds its way out into our actions, and we start being harsh and critical. We want more and more attention and become caustic and hostile toward those who threaten our sense of self-importance.

I don't know if John ever visited that church where Diotrephes threw his weight around, but John said in verse 10 that if he ever got there he would keep that man's brash behavior in mind. I also don't know what John planned to do, but wouldn't it have been much better if Diotrephes humbled himself before God instead of needing the apostle to confront him?

We all would do well to heed the words of the prophet in Micah 6:8: "He hath shewed thee, O man, what is good; and what doth the LORD require of thee, but to do justly, and to love mercy, and to walk humbly with thy God?"

5

Road Maps and Sign Posts

James 4:7 "Submit yourselves therefore to God. Resist the devil, and he will flee from you."

There are two signs posted at several locations throughout our church building; they both show a map of the floor plan. Why two maps? Well, an arrow on one of them shows the quickest path *out* of the building in case of fire. The other map shows the quickest path to a safe location *inside* the building in case of a tornado or other weather emergency.

The Bible also gives us signs—maps to guide us. God gives us instructions as to how we can live successful lives. Some of those instructions are to *flee*: fornication; (1 Corinthians 6:18) idolatry; (1 Corinthians 10:14) youthful lust; (2 Timothy 2:22) and the love of money. (1 Timothy 6:10-11) In these verses, God is telling us to run away from the things that dishonor God and bring sorrow and destruction to people.

Temptations to sin come from several sources; as the saying goes, we are tempted by "the world, the flesh, and the devil." The world will tempt us with enticing images and words, and even our own deceitful hearts will mislead us. Additionally, the wicked one and his followers are always willing to stir up our baser cravings.

Note that today's verse tells us to deal differently with the devil than with temptations. We are to *flee* from temptation, but we are to *resist* the devil. The difference here may be a little confusing, but keep this in mind; Satan *wants* us to sin, but *we* are the ones who actually yield to temptation. Regardless of what Satan tells us, *we* are the ones who choose to obey or disobey the Lord.

I believe that is what today's verse is saying. We must resist the devil's enticements to stay and be mesmerized by sin; rather, we must flee from it.

Now, you might ask, "How can I resist Satan's tempting influence?" We look again at today's verse for the answer. "Submit yourselves therefore to God." That is vitally important! If we are not submitting our wills to God, then resisting the devil is futile. We are operating in our own strength, and that is sure to fail.

"Submit yourselves therefore to God. Resist the devil, and he will flee from you."

So then, submit to God, resist the devil, and flee from sin.

6

The Forever Word

1 Peter 1:25 "But the word of the Lord endureth for ever. And this is the word which by the gospel is preached unto you."

Lately, I have been reading in Psalm 119. It speaks of God's Word, His testimonies, and His statutes. It declares many of the attributes of God's Word.

Today's verse reminds us of one of those attributes. Peter says God's Word "endureth forever." We generally understand the idea that God's Word will forever be in force. It is important for us to grasp that concept, for it is not just some stand-alone doctrine; it affects everything else God tells us because if He says something in a declaration that never ceases, it becomes sure and dependable.

Upon occasion when I was a child, one of my classmates would say something that someone else didn't like, and the offended person would say, "You take that back," as if to demand that the offending speaker un-say their unpleasant remarks. God knows *all* truth and never misspeaks, so He never has to "take back" any of His words. If He says something, we can count on it.

In this verse, Peter also mentions that it is by God's Word that the gospel is preached unto us. This should be a great comfort to us that God equates His eternal Word with the gospel. I take that to mean that the gospel is as enduring as God's Word itself. If God proclaims the gospel by way of a book that will always be, it is a sure and dependable thing.

We can rely on God's Word, and we can rely on the assurance of His gospel.

7

What Meaneth This?

Acts 2:12 "And they were all amazed, and were in doubt, saying one to another, What meaneth this?"

Today's verse records the public reaction to the disciples on the day of Pentecost shortly after the Resurrection of the Lord Jesus. People from a multitude of countries and regions—more than a dozen are listed—heard Peter and others speak. However, regardless of the language these

Galileans spoke, the people from all these other countries heard in their own language. The people ask what that means.

Peter used their question as a gate to lead them into the spectacular account of the cross of Christ. Additionally, Peter does not just give the account of the cross; he momentarily brushes up against the *reason* that the cross was necessary. "Men and brethren, let me freely speak unto you of the patriarch David, that he is both dead and buried, and his sepulchre is with us unto this day." (v29) In context, Peter mentioned David in the linage of Jesus, but the fact that David is in a tomb is the very reason for our *need* for the cross of Christ. Without the cross, we are without hope.

Recently, my son Mark posted a quote by Matt Chandler from his book, *The Explicit Gospel*: "The cross of Christ is the response of God to men for belittling His name. The cross of Christ exists because mankind— loved by God, created by God, set in motion by God—betrayed God and prefers his stuff to Him."

Adam and Eve abandoned God for "his stuff". They wanted the forbidden, not just the fruit, but also the glory. Satan tricked them into making the same disastrous choice that he made; he has been fooling us all ever since.

As Chandler says, God's response to our belittling rebellion is to forgive those who come to Him in repentance and faith, and yet, in order to forgive us, Christ had to take upon Himself the punishment due us for our sins.

What meaneth this? What it means is that the Almighty God, through the cross, has opened a window of forgiveness for all who take Him at His word. However, He gives a warning: the window will not stay open forever.

If you have not yet bowed before Him, do so now. If you already have bowed to Him, worship, praise, and thank Him for His forgiveness.

8

The Vanishing Point

Psalm 119:89 Forever, O LORD, thy word is settled in heaven. 90. Thy faithfulness is unto all generations: thou hast established the earth, and it abideth. 91. They continue this day according to thine ordinances: for all are thy servants."

Two things struck me while reading this passage. The first is the word "forever." It is the translation of a Hebrew word, which conveys the idea of a vanishing point. We see that when we look down a length of railroad tracks. The two rails appear to get closer and closer, then become one, and finally disappear from view. That is the idea this word portrays, but it also includes both directions. As far as existence extends into the future *and* into the past, God's word is settled in Heaven. It does not change no matter how far back we search or how far into the future we go.

The second thought I had was from verses 90 and 91 and was the idea of a "maverick molecule." I first heard that term many years ago from Bible teacher R. E. Rhoades. He said that if there was one molecule that did not come under the authority of the Almighty Creator, that one molecule might do something that set off a chain reaction, causing things to go differently than God has purposed. Mr. Rhoades' conclusion was that such an unruly particle does not exist and that everything falls under God's jurisdiction and authority.

That is the idea of today's passage. God has created the Earth, it exists in harmony with His plan, and the Earth—and by implication, all His creation—are His servants and do as He wills.

Of course, there are connotations in this, which go far beyond our understanding, even to that vanishing point mentioned earlier. However, we must come back to a realistic awareness; even in our redeemed and forgiven state, we are finite beings who cannot fully comprehend the infinite God. Furthermore, since we cannot fully grasp His being or His ways, we are incapable of passing judgment on His wisdom, pronouncements, and actions.

God has established the Earth, it stands the way He said for it to stand, and His faithfulness is to all generations. Including ours. Let us give Him thanks.

"O praise the LORD, all ye nations: praise him, all ye people." (Psalm 117:1)

9

Pride Goeth before Destruction

Proverbs 16:18 "Pride goeth before destruction, and an haughty spirit before a fall."

Today's verse is a familiar one. Many times, it is quoted in a condensed form: "Pride goes before a fall."

This same thought is in Psalm 99:3-5; it is not as clear on the surface, but the writer expresses it in a profound way: "Let them praise thy great and terrible name; for it is holy. The king's strength also loveth judgment; thou dost establish equity, thou executest judgment and righteousness in Jacob. Exalt ye the LORD our God, and worship at his footstool; for he is holy." The word translated exalt in Psalm 99:5 means, "rise, rise up, be high, be lofty, be exalted." It is appropriate that the psalmist uses this word to refer to the King of Glory as one who is lofty and lifted up.

However, like many Hebrew words, there is another flavor to this word, for it can also be used to describe lifting ourselves up in arrogant pride. In that sense, according to **Strong's Concordance**, the word takes on the flavor of something rotten or worm-eaten. Although the account in Acts 12 is in the New Testament, and therefore does not use Hebrew words, I find it to be quite eye-opening. Herod gave a speech and the crowd went wild, calling him a god. Herod was so proud of himself and all that he had done that he evidently embraced the people's claim to his deity. "And immediately the angel of the Lord smote him, because he gave not God the glory: and he was eaten of worms, and gave up the ghost." (v23)

These are hard words, but only if we think of ourselves "more highly than we ought to think." (Romans 12:3) We surely can take delight and pleasure that God uses us to bring glory to Himself and encouragement to others, but let us diligently guard our hearts against pride, for even if God does not do to us as He did to Herod, the worms of pride will surely cause rottenness and decay in our well-being.

Thankfully, the next verse following Herod's demise assures us that man's conceit—though it will injure the man—cannot hinder God's great purposes: "But the word of God grew and multiplied." (Acts 12:24)

Let us give God the glory. After all, it is rightfully His.

10
I Can't Get No Satisfaction

John 4:13-14 "Jesus answered and said unto her, Whosoever drinketh of this water shall thirst again: But whosoever drinketh of the water that I shall give him shall never thirst; but the water that I shall give him shall be in him a well of water springing up into everlasting life."

In 1965, British rock band, The Rolling Stones, released a song written by two of its members, Mick Jagger and Keith Richards. It was titled "(I Can't Get No) Satisfaction," and that refrain is heard repeatedly throughout the almost 4-minute song. It expressed **dis**satisfaction with everything from frustrating relationships and commercialization, to the seemingly endless and useless chatter on radio. I am not sure what they have found in their relationships during the last 50 years, but I am afraid commercialization and inane chatter have not improved much.

Along that same line, I was driving several days ago and pulled behind a boat on a trailer. The name on the boat was "Never Satisfied." I have heard that the two happiest days in a boat owner's life are the day they buy their boat and the day they sell their boat. I have never owned a boat, so I cannot attest to the accuracy of that maxim, but we mortals do tend to tire quickly of the shiny things that once held our attention.

As nice as they are, things that are special at first often become mundane and finally just fodder for a yard sale. I am not completely sure why that is, but I find it to be true that for many of us, and perhaps all of us who experience any level of affluence, satisfaction is a very elusive commodity. However, in the above verses, the Lord Jesus promised the woman at the well that the Living Water He provides would satisfy her longing for a meaningful life. He offers the same to all who come to Him in repentance and faith.

Six years after the Rolling Stones released their lamentation, another songwriter, Lanny Wolfe, penned these words of comfort to all who seek satisfaction in the only place in which it can be found:

> Only Jesus can satisfy your soul,
> And only He can change your heart
> And make you whole.
> He'll give you peace you never knew,
> Sweet love and joy, and heaven too
> For only Jesus can satisfy your soul.
> ~ Lanny Wolfe

11
Words Mean Things

Romans 3:24-25 "Being justified freely by his grace through the redemption that is in Christ Jesus: Whom God hath set forth to be a propitiation through faith in his blood, to declare his righteousness for the remission of sins that are past, through the forbearance of God;"

Today's verses contain a word we don't use much anymore: propitiation. It is the translation of a word that means "atoning victim," that is, someone who pays someone else's debt in order to make things right between the debtor and the one to whom the debt is owed. The late R. C. Sproul said it this way: "Propitiation brings about a change in God's attitude, so that He moves from being at enmity with us to being for us. Through the process of propitiation, we are restored into fellowship and favor with Him."

Many years ago, I heard a radio preacher reading this verse. As he did, he mispronounced the word as "perpetuation," which means to continue things the way they are. It was an innocent mistake, but what a stark contrast that mistake created.

God could have abandoned us to continue in our sins and face all their penalties; instead, He sent a substitute to take our place. The Lord Jesus came willingly to redeem us from a righteous death sentence. (Romans 6:23) He came as a propitiation so that our separation from God would not be perpetuated!

> "Man of Sorrows," what a name
> For the Son of God who came
> Ruined sinners to reclaim!
> Hallelujah! What a Savior!
> ~ Philip P. Bliss

12

Twice a Slave, Part 1

Romans 6:6 "Knowing this, that our old man is crucified with him, that the body of sin might be destroyed, that henceforth we should not serve sin."

A little boy built a toy boat. As he played with it, the string broke, and the boat washed downstream. Someone found it and sold it to a local store, and the boy had to purchase his own creation. He later proclaimed, "Little boat, you are twice mine; I made you, and I bought you." Jesus can say the same thing about His redeemed people. He made us, and He bought us with His precious blood.

There were two ways in which we were servants or slaves prior to salvation. God—by His tender mercies—redeems us from both, but it behooves us to understand how.

One of those enslavements was to sin. (Romans 6:16-18) However, the Bible teaches that the problem is not just the sins we commit, but the nature we have within. We do not become sinners because we sin; we sin because we are sinners. It is our nature as fallen creatures to disobey God. Even our mortal attempts to please Him are sin if they are not of faith; they are human attempts to do what only Christ's work can do. (Titus 3:3-6)

Furthermore, there are two elements to the sin problem—sins (plural, the acts) and sin (singular, the nature), and God deals with them in two different ways:

First, when we admit God is right and we are wrong (repentance), we come to Him in faith. He forgives the acts of our rebellion, and we stand before Him, completely justified by faith. (1 John 1:9) That is *positional* sanctification; our position before God is that we are holy, set apart for His use.

Second, there is the matter of the sin nature that still lives in us. It was crucified with Christ, (Galatians 2:20) but the old nature continues to seek its own way. The Holy Spirit calls for our cooperation in yielding less to our desires and instead following His divine leadership. This is *practical* sanctification. The old nature failed in our strength, but the new nature succeeds in God's strength. If I may say it this way, we *work out* what God has *worked in*. (Philippians 2:12)

Servitude to sin is one way we were enslaved. Tomorrow, we unfold more on this idea.

13

Twice a Slave, Part 2

Galatians 3:1-2 "O foolish Galatians, who hath bewitched you, that ye should not obey the truth, before whose eyes Jesus Christ hath been evidently set forth, crucified among you? This only would I learn of you, Received ye the Spirit by the works of the law, or by the hearing of faith?"

Last time, we reviewed the fact that before we came to Christ, we were slaves to sin. Even now, after we have become Christians, sin still grabs for our attention. I love and respect my dear fellow-believers who interpret 2 Corinthians 5:17b ("Old things are passed away; behold, all things are become new.") to mean that the old nature is eradicated. We know that the *verse* is true; there is no debate about that. However, if that is the proper *interpretation* of that verse, God would not have to tell us, as Christians, to lay aside troubling sins; (Hebrews 12:1) they would simply not be a problem. We must be diligent against old ways, and we must keep short accounts with God when we do sin.

However, there is a *second* enslavement, *another* one we face after we become believers. Actually, it too is a transgression, for it is the sin of slavery to the Law for righteousness.

Galatians is the only letter Paul wrote to a church in which he confronted a major flaw without first praising them for what they were doing right. And what was their fault? They believed they had to keep the law because Christ's work on the cross was not good enough. They had so distorted Paul's message that the apostle marveled they had so quickly abandoned the true gospel for a perverted fake. (1:6-7) He was afraid he had wasted his time on them. (3:4, 4:11) He said that their abandonment of the gospel of grace was not only simple man-pleasing, but it was dishonoring to Christ. (1:9-10) He also says those who distort the gospel that way should be accursed—anathema: "bound under a great curse." (1:8-9)

The two distortions here are the evil of sin and rebellion; and the arrogance and folly of depending on our works. Above it all is the Lord Jesus Christ who placed us out of the Law's reach by dying for our sins. I think Paul is telling us if our focus is on sin *or* the Law, it is not on Christ where it belongs.

14
Twice a Slave, Part 3

Galatians 6:14 "But God forbid that I should glory, save in the cross of our Lord Jesus Christ, by whom the world is crucified unto me, and I unto the world."

Should an article with the word "twice" in the title have a Part 3? Well, after a little chuckle, I decided yes, and here is my reasoning.

In my first Musing on this topic, I pointed out that sin enslaves us. Even after we trust Christ and are forgiven of all unrighteousness, (1 John 1:9) sin still entices us, and we must diligently resist it. (Hebrews 12:1)

However, what gives rise to the third writing in this trilogy is what I said yesterday, when I mentioned that we are not to be slaves to the Law either. As good as the Law is, we must not assume that keeping the Law is part of our righteousness. As true as that is, the fallen human heart will find ways to distort that also. (Jeremiah 17:9)

Keeping the Law is *not* part of our righteousness, but one distortion of that truth is the idea that once I trust God for His forgiveness, I am free to live as I please—I can live a "lawless" life.

I try to keep these Musings brief, so I was not able to expand on this thought last time. That is the subject for today's thoughts.

Lest we misinterpret grace without the Law as being license for lawlessness, we must recall that James reminds us that "faith, if it hath not works, is dead, being alone." (2:17) He goes on to say, "Shew me thy faith without thy works, and I will shew thee my faith **by** my works." (2:18, emphasis mine)

In addition, Paul balances the matter this way: "Therefore we conclude that a man is justified by faith without the deeds of the law. ... Do we then make void the law through faith? God forbid: yea, we establish the law." (Romans 3:28, 31)

Paul then says it outright: "What then? shall we sin, because we are not under the law, but under grace? God forbid." (Romans 6:15)

Friends, don't think of the Christian life as a tightrope-walking act hemming us in by dos and don'ts. It is a life of freedom, but freedom to honor God by walking in newness of life. Let us do so with faith, joy, and peace.

15

Twice a Slave, Part 4

Luke 18:10-13 "Two men went up into the temple to pray; the one a Pharisee, and the other a publican. The Pharisee stood and prayed thus with himself, God, I thank thee, that I am not as other men are, extortioners, unjust, adulterers, or even as this publican. I fast twice in the week, I give tithes of all that I possess. And the publican, standing afar off, would not lift up so much as his eyes unto heaven, but smote upon his breast, saying, God be merciful to me a sinner."

I suspect that a certain percentage of my regular readers who saw "*Twice* a Slave, Part 3" suspected that I would not stop at just three. You were right. I initially intended to cover everything in just one Musing, but each one left me with just a little more to say. Today's thoughts are the final entry on the subject. I trust that these reviews have been helpful.

As stated in the first three posts, even though we don't want to be slaves to sin **or** the Law, neither do we want to live lawlessly. Our delight and pleasure is to find ourselves as willing servants to the Lord of Glory. However, the sad fact is that we are fallen people living in a fallen world. Isaiah said it this way, "Then said I, Woe is me! for I am undone; because I am a man of unclean lips, and I dwell in the midst of a people of unclean lips: for mine eyes have seen the King, the LORD of hosts." (6:5)

We must never use that as an excuse for unrighteous behavior, either before or after the fact. Nevertheless, sometimes in our walk we find that by carelessness—or worse, by choice—we fall. We think, say, or do something that is **not** honoring to God. What then?

Whether we have given in to sin, or on the other hand, have drunk from the same cup of self-righteousness as the Pharisee, there is hope. However, it can only be found where the publican found it: in the mercy and loving kindness of our Savior. As John said it, "My little children, these things write I unto you, that ye sin not. And if any man sin, we have an advocate with the Father, Jesus Christ the righteous:" (1 John 2:1)

16

I Must Come to I AM

John 8:58-59 "Jesus said unto them, Verily, verily, I say unto you, Before Abraham was, I am. Then took they up stones to cast at him: but Jesus hid himself, and went out of the temple, going through the midst of them, and so passed by."

Someone might be surprised that Jesus would claim to exist before Abraham, a man who preceded Him by almost 2,000 years; however, we might be just as surprised by those who reacted so violently to a man who had claimed something so apparently ridiculous. Why were they so angry? Jesus' detractors were angry because He claimed to be equal with God. (Also see John 5:18.) Let's look closer.

The words Jesus used of Himself, "I am," are translated from the Greek words "ego eime." The lexicon in **Strong's Concordance** says the first word, pronounced eg-o' is "a primary pronoun of the first person, 'I' (only expressed when emphatic)." Whatever claim Jesus made, He was clearly making of Himself.

The second word, pronounced i-mee', is "first person singular present indicative; a prolonged form of a primary and defective verb; I exist (used only when emphatic)." The thing that struck me about that definition is the phrase "defective verb."

I don't claim to be a Greek scholar, but I know that one general defect in human languages is they can't adequately express eternal existence, simply because nothing in our personal experience is eternal. Plants die. Pets die. Friends and family die. One day, we will die.

I am currently sitting in a darkened house, typing this Musing on my cell phone. We have experienced the first ice storm of the season, and I am told that 60,000 people are without power. The thought came to me as I was typing, that just like those people who are disconnected from their power, we are all born disconnected from eternal life. Oh, we are indeed eternal beings who will exist forevermore, but there is a difference between existing forevermore and living forevermore.

That is why we need the eternal life of God, which is only available to us through the Lord Jesus Christ. He is I AM, one with the Father and the Holy Spirit, together, the Great God.

The lights literally just came back on at our house. I am glad we are reconnected to the power. I thank God that by grace, I am also connected to Him.

17

Generous

Romans 5:6-9 "For when we were yet without strength, in due time Christ died for the ungodly. For scarcely for a righteous man will one die: yet peradventure for a good man some would even dare to die. But God commendeth his love toward us, in that, while we were yet sinners, Christ died for us. Much more then, being now justified by his blood, we shall be saved from wrath through him."

John Davison Rockefeller was 21 years old when a tall, lanky lawyer named Abraham Lincoln became president of the United States in 1861. By his mid-70s, Rockefeller had accumulated around $900 million, the equivalent of almost $190 billion in current dollars. That is a staggering sum equal to the combined wealth of Warren Buffett and Bill Gates today.

Mr. Rockefeller had a habit of carrying around a bag of dimes, handing them to people that he met, often children, whom he encouraged to be wise in their money habits. In that day, even a small amount of money was a lot; for example, a dime back then could buy what might cost ten or fifteen dollars today. Over time, Mr. Rockefeller handed out around $35,000 in dimes, a sum that is equal to several million dollars today.

I do not know if Mr. Rockefeller was ever insulted, attacked, or beaten up, but if he was, my guess is that he didn't hand his attacker a dime. He was an incredibly generous man, but I suspect that he was generally not as generous to those who mistreated or maligned him.

Today's verses say that few of us would lay down our lives, even for good people; however, Christ did not lay down His life for good people, but for ungodly sinners. I do not minimize Mr. Rockefeller's kindness, but that is a rich man being generous to relatively innocent children. However, these verses are about the King of the Universe lavishing His generosity upon insurrectionists who spurned Him and even murdered Him.

> On yonder hill hung the King of the world;
> Bleeding, He died on the old, rugged tree.

There God did mark all my debt "Paid in full,"
And thus, He declares that now I am free.
~ W.F. Powers

In His generosity, God picked us up out of a staggering, incalculable, unpayable debt, and set us down in His family. That is inconceivable generosity.

18

Fame or Shame

1 Peter 5:6 "Humble yourselves therefore under the mighty hand of God, that he may exalt you in due time:"

I try to be careful when writing these Musings; I trust that I am yielding to the Holy Spirit and giving way to His leading. One of the reasons for my caution is that I find it misleading and even deceptive when someone plays games with words in the Bible. As an example, I knew a man who thought Santa Claus was an evil concept, and he "proved his case" by pointing out the similarity between the spellings of Santa and Satan. Regardless of what position one takes on that seasonal figure, that particular argument is unsound, among other reasons, because it does not work in all other languages. I don't know that man's heart, and perhaps he just intended to make a passing observation rather than a dogmatic tenet. Nevertheless, for that reason, I want to be clear that my thoughts here today are a passing observation, not a doctrine. A Hebrew scholar may be able to make a stronger case, but I can only make this as an observation.

Here is what I noticed in my reading this morning:

In Genesis 6:1-4, God described the mating of the "sons of God" (ben elohiym) with the "daughters of men" (bath adam) that produced giants (nᵉphiyl) who became "men of renown" (shem). In other words, the offspring from "ben elohiym" and "bath adam" made names for themselves, either famously or infamously. My observation is about the Hebrew word "renown" (shem) which, as I understand, is pronounced "shame" just like the English word for guilty humiliation.

Again, I am not building a doctrine here, but I do find the use of the words to be interesting, in when human beings lift themselves up in fame, it often leads to disaster, ruin, and shame. Truly, as today's verse says, we should be careful that a sense of self-importance doesn't overpower us. As Paul wrote to the church at Rome, "For I say, through the grace given unto me, to every man that is among you, not to think of himself more highly than he ought to think; but to think soberly, according as God hath dealt to every man the measure of faith." (Romans 12:3)

Genuine humility is a good thing; it causes us to decrease and God to increase. (John 3:30)

19

Victory on Display

2 Corinthians 4 "8 We are troubled on every side, yet not distressed; we are perplexed, but not in despair; 9. Persecuted, but not forsaken; cast down, but not destroyed; 10. Always bearing about in the body the dying of the Lord Jesus, that the life also of Jesus might be made manifest in our body. 11. For we which live are alway delivered unto death for Jesus' sake, that the life also of Jesus might be made manifest in our mortal flesh."

Here Paul is telling the saints at Corinth that he is going through sufferings, but he is not overwhelmed. I've always thought of that as an encouragement to believers that the stresses of our lives would not overcome us. Perhaps that is how you read that passage too, and I think that reading is correct.

However, there is more to that thought, which the apostle brings out in verses 9 and 10.

We aren't just surviving the struggles we have in life; those struggles and survivals are actually part of our testimony. We successfully go through difficulties, and by doing, so we demonstrate what Christ has been through and the victory he obtained by it. It is true that we **speak** of Christ as we witness for Him, but God also uses us to **demonstrate** the life of Christ to others. Christ suffered, but He also succeeded! We bear testimony to that fact through our struggles.

I recall to your mind the conversation mentioned in Luke 9:30-31. On the mount of transfiguration, the Lord Jesus spoke to Moses and Elias. What did they talk about? The death that Jesus was going to **accomplish** at Jerusalem! We don't usually think of death as an accomplishment, but that is what Jesus did; He accomplished death so that God can be just, and yet we no longer need to face God's just wrath.

God is using us as human canvases upon which He is painting a picture of His Son. We suffer, and yet it does not destroy us; we struggle, and yet we are not ruined. We are victorious in our dilemmas similar to Christ's victory. That gives to the world a testimony—a picture—of the spectacular grace of God.

Praise him! praise him! tell of his excellent greatness,
Praise him! praise him! ever in joyful song!
~ Fanny Crosby

20

Bob Was Right

Romans 4:11, 23-24 "And he received the sign of circumcision, a seal of the righteousness of the faith which he had yet being uncircumcised: that he might be the father of all them that believe, though they be not circumcised; that righteousness might be imputed unto them also: ... Now it was not written for his sake alone, that it was imputed to him; But for us also, to whom it shall be imputed, if we believe on him that raised up Jesus our Lord from the dead;"

Christian radio talk show host Bob Burney recently spoke about the difference between an implant and a transplant and made this observation: An implant, such as a pacemaker, is a nonliving device that is placed in a person and performs a specific function but never becomes an actual part of that person. A transplant is a living part from a living being that is placed into a person and actually becomes part of that person.

Mr. Burney then likened that to the righteousness of Christ, which is imputed to those who believe on His name. Bob said that something imputed is like a transplant, for it is the righteousness of a living being which is placed into another living being.

As I thought about this, I marveled at the glorious grace and kindness that our God has given us. It reminded me of the words of John, which we see in his first epistle: "Behold, what manner of love the Father hath bestowed upon us, that we should be called the sons of God:" (1 John 3:1a)

Our standing with God is not one of religion, but one of relationship. It is not one of rules, but of rest. It is not something lifelike, but rather something living. We have standing before God, not because we *do*, but because He *did*.

One of the most beautiful things in this broken world is when people are kind to each other; however, regardless of how good, how kind, and how helpful we are, our good works will never give us a right standing with God. The only thing that will cause us to be right with God is for Him to transplant His righteousness into us, thereby making that righteousness an integral part of us. Thankfully, that is what He does through Christ.

21

Psalm 119 and the Progression of Spiritual Life

Psalm 119:25 "My soul cleaveth unto the dust: quicken thou me according to thy word. 26. I have declared my ways, and thou heardest me: teach me thy statutes. 27. Make me to understand the way of thy precepts: so shall I talk of thy wondrous works."

Psalm 119 is separated into 22 divisions; each section contains eight verses and is titled with a letter of the Hebrew alphabet. Many print Bibles show these divisions; some electronic Bibles do not. Today's verses are the first three in the fourth division and are captioned by the fourth Hebrew letter, Dalet. I shall briefly mention the other five verses, but we shall concentrate on the first three.

In verse 25, the writer says his soul "cleaveth unto the dust;" it is as if he is dead, lying in the dirt. Indeed, he uses a Hebrew word translated "quicken," which includes the idea of being "restored to life." This is similar to Paul's thought in Ephesians 2:1, where he declares that God has quickened us from our dead, unregenerate state. This 25th verse reminds me of the beginning of spiritual life.

I am uncertain of verse 26; it reminds me of an immature believer demanding his own way: "I have declared *my* ways." (emphasis mine) I understand that *may* be a confession of his own weak thoughts rather than a demand for his own way; however, if it is a demand, he seems embarrassed when he realizes that the Almighty God was listening to his childish prattle: "thou heardest me." In either event, he concludes that God's ways are better than his are and asks the Lord, "Teach me thy statutes."

Finally, in verse 27, he wants not just to learn God's statutes; he wants to understand them. When that happens, he is sure he will "talk of thy wondrous works," and not ramble on about himself and his plans.

I encourage you to read the five remaining verses; they remind me of our growing relationship with God as we struggle with this life, but remain open, humble, and honest before the Lord about faults, fears, and our need for Him. I pray that we all find ourselves growing in that kind of transparent walk with God.

22

A Brief Thought on Thanksgiving

1 Chronicles 16:34 "O give thanks unto the LORD; for he is good; for his mercy endureth for ever."

This same thought is repeated in Psalm 106:1; Psalm 107:1; Psalm 118:1, 29; Psalm 136:1. We are to give thanks to the Lord, but notice the word "for"; it is used as a conjunction to show us the reason why we should give thanks to the Lord. There are many reasons we should give God thanks, but the two the psalmist lists here are huge:

- He is good. Sometimes the problems of this fallen world, as well as God's judgments, draw our attention away from the fact that He is good. However, He *is* good, and for that reason we are to give Him thanks.
- His mercy endures forever. We need to be honest with ourselves. If I know what God is like—at least in some part—and since I know what I am and what I am *not*, there is no reasonable response to everlasting mercy but a heart overflowing with thanksgiving to the One who is merciful to me.

I pray that you have a blessed Thanksgiving season.

23

Moms, Wives and Coats

Proverbs 3:5-6 Trust in the LORD with all thine heart; and lean not unto thine own understanding. In all thy ways acknowledge him, and he shall direct thy paths.

For the first five or six Christmas holidays after we got married, my wife and I went on vacation to our national capital, Washington, D.C. We often went alone, but one year we took three of our children. Though it was December, the temperatures were not too bad, so I dressed in layers rather than wearing a heavy coat. As we checked out of the motel, the young lady behind the counter asked good-naturedly, "You have a wife, and I know you have a mother. Where is your coat?" The inference was that I was not thinking my decisions through very well, and I needed some help.

That reminds me of a friend who is colorblind. If he happens to pick out his own clothes for the day, he will glance at his wife for approval as he comes down the stairs. Sometimes a dismissive wave of the hand is all it takes to cause his retreat back to the bedroom for another try.

Over the years, we have enjoyed a good laugh over the "Where is your coat?" episode. My wife has even laughingly used it to urge me to do something that made sense to her and that she thought would obviously make sense to my mother.

None of us make good decisions all the time. Indeed, in our natural condition, we are not capable of making good decisions in the spiritual realm. (1 Corinthians 2:14)

There is a saying in the business world: "Those who fail to plan, plan to fail." In other words, if you don't lay out specific steps to reach your goal, you will be fumbling in the dark, unable to make significant progress. For the believer, we thankfully have a perfect plan already laid out by the Perfect Planner—the Almighty God. He has even given us His Spirit to live in us and to guide us through His Word, which the psalmist describes as "a lamp unto my feet, and a light unto my path." (Psalm 119:105)

To paraphrase the young motel clerk, "You have a Savior, and I know you have His Spirit. Where's your guiding plan?" The best one lies between leather covers.

24

Deceitfulness

2 Corinthians 4:1-2 "Therefore seeing we have this ministry, as we have received mercy, we faint not; But have renounced the hidden things of dishonesty, not walking in craftiness, nor handling the word of God deceitfully; but by manifestation of the truth commending ourselves to every man's conscience in the sight of God."

In today's verses, Paul is renouncing dishonesty and deceit, committing himself to truth. Contrary to truth, deceit is an attempt to convince someone that something is true when it is not.

The Bible has much to say about deceit. Sometimes it is one person lying to another; sadly however, it is often us deceiving ourselves. Examples include: Riches that trick us into a false sense of security and well-being; (Mark 4:19) physical attraction that hides an unattractive person inside; (Proverbs 31:30) using the work of God simply for personal gain. (Jeremiah 48:10) Our lusts, our tongues, and our very hearts can deceive others and even our own selves. (Micah 6:12, Jeremiah 17:9)

The writer of Hebrews instructs believers to encourage each other to follow a good path so we are not deceived by those things that are contrary to Christ. "But exhort one another daily, while it is called To day; lest any of you be hardened through the deceitfulness of sin." (Hebrews 3:13) Note that the verse in Hebrews doesn't just say we can be deceived by sin, but that we are in danger of being hardened by it. We sometimes hear the phrase "little white lie," but in light of these Scriptures, lies don't seem so little or innocent anymore, do they?

25

Grasping Real Reality

1 Corinthians 13:11 "When I was a child, I spake as a child, I understood as a child, I thought as a child: but when I became a man, I put away childish things."

As we grow, we change. Our thoughts change. Our attitudes change. Our beliefs change. What we used to find important loses some of its appeal, and we turn a corner to find new realities coming into focus.

When I was in my twenties, I trusted Christ to save me from my sins. As I have grown in my faith, I have come to be awed by the magnificence of His glory. However, when I was still a young Christian, I used to think that God was part of my life; unfortunately, that way of thinking is a distortion. The point I am trying to convey—and I ask you please, stop a few moments to take this in—God is *not* part of *my* reality; He has made me a part of *His* reality!

Now, that may sound like a word game or merely two sides of the same coin; however, thinking that God is part of my life puts me on the face of the coin and God on the back. In truth, all Creation revolves around God. He is the God of *everything*, and I am *His* creation, not the other way around. He was here before me, and He will still be here when I am gone; I am therefore a part of *His* plan. The apostle Paul put it this way: "I am crucified with Christ: nevertheless *I live; yet not I*, but *Christ liveth in me*: and the life which I now live in the flesh I live by the faith of the Son of God, who loved me, and gave himself for me." (Galatians 2:20, emphasis mine)

God did not create us to feel insignificant or trivial, but neither is it His purpose that we think of ourselves more highly than we ought to think.

(Romans 12:3) The real and legitimate balance is that God is the center of all, and we who trust in Him are loved with an everlasting love by the True and Living God who *is* the center of it all.

26

Would You Fight an Unbeatable Giant?

Psalm 7:11b "God is angry with the wicked every day."

There is no nice way to say this. We mortals like to believe lies. At least some lies—the ones that make us feel good. We know that the doctor *should* be honest with us, but sometimes we don't want to hear what she has to say. If the plumber knows we do not like bad news and doesn't tell us about a problem, we may feel good, but probably not for very long. As hard as the truth is, if we know what it is, we can deal with the problem and perhaps fix it.

21st century Western society is fascinated with the idea of a god who loves everybody and who would never do anything to interfere with our lives. That is unless we call upon Him like a genie in a magic bottle to grant us health, riches, or some other goodies. Then he is supposed to go back to sleep until we beckon once more.

That mindset is suddenly disrupted when we read, "God is angry with the wicked every day." I do not know if Thomas Jefferson was a Christian believer, but he spoke of God being just and that His justice cannot sleep forever. I agree with Jefferson on that. How do we cope with the truth, that there is an angry aspect to God?

If we had any comprehension of the *power* of God, His anger would terrify us, as it should if that is all there is. However, the God who *is* angry with the wicked every day *is* loving, gracious, merciful, and tenderhearted too. The Holy One presents this complexity in a simplicity even a child can understand. He commands us to reason with Him that our transgressions be cleansed (Isaiah 1:18) and His anger be assuaged. The most startling thing is that God—who is angry with the wicked every day—has Himself made our forgiveness possible by punishing Jesus on the cross for our sins.

God is glorified in the justification of those who come humbly to Him in repentance and faith, and He will be glorified in His righteous anger against those who will not. The only two questions now are: In which group do you stand? And will you let your pride and arrogance pit you in an unwinnable fight against the Almighty God?

27

The Desolate and the Not Desolate

Psalm 34:21-22 "Evil shall slay the wicked: and they that hate the righteous shall be desolate. The LORD redeemeth the soul of his servants: and none of them that trust in him shall be desolate."

These verses should be a great comfort to believers, and they should also be a great warning to unbelievers. The problem is that unbelievers—by definition—do not believe, so they usually are not afraid of a biblical warning concerning their desolation. They **should** take heed though, for in another psalm, Asaph complained that the wicked were getting away with their evil ways and that his attempts to live a godly life were a waste of effort. Things changed for him when "I went into the sanctuary of God; then understood I their end." (Psalm 73:17) The end for unbelievers will be much different than they imagine.

However, there is another problem. Sometimes we believers do not believe either. The second of today's verses tell us that the opposite is true for us: "none of them that trust in him shall be desolate." We Christians sometimes live in much angst when we should be trusting God and what He says.

Do Christians have troubles? Of course we do. Asaph even admits that those who seek to be godly have troubles, (Psalm 73:13-14) but the difference is that God promises that He won't abandon us and that we shall never be desolate.

Let us face our trials, trusting the Holy Spirit for His wisdom and guidance, but let us **never** fear that we are deserted. God **promises** that we are not, and that we never will be. That is **wonderful** news!

28

One Murderous Year

2 Corinthians 6:2b "Behold, now is the accepted time; behold, now is the day of salvation."

Toward of the end of 2016, a year in which a number of famous people died, one fellow commented, "2016, you're one murderous year." Famous people are not better than those of us who are not famous, but their deaths do gain our attention simply because they are more widely known.

Musings

Closer to home though are the deaths of friends and relatives. How thankful we should be that those deaths are not as numerous or as often as the passing of celebrities! Still, we do lose those close to us, and it grieves us. Today is my late father's birthday. We lost him in March of 2010; we lost my mother later that same year and my wife's mother several years earlier. Last year we lost a sister, and awhile back, we lost another sister and her husband in consecutive years.

If God is good, why would He make such a place of sadness, sorrow, and death? The question is understandable, but it is based on a flawed assumption. The fact is that when God created this world, He pronounced it "very good." (Genesis 1:31) God was not the problem; our first parents who sin against Him were, and now, we are too.

There *is* a good side to this however. The same God, who made everything good, has purposed to *re*make everything good again. He did so by coming to this Earth and personally paying our sin debt. Now, all who trust Him are forgiven of their sin (John 3:16; Ephesians 1:7) and made righteous before Him.

However, there is a caveat, a warning, a "catch" if you will: those who refuse to come to Him on His terms will never experience that remaking. "He that believeth on the Son *hath* everlasting life: and he that believeth not the Son shall not see life; but the wrath of God *abideth* on him." (John 3:36, emphasis mine) Notice that *both* of the emphasized words are *present* tense. Those who believe *have* (now) everlasting life. Those who refuse His mercy and grace, *abide* (now) under His wrath.

Do not delay, my friend; do not stay in that dangerous place, that place of imminent wrath. "Behold, now is the accepted time; behold, now is the day of salvation."

29
Taps

Psalm 23:4a "Yea, though I walk through the valley of the shadow of death, I will fear no evil:"

A longtime friend died in late November, 2018. When we went to the visitation, a small, folded handout mentioned that Jim was in the Army in the early 1970s. The cover of that little bulletin had a military theme and listed the words of the somber music that is often played on a bugle or trumpet at funerals for service personnel. The tune is named "Taps" and consists of only 24 notes, played in 8 sets of 3 notes each. Do you know the words that go with that tune?

Day is done,
Gone the sun
From the lakes,
　From the hills
　　From the sky;
All is well,
Safely rest,
God is near.

Notwithstanding the Fall, this world still displays much of God's creativity. There is life, there is love, there is wonder and beauty. However, there are also reminders of our fallen brokenness and mortality, aren't there? The passing of loved ones is one such reminder.

Despite our brokenness, we can have hope. We do not need to despair, because—for those who trust in Christ's redemptive sacrifice—we have God's solemn promises of eternal life, restoration, peace with Him, and a home in Heaven forever. However, it is important to understand that God doesn't demand we clean up our lives before we come to Him; instead, just as the old invitation song tells us, we must come to God "Just as I am." It is true that we are to repent and turn from our sins and trust Him for His mercy and grace, but we cannot clean ourselves up. God Himself cleanses us when we confess our sins to Him, (1 John 1:9) and He will begin to change who we are, *after* we come to Him. Then, the more we walk in fellowship with Him, the more we experience His rest and peace.

Trust in Christ—that is what Jim did. How about you, my friend? I encourage you to turn to Him in faith today; there will never be a better time.

Then we find that—whether our "day is done, and our sun is gone" just for the night or because our bright, eternal, forever-day has dawned upon us—we as believers can say, "All is well, safely rest, God is near."

30

Let's Be Reasonable

Isaiah 1:18 "Come now, and let us reason together, saith the LORD: though your sins be as scarlet, they shall be as white as snow; though they be red like crimson, they shall be as wool."

Musings

One evening I was watching the news when they showed several video clips of people doing their after-Thanksgiving Christmas shopping. Well, for the people in the videos, it was actually their after-Thanksgiving Christmas brawl. One fellow flung a store employee into the shelves. Several other customers were pulling against each other over a large box containing a flat screen TV until the box began to tear open.

What causes people to behave that way? What causes people to loot and steal during natural disasters or riots? Whatever words we might use to describe it, "reason" isn't one of them. During these events, rational thinking is abandoned and chaos ensues. In striking contrast, God invites us to come and reason with Him. He does not create chaos; (1 Corinthians 14:33) that is Satan's tactic. (James 3:13-16) Instead, God calls us to be reasonable.

In the case of today's verse, the prophet is giving his people a message from the Lord; that same promise is ours today. To paraphrase God's offer, "Your hearts are stained with sin, but I have a remedy for that." Why would anyone turn down such mercy? Sadly, that is the natural bent of the lost soul. (1 Corinthians 2:14)

I find it interesting that God also addresses the consequences of sin and the offer of life through another prophet, Ezekiel. "Say unto them, As I live, saith the Lord GOD, I have no pleasure in the death of the wicked; but that the wicked turn from his way and live: turn ye, turn ye from your evil ways; for why will ye die, O house of Israel?" (Ezekiel 33:11)

Isn't reason a good thing? Isn't God being merciful when He invites us to come to Him while He offers such kindness? Never has a victorious general ever offered such startlingly generous terms of surrender.

Are we wiser than God is? Do we have a better plan? Or will we be reasonable and take the Almighty at His word?

The Lord tells us to come now and reason together with Him; though our sins bring consequences with them, He has created a solution at great personal cost.

I plead with you, come *now*!

DECEMBER

1

A Resting Place

Psalm 132:3-5 "Surely I will not come into the tabernacle of my house, nor go up into my bed; I will not give sleep to mine eyes, or slumber to mine eyelids, Until I find out a place for the LORD, a habitation for the mighty God of Jacob."

In Exodus 26, God gave instructions for building the tabernacle. It was a place where God would dwell among His people and a resting place for the Ark of the Covenant. As the people of Israel moved through the wilderness and into the Promised Land, they broke down the tabernacle into individual pieces and moved it from place to place.

In 1 Chronicles 17, we see that it was King David's great longing to build God a permanent place in Israel, a grand temple to replace the smaller, portable, tent-like tabernacle. David expressed that passion in today's verses, where he asked how he can live in a grand palace and sleep in his bed until he builds a suitable place for his God.

As I studied these verses, I looked up several of the words David used and found the word translated "habitation" to be very interesting. The word has uses that we might not think of being as grand as a house for God. For example, it means a residence, but could be used for a shepherd's hut or the lair of animals. However, one use of the word was what struck me because this word could also be used figuratively for a grave!

Regardless of the various meanings of the word David used, I suspect he never thought that a grave would ever be the "habitation for the mighty God of Jacob." Nevertheless, for three dark days, the grave is where the Savior lay. In spite of the darkness, the heart rejoices that just an hour or two before His precious body was laid in the tomb, He spoke words of grace: "teleo!" (tel-eh'-o), meaning 'It is finished.' (John 19:30) Our sin debt was paid in full.

As a result, instead of the God of Creation dwelling in a tabernacle or a temple, He now inhabits those who come to Him in repentance and faith.

How wonderful! "Make a joyful noise unto the LORD, all ye lands." (Psalm 100:1)

2

Furrows, Righteousness, and Cords

Psalm 129:2 "Many a time have they afflicted me from my youth: yet they have not prevailed against me. 3. The plowers plowed upon my back: they made long their furrows. 4. The LORD is righteous: he hath cut asunder the cords of the wicked."

God purposed that the psalmists, under the direct guidance of the Holy Spirit, wrote of their own experiences. As in so many of the psalms, the writer of today's verses addresses the affliction of God's people in Israel, but we can also see other meanings in this passage.

Though the psalmist probably lived before Isaiah and did not make the connection, his thoughts in verse 3 concerning plowers making long furrows on his back has a similarity to Isaiah's Messianic prophecy: "I gave my back to the smiters ... therefore have I set my face like a flint, and I know that I shall not be ashamed." (50:6-7) Several commentaries also mention a Messianic connection in this psalm.

As I was reading this passage recently, I noticed another similarity as well. I would not press the illustration too far since the oppressors of Israel—and the Lord's judgment on them—is clearly the focus of the writer. Nevertheless, I think it is at least fair to see a precious hint in verses 3 and 4. Though cutting the cords of the wicked surely applies to God's judgment upon them, if I may restate it reverently, "The plowers dug their furrows into Christ's back, but in His righteousness, the LORD has used the suffering Savior to cut asunder the cords which bound the wicked ones for whom He bled and died, thus making them free."

May we never cease to be in awe of God, not just for His works, but also for He Himself. Though this psalm declares that God brings judgment on those who practice wickedness, let us never forget that in times past, *we* too practiced wickedness. Whether we did so overtly or secretly in the recesses of our hearts, (Jeremiah 17:9) He has cut asunder the cords that bound us and set us free.

3

They Understood Not

Acts 7:25 "For he supposed his brethren would have understood how that God by his hand would deliver them: but they understood not."

In Acts chapter 6, certain religious people falsely accused Stephen of blasphemy; in chapter 7, he was given the opportunity to speak on his own behalf. In doing so, Stephen unfolded an outline of the history of his people. He recounted that Moses had defended a fellow Israelite from an abusive Egyptian. After that, Moses assumed that his people would accept him as a protector and leader, but as today's verse shows, they did not accept him. "They understood not."

As the passage continues, Stephen called the people stiff-necked and reminded them that they had not only rejected Moses, but the prophets as well. He then reminded them that Jesus too had come bearing witness of God, and they murdered Him also. At that, the religious leaders became enraged and murdered Stephen just as they had Jesus and the prophets before Him.

As I read that this morning, it reminded me of the parable Jesus gave in which He exposed the hearts of the religious leaders as those who "will not have this man to reign over us." (Luke 19:11-14)

As we read passages like this, it is easy to say, "Oh, those are some really bad people," but sadly it is not all that much different today. I don't want to paint with a broad brush, so to speak, but there are vast multitudes today who do not want God interfering with their lives. They don't mind wearing a little religious jewelry and going to church occasionally, but they don't want God calling for a changed life or renewed thinking. It is as if they say, "Thanks, God, for the nice religion and pretty music and good feelings, but my life is mine, and you can't have it."

As I said, I am not making an all-encompassing accusation; I truly thank God there is a strong faith in many of Christ's followers today. However, I encourage each of us to examine ourselves to see if our footsteps are in the same direction as the Master's. If they are not, now is the time to change.

4

The Authority and Purposes of God

Daniel 4:35, 37 "And all the inhabitants of the earth are reputed as nothing: and he doeth according to his will in the army of heaven, and among the inhabitants of the earth: and none can stay his hand, or say unto him, What doest thou? ... Now I Nebuchadnezzar praise and extol and honor the King of heaven, all whose works are truth, and his ways judgment: and those that walk in pride he is able to abase."

Nebuchadnezzar, king of Babylon in the time of the prophet Daniel, had become arrogantly proud. The Lord took away his kingdom *and* his sanity. Sometime later, God restored him. Today's verses record Nebuchadnezzar's reaction to God's gracious kindness.

Think of the rebellion of mankind throughout time: Adam and Eve, people in Noah's day, the tower of Babel, the golden calf, just to name a few. At any point in time, God could have done anything He purposed to do including ending it all. That was perfectly within His rights, and He would have been totally justified in doing so. On the other hand, if He purposed to pay for that sin Himself, that too was perfectly within His rights.

We *must* not think of God as a mean ogre; we must understand Him as a startlingly gracious God who has been slapped in His holy face. As distasteful as we may find it, we are members of a rebellious, human race; God is not obligated to us in *any* way, the *only* exception being in ways in which He obligates Himself. Understandably, those self-imposed obligations include His judgment of those who refuse to bow the knee in repentance and faith; inconceivably, it also includes His forgiveness of those who do.

I don't think it is a sin to ask God "Why?" if we ask so we can know Him better *and* if we are committed to obey whether we understand or not. However, we cross a breathtaking line when we question His wisdom and authority or if we base our obedience upon whether God satisfactorily explains Himself to us.

Any kindness God shows to us mortals is a gift of mercy and grace. "O come, let us worship and bow down: let us kneel before the LORD our maker. For he is our God; and we are the people of his pasture, and the sheep of his hand." (Psalm 95:6-7a)

December

5

Getting Old with the Faith of a Child

Mark 10:15 "Verily I say unto you, Whosoever shall not receive the kingdom of God as a little child, he shall not enter therein."
1 Corinthians 13:11 "When I was a child, I spake as a child, I understood as a child, I thought as a child: but when I became a man, I put away childish things."

Brian Aldiss, an English fiction writer, once made an interesting observation: "When childhood dies, its corpses are called adults ... That is why we dread children, even if we love them. They show us the state of our decay."

Childhood is filled with wonder and exuberance; however, we do not remain children, nor should we. It is truly a sad thing to watch a adult who refuses to grow up. However, it is a wonderful thing to retain *some* of the qualities of youth as long as we do not use them as an excuse to be childish. Today's verses help us maintain that balance.

In the passage in Mark, Jesus said that accepting God's authority requires a childlike approach. Note that this is not speaking exclusively of Heaven; the word translated "kingdom" is a word that means the authority to rule and have dominion. God does not only have dominion in Heaven, He has dominion everywhere, including here on Earth and in our lives. The natural man—the "adult" in us—does not want to yield to God, but Jesus calls upon us to let go of our ego and receive God as the authority in our lives.

Today's second verse tells us to "put away childish things." This addresses the matter from a similar but different angle, commanding us not to act childishly.

The merging of these two verses create a godly perspective on life: we are to grow up—to mature, to behave as adults—without giving up the awe we sense at the magnitude and glory of God. In other words, we are to "put away childish things" but at the same time receive the kingdom of God, and its authority and dominion, as a little child.

6

A Reason for Shame

Psalm 83:13-15 "O my God, make them like a wheel; as the stubble before the wind. As the fire burneth a wood, and as the flame setteth the mountains on fire; So persecute them with thy tempest, and make them afraid with thy storm."

As in many psalms, Asaph pleads with God to wreak havoc on the enemy. He starts this psalm by saying, "Keep not thou silence, O God: hold not thy peace, and be not still, O God. For, lo, thine enemies make a tumult: and they that hate thee have lifted up the head. They have taken crafty counsel against thy people, and consulted against thy hidden ones." (v1-3)

In fact, throughout the entire psalm from the first verse to the last, Asaph describes the evil works of his enemies and then calls upon God to crush them. It is a repeated cycle—evil works, please crush; evil works, please crush; evil works, please crush—except for verse 16.

Verse 16 is like a cool breeze that enters a sweltering, stale room. In those few words, the psalmist offers a ray of hope when he writes, "Fill their faces with shame; that they may seek thy name, O LORD."

How kind and merciful the Lord is that He would give us that glimmer of expectation. Maybe it is because He knows the damaged human heart all too well and knows the utterly helpless condition of fallen men and women. In any case, He purposes to brush aside all of our pompous braggadocio and arrogant bluster, and to use the tools of suffering, fear, and shame to bring about good.

Consider Naomi and Ruth in Moab. Consider Joseph in Egypt or Jonah in the great fish. Consider Jairus and his little girl, or the woman who had an issue of blood. Or the greatest example in all history: consider Jesus and His sufferings and the inconceivable good that God brought forth from that.

God does nothing without purpose—including suffering, fire, tempest, trouble, and yes, even shame—that people may seek His name, and "that men may know that thou, whose name alone is JEHOVAH, art the most high over all the earth." (v18)

7

The Package and the Product

Matthew 11:28-30 "Come unto me, all ye that labour and are heavy laden, and I will give you rest. Take my yoke upon you, and learn of me; for I am meek and lowly in heart: and ye shall find rest unto your souls. For my yoke is easy, and my burden is light."

For much of my adult life, I did electrical design for a couple of printing press manufacturers. Some of the machines we built were used in the food industry to make packaging for cereal boxes, soft drink foil packs, bottle labels, and more.

There was a saying in the packaging industry: "The package makes the first sale, but the product makes the second sale." In other words, if the *picture* on the package was appealing enough the customer might buy it, but if the *product* was not good, the customer would not be fooled the second time.

Sadly, Satan knows how to package things too. Remember that he told Eve the fruit would make her wise and that she would be like God. The problem was that though the "package" *looked* good, a few years later the "product" led Eve to a gravesite where she buried one of her sons.

Ever since that tragic day, the wicked one has been presenting rebellion against God in very enticing ways. Satan has nothing to offer that is of true value, so instead, he offers trinkets, bobbles, and shiny things to mesmerize us. He did that before we were saved to distract us from God's offer of forgiveness; even now, he does that to us as followers of Jesus to sidetrack us from our efforts to honor our Savior.

There is a reason why God calls the devil the "wicked one." (Matthew 13:19) Jesus also pictured Satan as a thief who "cometh not, but for to steal, and to kill, and to destroy:" Thankfully, Jesus said of Himself, "I am come that they might have life, and that they might have it more abundantly." (John 10:10)

I plead with you my dear reader, if you have not yet come to God for forgiveness, turn from your sins and come humbly before Him now, confessing your sins, and trusting Him for His pardon and grace. If you have already trusted in Him, keep pressing in, ever closer to Him; learn His ways and follow Him gladly.

8

Facts and Figures

Hebrews 11:17-19 "By faith Abraham, when he was tried, offered up Isaac: and he that had received the promises offered up his only begotten son, Of whom it was said, That in Isaac shall thy seed be called: Accounting that God was able to raise him up, even from the dead; from whence also he received him in a figure."

The Bible uses the term "figure" when describing something that actually existed or happened but which also gives an illustration of something else. We also call these "types" or "symbols." We find one example of this in the tabernacle, which God later replaced with the temple. These two buildings were where God dwelt near His people; God says that in the end, He will dwell with those who love Him. (Revelation 21:3)

In today's verses, Abraham planned to sacrifice Isaac and then received him in a figure. What does that mean? Well, just before that we read, "In Isaac shall thy seed be called." Abraham knew two things as that event started unfolding: first, Isaac would carry on Abraham's name, (Genesis 21:12) and second, he was supposed to sacrifice Isaac as a burnt offering. (Genesis 22:2) The only way Abraham could imagine both things happening was if God raised Isaac from the ashes. (Hebrews 11:19) As further evidence of his conviction, Abraham knew what he was going to do and still told his servants to remain at the base of the mountain with this promise: "*I and* the lad [both of us] will go yonder *and* worship, *and* come again to you." (Genesis 22:5, emphasis mine)

There are actually two types here: what Abraham expected reminds us of God's New Testament promise to raise His people back to life. There are two aspects to this type. First, God is able to raise physically dead people back to physical life just as He says, (Acts 26:8; 1 Corinthians 6:14; 2 Corinthians 4:14) and second, He is able to raise spiritually dead people to spiritual life, just as He says. (Ephesians 2:1; John 3:3; John 3:16; Romans 6:4)

The second type is the "ram caught in a thicket" (Genesis 22:13)— the replacement sacrifice—a picture of the Lord Jesus who died in our place that we might be redeemed, just as Isaac was spared.

Thank God for His "types," and thank Him especially for the realities they represent.

9

Facts and Figures, Part 2

Ephesians 5:31-32 "For this cause shall a man leave his father and mother, and shall be joined unto his wife, and they two shall be one flesh. This is a great mystery: but I speak concerning Christ and the church."

Yesterday we looked at several "types"—real life things or events that create an illustration of something else. We saw that God dwelling with His people in the tabernacle reminds us of His dwelling with His people in eternity. Last time, we saw several types in the account of God telling Abraham to sacrifice Isaac on the mountain.

God uses historical people, occasions, and institutions as illustrations of His unfolding plan. Today, we look at two facets of human relationships as pictures of God's connection to His people. Chapters 5 and 6 in Paul's letter to the Ephesians speak of relationships; God describes how people are to get along with each other.

First, let us look at the "type" of marriage as a picture of Christ's relationship to the church, the husband being a picture or "type" of Christ and the wife being a picture of Christ's beautiful bride, the church. Often in this fallen, broken world, that picture is mocked as archaic, but in truth, there is no sweeter love story than that of Christ for His church.

One side note: in reality, we men do not live up to that picture nearly as well as we should. Ladies, please forgive us. And guys, let us be gentle and gracious with our dear wives even as Christ is with the bride of His love. However, may we all see that type as a beautiful pattern for our marriages.

The second relationship picture I draw to your attention is in the first verses of both chapters 5 and 6. "Children, obey your parents in the Lord: for this is right." (6:1) God literally instructs children how to relate to their parents, but also compares that to how we, as children of God, are to relate to Him: "Be ye therefore followers of God, as dear children." (5:1) God is all wise, and we are just young learners. We must trust His wisdom and guidance, and yield to Him even when we, as children, do not understand His ways or perhaps think we know better.

10

Mosquitoes, Windshields, and the Wisdom of God

Acts 26:14 "And when we were all fallen to the earth, I heard a voice speaking unto me, and saying in the Hebrew tongue, Saul, Saul, why persecutest thou me? it is hard for thee to kick against the pricks."

The other day a mosquito got into our car. I concentrated on my driving but could not help but notice him buzzing all across the windshield. It was as if he could see the sky and couldn't understand what was preventing him from rising.

Mosquitoes do not understand glass. There was a simple reason why he could not fly upward. If he had understood, he would have abandoned his attempts to fly through a piece of glass and flown over to the side window that I had opened for him. Instead, he continued to wear himself out by pushing against the glass that he could never break.

Do we ever do that? Jesus used a word picture in today's verse when addressing Saul, who we know as Paul. God had knocked the future apostle off his horse. Sharp sticks, called pricks, were used to keep cattle in line when they were being herded along. (We would call them cattle prods.) Jesus asked Paul, "Why persecutest thou me?" and then reminded him that his resistance was as useless as a cow kicking against a pointed stick; he was hurting himself, not actually changing anything.

I don't know this for sure, but I sometimes wonder what will happen when we get to Heaven and God reveals some of what He was doing in us. I suspect that I might say, "Oh, *that's* what You were doing," and sorrow that I didn't trust Him better. I find it interesting that the phrase "wipe away all tears" appears in Revelation 21:4, right toward the end of the Bible. That means for a brief period, there will be tears in Heaven, probably tears of regret. They could be tears of joy, but why would God wipe away tears of joy?

I genuinely look forward to Heaven without dread for my failures. We shouldn't spend a lot of time concentrating on our defeats, but rather that we confess them and embrace forgiveness. However, let's also not continually bang our heads against the "glass" of the Lord's guidance and protection. We should trust Him every day as a good, wise, and faithful God.

11

Don't Buy the Lie

Genesis 3:4-5 "And the serpent said unto the woman, Ye shall not surely die: For God doth know that in the day ye eat thereof, then your eyes shall be opened, and ye shall be as gods, knowing good and evil."

Human pride is like a leash on an animal. Satan grabs onto our pride and leads us around as we would lead a horse or a dog. The problem is he never leads us in the right direction.

Granted, he will throw in some promises to sugarcoat what he offers. In Eden, the promise was being on a level with God, able to know good and evil. At the end of Christ's 40 days in the wilderness, Satan's tools were physical hunger, careless presumption, and materialistic power.

Ask yourself: what is the difference between what happened in Eden and what happened in the wilderness? The difference is that the first couple followed the devil when he pulled their leash, and Jesus did not. Someone might say that since Jesus was perfect he had no arrogant pride, and that is true. Nevertheless, the lesson is the same: the humans destroyed their world, their lives, and the lives of everyone who would ever be born, but Jesus resisted every temptation even though He knew the hellish death that awaited Him.

All the problems in this world—murder, terrorism, greed, perversion, hate, and all the rest—resulted from Two People believing One Lie and acting on it. Thankfully, salvation is ours by grace through faith because Jesus believed the truth and acted on it. What a glorious Savior!

Every one of us is tempted—*every one of us*, so I am not pointing fingers or making accusations. Instead, I just want to shine the light on the fact that the wicked one wants to lead us by the leash into danger, destruction, and ruin, and he makes his offers very enticing. However, they are lies. "There is a way which seemeth right unto a man, but the end thereof are the ways of death." (Proverbs 14:12)

Please don't go down that path. Don't let the wicked one lead you around by your pride-leash. Let us all join together in handing the reins of our hearts to the One who loves us, who died for us, and who will lead us "in the way everlasting." (Psalm 139:24)

12

What Satan Does Not Understand

Revelation 12:9-10 "And the great dragon was cast out, that old serpent, called the Devil, and Satan, which deceiveth the whole world: he was cast out into the earth, and his angels were cast out with him. And I heard a loud voice saying in heaven, Now is come salvation, and strength, and the kingdom of our God, and the power of his Christ: for the accuser of our brethren is cast down, which accused them before our God day and night."

Realistically, we could assume there are many things that Satan does not understand; however, today's verses give us a peek at one of them—Satan does not understand God's grace. I suppose that makes sense since he has never experienced it, and Scripture indicates that he never will.

Consider this. Isaiah 14:12 tells us that Lucifer was cast down from Heaven a long time ago, but chapters 1 and 2 of Job tell us that in some way, he still appears before God. What does he do when he is there? John tells us one of the things in today's verses: he is "the accuser of our brethren." He accuses us "before our God day and night," but why? I believe he wants to impugn the justice of God. It is as if he is saying,

"God, did you see what he (she) did? If you forgive *that*, you cannot call yourself just."

That is why I say Satan does not understand God's redemptive grace. In accusing us before God, the wicked one is implying that my standing in God's eyes is based on my behavior; however, it is not. My righteous standing before God is because of His judicial finding that there is no sin on my account! Then you might ask, "Are you saying you have never sinned?" I am not saying that at all. What I am saying is that there is no record of sin on my account. Do you know why? It's because all of my sins have already been paid for by a perfect substitute. Now I have a clean record because every one of my sins is paid in full. *none remain on my account!*

For those who come to God on the merit of Christ's finished work on the cross, our sins are forgiven—our record is clean. Let's live joyfully and holy.

Praise God from whom ALL blessings flow!

13

Being Humbly Proud

2 Timothy 4:6-8 "For I am now ready to be offered, and the time of my departure is at hand. I have fought a good fight, I have finished my course, I have kept the faith: Henceforth there is laid up for me a crown of righteousness, which the Lord, the righteous judge, shall give me at that day: and not to me only, but unto all them also that love his appearing."

"You cannot be both humble and proud," one might say. If by proud you mean arrogant and assuming superiority, then yes, that kind of pride is obviously incompatible with humility. However, there is another use of the word pride, which is to describe a sense of accomplishment— pride in a job well done, for example.

Now, I will grant you that even *that* pride could *become* arrogant and boastful, even if it does not start out that way. However, wasn't it the good kind of satisfaction that Paul had in mind when he told Timothy, "I have fought a good fight, I have finished my course, I have kept the faith"? You see, our frail human nature naturally bends toward straying away from God. Perhaps Paul was acknowledging that difficulty and therefore was excited finally to see the finish line just ahead, along with the end of his struggle.

That should encourage us. Maybe *we* look back with regret for *our* failings too. Maybe we find it easy to condemn ourselves, but hard to

336

accept God's forgiveness. Be careful here my friends; don't fall into thinking, "Oh woe is me. I am so bad that God cannot love me and forgive me." Dear reader, that *too* could be a form of pride, to think we are special cases and that God can love everyone except us.

There are two dangers about sin. One is to think we are not bad enough for God to notice—after all, I am not as bad as my neighbor is; this is self-righteousness. The other danger is to believe that our sins are *so* bad and *so* numerous that they are unforgivable; this is denying Jesus' claim that He will save any who come to Him. (John 6:37)

We really must be careful not to let our pride lead us in *either* of those directions, dear friends. Instead, like Paul, we must focus on God; we must fight a good fight, finish our course, and keep the faith.

14

Misconceptions about the Gospel

Romans 6:18 "Being then made free from sin, ye became the servants of righteousness."

Theologians can't plumb the depths of the gospel, and yet God expresses it so simply that even children can grasp its essential truths. However, Satan will do whatever he can to confuse us, so let's shine some light into his darkness.

One common misunderstanding about the gospel, particularly from today's verse ("free from sin") is that upon salvation we become sinless for the rest of our lives. I personally wish that *were* true, but 1 John 1 rejects that position. Instead, Paul is telling the Romans that the gospel makes believers judicially sinless in the eyes of the Almighty Judge before whom we will all one day stand: believers at one judgment and unbelievers at another.

Another way that the devil confuses many is by convincing them that if they say a few magic words inside a religious building, they automatically receive a get-out-of-hell-free card and can continue living sinful lives. Nothing could be farther from the truth. The gospel of Christ is not a fire insurance policy to save us from Hell; it is a peace treaty to save us from the wrath of God's offended justice. What is amazing is that the entire cost of that treaty was paid in full by the side that was wronged!

One last point: Christian *maturity* is a process, but *becoming* a Christian is an event. Trusting God for His forgiveness *is* the starting point for our Christian lives and growth. However, we don't start with the gospel and then *add* to it by our works; Ecclesiastes 3:14 dismisses that whole thought. Please hear me: Christ died to save us and rose to show He had succeeded. Now, through that gospel, God forgives rebels who lay down the fight and surrender to His mercy.

Some argue, "It *cannot* be that simple." Oh yes, it is *exactly* that simple. We have turned away from God and sinned against Him. (Romans 3:23) God commands us to repent and turn back to Him; (Acts 17:30) those who do so are forgiven, but those who do not, remain in their sins.

It *is* that simple. It is only complex when we try to understand its mysterious depths. The depths of God's grace are good too, we just cannot see it all yet.

15

Love Is Good and so Is the Right Kind of Hate

Psalm 119:113 "I hate vain thoughts: but thy law do I love."

This is an interesting verse comprised of two statements, one expressing hatred and the other one love.

Both of these words seem to be emotionally charged, not just in the English language, but also in Hebrew. The word translated hate is a word meaning a personal hatred of an enemy. It is elsewhere translated "odious," which the dictionary describes as extremely unpleasant or repulsive. The word translated "love" also expresses a powerful emotion and describes a passionate affection.

Now that we have defined the two verbs, let's look at their targets. For love, the target is God's Law; for hate, the target is vain thoughts.

First, let's look at the psalmist's expression of love. The Hebrew word for love's object—Law—is the word we pronounce "torah." You might recognize this as the word we use for the writings of Moses (Genesis through Deuteronomy), but the lexicon in **Strong's Concordance** says the broader meaning includes "precepts and statutes," suggesting that it covers all of God's instructions.

As for the object of hate, notice the phrase "vain thoughts." In translations that use such distinctions, the word vain is italicized, indicating that the translators supplied it to enhance an English word that does not fully convey the Hebrew meaning. The word translated "thoughts" expresses more than just concepts, ideas, or beliefs; it also suggests the divided opinions of a skeptic—someone who is not sure that God is telling the truth. This sounds like the double-minded man in James 1:8 and the church at Laodicea whom the Lord Jesus chides for being wishy-washy. (Revelation 3:14-16) This is not just arrogant and self-centered thoughts that the psalmist abhors; he hates the undecided, vacillating thoughts that distort our understanding of God's authority by suggesting that He doesn't mean what He says. That should also remind us of the subtle serpent in Genesis 3:1.

So then, the conclusion is that we must love and embrace God's truth and vehemently reject attempts to diminish His Word or its authority.

16

The Old Man in Me

Ephesians 6:12 "For we wrestle not against flesh and blood, but against principalities, against powers, against the rulers of the darkness of this world, against spiritual wickedness in high places."

The older I get, the godlier I should become, but sometimes it seems the opposite is true. As we draw closer to God, we will more acutely sense our mortal weaknesses. It just seems that God has so much left to do in many areas of my life.

As an example, let me confess one of the things that is my struggle. When I see violence and evil, it makes me very angry, very suddenly. When people deliberately commit murder and other evils, rage wells up in me, desiring immediate revenge. It is good that my anger quickly falls back within godly boundaries, because "the wrath of man worketh not the righteousness of God." (James 1:20)

Injustice *should* make us angry, but *excessive* anger disconnects us from a godly perspective and a godly response.

Let me give an example of my conflict between selfish rage and godly thinking. I recently saw a photograph of a Muslim woman lying on the ground. She tried to attack an Israeli border guard and was shot and killed. My anger is at people like her who shed, or try to shed, innocent blood. Then I consider her from a biblical perspective. She was a human being who was fooled by the same wicked one who tries to fool me, sometimes successfully.

I rejoice that the guard avoided injury, but when my anger subsides, my heart grieves for that woman and those like her. Someone so mislead and so angry has, through her own hateful actions, sealed her own fate. I am no one's judge, but if I understand the Scriptures correctly, it is very possible she was not ready to enter eternity. Now she is there forever. How sad.

The point of today's verse is that though mortals rebel against God—for which we are accountable—we should never dismiss principalities, powers, rulers of darkness, and spiritual wickedness in high places. Those are our real enemies.

By His grace, God continues to harvest precious souls who were blinded by hatred and other sins. I rejoice that He does so "out of every kindred, and tongue, and people, and nation." (Revelation 5:9)

Praise Him. He is good. He is God.

17

With Liberty and Justice for All

Leviticus 25:10 "And ye shall hallow the fiftieth year, and proclaim liberty throughout all the land unto all the inhabitants thereof: it shall be a jubile unto you; and ye shall return every man unto his possession, and ye shall return every man unto his family."

Part of this verse—"proclaim liberty throughout all the land unto all the inhabitants thereof"—is inscribed on the American Liberty Bell, which is housed in a memorial building in Philadelphia, Pennsylvania. That got me to thinking about the American Pledge of Allegiance, which concludes with the words "with liberty and justice for all."

There is a lot of anger today among people who think they have been denied liberty or have not received justice. The Lord teaches that we should do justly, so Christians *should* be concerned that what is right should *prevail*. I encourage each of us to do justly and pursue righteous dealings with others. However, as I was thinking about that, I realized there is another aspect to liberty and justice.

We all came into this world as enemies of God. "And you, that were sometime alienated and enemies in your mind by wicked works, yet now hath he reconciled in the body of his flesh through death, to present you holy and unblameable and unreproveable in his sight." Colossians 1:21-22) We have been made righteous before God; we have been set free from our sins and the just punishment we earned because of them. By His grace, through faith, He has reconciled believers to Himself. (Ephesians 2:8-9)

Christians live in the perfect liberty we have in Christ, (Romans 8:21) but the pledge's phrase is "liberty *and* justice." So where is the justice? Well, I am afraid that in the biblical context, it is liberty *or* justice, for there is only justice for those who refuse the forgiveness and the liberty Christ has bought for us. They place themselves—by their unbelief—under the justice for which their sins cry out.

Actually, the forgiveness and liberty that believers enjoy are also just, for they have been paid for. (Romans 3:26) However, those who refuse to bow their knee to God willingly shall one day bow their knee to Him anyway. (Philippians 2:9-11) Sadly, it will then be too late.

"Behold, now is the accepted time; behold, now is the day of salvation." (2 Corinthians 6:2b)

18

Crazy Rhoda and the Prayer Meeting

Acts 12:13-15 "And as Peter knocked at the door of the gate, a damsel came to hearken, named Rhoda. And when she knew Peter's voice, she opened not the gate for gladness, but ran in, and told how Peter stood before the gate. And they said unto her, Thou art mad. But she constantly affirmed that it was even so. Then said they, It is his angel."

Harod killed James, the brother of John, then put Peter in prison, evidently with the same intentions. Peter's Christian friends started praying for him, but when Rhoda returned from the door with news of Peter's freedom, the others told her she was crazy. Do we do that? Do we ask God to meet our needs and then expect Him not to? Why do we do that?

I know that I can trust God if He answers my prayer with a "wait" or even a "no." He is wiser than I am and therefore may deny my petition or adjust the timing. Even so, I should not be surprised when God is merciful and kind to me. After all, "He that spared not his own Son, but delivered him up for us all, how shall he not with him also freely give us all things?" (Romans 8:32)

Let's expect God to overrule us if we ask amiss, as we sometimes do; (James 4:3) however, let's stop thinking of God as a stingy ogre who takes pleasure in withholding good. As Jesus taught us, "Ask, and it shall be given you; seek, and ye shall find; knock, and it shall be opened unto you: For every one that asketh receiveth; and he that seeketh findeth; and to him that knocketh it shall be opened. Or what man is there of you, whom if his son ask bread, will he give him a stone? Or if he ask a fish, will he give him a serpent? If ye then, being evil, know how to give good gifts unto your children, how much more shall your Father which is in heaven give good things to them that ask him?" (Matthew 7:7-11)

As a good Father to His children, sometimes God says, "Yes;" sometimes He says, "Not yet;" and sometimes He says, "No." Nevertheless, He is good, and He is kind. *Always*.

19

His Classical Failure Was a Success

Romans 14:4 "Who art thou that judgest another man's servant? to his own master he standeth or falleth. Yea, he shall be holden up: for God is able to make him stand."

I like a broad spectrum of musical styles. In my late teens, I discovered a classical piece by French composer Maurice Ravel; his "Bolero" has been one of my favorites ever since. It starts out with a very soft, almost inaudible tapping rhythm on a snare drum, augmented with the light plucks of some stringed instruments. As the piece progresses, Ravel adds an instrument playing a simple tune; next, a different instrument plays the same tune, and then another and another. Then multiple instruments begin to play together, at first just a couple, followed by more and more, always repeating the same simple patterns, building to a regal crescendo. When performed well, it is both delicate and majestic.

Sadly, I have read several articles that indicate Ravel was not happy with that piece—that he later thought he overused the repeated patterns. Being something of a perfectionist myself, I can understand his dissatisfaction. Perfectionists tend to over-analyze our work, and yet I for one, along with many others, find Mr. Ravel's "Bolero" to be eminently pleasing and delightful.

Perhaps this is a good illustration of today's verse. In context, Paul is cautioning believers not to judge how someone else walks before God. Why? Because each of us is answerable to our Master and He can rightly judge our walk; no one else can. In reality, like Ravel, even we cannot always rightly judge our own efforts.

Now obviously, if someone is living in open sin—sexual immorality, stealing, lying, and so forth—the Scripture is clear that we can know that such behavior is wrong. (1 Corinthians 5:1 & 11; 2 Thessalonians 3:14) However, here Paul is talking about matters of personal preference and says we should not judge others whether in the observance of certain days or in eating certain foods.

Let us remember what Paul says, "Every one of us shall give account of himself to God." (Romans 14:12) Trying to walk in a way that honors our Lord should keep us all busy enough without us trying to run other people's lives.

20

An Invitation from the Incomprehensible God

Matthew 6:13b "For thine is the kingdom, and the power, and the glory, for ever. Amen."

His disciples asked Jesus to teach them to pray. I know they had seen Him pray, but my guess is that they had never seen anyone pray like Jesus. His prayers were intimate prayers to God as His Father, and His prayers were answered! The disciples wanted to know how to pray like that.

Both Matthew and Luke record this. In his discourse, the Lord taught them to approach God intimately (Our Father); but with great respect (Hallowed be thy name); and to acknowledge His sovereign purposes (Thy kingdom come. Thy will be done in earth, as it is in heaven). He went on to teach them to ask the Father for their physical needs (Give us this day our daily bread); pardon for their sins (forgive us our debts, as we forgive our debtors); and preservation and guidance in trials (lead us not into temptation, but deliver us from evil).

Matthew also records these closing words from the Lord: "For thine is the kingdom, and the power, and the glory, for ever. Amen."

In those words, Jesus was teaching them, and us by extension, that the Father they were approaching—to whom they were giving honor and from whom they were making requests—owned and ruled over all that exists, has the power and authority to use and dispense it as He purposes, and is majestic in all His Being!

The Unapproachable and Incomprehensible God, who is Holiness and Light, invites us to approach Him and learn of Him and of His great love, mercy, and grace that He has demonstrated at the cross. *That* is the God we worship and serve! He is majestic in all of His being, and yet He invites us, even with our weaknesses and limited abilities, to learn of Him, to know Him, and to approach Him intimately as our Abba, Father.

Years I spent in vanity and pride,
Caring not my Lord was crucified,
Knowing not it was for me He died
On Calvary.

By God's Word at last my sin I learned;
Then I trembled at the law I'd spurned,

Musings

Till my guilty soul imploring turned
To Calvary.

Mercy there was great, and grace was free;
Pardon there was multiplied to me;
There my burdened soul found liberty
At Calvary.
~ William R. Newell

21
Sent

Galatians 4 "3 Even so we, when we were children, were in bondage under the elements of the world: 4. But when the fullness of the time was come, God sent forth his Son, made of a woman, made under the law, 5. To redeem them that were under the law, that we might receive the adoption of sons. 6. And because ye are sons, God hath sent forth the Spirit of his Son into your hearts, crying, Abba, Father. 7. Wherefore thou art no more a servant, but a son; and if a son, then an heir of God through Christ."

When a company wants to accomplish a task, they put someone in charge of getting it done. If the task is at another location, they send the assigned agent to where the task is.

In His infinite knowledge, even before He created the world, God knew about the ghastly tragedy at Eden and the darkness that followed. As a result, God purposed to send His Son to redeem us from Eden's horror. "For God so loved the world, that he gave his only begotten Son, that whosoever believeth in him should not perish, but have everlasting life." (John 3:16)

That was a staggeringly wondrous event, but there is even more. Today's passage tells us that God sent His Son, (verse 4) but God also sent the Holy Spirit (verse 6) who teaches us to call God by the close and intimate name, "Abba, Father."

God has given us everything that is important to this life and to the next life. He has not only given us a Savior—our Redeemer, our Friend, and the Lover of our souls—He has also given us His Spirit to make us sons and heirs in Christ. Peter said it this way: "According as his divine power hath given unto us all things that pertain unto life and godliness, through the knowledge of him that hath called us to glory and virtue." (2 Peter 1:3)

344

God sent His Son to do FOR us what we could not do for ourselves and then sent the Spirit to do IN and THROUGH us what we could not do without His wisdom, guidance, and power. Praise God for the wisdom and grace, mercy and love that saved—and continues to save—the otherwise helpless and hopeless.

22

Three Great Mysteries

1 Corinthians 15:51-52 "Behold, I shew you a mystery; We shall not all sleep, but we shall all be changed, In a moment, in the twinkling of an eye, at the last trump: for the trumpet shall sound, and the dead shall be raised incorruptible, and we shall be changed."

Throughout 1 Corinthians 15, Paul taught about the resurrection of believers. In today's verses, the Greek word for mystery is "musterion" (moos-tay'-ree-on). We often think of a mystery as something we don't understand because we lack pieces of information. There is an element of that here, but this Greek word suggests something that has been withheld from those who were not ready for it. Here Paul is revealing to the believers at Corinth something for which their hearts are now prepared—that a day will come when those who have died shall be raised to new life, and then we who are still alive shall be changed in the same way.

How can that be? It is possible because of *another* event which we cannot fully grasp. Charles Wesley put it this way in his hymn, "And Can It Be That I Should Gain:"

'Tis mystery all: the Immortal dies:
Who can explore His strange design?
In vain the firstborn seraph tries
To sound the depths of love divine.
'Tis mercy all! Let earth adore,
Let angel minds inquire no more.

We have the promise of a new life with God forever because of the incomprehensible sacrifice Jesus made when He laid down His life as a ransom for many. (Matthew 20:28)

Now the question is, how could Jesus purchase our redemption? What makes Him a suitable sacrifice? The answer to this third mystery is that He was not just a man as some suppose. He was the Lord of Glory who was born as a baby and laid in a feed trough in preparation for the day when He would redeem us from our sins and give us new life with him forever. Keith Getty and Stewart Townend expressed it well in their song, "Joy Has Dawned":

> Son of Adam, Son of heaven,
> Given as a ransom;
> Reconciling God and man,
> Christ, our mighty champion!
>
> What a Savior! What a Friend!
> What a glorious myst'ry!
> He a babe in Bethlehem,
> Also Lord of hist'ry.

As Christmas approaches, I wish great joy for you all.

23

Aliens

John 17:14-17 "I have given them thy word; and the world hath hated them, because they are not of the world, even as I am not of the world. I pray not that thou shouldest take them out of the world, but that thou shouldest keep them from the evil. They are not of the world, even as I am not of the world. Sanctify them through thy truth: thy word is truth."

The King James Bible uses the word "alien" five times. I am sure you know that the Scriptures are *not* talking about space creatures. The three Hebrew words translated "alien" refer to people who are not where they would normally be found. As a word picture, daffodils and orchids are each beautiful in their own right, but in a rose garden, both would be foreign, alien, and out of place.

In that same sense, Christians are aliens. We are in this world but not of it. We should function as good citizens of this world, but that is temporary and our spirits sense that. Ultimately, we are citizens of Heaven, and *that* world should be drawing us to an ever-increasing longing to be there. In God's timing, of course, but longing nevertheless.

We belong on the Earth for now; that is where God has placed us. However, we *are* aliens. Former atheist-turned-Christian C.S. Lewis mentioned this very thing, citing evidence within our very beings that whisper to our souls:

"Creatures are not born with desires unless satisfaction for those desires exists. A baby feels hunger: well, there is such a thing as food. A duckling wants to swim: well, there is such a thing as water. ... If I find in myself a desire which no experience in this world can satisfy, the most probable explanation is that I was made for another world. ... If that is so, I must take care, on the one hand, never to despise, or to be unthankful for, these earthly blessings, and on the other, never to mistake them for the something else of which they are only a kind of copy, or echo, or mirage. I must keep alive in myself the desire for my true country ... I must make it the main object of life to press on to that country and to help others to do the same."

That explains a lot, doesn't it?

24

Three Profound Words

Isaiah 9:6 "For unto us a child is born, unto us a son is given: and the government shall be upon his shoulder: and his name shall be called Wonderful, Counsellor, The mighty God, The everlasting Father, The Prince of Peace."

Familiarity is an enemy to learning. The more we think we know about a subject, the easier it is for our minds to slide into a valley of complacency—a place where it thinks, "I already know this." Then learning becomes difficult and even impossible. Such is the case with today's verses. With the exceptions of John 11:35 ("Jesus wept.") and Psalm 23, few passages in the Bible are better known to us than the birth of the Savior as prophesied by Isaiah and recounted in Luke 2.

Most of us are aware of the distinction in the first two phrases: the child is born, but the son is given. We see this as confirming our understanding of the dual nature of the person of Christ—"a child is born" speaks of His humanity being born, and "a son is given" speaks of the Eternal Son who came to save His people from their sins. (Matthew 1:21) We also see that He will rule ("government shall be upon his shoulder,") and He shall be worthy of many titles ("Wonderful, Counselor, The mighty God, The everlasting Father, The Prince of Peace").

However, so often we overlook three simple words in this passage. We must not miss them, for the words God gives us in Scripture are there for our learning, and these three words are an integral part of the message here. Those three words are, "For unto us."

The coming of Christ at that miraculous birth was not just a historic event. Oh, it *was* that, but He didn't just come to make Bethlehem famous or to entice gifts from the wise men from the East. The news of His birth was not just to give the newspapers a headline for the next day. He came "for unto us." He came to show us what the Father is like; to teach us the ways of godliness, righteousness, and faith; and ultimately, He came to redeem our sinful selves by laying down His life and shedding His own precious blood.

We can rejoice that He came, but we rejoice so much more when we consider He came "for unto us."

25

Christmas

Luke 2:13-14 "And suddenly there was with the angel a multitude of the heavenly host praising God, and saying, 'Glory to God in the highest, and on earth peace, good will toward men.' "

In 1861, the first year of the American Civil War, American poet Henry Wadsworth Longfellow lost his wife in a tragic fire. Two years later, in the spring of 1863, his son Charles joined the army against Longfellow's wishes and was severely injured in November of that same year. Just weeks later, on Christmas Day, the poet wrote a poem that was later set to music; we know the song by the title "I Heard The Bells On Christmas Day."

Longfellow penned seven verses, but two of them are usually missing from our hymnals. That is understandable as they speak directly of that war, recounting the soot-blackened mouth of the thundering cannons that were robbing his fellow citizens of peace on Earth; after all, Christmas was a time of remembrance of the Savior's birth that promised that peace would eventually come. However, that omission is also unfortunate because those verses breathe life into our understanding of Longfellow's angst over the war that almost ended his son's life.

I pray you will take the time to read all seven verses. As you do, you may identify with Mr. Longfellow's despair, for we *still* live in unsettling times. I also pray that you identify with the peace that the Savior brings to those who trust in Him, even if that peace over the whole Earth is yet to come.

Wishing for you a blessed time of remembering the birth of Jesus who loved us and gave Himself for us. (Galatians 2:20)

December

I heard the bells on Christmas Day
Their old, familiar carols play,
And wild and sweet the words repeat
Of peace on earth, good-will to men!

And thought how, as the day had come,
The belfries of all Christendom
Had rolled along the unbroken song
Of peace on earth, good-will to men!

Till ringing, singing on its way,
The world revolved from night to day,
A voice, a chime, a chant sublime
Of peace on earth, good-will to men!

Then from each black, accursed mouth
The cannon thundered in the South,
And with the sound the carols drowned
Of peace on earth, good-will to men!

It was as if an earthquake rent
The hearth-stones of a continent,
And made forlorn the households born
Of peace on earth, good-will to men!

And in despair I bowed my head;
"There is no peace on earth," I said;
"For hate is strong, and mocks the song
Of peace on earth, good-will to men!"

Then pealed the bells more loud and deep:
"God is not dead, nor doth He sleep;
The Wrong shall fail, the Right prevail,
With peace on earth, good-will to men."

26
Seasons

Ecclesiastes 3:1-8 "To every thing there is a season, and a time to every purpose under the heaven: A time to be born, and a time to die; a time to plant, and a time to pluck up that which is planted; A time to kill, and a time to heal; a time to break down, and a time to build up; A time to weep, and a time to laugh; a time to mourn, and a time to dance; A time to cast away stones, and a time to gather stones together; a time to embrace, and a time to refrain from embracing; A time to get, and a time to lose; a time to keep, and a time to cast away; A time to rend, and a time to sew; a time to keep silence, and a time to speak; A time to love, and a time to hate; a time of war, and a time of peace."

Here in the Northern Hemisphere, we passed into Winter several days ago and experienced the shortest day of the year; for our friends in the Southern Hemisphere, they are just starting their Summer.

As we close out another year, I was thinking about seasons, both the seasons of this Earth and the seasons of life. Today's verses remind us of some of those shorter seasons: seasons of planting and harvesting, tearing down and building up, mourning and dancing, getting and losing.

These are some of the seasons *during* life, but life *itself* is a series of seasons too. There is the spring of life when we are new and everything around us is new for the discovering. Then comes summer when we reach our strength and stamina. Next comes the autumn with its relaxing and reflections. Finally comes winter, a time when strength and stamina fade, and we sense the effects of Adam's fall. (Ecclesiastes 12:3)

It is interesting that we sometimes use the English word "fall" interchangeably with the word "autumn" because Adam's "fall" ushered the entire world into a frigid winter with no human way of escape. However, one spring many years ago, Christ arose from the grave and opened the beauty and warmth of eternal summer to those who come to Him in repentance and faith.

"The gift of God is eternal life through Jesus Christ our Lord." (Romans 6:23b) Thank You, Lord.

27
Paul's Last Days

2 Timothy 4:6-8 "For I am now ready to be offered, and the time of my departure is at hand. I have fought a good fight, I have finished my course, I have kept the faith: Henceforth there is laid up for me a crown of righteousness, which the Lord, the righteous judge, shall give me at that day: and not to me only, but unto all them also that love his appearing.

Verses 9-11. "Do thy diligence to come shortly unto me: For Demas hath forsaken me, having loved this present world, and is departed unto Thessalonica; Crescens to Galatia, Titus unto Dalmatia. Only Luke is with me. Take Mark, and bring him with thee: for he is profitable to me for the ministry."

In the first three verses, Paul foresees that he is coming to the finish line of his life. He doesn't have an unhealthy death wish, but he seems pleased that he has stayed on course and is arriving at his long-sought destination. He even anticipated the crown of righteousness he would receive.

However, in the next three verses, the apostle shows what I interpret as being vulnerable. He asks Timothy to come quickly to be with him. One person had abandoned the old saint, and a couple of others seem to be away on other missions. Only Luke remained there with Paul, and he wanted Timothy to come and bring Mark with him, a young man with whom Paul had previously had a falling out. I think Paul really craved company as he ran the final lap of his race.

Note that I used the word vulnerable rather than weakness. It was not weak for Paul to want the fellowship of his Christian friends as he approached the end. The Lord even tells us not to forsake the assembling of ourselves together like some people do but rather to encourage one another. (Hebrews 10:25)

Most of us would like the encouragement and companionship of loved ones as we see the horizon approaching. Can we do that with a phone call, email, or letter? Somewhat, but not like when we are together. If we cannot get to church, God will provide for us, but I believe our spiritual health will suffer if we *could* get there but rather choose to forsake assembling together. (Hebrews 10:25)

Let us each run our own race, but let's not run it alone.

28

How Long, O Lord?

1 Thessalonians 5:17 "Pray without ceasing."

Revelation 6:10 "And they cried with a loud voice, saying, How long, O Lord, holy and true, dost thou not judge and avenge our blood on them that dwell on the earth?"

One of the things I don't like about social media is all of the sufferings that people post. Struggles, pain, sorrow, hate, and anger. However, do you know one of the things I *do* like about posts on social media? The sufferings, struggles, pain, sorrow, hate, and anger. Do you know why I like and don't like the same things? Because there is a certain honesty about it all.

Those displays of brokenness grieve me a lot. I am not saying that every discouraging post is truthful; there are plenty of false posts. In fact, the lies and distortions of false posts are actually just more of the same kind of brokenness as the other things I listed. However, the bright ray I find in the whole mix is that those posts remind me to pray for those who are in anguish of body, soul, and spirit.

The post that prompted this Musing included a picture of a woman in a hospital bed and a plea for prayer on her behalf. That post was made by someone outside my country, but the problems are the same everywhere. There are murders, accidents, sickness, and addictions in my country too, as well as in almost every city, town, and hamlet in the world. Human suffering is global. The widespread character of this suffering is a result of the Fall, and thankfully, the gospel of Christ is to be preached to all the world and to be offered to all who will listen. One other sad thing we can add to the list is that many will never repent of their sins and come to God by faith.

Today's first verse commands us to pray continuously. The second one reminds us that in the future, some of God's people who have been murdered will ask, "How long, O Lord...?" Let us preach the gospel, and let us do what we can to reduce suffering and sorrow, (Galatians 6:10) but I believe it is also proper—reverently and respectfully—to ask, "How long, O Lord?"

29

The Answer to "How Long, Oh Lord?"

2 Peter 3:9 "The Lord is not slack concerning his promise, as some men count slackness; but is longsuffering to us-ward, not willing that any should perish, but that all should come to repentance."

Yesterday, we looked at the question posed by Christians who had been murdered for their faith, "How long, O Lord?" (Revelation 6:10) My heart grieves for the Lord's people in our sufferings, some of which come by persecution and others simply because we are sojourners in a fallen world.

However, there is an answer to that question. For example, shortly after writing yesterday's Musing, I came across an article that said, "God is moving in the homosexual community! He is turning hearts towards Himself and leading many to repentance, setting them free from their bondage." Is *that* why the Lord seems to us to be delaying His judgment? Is it because He is patiently working His redemptive purposes amidst our brokenness?

The lexicon in ***Strong's Concordance*** says the word Peter uses in today's verse, the word translated "longsuffering," means "patience, forbearance, longsuffering, slowness in avenging wrongs."

It is sad, and part of our damaged state, that we tend to think of ourselves better than others—you know, those who are "a lot worse than us." However, the truth is that we are all broken with the same brokenness, the brokenness of being dead in our trespasses and sins. (Ephesians 2:1) That brokenness manifests itself in different forms—murder, adultery, homosexuality, hatred, bigotry, idolatry—but all of it is just our sinfulness oozing out of whatever cracks it finds in us.

God is working all throughout this world. My heart melts in worship and praise as I hear of multitudes of Muslims coming to the Savior. He is doing the same for those in prison, for the wretched and wicked, for the lonely and brokenhearted. In fact, God is redeeming people from every situation. Thankfully, He even breaks and then redeems those who thought they were good enough without Him.

May we be thankful, and may we simply be beggars telling other beggars where to find bread. (Mark 16:15)

I never get used to what You do—
I never get used to watching You

Take a life beyond redemption,
Make it yours and make it new.

I never outgrow the miracle—
A heart that was empty flowing full.
I never get used to what You do.
~ Twila Paris

30

If

Matthew 4:3 "And when the tempter came to him, he said, If thou be the Son of God, command that these stones be made bread."

Satan's earliest recorded act against God was lifting his heart in pride; as a result, God cast him out of Heaven. Ever since then, he has attacked the children of faith, tempting us to "leave the God we love," as Robert Robinson put it in his hymn, "Come Thou Fount of Every Blessing." As if that were not enough, the devil didn't stop at tempting humans; rather, he demonstrated unmitigated gall in tempting his Creator, the Lord of Glory.

Today's verse recounts the first of the three temptations Satan placed before the Savior just after His forty-day fast. Twice he questioned Jesus' deity ("if thou be the Son of God" - v3 & 6) and once His judgment ("if thou wilt fall down and worship me" - v9). True to His being, Jesus not only did not yield, but also gave the wicked biblical reasons why He should not and would not. (Matthew 4:4, 6 &7)

Satan comes to us the same way. "*If* you *really* were a child of God ...." "*If* you *really* had faith ...." "*If* you *really* loved God ...." If, if, if! Oh, when will we learn his lying ways?

He is a fraud, so he tells us we are too. The devil tries to use our immaturity and weakness to convince us we are frauds like he is. In truth, we are frauds *only* when we try to live the Christian life in our own strength, for the Christian life *cannot* be lived in the power of the flesh.

That is why Jesus promised He would send the Holy Spirit because "when he, the Spirit of truth, is come, he will guide you into all truth," (John 16:13a) that truth being God's Word. (John 17:17) The Comforter, whom Jesus sent, leads us away from willfulness and doubt. That is *not* to say we will not naturally *be* willful and doubtful; that is what the old nature is like. That is why we need the Holy Spirit to lead us *away* from that which is natural and fleshly and toward God's Word. Our proper response is to cooperate with Him—to follow His leading—thereby walking in the Spirit, and not fulfilling the lust of the flesh. (Galatians 5:16)

31

Homing Pigeons

John 14:1-6 "Let not your heart be troubled: ye believe in God, believe also in me. In my Father's house are many mansions: if it were not so, I would have told you. I go to prepare a place for you. And if I go and prepare a place for you, I will come again, and receive you unto myself; that where I am, there ye may be also. And whither I go ye know, and the way ye know. Thomas saith unto him, Lord, we know not whither thou goest; and how can we know the way? Jesus saith unto him, I am the way, the truth, and the life: no man cometh unto the Father, but by me."

I read an article recently about a businessman who spends a lot of time traveling. He enjoyed seeing new places and meeting new people, but he has come to appreciate arriving back home.

That got me to thinking about homing pigeons, a special breed of pigeons with an amazing sense of direction. They can find their way back to their nests over a distance of hundreds of miles and can fly at speeds greater than fifty miles per hour.

In turn, all that got me to thinking about the eternal home that awaits me. In today's verses, Jesus talks about the home He has gone to prepare for His people. The homing pigeon can find its way home, and the businessman—or at least the pilots and cab drivers he uses—can get him home. However, Thomas asks a question about arriving at a desired destination and gets a much different answer than he was expecting: "Thomas saith unto him, Lord, we know not whither thou goest; and how can we know the way? Jesus saith unto him, I am the way, the truth, and the life: no man cometh unto the Father, but by me."

Jesus does not tell us about a home He is preparing and then give us a compass or map. In essence, He tells His disciple, "I am not going to just show you the way, Thomas; I *am* the way."

What comfort it is that the One who is preparing our eternal home has not just made a way or just shown the way. He *is* the way, and one day shall take us to the home He has prepared for us.

PERSONAL

The author, William F. Powers, is married to Jerian Powers; they live in Southwestern Ohio. Together they have 8 children and a growing number of grandchildren. Several months prior to the release of this book, they were blessed with their first great grandchild, Liam.

Contact Information:
  Musings@WilliamFPowers.com

The author's works are listed at his website:
  www.WilliamFPowers.com